OPENING THE SEALED BOOK

OPENING THE SEALED BOOK

*Interpretations of the Book of Isaiah
in Late Antiquity*

Joseph Blenkinsopp

WILLIAM B. EERDMANS PUBLISHING COMPANY
GRAND RAPIDS, MICHIGAN / CAMBRIDGE, U.K.

Published 2006 by
Wm. B. Eerdmans Publishing Co.
2140 Oak Industrial Drive N.E., Grand Rapids, Michigan 49505 /
P.O. Box 163, Cambridge CB3 9PU U.K.

Printed in the United States of America

10 09 08 07 06   7 6 5 4 3 2 1

Library of Congress Cataloging-in-Publication Data

Blenkinsopp, Joseph, 1927-
Opening the sealed book: interpretations of the book of Isaiah
in late antiquity / Joseph Blenkinsopp.
p.   cm.
Includes bibliographical references and index.
ISBN-10: 0-8028-4021-3 / ISBN-13: 978-0-8028-4021-9 (pbk.: alk. paper)
1. Bible. O.T. Isaiah — Criticism, interpretation, etc.   I. Title.

BS1515.52.B44   2006
224'.1060901 — dc22

2006019375

www.eerdmans.com

Contents

Contents

Abbreviations

AASF	Annales Academiae scientiarum fennicae
AB	Anchor Bible
ABD	*Anchor Bible Dictionary,* ed. David Noel Freedman
ANET	*Ancient Near Eastern Texts,* ed. James B. Pritchard
ASNU	Acta seminarii neotestamentici upsaliensis
AUM	Andrews University Monographs
BA	*Biblical Archaeologist*
BETL	Bibliotheca ephemeridum theologicarum lovaniensium
BHT	Beiträge zur historischen Theologie
Bib	*Biblica*
BJRL	*Bulletin of the John Rylands Library*
BN	*Biblische Notizen*
BRS	Biblical Resource Series
BZ	*Biblische Zeitschrift*
BZAW	Beihefte zur Zeitschrift für die alttestamentliche Wissenschaft
CAH	*Cambridge Ancient History*
CBC	Cambridge Bible Commentary
CBQ	*Catholic Biblical Quarterly*
CBQMS	Catholic Biblical Quarterly Monograph Series
DJD	Discoveries in the Judaean Desert
DSD	*Dead Sea Discoveries*
EBib	Etudes bibliques
EDNT	*Exegetical Dictionary of the New Testament,* ed. Horst Balz and Gerhard Schneider

EDSS	*Encyclopedia of the Dead Sea Scrolls,* ed. Lawrence H. Schiffmann and James C. VanderKam
EKK	Evangelisch-katholischer Kommentar
EncJud	*Encyclopaedia Judaica,* 16 vols. (New York: Macmillan, 1972)
ErIsr	*Eretz-Israel*
FRLANT	Forschungen zur Religion und Literatur des Alten und Neuen Testaments
GKC	*Gesenius' Hebrew Grammar,* ed. E. Kautzsch, trans. A. E. Cowley, 2nd ed.
Herm	Hermeneia
HeyJ	*Heythrop Journal*
HKAT	Handkommentar zum Alten Testament
HSAT	Die Heilige Schrift des Alten Testaments
HTR	*Harvard Theological Review*
HTS	Harvard Theological Studies
HUCA	*Hebrew Union College Annual*
ICC	International Critical Commentary
IDBSup	*Interpreter's Dictionary of the Bible, Supplementary Volume,* ed. Keith Crim
IEJ	*Israel Exploration Journal*
Int	*Interpretation*
IOS	*Israel Oriental Studies*
JBL	*Journal of Biblical Literature*
JCS	*Journal of Cuneiform Studies*
JJS	*Journal of Jewish Studies*
JNES	*Journal of Near Eastern Studies*
JPS	Jewish Publication Society
JQR	*Jewish Quarterly Review*
JSOT	*Journal for the Study of the Old Testament*
JSOTSup	Journal for the Study of the Old Testament: Supplement Series
JSPSup	Journal for the Study of the Pseudepigraph: Supplement Series
JSS	*Journal of Semitic Studies*
JTS	*Journal of Theological Studies*
KHC	Kurz Hand-Commentar zum Alten Testament
LEC	Library of Early Christianity
LS	*Louvain Studies*
LXX	Septuagint

MT	Masoretic Text
NCBC	New Century Bible Commentary
NEB	New English Bible
NovTSup	Supplements to Novum Testamentum
NRSV	New Revised Standard Version
NTS	*New Testament Studies*
NumenSup	Supplements to Numen
OBO	Orbis biblicus et orientalis
OIP	Oriental Institute Publications
OLA	Orientalia lovaniensia analecta
OTL	Old Testament Library
OtSt	*Oudtestamentische Studiën*
PAAJR	*Proceedings of the American Academy of Jewish Research*
PIBA	*Proceedings of the Irish Biblical Association*
PL	*Patrologia latina*, ed. J.-P. Migne
RB	*Revue biblique*
RevQ	*Revue de Qumran*
RHPR	*Revue d'histoire et de philosophie religieuses*
SBL	Society of Biblical Literature
SBLEJL	Society of Biblical Literature Early Judaism and Its Literature
SBLMS	Society of Biblical Literature Monograph Series
SBLSymS	Society of Biblical Literature Symposium Series
SBLTT	Society of Biblical Literature Texts and Translations
SBT	Studies in Biblical Theology
SJLA	Studies in Judaism in Late Antiquity
SNTSMS	Society for New Testament Studies Monograph Series
ST	*Studia theologica*
STDJ	Studies in the Texts of the Desert of Judah
SUNT	Studien zur Umwelt des Neuen Testaments
TBC	Torch Bible Commentaries
TDNT	*Theological Dictionary of the New Testament*, ed. Gerhard Kittel and Gerhard Friedrich
TDOT	*Theological Dictionary of the Old Testament*, ed. G. Johannes Botterweck, Helmer Ringgren, and Heinz-Josef Fabry
TLOT	*Theological Lexicon of the Old Testament*, ed. Ernst Jenni and Claus Westermann
VT	*Vetus Testamentum*
VTSup	Supplements to Vetus Testamentum
WBC	Word Biblical Commentary

WMANT	Wissenschaftliche Monographien zum Alten und Neuen Testament
ZAW	*Zeitschrift für die alttestamentliche Wissenschaft*
ZBK	Zürcher Bibelkommentare
ZNW	*Zeitschrift für die neutestamentliche Wissenschaft*
ZTK	*Zeitschrift für Theologie und Kirche*

The vision of all this has become for you like the words of a sealed book. When they hand it to one who knows how to read, saying, "Read this please," he replies, "I can't, for it is sealed." When the book is handed to one who can't read, with the request, "Read this please," he replies, "I don't know how to read."

Isaiah 29:11-12

Introduction

The main focus of the following chapters is the interpretation of texts, and the main point I want to make is the powerful impact that the interpretation of biblical texts can have on social realities. At a time and in a culture in which biblical texts can be cited in support of specific social and political agendas, not always with reassuring results, and when books featuring apocalyptic scenarios based on the Bible sell in the millions, this should not require much emphasis. The specific instantiation of this general thesis will be the interpretation of the book of Isaiah as an essential and irreplaceable factor in the legitimizing, grounding, and shaping of dissident movements in late Second Temple Judaism, with special reference to the Qumran sects and the early Christian movement. The interpretation of texts is generally understood to be a scholarly and scribal activity; it is that, but it is also a social phenomenon and, typically, a group activity. Our inquiry into the different ways in which the interpretation of texts from Isaiah played a part in the turmoil of the late Second Temple period should provide another demonstration of the power of a textual tradition to move the course of history in a certain direction and thus to make a difference in "the real world."

What makes interpretation possible is that any text, except possibly a text which is purely factual, is open to multiple readings and meanings. Interpretation is what happens between text and reader. Each reader brings to the text an agenda dictated by personal needs, presuppositions, and prejudices and, no less significantly, the needs, presuppositions, and prejudices of the social class, or political and religious interest group, to which he or she belongs, and the requirements of its agenda to which he or she subscribes. The same text can therefore generate conflicting interpretations which can in their turn spill over into social conflict. The history of Christianity provides numerous examples of these conflicts of interpretation, the effects of which have not always been confined to polite debate. Think, for example, of the Protestant Reformation and the conflicting interpretations of Rom 1:17, itself one of several possible interpretations of Hab 2:4 ("The righteous live by their faith"). We happen to have a Qumran interpretation of the same prophetic text, according to which it refers to the members of the group who will survive the final judgment on account of their faith in the Teacher of Righteousness (1QpHab VIII 1-3).

The study which follows also aspires to make a modest contribution to the history of the rise of sectarianism in early Judaism by a kind of comparative hermeneutics based on the ways in which the book of Isaiah was appropriated and interpreted in those liminal groups for which some evidence exists. These include the group for and within which the book of Daniel was written, the Damascus sect, the Qumran *yahad*, the followers of John the Baptist, and the early Christian movement. About the other major sects *(haireseis)* mentioned by Josephus, the Pharisees and Sadducees, no data relevant to this project is available. Most specialists identify the Qumran sectarians with the Essenes. While I accept this as the best available hypothesis, serious alternatives are on the table, and therefore I have been careful not to base any arguments or stake any claims on the Essene hypothesis being the correct option.

Since the topic of the book also concerns the origins of the Christian movement, it is necessary to insist that Christianity originated as a Palestinian Jewish sect in the mid-1st century C.E. Its origins are therefore to be sought not just in Second Temple Judaism in general but in late Second Temple *sectarian* Judaism. It is therefore legitimate, and historically necessary, to compare it with other sectarian groups both contemporaneous with it and prior to it. It is understandable that there will be something unsettling about this approach for the committed Christian reader. We can only repeat that Christianity cannot avoid the implications and the challenges arising from being a historical religion. To affirm the doctrine of the incarnation implies accepting the challenge of history, and it is entirely possible to do so in the expectation of acquiring a deeper understanding of and appreciation for the faith professed by the Christian.

One aspect of Isaianic interpretation which is easily overlooked, but which we will try to keep in mind during our inquiry, is that it begins in the book itself. All critical commentators on Isaiah agree that, in spite of the attribution of all 66 chapters to the one author named in the superscript, the book is a collection of miscellaneous material deriving from a number of anonymous (or pseudonymously Isaianic) authors, compiled over a long period of time, from the 8th century B.C.E. to perhaps as late as the 3rd century B.C.E., therefore about half a millennium. While it is not always easy to detect connections between successive passages or other intertextual links in the book, the overall impression is not of a disarticulated and haphazard collection of literary scraps but rather an ongoing incremental and cumulative interpretative process. In the course of our inquiry we will see many examples of texts which take off from existing texts, amplifying and updating them, either applying them to a new situation or developing them in a different direction. The same process is, of course, more clearly visible after the point had been reached when such commentary could no longer be incorporated in the book itself. This is especially the case with the Qumran pesharim, the earliest commentaries on the book of Isaiah, and early Christian appropriation of the book as exemplified in the series of fulfillment sayings in Matthew's gospel.

Viewing this issue from a broader perspective, I will argue that three very influential interpretative trajectories about the function and place of prophecy and the prophetic role originate in the book. There is, first, the profile of the prophet who insists on justice and righteousness in public life, speaks out on behalf of the marginal classes of society, refuses to confer absolute validity on existing political and religious institutions, directs an unsparing criticism against political and religious elites, and, in general, plays a deliberately critical and confrontational role in society. In contrast to this "classical" prophetic role, there is the prophet in the guise of apocalyptic seer who predicts and heralds the final and decisive intervention of God in human affairs and the affairs of Israel in particular, announcing imminent judgment for the many and salvation for the few. There is, finally, the prophet as "man of God" who counsels, intercedes, chides occasionally, heals, and works miracles — who, in other words, does what the "man of God" was expected to do in ancient Israel. It is in this capacity that the Isaiah of the few narrative passages in the book very soon became the subject of biographical interest, in the same way, if not to the same extent, as Jeremiah in the book which bears his name.

While it is clearly possible for an individual prophetic figure to incorporate elements of more than one of these roles, they can be shown to represent, as a historical fact, distinct and distinctive lines of interpretation. All three have their points of departure in the book, but as we follow the thread beyond the confines of the book we observe how the last of the three options, according to which the prophet is spoken of biographically, as belonging to the past rather than the present or the future, is carried forward throughout the Second Temple period and beyond, from Chronicles to Josephus and *The Martyrdom of Isaiah.* I hope to show that this biographical option represented, in its origin, a deliberate strategy to neutralize the prophet as a destabilizing influence in society, that is, as filling the first of the three roles outlined above. The strategy was, moreover, so successful that we have to come all the way down into the early modern period for this first role, the prophet as critic and reformer, to emerge clearly into the light of day. We can find this interpretative option, for example, in Heinrich Ewald's *Die Propheten des Alten Bundes* (1840) and, in the English-speaking world, in the writings of such influential figures as F. D. Maurice and Walter Rauschenbusch.

The line of Isaianic interpretation with which we will be most occupied in what follows is, however, the one which connects the inchoate apocalyptic eschatology of the book of Isaiah with Daniel, the Qumran sects, and early Christianity. Taking over from Amos the old motif of the remnant of Israel, the Isaianic authors associated it with those who returned as penitents from exile and are presented as the nucleus of a new community — an idea which was to have a decisive place in sectarian self-understanding in the late Second Temple period. I regard the identification of the remnant with the survivors of the Babylonian exile as the principal Isaianic contribution to the sectarianism of the late Second Temple period. Another motif which would be prominent in writings emanating from the sects was the sealed book alluded to in Isaiah (Isa 8:16; 29:11-12). This theme, common in apocalyptic circles ancient and modern, links with the idea of interpretation as a form of decryption, in the sense that God had implanted secret revelations in the book of Isaiah. The code to decipher these prophetic cryptograms would be revealed only much later to chosen intermediaries living in the last age of the world. These revelations consisted in coded reference to situations in the life of the receptor community, and in particular to the mission and destiny of its founder, the Teacher of Righteousness for Qumran, Jesus of Nazareth for his first followers. But there was also much in Isaiah which could be read in plain text as a guide to the collective self-understanding of the group in question and the moral qualities which it aspired to embody. Some indications of this are presented in the chapter on the comparative study of titles in Qumran and early Christianity (the Elect, the Servants of the Lord, etc.).

The apocalyptic understanding of history, and the corresponding cryptogrammatic type of interpretation applied to Isaiah, still very much with us, will inevitably raise serious questions for the thoughtful reader of the Bible today. Leaving aside the somewhat tenuous links between Essenes and the small Karaite communities in Israel and one or two other countries, the Qumranites did not survive the war with Rome, and therefore we do not know how they would have evolved. The Christian movement did survive and evolved beyond its sectarian origins, impelled by the requirement of a universal mission proclaimed by its founder. In the process of doing so it was compelled to abandon or, better, reformulate the apocalyptic expectations cherished in the earliest period of its existence. But no matter how reinterpreted, the texts in which this apocalyptic matrix was articulated remained for future generations of Christians to reactivate, hence the tension throughout Christian history, and at the present time, between apocalyptic despair of influencing the course of history and prophetic realism in dealing with the affairs of the world from a critical, religious perspective — the first of the three options listed above.

On a more personal note, I want to add that this study of the interpretation of Isaiah in late antiquity began in earnest while I was working on the three-volume Anchor Bible commentary on the book, published between 2000 and 2003. Including even part of this material into the commentary would have increased its length beyond reasonable measure and risked testing the reader's patience beyond endurance. Unless otherwise indicated, translations of Isaiah are from these three volumes.

It is a pleasure to express my appreciation to T. & T. Clark/Continuum International for permission to reprint, in slightly revised form, part of my contribution to *New Directions in Qumran Studies,* edited by Jonathan G. Campbell, William John Lyons, and Lloyd K. Pietersen (2005), the chapter entitled "The Qumran Sect in the Context of Second Temple Sectarianism" in Chapter 3 of the present work. I also wish to acknowledge permission granted by Neukirchener Verlag for permission to reprint part of my contribution to *Minḥa: Festgabe für Rolf Rendtorff zum 75. Geburtstag,* edited by Erhard Blum (2000), the chapter entitled "The Prophetic Biography of Isaiah," a slightly revised version of which appears in Chapter 2 of the present work.

I am not a specialist in Qumran studies, and therefore the debt owed to the goodly fellowship of Qumran scholars will be evident throughout. Listing names would be invidious, but a special mention is due to Philip Davies, with whom I had many conversations, in pubs and other congenial settings, on the subject of the book during the academic year 2003-4 spent in Sheffield. It is also a pleasure to thank Dr. Angela Kim Harkins, who read parts of the work and made valuable suggestions, as well as doctoral student Mr. Sam Thomas, who helped with research. Not least, I owe a special debt of gratitude to the Andrew W. Mellon Foundation for the award of an Emeritus Research Grant which greatly facilitated the work at every stage. Finally, as on previous occasions, my thanks to my wife for help in clarifying issues related to the work and for her unfailing love and support.

· CHAPTER 1 ·

Isaiah: The Book

What Is a Book?

We speak of "the book of Isaiah," but it would be a good idea to be clear
at the outset as to what we mean when we speak of a biblical book. Our
understanding of a book as a composition written by one or more authors, usually identified by name and protected legally from the intrusion, well-meaning or otherwise, of later hands, is a product of the early
modern age. We cannot assume that this is the way books were understood in antiquity. Some ancient compositions included a colophon in
which the owner of the tablet or the scribe who copied it is named. *Gilgamesh,* for example, was copied by a certain incantation priest named
Sin-leqe-unninni. He may also have collated and arranged existing
Gilgamesh material, but we may doubt whether he qualifies realistically
as author of the poem. At any rate, the collating, classifying, and archiv-
ing of what can be called canonical texts, but without much regard for
authorship, is well attested for ancient Mesopotamia.[1] In Greece, hand-
books and technical manuals on such subjects as medicine and rhetoric
were being produced from the 5th century B.C.E. These would have circulated among specialists without in any way presupposing widespread
literacy or, much less, the existence of a book-publishing industry. The
Histories of Herodotus (ca. 420 B.C.E.) and Thucydides (ca. 390 B.C.E.)

---

1. Wilfred G. Lambert, "Ancestors, Authors, and Canonicity," *JCS* 11 (1957): 1-14;
Francesca Rochberg-Halton, "Canonicity in Cuneiform Texts," *JCS* 36 (1984): 127-44.

would have been read by the few and heard read in public recitations by the illiterate many. The same would be true of the works of the great tragedians. In preindustrial societies like ancient Greece and ancient Israel, the great majority of the population had neither the competence nor the motivation to read and write.[2]

In the Jewish context, books in anything like the modern understanding of the term only begin to appear in the Hellenistic period. J. B. Bury pointed out long ago that the concept of *littérateur* or author is a creation of that time. He added, perhaps somewhat hyperbolically, that from one end of the Mediterranean to the other people were expressing themselves in writing, and that since education was by then quite widely (if thinly) spread there was no lack of readers.[3] An early commentator on Qoheleth who, not untypically, is identified only by a pseudonym, may also have been guilty of hyperbole when he complained that in his day, probably the second half of the 3rd century B.C.E., there was no end of making books (Qoh 12:12).

As far as we know, the first Jewish composition in which the author identifies himself is *The Wisdom of ben Sira.* He gives us his full name towards the end of the treatise ("Jesus son of Eleazar son of Sirach of Jerusalem," Sir 50:27), and his composition is recommended to the public at the beginning in a blurb written by his grandson. Needless to say, we are at the mercy of the few sources which have survived from the obscure period of early Jewish history that covers the last century of Persian rule and the Diadochoi down to the Maccabees. One or other of the Jewish historians writing in Greek, whose work has survived only in scraps handed down by later authors including Josephus, Clement of Alexandria, and Eusebius, may antedate Sirach. Demetrius and Pseudo-Hecataeus in particular come

2. On literacy in antiquity, see William V. Harris, *Ancient Literacy* (Cambridge, Mass.: Harvard University Press, 1989), 66-93 (an average of 10 per cent of the population); Susan Niditch, *Oral World and Written Word: Ancient Israelite Literature* (Louisville: Westminster/John Knox, 1996), 39-45. Aaron Demsky, "Writing in Ancient Israel and Early Judaism, Part One: The Biblical Period," in *Mikra: Text, Translation, Reading and Interpretation of the Hebrew Bible in Ancient Judaism and Early Christianity,* ed. Martin Jan Mulder (1988; repr. Peabody: Hendrickson, 2004), 10-20, is too optimistic in assessing the degree of literacy in Israel of the biblical period, and is certainly mistaken in claiming that his maximalist view represents a consensus (15). On literacy in early Christianity, see Harry Y. Gamble, *Books and Readers in the Early Church* (New Haven: Yale University Press, 1995), 1-41.

3. J. B. Bury, *The Hellenistic Age: Aspects of Hellenistic Civilization* (New York: W. W. Norton, 1923), 32-33.

to mind.[4] Literary activity at that time also included putting texts which had become part of the national patrimony under the name of a great figure from the past: Moses as author of the Pentateuch, David of Psalms, Solomon of Proverbs and much else besides. About the same time, names were attached to prophetic books. It is unlikely that all of the names assigned to the 15 prophetic books in the biblical canon had been passed down from the time when the prophecies were first spoken or written. Some names would have been known since they occur in the text (Isaiah, Jeremiah, Ezekiel, Hosea, Amos) or in a different text (Micah in Jer 26:17-19), but in several cases (Joel, Obadiah, Nahum, Habakkuk, Zephaniah) the name of the putative author appears only in the superscription, not in the text itself. (The attribution to Habakkuk of the poem in Hab 3:1-19 is dependent on the title of the book in 1:1). One of the Twelve, Malachi, is clearly fictitious, others are not above suspicion, and for most of the units in the *Dodekapropheton* independent confirmation of authorship is lacking. The question of Isaianic authorship will be taken up in the following chapter.

Books (Heb. *sĕpārîm*) were in the form of a roll of papyrus or animal skin *(mĕgillâ)* rather than a codex. When Isa 34:4, followed by Rev 6:14, says that on judgment day the sky will be rolled up like a book, the authors are obviously thinking of a scroll, a *mĕgillâ*. The gradual transition from scroll to book in codex form, the form still in use, took place between the 1st and the 4th centuries C.E., and the spread of Christianity had much to do with it. The codex made finding a specific passage much easier and was more capacious, probably less expensive, and much easier to work with. A person needed two hands to manage a scroll, only one for a codex.[5]

In biblical texts, the term *sēper* refers to a range of products to which we would not assign the word "book."[6] These include lists, records, con-

---

4. Carl R. Holladay, *Fragments from Hellenistic Jewish Authors*, vol. 1: *Historians*. SBLTT 39 (Chico: SBL, 1983); Harold W. Attridge, "Jewish Historiography," in *Early Judaism and its Modern Interpreters*, ed. Robert A. Kraft and George W. E. Nickelsberg (Atlanta: Scholars, 1986), 311-16; Pieter W. van der Horst, "The Interpretation of the Bible by the Minor Hellenistic Authors," in Mulder, *Mikra*, 528-46.

5. On books in early Christianity, see Gamble, 42-81.

6. In a stimulating article Edgar W. Conrad stresses the need to clarify the different meanings of *sēper* in biblical texts and argues against the common assumption that orality was displaced by writing; on the contrary, in many instances the written word was the basis for oral performance. See his "Heard But Not Seen: The Representation of 'Books' in the Old Testament," *JSOT* 54 (1992): 45-59.

tracts, and other legal documents. Letters *(sĕpārîm)* are mentioned in Isaiah (37:14), as is a decree of divorce *(sēper kĕrîtût,* 50:1). In one cryptic aside (34:16), the reader is urged to consult a "Book of Yahveh." The passage immediately preceding (34:5-15) describes the impending devastation of Edom, destined to be handed over to satyrs and other unpleasant creatures under the sway of the demoness Lilith. There follows the invitation to consult this Book of Yahveh *(sēper YHVH),* a passage which Bernhard Duhm, one of the great names in Isaianic interpretation, described as one of the strangest in the prophetic corpus.[7] The idea seems to be that consulting this "book" will verify that the ecological degradation of Edom will indeed take place and that that country has been, as it were, juridically handed over to wild animals. The *sēper* in question is not further identified. It could be a lost work, like "The Book of the Wars of Yahveh" or "The Book of Yashar" (Num 21:14; Josh 10:13; 2 Sam 1:18), one which contained oracular utterances directed against hostile peoples like Edom; we are not told. At any rate, this "Book of Yahveh" is not to be confused with "the Book of God" or "the Book of the Living" which contain the names of the elect, those recorded by God for life (Isa 4:3). The "Book of Truth" of Dan 10:21 is different again, closer to the Mesopotamian "Tablets of Destiny."

From Scraps to Scrolls[8]

Since our inquiries are concerned with the future rather than the past of the book of Isaiah and, specifically, how it was received and interpreted in late antiquity, it will not be necessary to rehearse once again, in good historical-critical fashion, the history of the formation of the book. But for future reference, some issues relevant to our main theme need a brief mention.

1. The book of Isaiah is a component of Prophets *(Neviim),* the midsection of the tripartite Hebrew Bible canon. This section contains four historical books: Joshua, Judges, Samuel, Kings, and four prophetic books: Isaiah, Jeremiah, Ezekiel, the Twelve or, in the order set out in the famous baraita in the Babylonian Talmud: Jeremiah, Ezekiel, Isaiah, the

7. *Das Buch Jesaja,* 2nd ed. HKAT (Göttingen: Vandenhoeck & Ruprecht, 1922), 253.

8. I borrow this genial formulation from Philip R. Davies, "'Pen of iron, point of diamond' (Jer 17:1): Prophecy as Writing," in *Writings and Speech in Israelite and Ancient Near Eastern Prophecy,* ed. Ehud Ben Zvi and Michael H. Floyd. SBLSymS 10 (Atlanta: SBL, 2000), 72.

Twelve (*b. B. Bat.* 14b). In the following section of the baraita, dealing with the authorship of the biblical books, the order is different again. Jeremiah authored the book that bears his name together with the book of Kings and Lamentations. Hezekiah and his colleagues wrote Isaiah, Proverbs, Canticles, and Qoheleth (Ecclesiastes), while "the Men of the Great Assembly" wrote Ezekiel and the Book of the Twelve. The surprising information that King Hezekiah wrote Isaiah is explained by Rashi on the grounds that Isaiah was murdered by Manasseh before he had time to write up his prophecies himself; a more probable explanation is that "wrote" here means "copied."[9] The inclusion of history under the rubric of prophecy also calls for an explanation. Whatever else it implies, it reflects one of the transformations which prophecy was undergoing in the postdestruction phase of the history, transformations of profound and enduring importance. The profile of the prophet as critic of social mores and powerful counterforce to corrupt political and religious elites recedes into the background. It becomes the road not taken. One of its substitutes is the prophet as historian. In his polemical treatise *Against Apion,* Josephus, not unmindful of his own role as historian and his own claim to prophetic endowment, makes the remarkable claim that in Judaism "the prophets alone had this privilege (of writing historical records), obtaining their knowledge of the most remote and ancient history through the inspiration which they owed to God" (*C. Ap.* 1:37). By that time, however, the idea was familiar. According to the author of Chronicles, the prophet Isaiah was the historian of the reigns of Uzziah and Hezekiah (2 Chr 26:22; 32:32), and the Chronicler refers to several other prophets as historical sources. The ideological shift is apparent. On this showing, the authority of the prophet bears on the past, not on the present or the future, and therefore the ability of the prophet to question and even destabilize the power structures of society is neutralized.

2. Within this overall structure of the Neviim there lurks a counterstructure comprising the three (Isaiah, Jeremiah, Ezekiel) and the twelve (the *Dodekapropheton*). If, as seems probable, the final paragraph of Malachi, the last of the twelve, is the finale to the entire prophetic collection (Mal 3:23-24 [Eng. 4:5-6]), its allusion to the return of Elijah in the end time and his task of reconciliation seems to insinuate an eschatologi-

9. See the recent discussion of the baraita in Jed Wyrick, *The Ascension of Authorship* (Cambridge, Mass: Harvard University Press, 2004), 21-58.

cal reading of the collection as a whole, with a focus on the reintegration and reformation of Israel. This reading of the passage is confirmed by its earliest extant interpretation. Of Elijah, Jesus ben Sira writes:

> At the appointed time, it is written that you are destined
> to calm the wrath of God before it breaks out in fury,
> to turn the hearts of parents to their children,
> and to restore the tribes of Israel. (48:10)

This eschatological thrust into the future, towards the creation of a renewed or new community, is found in almost all the prophetic books. Its identification in Isaiah is one of the chief aims of the present study.

3. Isaiah, a collection of many "scraps" and several compilations differing in linguistic character and theme, therefore much closer to the *Dodekapropheton* than to Jeremiah and Ezekiel, is nevertheless presented as a unity, a *book*. The intent is implicit in the literary phenomenon of inclusion, that is, a deliberate linguistic and thematic parallelism between the beginning and the end of the compilation. The existence of this parallelism can be checked even without referring to the Hebrew text by comparing chapter 1, especially 1:27-31, with chapters 65–66. A unifying intention is also indicated by affixing the name Isaiah to the beginning of the scroll (1:1; 2:1), thus affirming authorial unity, though according to an understanding of authorship quite different from ours today. We will have more to say about the authorship of the book in the following chapter.

4. The prophet was, in the first instance, a public speaker, a demagogue in the etymological sense of the term. Much prophetic discourse in early Israel doubtless went unrecorded, but some survived by being recorded in writing by disciples, or committed to memory and written down subsequently, or deposited in temple archives. Since Baruch did not know Jeremiah's prophecies by heart, they had to be written down for him to read to the public during a festival in the precincts of the temple from which Jeremiah was debarred — not surprisingly since he had predicted its destruction (Jer 36:4-6). Ezekiel's chariot-throne vision appears to have been expanded and elaborated by a "school" of devotees who expatiated on the living creatures, the chariot wheels *('ôpannîm),* and the lapis throne. Isaiah confided his testimonies and teachings to his disciples in order to guarantee the authenticity of the predictions they contained after the failure of his first incursion into Judean foreign affairs (Isa 8:16).

6

This written copy is called a "testimony" *(tĕʿûdâ)*, an indication that predictive prophecies could take on a quasilegal status when written and notarized for purposes of authentication, comparable to the prophetic "witness" written in a "book" alluded to at Isa 30:8-11, a text to which we shall return.

5. The history of the interpretation of Isaiah begins in the book itself. There are numerous instances in the book of exegetical addenda attached to existing sayings. By way of example, we might consider the four brief prose addenda in the Isaianic first person narrative or Memoir (7:18-25) and the five appended to a discourse directed against Egypt (19:16-25). These latter cover a period of centuries, moving from the oracular poem condemning Egypt and mocking Egyptian claims to wisdom (19:1-15) to what is surely one of the most eirenic statements in the entire Hebrew Bible: "Blessed be my people Egypt, Assyria the work of my hands, Israel my possession" (19:25). All of these are introduced with the formula "on that day," which redirects them to a future very different from the unsatisfactory present. We can detect throughout the book an ongoing process of commentary and supplementation, of cumulative and incremental interpretative activity, until the point is reached where such activity had to be carried on outside the book, in the form of commentary on it. Hence the capacity to generate commentary, of which the earliest examples are the Qumran pesharim, is one of the surest indications that the text in question is considered authoritative, a candidate for canonical status.

This feature of the book raises the question of authorization: on what basis did the anonymous authors of these addenda in Isaiah justify their activity? Take, for example, the sayings directed against Moab, one of Judah's neighbors, which is to say, enemies. The long poem in the form of an ironic lament over the misfortunes of Moab, a poem which is a masterpiece of *Schadenfreude* (Isa 15:1–16:11), is rounded off with a comment on the ritual lamentations going on in Moab's national sanctuary referred to in the poem (15:2):

> When Moab wears himself out presenting himself at the hill-shrine, when he comes to his sanctuary to pray, he will not succeed. (16:12)

This codicil to the poem hardly called for much by way of prophetic inspiration, but a later hand has added a further "oracular," that is, predictive, statement:

7

This is the saying which Yahveh addressed to Moab a long time ago, but now Yahveh says, "Within three years, the length of employment for a hired laborer, the pomp of Moab will be humbled in spite of its great population. Those who are left will be few and of no account. (16:13-14)

This statement presupposes a claim to speak in the name of the same God who spoke years earlier through another anonymous prophet. The nexus is created by the conviction that the God who spoke then is still actively communicating through chosen intermediaries. The new pronouncement does not follow logically from the older one, is not even presented as a comment on it, yet clearly follows from a reading of the text as in some sense an inspired and authoritative utterance. It can be considered interpretation only in the broadest understanding of that word. We do not know on what basis the one responsible for the addendum considered himself authorized to create, so to speak, new prophecy out of old. Since one of the tasks of temple prophets was to denounce, curse, and predict bad fortune for the enemies of the state, he could have been one of their number.[10] At all events, the claim implied in the prediction is comparable to the authorization assumed by the Levitical scholars who expounded the laws read out by Ezra (Neh 8:7-8) or the *maśkîlîm*, the wise and learned leaders of the Daniel conventicle who also scrutinized the prophetic books (Dan 9:1-2), and of whom we shall have more to say later. The claim to authorization as a mouthpiece of the deity characteristic of prophecy has now been taken over by the interpreter of prophecy. The exegete is now the prophet.

The Literate and Illiterate
Are Invited to Read a Sealed Book

Even stranger than the allusion in Isa 34:16 to a book of Yahveh that the reader is urged to consult is the reference in 29:11-12 to a sealed book. This is one of several cryptic sayings in the book which give the impression of being intended for a limited circle of readers who can be expected to get the point:

10. Compare the case of Hananiah, whose altercation with Jeremiah in the temple precincts included a similar short-term, high-risk prediction, in this instance a prediction of the defeat of Nebuchadnezzar within two years (Jer 28:1-11).

8

The vision of all this has become for you like the words of a sealed book. When they hand it to one who knows how to read, saying, "Read this please," he replies, "I can't, for it is sealed." When the book is handed to one who can't read, with the request, "Read this please," he replies, "I don't know how to read."

It is pointless to ask an illiterate person to read a book, a fortiori a sealed book, and no less pointless to ask a person who is literate but unauthorized to break the seal to do so. But it is precisely the pointlessness which provides the clue to the function of this brief dramatic cameo. We could read it as the literary deposit of one of those prophetic sign-acts which function as a form of interaction further along the spectrum of communication from hortatory or comminatory discourse. A parallel would be Jeremiah offering wine to the Rechabites in the temple precincts (Jer 35:1-11). Jeremiah knew in advance that the members of this radically rejectionist group which eschewed alcohol would decline the offer, but the idea was to make a point for the benefit of others, in this case about fidelity to religious traditions. As the initial sentence indicates, the point being made in the present instance has something to do with failure to grasp the prophetic message, but its more precise import can be determined only in the context of the book as a whole.

So perhaps, then, there is more to this passage than meets the eye. In the first place, Isa 29:11-12 is one of those addenda referred to earlier, generally in prose rather than the usual accented "recitative" of prophetic discourse. These addenda are attached to and are generated by reflection on existing prophetic sayings, updating earlier pronouncements in light of later situations, creating in effect new prophecy out of old. They are of various kinds, but most of them serve to extend the scope of the original saying into the future. Many of these addenda are prefaced with the phrase "on that day" or a similar formula. This type of superscript introduces future projections, often expressing national and ethnic aspirations — or sometimes fantasies — including the end of the diaspora, the destruction or subjection of hostile nations, scenarios of cosmic upheaval and disintegration, and the like. Others deal with such themes as the end of idolatry (2:20; 17:7-8; 31:6-7), the abolition of warfare (2:2), the prospect of abundance, fertility, and healing (30:23-26).[11] The "on that day" formula con-

---

11. There are 44 of these "on that day" *(bayyôm hahû')* addenda in Isa 1–39 and only

nects with the prophetic topos of the "day of Yahveh" (*yôm YHVH*, Amos 5:18-20, etc.), variously described in Isaiah as "a day of burning anger" (Isa 13:13), "a day of tumult" (22:5), "a day of vengeance" (34:8; cf. 63:4), and, ominously, "a day of great slaughter when the towers come crashing down" (30:25). Taken together, these addenda contribute to an interpretative continuum leading in the direction of the kind of final resolution attested in Daniel and the Qumran sectarian writings.

This cryptic text is, then, a comment on or addendum to the passage immediately preceding:

> Be in a daze, be in a stupor, close your eyes fast, be blind;
> be drunk, but not with wine, stagger, but not with strong drink!
> For Yahveh has poured out upon you a spirit of deepest slumber;
> he has closed your eyes [the prophets], he has covered your heads
>   [the seers]. (29:9-10)

The defective syntax suggests that the phrases "the prophets" *('et-hannĕbî'îm)* and "the seers" *(haḥōzîm)* have been inserted into the saying by a Second Temple glossator with the purpose of redirecting the charge of religious insensitivity onto those officially designated as prophetic personnel at the time of writing. They were probably inserted quite early; they are, in any case, present in the Greek version (LXX), which, however, substitutes "rulers" for "seers," and in the fragmentary Qumran commentary on this verse (4QpIsa^c fr. 15-16). The scribe who added the words in parenthesis evidently shared the low opinion of officially designated prophets which seems to have been widespread during the Second Temple period (e.g., Neh 6:14; Zech 13:2-6). Compare a similar but briefer instance in 9:13-14 (Eng. 14-15):

> *lemma:* "Yahveh cut off from Israel both head and tail"
> *gloss:* "elder and dignatory are the head, the prophet [who is] the
>   teacher of falsehood, the tail"

Leaving these glosses aside, the seer is accusing his public of spiritual imperception and obduracy when faced with the prophetic word — a common Isaianic theme expressed programmatically in the vision in the

---

one in 40–66, i.e., 52:3-6. I take this to be one of several indications of the great difference between the two parts of the book at the literary level.

heavenly throne room (6:9-10). This condition is described metaphorically as blindness, a drunken stupor, and sleep.[12] The metaphors may in turn have been suggested by the no doubt hyperbolic language in which the lifestyle of the religious elite in Samaria is described in 28:7-8:

> These too stagger with wine, lurch about with strong drink;
> priest and prophet stagger with strong drink;
> they are befuddled with wine, they lurch about with strong drink;
> stagger as they see visions, go astray in giving judgment;
> all tables are covered in vomit, no place free of filth.

This very physical description of a state of serious inebriation prompts the idea of spiritual stupor and hebetude confronted with the prophetic message, which is then expressed metaphorically as an inability and perhaps also an indisposition to read the written word. And to take this one stage further, the last link in this interpretative catena is the promise that this condition — stupor, blindness, incomprehension — will eventually be removed: "The eyes that can see will no longer be closed, the ears that can hear will listen" (32:3).

Is the Sealed Book the Book of Isaiah?

Based on what has been said so far, 29:11-12, read as commentary on 29:9-10, could be explained simply as another way of expressing, through the metaphor of a sealed book, the incomprehension of the public confronted with the prophet's oral message. But a closer reading of the passage may persuade us that further layers of meaning underlie the metaphor of the sealed book.

The first question is about the meaning of the phrase "the vision of all this" *(ḥāzût hakkōl)*. The substantive *ḥāzût* is one of a cluster of Hebrew terms meaning an extraordinary visual experience, in short, a vision. The

---

12. The sleep *(tardēmâ)* is the special kind which Yahveh placed on the Man in the garden (Gen 2:21), which overcame Abraham during "the covenant of the pieces" (Gen 15:12), and which prevented Saul and his men from noticing David's entrance into their camp (1 Sam 26:12). The corresponding verb *(rdm)* describes the trance state in which Daniel experienced his visions (Dan 8:18; 10:9). Jonah, asleep in the hold of the ship, is a *nirdām*, perhaps insinuating a lack of spiritual awareness in addition to fatigue (Jonah 1:5-6).

word occurs exclusively in Isaiah and Daniel, but only in one instance apart from 29:11 is its meaning entirely clear, namely, the grim or hard vision *(ḥāzût qāšâ)* in which a prophet foresees the fall of Babylon (Isa 21:2).[13] In the context it is clearly synonymous with *ḥāzôn*, comparable to the similar description of the reception of a *ḥāzôn* in Hab 2:2. Since the book of Isaiah as a whole is presented under the rubric of a vision, the use of the word "vision" with the qualification "of all this" *(hakkōl)* in this addendum suggests the possibility that "the vision of all this" alludes to the book of Isaiah in whatever shape it existed at the time of writing. The book contains three titles: it is introduced as "The Vision of Isaiah" (1:1), there is a similar superscription at the beginning of the second chapter, "The word that Isaiah . . . saw in vision" (2:1), and the anti-Babylonian saying in Isaiah 13 is also introduced as a vision (13:1). There is critical agreement that all three titles were inserted at a relatively late period, and a late date is also indicated by 2 Chr 32:32, where Isaiah's prophecies are described comprehensively as "the vision of Isaiah ben Amoz the prophet." By that time the term *ḥāzôn* had undergone a semantic expansion, taking in much the same connotation as our word "revelation," including revelation available in writing. I suggest, therefore, that "the vision of all this" refers to a book containing Isaianic revelations, an earlier edition of the book of Isaiah as we know it, with which the scribe who added this cryptic note was familiar.

If, therefore, 29:11-12 was the work of a Second Temple scribe, perhaps the same scribe who added the prejudicial glosses about prophets and seers, it presupposes a shift towards the written end of the oral-written spectrum with respect to prophetic material, consistent with the widespread evidence for the *scribalization* of prophecy in the Second Temple period. There is some evidence that writing was, in some measure, a reaction to the nonreception of prophetic utterances. We considered earlier the case of Jeremiah, who had his prophecies, delivered orally over a 23-year

---

13. Translators ancient and modern have failed to find an entirely satisfactory explanation for *qeren ḥāzût* and *ḥāzût 'arba'* in Dan 8:5 and 8:8, respectively. When it is not emended or omitted as a gloss it is usually translated "conspicuous," qualifying the horn of the mythic ram. See the detailed textual note on Dan 8:5 in James A. Montgomery, *A Critical and Exegetical Commentary on the Book of Daniel.* ICC (Edinburgh: T. & T. Clark, 1926), 331-32. The terms *ḥōzeh* in Isa 28:15 and *ḥāzût* in 28:18 seem to allude to a pact, the "deal with death" that the ruling classes in Jerusalem boast of having made. On this passage, see my *Isaiah 1–39.* AB 19 (New York: Doubleday, 2000), 391-95, and "Judah's Covenant with Death (Isaiah XXVIII 14-22)," *VT* 50 (2000): 472-83.

period, written out on a *mĕgillat sēper,* a book in scroll form, after having been forbidden entrance into the temple, in effect, excommunicated (Jer 36:4-8). Habakkuk was told to write his vision on tablets, probably stone tablets, to guarantee its authenticity when its predictions were fulfilled (Hab 2:2-3). Since the public addressed refused to heed his message, Isaiah also had to write it on a tablet *(lûaḥ)* and inscribe it in a book *(sēper)* that it might be there in time to come as a witness forever (Isa 30:8-11).

Earlier in the book we heard that, after the failure of his first intervention in international politics, Isaiah was told to secure the message and seal his teachings among his disciples in the expectation of the eventual vindication of their truth and relevance (8:16). This is the only other mention of a sealed document in Isaiah, and in view of what has just been said, it seems likely that the sealed "vision of all these things" is a reference to Isaiah's sealed testimony confided to his disciples. To be a disciple *(limmud,* lit., "one taught") is to hold in trust and internalize the teaching of the master, whether in oral or in written form, but in this instance the latter, since only the written word can serve as a *tĕʿûdâ,* a witness for future generations. The passage about the sealed book, therefore, deals with the reception or nonreception of *written* prophecy. As a sealed real estate transaction serves to guarantee proof of title (e.g., Jer 32:9-15), so the written text committed to the prophet's disciples and protected by its seal guarantees the authenticity of the prophecy.

But why a *sealed* book? During the time of the kingdoms and in early Judaism, important documents would have been sealed with a lump of hot wax or wet clay (a bulla) on which the sender's name or some form of identification would be impressed.[14] Rulers and high officials would make the impression with a signet ring (e.g., Esth 8:8, 10), with a view to indicating the status of the sender and guaranteeing the authenticity and security of the document. The document in question could be, *inter alia,* a letter (1 Kgs 21:8), a royal edict (Esth 3:12), a notarized agreement or pact (Neh 10:1), a sealed real estate purchase document which could be produced as proof of title (Jer 32:9-15), or a divorce document (Isa 50:1; Jer 3:8; Deut 24:1-4). Important documents would require notarization by two wit-

---

14. Naḥman Avigad, "Seal, seals," *EncJud* 14: 1072-74, with many examples in the same author's *Bullae and Seals from a Post-Exilic Judean Archive* (Jerusalem: Hebrew University, 1976); and *Hebrew Bullae from the Time of Jeremiah* (Jerusalem: Israel Exploration Society, 1986).

nesses, like the tablet on which Isaiah wrote "Property of Maher-shalal-hash-baz" (Isa 8:2). We have good examples of such documents dealing with marriage and real estate among the Elephantine papyri.[15] And to come to the point, sealing a predictive prophecy had the purpose of providing irrefutable proof of its authenticity, and therefore its divine origin, at the time of fulfillment. When that happened, and the prophet was sure that it would, the situation envisaged in Isa 29:11-12 would be reversed. The book would be unsealed and its meaning would become clear to those now capable of hearing and understanding:

> On that day the deaf will hear the words of a book,
> and free of all gloom and darkness
> the eyes of the sightless will see. (29:18)

The Isaianic-Danielic Interpretative Trajectory

In biblical texts sealed prophetic books are mentioned only in Isaiah and Daniel (Dan 8:26; 9:24; 12:4, 9). The sealed book containing secrets hidden in the mind of God, coded messages awaiting decryption, is one of the more expressive motifs of apocalyptic discourse in Daniel, Qumran, and early Christianity. That the book is sealed is sometimes implied rather than stated explicitly, especially in apocalyptic texts. We are not told that the 70 esoteric books copied by Ezra and his team of scribes and reserved for "the wise among your people" were sealed, but since they contained apocalyptic revelations they probably were (4 Ezra 14:45-48). It would therefore be imprudent not to consider the possibility that there exists a connection of some kind between the sealed book of Isa 29:11-12 and later apocalyptic references to such books, especially since the thrust towards the apocalyptic worldview is in evidence throughout the book of Isaiah. The thematic and linguistic affinities between Isaiah and Daniel, not much noticed in the commentaries, at least justify taking this inquiry a little further.

To begin with the broad view, what is central to both books is a critique of the great empires. In Isaiah the empires are Assyria, Babylonia, Persia; in Daniel, Babylonia, Media, Persia, and the Greeks, to which list

15. A. E. Cowley, *Aramaic Papyri of the Fifth Century B.C.* (1923; repr. Osnabrück: Otto Zeller, 1967), nos. 6, 8, 13, 15, 18, 36.

Qumranic and early Christian apocalyptic will add the Romans. Daniel therefore overlaps with Isaiah and takes the sequence further. In Daniel, written and circulated during the persecution of Antiochus IV about the year 165 B.C.E., the historical panorama is viewed from the perspective of the Babylonian exile in the Neo-Babylonian and early Persian period, and this perspective dominates the way later sectarian movements view the history and their place in it. This too is Isaianic, since the exile serves as the fulcrum of the book and the most important point of reference for its theological meaning. The interpretation in Daniel's third vision of the 70 weeks of exile, based on Jer 29:10, is dictated by a view of history according to which events are predetermined by divine decree. At this point the language is too close to Isaiah for it to be coincidental. Gabriel reveals that desolations are decreed, leading to an end that is foreordained:

> After the sixty-two weeks an anointed one will be cut off and no one will support him. The people of the prince that is to come will destroy the city and the sanctuary. His end will be in a cataclysm, and towards the end there will be war. *Desolation is decreed.* He will make a strong pact with the many for one week, and for half a week he will put a stop to sacrifices and offerings. In the train of these abominations there will be one who creates desolation, until the *destruction that is decreed* is poured out upon the desolator. (Dan 9:26-27)[16]

Compare the following passages from Isaiah:

> The Sovereign Lord Yahveh of the hosts will bring about *the destruction that is decreed* in the midst of the earth. (10:23)

> I have heard (in vision?) *destruction decreed* by the Sovereign Lord Yahveh of the hosts over all the earth. (28:22b)[17]

---

16. There are several uncertainties in this passage and therefore in the translation offered. At 9:26 I have translated *wĕ'ên lô* with "and no one to support him," which is speculative but makes better sense than "and shall have nothing" (NRSV). "Cataclysm" translates *šeṭep*, lit., "flood"; the substantive does not occur in Isaiah but the corresponding verb *(šṭp)* is used frequently in contexts describing annihilating judgment (Isa 8:8; 10:22; 28:2,15; 30:28). "In the train of these abominations" translates *'al kĕnap šiqqûṣîm*, (lit., "on the wing of abominations"), following NEB.

17. The verb *ḥrṣ* (Niphal), "decree," appears only in these two texts of Isaiah and in Dan 9:26-27; 11:36. Note the unusual phrase *kālâ wĕneḥĕrāṣâ* ("the destruction that is de-

At several other points in Daniel we hear echoes of Isaiah. In the first of the four visions (Dan 7:1-28), the throne room scenario is reminiscent of Ezekiel 1 but also of Isaiah 6, the vision of the heavenly audience chamber. In the vision of the Ram and the Goat (8:1-27), the description of Little Horn, a disparaging sobriquet for Antiochus IV, who ascends as high as the host of heaven, seems to have been inspired by the Isaianic poem about the fate of the king of Babylon, "Star of the dawning day, fallen to the ground" (Isa 14:12-15). This would suggest that the Daniel group read this chapter (Isa 14:3-23) as referring to the contemporary tyrant, a procedure familiar from the Qumran pesharim.[18] In the third vision (Dan 9:1-27), Daniel's confession of sin, spoken in the name of Israel past and present (9:1-19), is similar in form and language to the communal lament of Isa 63:7–64:11 (Eng. 12). This kind of prayer, well-attested in the Second Temple period (e.g., Ezra 9:6-15; Neh 9:6-37), is also represented at Qumran in 4Q504, a text published by Maurice Baillet under the title "Paroles des Lumières" ("Words of the Heavenly Luminaries").[19]

Affinity with Daniel, and with the worldview of the apocalyptic sects of the late Second Temple period, is especially in evidence in Isaiah 24–27, somewhat misleadingly referred to as the "Isaian Apocalypse." In his discussion of the authorship of this section of the book, Bernhard Duhm remarked that Isaiah could as well have written the book of Daniel as Isaiah 24–27.[20] While there are significant differences compared with later apocalyptic writings — there is no periodization of history, for example, and no consistent dualism — several typically apocalyptic themes appear in this section. Judgment is passed on the whole world, not just on the unnamed city (24:1-13, 17-20), and is accompanied by cosmic disturbances (24:21-23); in the last days death will be abolished (25:8) and the dead will be raised (26:19), though not all commentators agree that this is to be understood literally; the motifs of the messianic banquet (25:6) and the final harvesting (27:12) are also adumbrated. One passage in particular deserves a closer

---

creed"), hendiadys, in Dan 9:27 and Isa 10:23; 28:22; also *'ad-kālâ za'am* ("until the time of wrath is completed") in Dan 11:36b (cf. Isa 26:20). Similar language occurs in the Qumran texts, e.g., 1QS IV 25 *qēṣ neḥĕrāṣâ* ("the predetermined end").

18. See the remarks of Michael A. Knibb, "'You Are Indeed Wiser Than Daniel'. Reflections on the Character of the Book of Daniel" in *The Book of Daniel in the Light of New Findings*, ed. A. S. van der Woude. BETL 106 (Leuven: Leuven University Press, 1993), 400-411.

19. *Qumrân Grotte 4, III (4Q482-520)*. DJD 7 (Oxford: Clarendon, 1982), 137-75.

20. *Das Buch Jesaja*, 172.

look. Following on a description of a state of general religious euphoria in the Jewish world inclusive of the eastern and western diasporas (24:14-16a), we come upon one of several instances in the book of the intrusion of an authorial voice:

> But meanwhile I thought,
> "I have my secret! I have my secret!
> Woe to the unfaithful ones who deal faithlessly,
> who deal with an utter lack of faith!
> Terror, the trap, the deep pit
> await you who dwell on the earth!" (24:16b-17)

In biblical texts the Aramaic word *rāz* ("secret"), a loanword from Old Persian, occurs only here and in Daniel, where it functions as a key component of the interpretative process.[21] The thing to be interpreted, the *interpretandum* or "the text," can be a dream in the head of a mad king, a dream he doesn't even remember (Dan 2:18-19, 27-30, 47; 4:6). It can be a ghostly message written on a wall (5:25), or a dream-vision featuring strange and fearsome beasts (7:1-14). It can also be a biblical text like the 70 years of Jeremiah (Jer 25:11-12; 29:10), the correct interpretation of which is revealed *for the first time* to the seer (Dan 9:2), just as the real meaning of Habakkuk is revealed *for the first time* to the Teacher of Righteousness (1QpHab VII 1-2). The true meaning of these "texts," encrypted in the mind of God, is inaccessible to the uninitiated reader. God it is who "reveals mysteries" (Dan 2:28) and "seals up mysteries and reveals hidden things" (4QHodayot[a] 7 I 19). The encrypted message is the *rāz*, the key to decoding of which is communicated to a chosen individual in an ambient of prayer, fasting, penitential practices, and conversation with angels. On the reading of Isa 24:16b-17 proposed here, the Isaianic seer claims to be the recipient of such a message, in this case a message of judgment at odds with the prevalent mood of religious euphoria.

---

21. Dan 2:18-19, 27-30, 47; 4:6. NRSV "I pine away, I pine away" for *rāzî-lî, rāzî-lî* assumes a verbal stem *rzh*, "to be thin," "to waste away," but this seems incongruous in the context, and "I have my secret!" is supported by several of the ancient versions (Syriac, Lucianic, Symmachus, Theodotion, Vulgate) as well as the Targum. See my *Isaiah 1-39*, 352-57. In the Qumran sectarian writings, *rāz* is a key word of frequent occurrence (1QpHab VII 4, 8; 1QS III 21; XI 3-4; 1QH I 11-12; 1QM III 9; XIV 14; XVI 11, 16). See Otto Betz, *Offenbarung und Schriftforschung in der Qumransekte* (Tübingen: Mohr, 1960), 82-86.

A final example of this trajectory from Isaiah to Daniel and beyond can be found in the final verse of the book of Isaiah, a verse which has induced a feeling of dismay in several commentators:

> They will go out and gaze on the corpses of those who rebelled against me; for neither will the worm that consumes them die nor the fire that burns them be quenched; they will be an object of horror to all flesh. (Isa 66:24)

This dantesque scenario of fire and corruption is replicated in several texts from the Hasmonean and early Roman periods, including early Christian texts. It does not appear in these terms in Daniel, but it is worth noting that the word *dērā'ôn* ("object of horror") occurs only here and in Dan 12:2 with reference to those whose final lot is shame and everlasting contempt.

This ideological alignment between the book of Isaiah in its development towards its final form and the book of Daniel strengthens the impression that the sealed book of Isa 29:11-12 is the "instruction" *(tôrâ)* and the "testimony" *(tĕ'ûdâ)* of Isa 8:16, but now to be read as a corpus of eschatological teaching intelligible only in the context of the apocalyptic worldview.

The Sealed Book in Daniel

These examples of what we may call Danielic themes and expressions in Isaiah, or Isaianic themes in Daniel, exemplify the kind of learned retrieval and reworking of existing prophetic material by means of which religious traditions were formed and consolidated. They also provide an appropriate preface to the theme of written and sealed eschatological prophecy in both books. The sage Daniel committed to writing the first of the four dream-visions together with its decoded meaning provided by an intermediary, the angelic interpreter or go-between in this interactive vision (Dan 7:1), but we are not told that he sealed it. This is the vision of the four beasts emerging from the sea, which draws on ancient mythic themes also represented in Isaiah — Leviathan, the dragon in the primeval sea; Rahab, symbol of oppressive Egyptian imperial power (Isa 27:1; 30:7). The vision of the Ram and the Goat, zodiacal symbols of Persia and Syria, respectively (8:1-14), also receives its interpretation in the course of an interactive exchange in the vision (8:15-25). We pick up several Isaianic echoes in this second vision narrative, beginning with Little Horn (Antiochus IV), who "magnified himself" up to the host of heaven, language which recalls the poem about the fate of the king of Babylon (Isa 14:12-15). At the conclusion of the interpretation given by Gabriel, Daniel is told to "keep the vision secret for it is for many days hence" (8:26). Though he had not been told explicitly to write it, writing is clearly implied throughout the vision sequence, and the only way to keep a written prophecy secret was to seal it. There is therefore practically no difference between keeping secret (Heb. verb *stm*) and sealing *(htm)*. The eschatological meaning of the vision is repeatedly emphasized: Gabriel informs the seer that "the vision is for the end time" (8:17); it is reserved for the terminal period of wrath (8:19), the predestined time of the end (8:19). And he is told to seal it since "it is for many days hence" (8:26).

In keeping with the conventions of pseudepigraphy, the chronological frame of reference adopted by the writer, the "many days" of Dan 8:26, corresponds to the interval between the Neo-Babylonian period (ca. 550 B.C.E.) and the reign of the Seleucid king Antiochus IV (175-164 B.C.E.), a span of time therefore not far short of four centuries. The sealing of the vision narrative in the Neo-Babylonian period was necessary to explain why the momentous events mentioned in the vision remained unpublished and unknown during the intervening centuries. It also allowed the seer responsible for this *vaticinium ex eventu* to take the long view, to locate present situations and events of relevance to the sect in the context of a teleological view of history. He was thereby enabled to present a theological interpretation of events as foreseen and preordained by God, and thus to assure his associates of their eventual outcome in the destruction of the tyrant, an event which would come about by nonhuman agency (8:25). Locating the seer and his associates in the eastern diaspora in the last years of Babylonian rule served, finally, to underline the conviction of the conventicle in which the book was produced that they were the legitimate heirs of the "holy remnant" of the exilic period. This link with the few faithful survivors of the destruction of the Judean state and subsequent deportations is not confined to Daniel. It corresponds to the account of the origins of the Damascus sect in CD I 1–II 1, where the 390 years beginning with Nebuchadrezzar's conquest of Judah (CD I 5-6) corresponds to the period in Daniel 8 during which the book containing the vision remained sealed. We shall see that the same perspective on the exilic and postexilic periods appears in the Enoch cycle (*1 En* 93:8-10) and Jubilees (*Jub* 1:13-18).

In the third vision (Dan 9:1-27), Daniel is discovered poring over "the books" (*sĕpārîm*, 9:2) and specifically over Jeremiah's prediction of 70 years exile (Jer 25:11-12; 29:10). Since this vision is presented as taking place in the first year of Darius, therefore for the author at the very beginning of the period of Persian rule (cf. 5:30-31),[22] the 70 years would have just run their course, thus facilitating their reinterpretation. The period of 70 years is extended to 70 times seven, therefore 490 years, parallel to the period during which the previous vision remained sealed.[23] On this occasion Daniel receives no instructions, but Gabriel tells him that the 70 weeks of years are decreed "to seal the prophetic vision" (9:24; lit., "vision and prophet"; hendiadys). Since the purpose of sealing is to authenticate, the point is that the truth and authenticity of both the vision and its recipient will be ratified only after the passage of 490 years, after which it will no longer be necessary to keep the written vision sealed. The author therefore revises the earlier interpretation of the 70 years in 2 Chr 36:22, according to which the 70 years came to an end in the first year of Cyrus; his calculation begins where the one in Chronicles ends (Dan 9:25). The period of 490 years was necessary to finish transgression, fill up the measure of sin, expiate iniquity, bring in righteousness at its conclusion, seal the prophetic vision, and anoint a holy place (9:24). The last phrase indicates the end of this long span of time with the rededication of the temple in 164 B.C.E. The implied negative judgment passed on the entire postexilic period down to the time of writing becomes explicit in Gabriel's exposition, where it is described as a time of distress (9:25),[24] and we find the same negative judgment in the historical perspective of the Damascus Document (CD I 5-6) and the Enochian Apocalypse of Weeks (*1 En* 93:9). This theologically inspired historiographical perspective will occupy us in a later chapter.

22. It will not be necessary to discuss the complicated and confused historical references in the book. The perspective is drastically foreshortened, since according to the author Belshazzar is the son of and successor to Nebuchadnezzar and is followed directly by Darius.

23. On the 70 years of Jeremiah and Daniel there is, unsurprisingly, a very substantial bibliography. I mention only John J. Collins, *Daniel*. Herm (Minneapolis: Fortress, 1993), 352-53; and Devorah Dimant, "The Seventy Weeks Chronology (Dan 9, 24-27) in the Light of New Qumranic Texts," in van der Woude, *Book of Daniel*, 57-76. She brings 4QPseudo Moses (4Q390) to bear on the discussion.

24. On the phrase *bĕṣôq ha'ittîm*, see Montgomery, 380-81; Collins, 356. R. H. Charles, *A Critical and Exegetical Commentary on the Book of Daniel* (Oxford: Clarendon, 1929), 244, emends to *bĕqēṣ ha'ittîm*, following LXX and Syr, an emendation which seems to me to be unnecessary.

The fourth vision (Dan 10–12), like its predecessor, takes place in an atmosphere of penitential prayer, the confession of sin, fasting, and abstinence (10:1-3; cf. 9:3-21). The vision is described as an authentic utterance (10:1) transcribed from a heavenly "Book of Truth" (10:21). This topos, no doubt deriving from the Mesopotamian Tablets of Destiny, implies a strong sense of predestination. In the Enochian *Book of the Heavenly Luminaries* (1 *En* 81:1-2) the angel Uriel instructs Enoch to read the heavenly tablets which contain the record of all human history, while in the *Apocalypse of Weeks* (1 *En* 93:2) the epitomized history from Enoch's birth to the actual time of writing is cited from the heavenly tablets. Likewise, at the outset of this fourth vision, Gabriel's detailed account of events from the Persian period to Antiochus IV draws on "the Book of Truth," which also contains the names of the elect (10:21; 12:1). The same idea is adumbrated in the census of the restored community in Jerusalem whose names are "recorded for life" according to Isa 4:3, and this idea of a saved community, an anticipation of the saints of the final age, a kind of realized eschatology, may well be behind the actual list of citizens of the new commonwealth in Nehemiah 7. The eschatological import of the vision in Daniel is, in any case, explicit: it is for the last days, and only a short time remains for its fulfillment (10:14). Every event in the progress towards this consummation happens at its preordained time (11:29). After the "time of anguish" (12:1; cf. Isa 33:2), the faithful people will be delivered and will enjoy astral immortality (12:1-3). Daniel is then instructed to write the vision and seal it until the end time, when all of this is to happen (Dan 12:4). The injunction is repeated by an interlocutor in a follow-up to this interactive vision, after which Daniel is dismissed now that the words of the vision are sealed until the end time (12:9).

The claim implicit in this presentation is one of remarkable audacity. The period from the Babylonian exile to the emergence of the Danielic sect is seen as a time of distress, spiritual blindness, and failure, a situation comparable to that of those unable to read the sealed book in Isa 29:11-12. It appears that, according to the author, the basic problem during this long period was lack of access to the revelation which he represents as having been sealed up in the early Persian period. The point is perhaps being made in Dan 12:4, where, by emending *haddāʿat* ("knowledge") to *hārāʿâ* ("evil"), we have the plausible reading "Many shall run to and fro and evil will increase." This would then find its explanation in Amos 8:12, "They shall run to and fro seeking the word of Yahveh but they will not find it."

The Danielic group sees itself as directly linked with those who survived the exile with their faith intact, those who, in another Isaianic borrowing, will be known in Qumran as "the penitents of Israel." It is this conviction which explains the juxtaposition of the diaspora tales in chapters 1–6 with the visions in chapters 7–12. The four Judean youths at the Babylonian court combined comprehensive learning with intense piety; they were "versed in all (aspects of) wisdom" (1:4), for God had given them knowledge, literary skill, and wisdom. Daniel, renamed Belteshazzar, as one of the group, shared in these endowments, but his insight into visions and dreams, illustrated in the following tales, set him apart (1:17). The language seems to suggest a small-scale representation of the *rabbîm* and *maśkîlîm*, respectively, the Danielic sectarians and their leaders, as recipients of the revelations to follow.[25]

The most impressive and, in its effects, the most significant borrowing from Isaiah in Daniel is the characterization of the group within which and for which the book was written as *maśkîlîm*, "the wise among the people" (11:33). These are the ones who are gifted with supernatural enlightenment enabling them to understand what is really going on (12:10). They face persecution and death (11:33-35), but are consoled with the prospect of resurrection and immortality (12:3). In these respects they replicate the fate of the Servant of the Lord who, after suffering and death, will be greatly exalted and will see light (Isa 52:13; 53:11). The linguistic connections begin rather tenuously with the opening line of the Isaianic poem, "See, my Servant will achieve success" (52:13),[26] but it comes into sharper focus in the relation between the *maśkîlîm* and the *rabbîm*, "the Many," a term which, in the Danielic context, in Qumran, and perhaps in early Christianity, refers to the author's fellow sectarians. The former will not only instruct the latter (Dan 11:32-33) but will vindicate them or lead them to righteousness (12:3) following the example of the Servant ("My servant will vindicate/ lead to righteousness the Many," Isa 53:11b). How this is to happen we are not told, but the association of the Danielic sages with the Servant suggests that it would come about, in some way, through their suffering and the

25. In Dan 12:10 the *rabbîm*, who are to be purified, cleansed, and refined, are differentiated from the *maśkîlîm*, and both are differentiated from the *rěšā'îm*, the reprobate. But in 11:35 all those who are to undergo the same cathartic process are called *maśkîlîm*. The usage is therefore not entirely consistent.

26. *hinnēh yaśkîl 'avdî*, in which *yaśkîl* ("will achieve success" or "will be wise") is from the same verbal stem as *maśkîl(îm)*.

death of those who had already fallen victim to persecution (Dan 11:33-35). In Daniel, therefore, the Servant of Isaiah 53 receives, for the first time, a collective interpretation.

Sealed and Secret Books after Daniel

Apocalyptic writings subsequent to Daniel which have survived from the Hasmonean and Roman periods — some even later — refer to secret books, sealed books, and heavenly books as the source of esoteric knowledge communicated to a chosen intermediary. Examples can be found in the Enoch cycle (*1 En* 81:1-2), *The Ascension of Isaiah* (9:22-23), and the *Odes of Solomon* (9:11). The book of *Jubilees* opens with the revelation to Moses on Mount Sinai of the tablets of the law together with a second revelation, "the law and the testimony." The relevant Qumran manuscript of *Jubilees* (4Q216 = 4QJubilees[a]) is fragmentary, but this additional revelation is clearly referred to as *hattôrâ wĕhatĕ'ûdâ,* using the same terms as in Isa 8:16: "Secure the testimony *(tĕ'ûdâ),* seal the instruction *(tôrâ)* among my disciples" (I 11-12; IV 4 corresponding to *Jub* 1:4, 26). The most interesting point is that in *Jubilees* the testimony and instruction consist in "what was in the beginning and what will happen in the future" or "an account of the division of all the days" (*Jub* 1:4). The reference is to the book of *Jubilees* itself as consisting in an account of events to the time of Moses followed by predictions, mostly unfavorable, of the future leading to the final epoch of history. This will witness a new creation, the erection of the eschatological temple, and the self-manifestation of God in Jerusalem (1:27-28). In this context, therefore, Isaiah's sealed testimony is in effect a transcription of the heavenly tablets containing these revelations, which itself is a transcription made by the Angel of the Presence or by Moses himself. The author of *Jubilees* seems, then, to have understood the sealed document confided by Isaiah to his disciples as an esoteric record revelatory of future events.[27]

In most instances the sealed book contains the names of the elect and is to be opened or unsealed only at the end of time (*4 Ezra* 6:20-21; *Odes Sol.* 23:5-6). In one late text the seer observes the heavenly archivist taking the scroll out of its container, breaking the seal, and handing it to the En-

---

27. See Cana Werman, "'The תורה and the תעודה' Engraved on the Tablets," *DSD* 9 (2002): 75-103.

throned One (3 *En* 27:1-3). But the idea of apocalyptic as esoteric, book knowledge comes to clearest expression in the Ezra apocalypse composed in the late 1st century C.E. but purporting to come from 30 years after the fall of Jerusalem, therefore from 556 B.C.E. (4 *Ezra* 3:1). With the assistance of five amanuenses and fortified by a fiery liquid, Ezra reproduced in 40 days the 94 books destroyed during the sack of Jerusalem. Of these, 24 were the scriptural books available to all, worthy and unworthy alike, while the remaining 70 contained esoteric knowledge destined for "the wise among your people," a designation taken from Dan 11:33 *(maśkîlê 'ām)*. These were to remain secret, and therefore presumably sealed (4 *Ezra* 14:44-48). The allusion is clearly to apocalyptic writings which, at least from the point of view of their esoteric nature and restricted readership, are considered to be on a higher level than the other writings made publicly available. This, too, corresponds to a common belief among apocalyptically-minded sectarian groups who tend to value nothing more than their esoteric doctrine.

It is hardly surprising that the Qumranites were intensely concerned with mysteries hidden from previous generations and now revealed to their founder and, through him, to the members of the community. Secrecy and esotericism are connatural with sectarianism. Josephus, for example, reports that the Essenes took an oath to guard the secrecy of their books and the names of the angels (*War* 1:142). In the rule books, hymns, and prayers from Qumran the authors speak with awe of God's wonderful mysteries *(rāzê pele')* and the mysteries of his knowledge *(rāzê da'at)*.[28] The community itself constitutes or encapsulates a "sealed mystery": "He who makes the holy shoot grow into the true planting hides its sealed mystery, unknown and unregarded." The community as God's planting is an Isaianic image,[29] and the mystery has to do with the understanding of history, the place of the community in the great scheme of things, the divinely predestined and guided flow of historical events, and their proximate consummation, "the mystery of the future."[30] These mysteries concerning the

---

28. CD III 18; 1QS III 23; IV 6; XI 5, 19; 1QH^a V 8; IX 21; 1QM III 9, etc.

29. 1QH^a XVI 10-11; cf. Dan 11:7; CD I 7. In Isa 60:21 the new people of God will be "the shoot that I myself planted, the work of my hands that I may be glorified."

30. This I take to be the meaning of *rāz nihyeh* rather than "the mystery of existence" as rendered by Florentino García Martínez and Eibert J. C. Tigchelaar; see 1QS XI 3; 1Q Instruction (1Q26); 1QMysteries and 4QMysteries^b. The expression also occurs about 20 times in 4QInstruction. See Matthew J. Goff, *The Worldly and Heavenly Wisdom of 4QInstruction.* STDJ 50 (Leiden: Brill, 2003).

final consummation of history have been revealed to the Teacher of Righteousness (1QpHab VII 5-8). That the author of the *Hodayot* frequently claims to be the privileged recipient of God's wonderful mysteries and the one who mediates them to the members of his group (e.g., 1QH^a IX 21; X 13; XII 27-28) adds plausibility to the hypothesis identifying him with the Teacher of Righteousness.

Unfortunately, no pesher has survived on Isa 24:16a, the seer's exclamation about the secret *(rāz)* confided to him, but the passage immediately following (24:16b-17), pronouncing judgment on the faithless ones and disaster on the inhabitants of the earth, was appropriated by the Qumran sectarians. The alliterative *paḥad wĕpaḥat wĕpaḥ* ("terror, the trap, the deep pit") received its own pesher in the Damascus Document, where it is identified with the three nets of Belial, namely, fornication, wealth, and desecration of the temple (CD IV 14). The title *bōgĕdîm* ("faithless ones") also served to characterize those who broke away and founded their own conventicle (or from whom the Damascus group splintered off), referred to in the Damascus Document as "the congregation of the faithless ones" (CD I 12), language typical of intrasectarian polemics.

The claim to be the privileged recipients of esoteric knowledge was central to the Qumran sectarians' self-understanding, and since they formed a learned, scribal, and priestly society, this knowledge was transmitted by means of texts. One unfortunately fragmentary text, 4QMysteries^b, appears to reflect a dispute between rival esoteric schools. One of these is said to be foolish since "the seal of the vision has been sealed up from you, you have not looked on the eternal mysteries, and you have not grasped (true) knowledge." The result is that "if you (try to) open the vision, it will be closed to you." Here, too, as it seems, the mystery *(rāz)* deals with knowledge about the past and future accessible only through divine revelation disclosed in vision to chosen intermediaries. We are also reminded that there may have been more of these small conventicles claiming esoteric knowledge and special revelations than the few we know about from the sources at our disposal.

In the first Christian apocalypse, the first of many, the heavenly scenario presents the Enthroned One holding a book with seven seals that no one in heaven or earth could open. When, notwithstanding, the seals are progressively broken by the Lamb that is Slain (a representation adopted from the so-called Animal Apocalypse, *1 En* 90:8), the book reveals a sequence of disasters in store for humanity described in terms taken over from the canonical prophetic books. After the breaking of the seventh seal, the seer is instructed to seal up what the seven thunders had spoken and yet not to write it down (Rev 10:1-4). However this is to be understood, at the end of the vision he is told not to seal the words of the prophecy since the time of the end, and therefore the time of ultimate disclosure, is near (Rev 22:10).

The complicated and hallucinatory scenarios in Revelation draw on a wide range of biblical texts, among which Isaiah is understandably prominent. The borrowings include descriptions of cosmic upheaval (Rev 6:12-14; cf. Isa 13:10; 34:4; 50:3), the attempt to survive the final judgment by hiding in caves and holes in the ground (Rev 6:15; cf. Isa 2:10, 19), and the consoling scene of God wiping away tears from every face (Rev 7:17; cf. Isa 25:8). The flight into the wilderness of the Woman Clothed with the Sun (Rev 12:5-6) is a special case since her flight resulted from a mistranslation in the Old Greek version of the Hebrew verb *mlṭ* (Hiphil) in Isa 66:7, which, in addition to the more usual meaning "escape," "take flight," can also mean "bring to birth,"[31] one of the more interesting examples of the generation of new narrative from the assiduous reading of biblical texts.

The argument presented in this chapter may be summarized as follows. The cryptic saying in Isa 29:11-12 about a sealed book and its implied readers (or implied nonreaders) refers to the sealed document of Isa 8:16, understood as the book of Isaiah read and interpreted from an eschatological-apocalyptic perspective. As such, it indicates what kind of a "book" Isaiah is in its final form, that is, the form it attained by the time it began to generate independent commentary. It provides an essential clue to the shift from oral to written prophecy and from prophetic eschatology to apocalyptic eschatology, in other words, a kind of discourse and an assemblage of themes with significant affinities to the apocalyptic scenarios and images represented primarily by the book of Daniel. While agreeing that the apocalypticism of Daniel and Enoch is a more developed and complex phenomenon than anything in Isaiah or, for that matter, any of the other prophetic books,[32] I maintain that there are enough indications

---

31. As in Isa 34:15, where *mlṭ* refers to owls laying eggs. See my *Isaiah 56-66*. AB 19B (New York: Doubleday, 2003), 302-3.

32. A point emphasized by John J. Collins, "From Prophecy to Apocalypticism: The Expectation of the End," in *The Encyclopedia of Apocalypticism*, vol. 1: *The Origins of Apocalypticism in Judaism and Christianity* (New York: Continuum, 1998), 130-34.

in Isaiah, one or two of which I have mentioned, to demonstrate a development in its literary history in the direction of the apocalyptic worldview, a position which many critical commentators would accept. The two categories of potential readers, the competent and the illiterate, would then refer, respectively, to those who do not share the eschatological consciousness which alone renders the message intelligible and those for whom any kind of prophetic discourse is unintelligible. Neither has the key to crack the code, and so for both the offer falls on deaf ears.

And finally, if this is so, it must raise serious questions for the widely accepted view of canonicity as the outcome of deliberations and decisions emanating from the religious leadership, in this instance primarily the Jerusalem priesthood, and as embodying a self-consistent set of normative and authoritative beliefs. Apocalyptic eschatology is essentially a group phenomenon, and the groups which draw their spiritual sustenance from this view of reality are typically not at the center of power. On the contrary, they tend to reject either explicitly or implicitly the claims of the religious authorities and redefine the redemptive media according to their own lights. Hence a book like Isaiah, in the final form of which the apocalyptic worldview is clearly if unsystematically inscribed, does not fit this idea of normative and authoritative canonicity.[33] This situation clearly problematizes the canonical status of the book of Isaiah while raising some hard questions for the proponents of "canonical criticism" in general. Questions also arise about the role of Isaiah himself as putative author of the book, an issue which will occupy us in the following chapter.

---

33. See my paper, "The Formation of the Hebrew Bible Canon: Isaiah as a Test Case" in *The Canon Debate*, ed. Lee Martin McDonald and James A. Sanders (Peabody: Hendrickson, 2002), 53-67.

· CHAPTER 2 ·

Isaiah: Author, Prophet, Man of God

Isaiah as Author

A major issue for the interpreter of Isaiah 1–39 is the presence in these chapters of two distinct and contrasting profiles of the prophet. There is the Isaiah of the sayings, an uncompromising critic of the political and religious establishment of his day; and there is the "man of God" of the narrative sections — of the type represented by Elijah and Elisha — in which capacity Isaiah plays a positive and corroborative role in society, doing what the "man of God" in ancient Israel was expected to do — advising, comforting, healing, and, in general, being supportive. This poses a problem for the interpreter: Are the differences merely perspectival or must we conclude that they are irreconcilable? And if the latter, how did this basic incompatibility within the first part of the book come about?

Before addressing these questions, a word should be said about Isaiah as author of the book which bears his name. Since it would be difficult to think of Isaiah in any realistic sense as author of the narrative passages which refer to him in the third person and in which he is presented in the role of a typical "man of God," we are dealing essentially with the authorship of the sayings which make up the bulk of the material in the book. Limiting ourselves, then, to this discourse material, we would have to say that Isaianic authorship is not strongly attested. Isaiah is not mentioned in any source external to the Bible, and in his capacity as author he is named only in three titles (1:1; 2:1; 13:1), which critical commentators agree were added long after the time of the putatively historical Isaiah active in the 8th century B.C.E. Furthermore, the title in 13:1 introduces a pronouncement against Babylon which all admit to be pseudonymous since, given the historical situation, a writer in the 8th century would have had no reason to anticipate or celebrate the fall of Babylon which happened two centuries later. Apart from these titles, the prophet's name appears only in the three narrative sections of chapters 1–39 which feature the alternative "man of God" role. It occurs once in the account of the campaign of Syria and Samaria against Jerusalem in chapters 6–8 (7:3), twice in the account of Isaiah's disconcerting intervention in an Assyrian campaign against Egyptians and Ethiopians in chapter 20 (20:2, 3), and 10 times in the long narrative relating Sennacherib's siege of Jerusalem in chapters 36–39 (= 2 Kgs 18–20). The absence of cross-referencing between narratives and discourses reinforces the impression that they are of quite different origin.

According to the critical consensus, the titles were added at some point in the Second Temple period, and later in that period rather than earlier. The first, "the Vision of Isaiah" *(ḥăzôn yĕšaʿyāhû)*, the title of the book as a whole, is identical with the title of a book attributed to Isaiah by the author of the books of Chronicles (hereafter the Chronicler) writing in the late Persian or early Hellenistic period (2 Chr 32:32). According to the Chronicler, Isaiah ben Amoz was the historian of the reigns of Uzziah and Hezekiah (2 Chr 26:22; 32:32); he is therefore one of several prophets whom the author has transformed into historians: Samuel, Nathan, and Gad for David's reign (1 Chr 29:29), Nathan, Ahijah, and Iddo for Solomon (2 Chr 9:29), Shemaiah and Iddo for Rehoboam (12:15), Iddo for Abijah (13:22), and Jehu ben Hanani for Jehoshaphat (20:34). Jesus ben Sira also speaks of Isaiah's Vision (Sir 48:22). Another indication is the term *ḥăzôn* ("vision") in the title of the book, also the title of the much smaller books of Obadiah and Nahum. This term occurs predominantly and perhaps exclusively in late biblical texts — seven times in Ezekiel, 12 times in Daniel — and has undergone a semantic expansion similar to the transformation of the term *nābî*, "prophet," coming eventually to be practically synonymous with "revelation" or "revealed teaching."

There are other clues pointing to the late date of these superscripts. Both Isa 1:1 and 2:1 refer to "Judah and Jerusalem," which is the standard formula in the postexilic period[1] but the reverse of the order in sayings

---

1. 2 Chr 11:14; 20:17; 24:6, 9; Ezra 9:9; 10:7.

generally taken to be of early date.[2] There are seven other Isaiahs named in biblical texts, and all are from the time of the Second Temple. One belongs to the Judean dynastic line (1 Chr 3:21), one is a Judeo-Babylonian belonging to the Elam phratry who did aliyah with Ezra (Ezra 8:7), and another is an eponym of Benjaminites living in Jerusalem at the time of Nehemiah (Neh 11:7). The remaining four are all Levites: three from different guilds of temple musicians (Ezra 8:19; 1 Chr 25:3, 15) and the fourth a temple treasurer (26:25).[3] The name also occurs in the Elephantine papyri from the 5th century B.C.E. and on two seals of uncertain origin.[4]

The late date of the titles inevitably raises questions about the literal understanding of authorship as applied to the book of Isaiah, but attribution to any one author is in any case ruled out by the abundant evidence that the book was compiled from the work of different hands over several centuries, with sayings expanded, commented on, and reinterpreted by other sayings from a later time. The same conclusion is indicated by the considerable amount of overlap between the book of Isaiah and the Book of the Twelve. A detailed demonstration is not possible at this point, but I believe it would confirm a high level of fluidity and artificiality in assigning discourses and sayings to named individuals in the Book of the Twelve (*Dodekapropheton*). The artifice is clearly in evidence at the end, where adjustments had to be made and an additional prophetic *persona* created (i.e., Malachi) in order to maintain the number twelve.[5] But indeterminacy and fluidity are not confined to the last section, and Malachi may not

2. Isa 3:1, 8; 5:3; 22:21.

3. We cannot make a distinction of earlier and later on the basis of the incidence of the shorter *(yĕša'āh)* and longer form *(yĕša'yāhû)*, since both occur in 1 Chronicles and Ezra-Nehemiah.

4. For the Isaiahs of the Elephantine papyri, see Abraham Cowley, *Aramaic Papyri of the Fifth Century B.C.*, 11 (AP 5:16), 23 (AP 8:33), 26 (AP 9:21). For the seals, see Naḥman Avigad, "The Seal of Yesha'yahu," *IEJ* 13 (1963): 324. Avigad translated the inscription on the seal found on the surface at the site of Kiriath-jearim (Abu Gosh?) "(belonging) to Yesha'yahu (son of) Marayahu," but the name in his transcription lacks the final waw and should therefore be the shorter form. He dates it to the early 7th or early 6th century B.C.E. but offers no reasons. Three of the batch of 255 unprovenanced bullae which came on the antiquities market in 1975, and which Avigad published in 1986, bear the name Isaiah in the long form. Avigad dates them to the time of Jeremiah on the basis of analogy with biblical names; see Avigad, *Hebrew Bullae from the Time of Jeremiah*, 66-67, 70.

5. I discussed the significance of the duodecimal system in the formation of the Twelve in *Prophecy and Canon* (Notre Dame: University of Notre Dame Press, 1977), 96-123.

be the only name created *ad hoc* for inclusion in the Twelve. The names of authors which appear only in the superscriptions — Joel, Obadiah, Nahum, and Zephaniah — occur with a high rate of frequency in Ezra-Nehemiah and Chronicles, and three of the four are, like Isaiah, the names of Levites.[6] As a compilation of diverse material, Isaiah is closer to the Twelve than it is to Jeremiah and Ezekiel. In this respect, it is interesting that the Babylonian Talmud notice about the authorship of biblical books (*b. B. Bat.* 14b) lists Isaiah after Jeremiah and Ezekiel and immediately before the Twelve.

In spite of the overwhelming weight of evidence in favor of plurality of authorship in the first 39 chapters of Isaiah, there seems to be no good reason to disallow a solid 8th-century B.C.E. substratum attributable to one individual who took over and took further the fundamental critique of contemporary society articulated by Amos. Prophetic writings are notoriously nonself-referential, but intertextual connections and borrowings can nevertheless be detected. The poem about the anger of God in Isa 9:7-20 (Eng. 8-21) resounds with echoes of Amos, and its opening verse ("Yahveh sent a message against Jacob, and it will fall on Israel") may well be an allusion to the preaching of Amos.[7] From the very outset Isaiah's critique of Judah's political and religious elite is radical and unsparing. Those condemned are "the rulers of Sodom" and "the people of Gomorrah" (1:10); Yahveh has abandoned his people (2:6); their leaders have trampled on the faces of the poor (3:15), and more of that nature. The Isaiah of these denunciations well illustrates the remark of Abraham Heschel, that God is raging in the prophet's words.[8]

The heterogeneous character of the book and the contrasting profiles of Isaiah which it contains could lead us to review common understandings of the concept of authorship. Affixing the name Isaiah to such a collection of diverse material with a long production history is in the same order as attributing the Pentateuch to Moses — about whom preexilic texts are almost completely silent — Psalms to David, and a wide range of didactic, aphoristic, and reflective writings to Solomon. This practice was

---

6. Joel is a common Levitical name in Chronicles, a Levite named Zephaniah is mentioned in 1 Chr 6:21 (Eng. 36), and one named Obadiah in Neh 12:25. Nahum occurs only in the title to the prophetic book.

7. See my *Isaiah 1–39*, 215-19.

8. Abraham J. Heschel, *The Prophets: An Introduction* (New York: Harper and Row, 1962), 5.

not confined to ancient Israel; it was not uncommon, for example, for the name of the founder of a philosophical school (Hermes Trismegistos, Pythagoras, Plato) to be attached to writings of a disciple. The practice had the effect of placing the work in question within a tradition which endowed it with an authority that otherwise it would not have.

As to why the book of Isaiah became the depository for so much additional material we can only speculate. Readers may have been impressed by a certain self-authenticating quality about Isaianic discourses and the prestige of one who was the confidant of kings. The overriding concern for the fate of Jerusalem would also have attracted attention. Perhaps, too, the sealed prophetic testimony confided to disciples (Isa 8:16) elicited interpretative comment from future generations of readers, one example of which would be the passage about the sealed book in 29:11-12 discussed in the previous chapter.

Contrasting Profiles of Isaiah in the Book

So much for Isaiah as author of the sayings. When we turn to the narratives we find a very different situation and a much more solid prophetic profile. To repeat: apart from titles, Isaiah is named only in these narratives, and he functions no longer as a critic of the political and religious establishment but as a "man of God" (*'îš 'ĕlohîm*), a gentler, kinder version of Elijah or Elisha who heals, works miracles, performs prophetic sign-acts, and provides religious support — however qualified — for the political establishment. In short, he is a completely different kind of character.

The first of the three narrative passages of unequal length calling for discussion is the so-called Isaian Memoir or Memorandum in chapters 6–8 dealing with the prophet's intervention in hostilities between Judah under Ahaz and Syria under Rezin allied with Samaria under Pekah.[9] It begins

9. The idea of a memoir or memorandum *(Denkschrift)* goes back to Karl Budde, *Jesajas Erleben: Eine gemeinverständliche Auslegung der Denkschrift des Propheten (Kap. 6,1–9,6)* (Gotha: Leopold Klotz, 1928). Budde included 9:1-6 in his *Denkschrift* since it seemed to him that 6:1–9:6 formed a distinct source inserted into the poem about Assyria as an instrument of Yahveh's judgment on Israel (Isa 5:26-30 + 9:7-11). Ronald E. Clements, "The Prophet as an Author: The Case of the Isaiah Memoir" in Ehud Ben Zvi and Michael H. Floyd, *Writings and Speech in Israelite and Ancient Near Eastern Prophecy,* 89-101, defends the essential authenticity of the Memoir.

and ends in the autobiographical mode (6:1-13; 8:1-23a [Eng. 9:1]), with third person narrative sandwiched in between (7:1-17, omitting the addenda in 7:18-25). The speaker does not identify himself in the first person sections, but in view of the nonreferential character of prophetic writings this is not surprising. The name Isaiah does, however, occur in the midsection, which reports how he was sent on a mission to king Ahaz (7:3). The first sentence of this third-person section is taken, with only slight modifications, from the account of the reign of Ahaz in the Deuteronomistic History.[10] It reads:

> In the days of Ahaz son of Jotham son of Uzziah, king of Judah, Rezin, king of Syria, and Pekah son of Remaliah, king of Israel, went up to fight against Jerusalem but were unable to win a decisive victory against it. (Isa 7:1)

The relevant passage in the History (2 Kgs 16:5) reads:

> Then Rezin, king of Syria, and Pekah son of Remaliah, king of Israel, went up to fight against Jerusalem and laid siege to Ahaz, but were unable to win a decisive victory.

The transcriber has simply substituted the reference to rulers for the simple temporal adverb "then" ('āz) in 2 Kgs 16:5, no doubt to provide the correct historical context. He has also omitted mention of a siege, probably because it would have ruled out the meeting between king and prophet at the conduit of the Upper Pool (Isa 7:3). The borrowing suggests that the author of the History, or an associate, was responsible for providing the historical context for Isaiah's positive message to the king in Isa 7:1-17. If this is so, we would have parallel versions of the reign of Ahaz: one decidedly unfavorable in the History, in which Ahaz submits to Assyria and introduces reprehensible cultic innovations and from which Isaiah is absent (2 Kgs 16:1-20); the other, much more positive, or at least much less negative, in which Ahaz consults with Isaiah and even exhibits religious scruples about putting Yahveh to the test (Isa 7:1-17). This is the reverse of the situation with the reign

10. Hereafter "the History" *tout court* and "the Historian" for its author, leaving aside the issue of multiple editions and therefore multiple authorship. I propose therefore to ignore the terminological distinction between "Deuteronomic" and "Deuteronomistic" and will use only the latter — and as sparingly as possible — to indicate the final edition of the book and associated writings in the postexilic period

of Jeroboam II, where we have a quite positive account in the History featuring a supportive prophet called Jonah ben Amittai but no Amos (2 Kgs 14:23-29) and a more negative version in the one and only narrative passage in the book of Amos, in which Amos condemns both the Jehu dynasty and the state temple at Bethel (Amos 7:10-17).[11]

The next narrative passage in the book is the one in which Isaiah acts out the defeat and humiliation of the Egyptians by Sargon II of Assyria by walking barefoot and naked through the city, perhaps accompanied by followers (Isa 20:1-6; cf. Mic 1:8, "I will lament and wail, I will go barefoot and naked"). The wording of this passage shows it to be closely connected with the History and suggests that Judah was involved to some degree in the Philistine revolt of 713-711 backed by the Egyptians. This appears to be the historical background to this remarkable prophetic sign-act. The narrative opens with the annalistic formula for a military campaign which is routine in the History: "In the year that the Tartan (Akk. *turtanu*, "viceroy") despatched by Sargon king of Assyria came to Ashdod, fought against it, and took it . . ."[12] There are also several turns of phrase common in the History but absent from the book of Isaiah.[13] But the clearest indication that this brief narrative segment originated in the History is the reference to Isaiah as the *ʿebed* ("servant") of Yahveh, since this is the standard designation for the prophetic office in Deuteronomistic writings but is attached to Isaiah in the book of Isaiah only here.[14] The idea of both prophecy and kingship as forms of service or "servanthood" is without doubt a Deuteronomistic contribution.

We come now to the longest of the narrative sections, one which

11. See Peter R. Ackroyd, "A Judgment Narrative between Kings and Chronicles? An Approach to Amos 7:9-17" in *Canon and Authority: Essays in Old Testament Religion and Theology*, ed. George W. Coats and Burke O. Long (Philadelphia: Fortress, 1977), 71-87; repr. in Ackroyd, *Studies in the Religious Tradition of the Old Testament* (London: SCM, 1987), 195-208.

12. 1 Kgs 14:25-26; 2 Kgs 12:18; 15:29; 16:5; 18:9, 13; 24:10; 25:1.

13. The opening temporal phrase *bĕʿēt hahîʾ* ("at that time") occurs at numerous points in the History but only once in Isaiah, and that a prose addendum (18:7; 39:1 is taken from the History). That Yahveh communicates *bĕyad yĕšaʿāhû* ("by means of Isaiah") is an expression absent from Isaiah but of a kind very frequent in the History (1 Kgs 8:53, 56; 12:15; 14:18; 15:29; 16:7, 12, 34; 17:16; 2 Kgs 9:36; 10:10; 14:25; 17:13, 23; 21:10; 24:2).

14. 2 Kgs 9:7; 17:13, 23; 21:10; 24:2; Jer 7:25; 25:4; 26:5; 29:19; 35:15; 44:4. It is also predicated of individual prophets: Ahijah (1 Kgs 14:18; 15:29); Elijah (2 Kgs 9:36; 10:10); Jonah ben Amittai (14:25).

runs more or less parallel with 2 Kings 18–20. Significantly, only here is Isaiah referred to explicitly as a prophet (*nābî'*, 37:2; 38:1; 39:3). It contains four incidents involving the intervention of Isaiah:

1. 36:21–37:7 (2 Kgs 18:37–19:7): a solicited intervention during Sennacherib's punitive campaign in Judah.
2. 37:21-35 (2 Kgs 19:20-34): an unsolicited intervention in the same situation.
3. 38:1-8, 21-22 (2 Kgs 20:1-11): Isaiah heals King Hezekiah and works a miracle.
4. 39:1-8 (2 Kgs 20:12-19): Isaiah predicts exile in Babylon.

There is no question of discussing the entire range of issues which this complex narrative raises,[15] but one or two points relevant to the argument need to be made. The first two sections appear to be alternate accounts of the same incident. The Assyrian generalissimo makes two harangues (36:4-20; 37:10-13), in which the same cities conquered by the Assyrian armies are named (36:19; 37:12-13); Isaiah intervenes twice and makes much the same oracular prediction on each occasion (37:2-7, 21-35); and Hezekiah visits the temple twice (37:1, 14-20). That chapters 36–39 have been copied into the book of Isaiah from the History is occasionally questioned,[16] but it seems to me that the arguments for the priority of the account in the History are decisive. The principal arguments are as follows:

(1) The promise made to Hezekiah of 15 additional years of life (38:5) is calculated on the basis of chronological data in the History, according to which Hezekiah reigned 29 years and the Assyrian attack took place in the 14th year of his reign (2 Kgs 18:2, 13).
(2) Consulting a prophet who gives good news for the short term and bad news further into the future, as Isaiah does apropos of the Babylonian delegation (37:2-4; 39:5-8), corresponds to a theme in the His-

---

15. See my *Isaiah 1–39*, 458-89.

16. Klaus A. D. Smelik, "Distortion of Old Testament Prophecy: The Purpose of Isaiah xxxvi and xxxvii," *OtSt* 24 (1986): 70-93; Jacques Vermeylen, "Hypothèses sur l'Origine d'Isaïe 36–39," in *Studies in the Book of Isaiah*, ed. J. van Ruiten and M. Vervenne (Leuven: Leuven University Press and Peeters, 1997), 95-118; see further the discussion of the issue in Christopher R. Seitz, *Zion's Final Destiny* (Minneapolis: Fortress, 1991), 66-71, 136-40; and H. G. M. Williamson, *The Book Called Isaiah* (Oxford: Clarendon, 1994), 189-94.

tory. In 1 Kgs 11:31-36 the prophet is Ahijah, and in 2 Kgs 22:11-20 it is Huldah, the Hebrew Cassandra.

(3) The direction from the History to the book of Isaiah is attested clearly in the other two narrative sections in chapters 1–39, as we have just seen, and this creates a presumption in favor of the same direction in this third instance.

(4) The same conclusion is suggested by the last chapter of Jeremiah, which has certainly been taken from the History even though Jeremiah himself is not mentioned in it (Jer 52; 2 Kgs 24:18–25:30).

The situation is somewhat complicated by the indications that the author of the account of Hezekiah's miraculous deliverance was familiar with and has drawn on Isaian sayings, in whatever form they were available at that time. The Rabshakeh's bragging about Assyrian conquests parallels Isa 10:8-14 and even names some of the same conquered cities. His low opinion of Egypt as an ally (36:6) reflects the frequent polemic against Egyptian alliances in the sayings,[17] and in asking the defenders of the city about the source of their confidence and their plan of action he touches on two of the most basic themes in the first part of the book.[18]

In Isaiah 1–39, therefore, we have a number of legends[19] about a man of God called Isaiah who performs sign-acts, intercedes, heals, works miracles, and predicts the future. These probably represent only a selection of stories about this "man of God" in circulation at that time. Herodotus (2.141) reproduces a legend about the defeat of Sennacherib in Egypt which, though it does not feature Isaiah, reinforces the sense that the western campaigns of that ruler occasioned a rash of storytelling. In this case the defeat came about not through the Destroying Angel but by mice gnawing through the Assyrian bowstrings, leaving their owners helpless in battle. The story concludes, perhaps tongue in cheek, with a grateful peo-

---

17. Isa 19:1-7; 20:1-6; 30:1-5; 31:1-3.

18. The verb *bṭḥ*, "trust," occurs seven times in the Rabshakeh's address; cf. Isa 12:2; 26:4. On the plan or agenda (*'ēṣâ*) of YHVH, see Isa 5:19; 14:26; 19:17; 25:1; 28:29; 29:15-16; 30:1-2.

19. Form-critical scholars use the term "legend" or "legendum" to indicate a specific literary type of narrative consisting in the life of an extraordinary or extraordinarily holy man or woman, generally with miraculous episodes especially at the birth and death of the subject. The classic study of the genre is still André Jolles, *Einfache Formen,* 2nd ed. (Darmstadt: Wissenschaftliche Buchgesellschaft, 1958), 23-61.

ple erecting a statue to the pharaoh holding a mouse in his hand. Some of these legends were taken up into the History with appropriate editorializing and, at a later time, inserted into the book of Isaiah. Since the interpolator was familiar with sayings attributed to Isaiah, it seems that they were inserted deliberately to create a prophetic profile and a model of ruler-prophet relationship to set over against the dissident figure behind the sayings, whose relationship to the political leadership was almost invariably adversarial. Scholars have noted a somewhat similar procedure attributed to Deuteronomists in the book of Jeremiah, where the editor has inserted material mostly in prose to built up a prophetic profile more in keeping with the ideology of the Deuteronomistic school.

To make the further point that the difference between these two profiles is fundamental and irreconcilable and not merely perspectival, we need only take account of the prophetic diatribe in Isaiah 1–35 which can, with a reasonable degree of probability, be taken to reflect Judah's revolt against Assyria instigated by the death of Sargon II and the accession of Sennacherib in 705 B.C.E., a revolt which ended with the devastating punitive campaign in Judah five years later. Many, perhaps most, scholars have concluded that these events provide the background to the first diatribe in the book (1:2-31). Judah is devastated and Jerusalem left like a "lean-to in a vineyard" (1:8), a metaphor which brings to mind Sennacherib's description of Hezekiah shut up in Jerusalem "like a bird in a cage."[20] The tone is one of uncompromising hostility towards "the rulers of Sodom" (1:10), and the impression is conveyed that they are responsible for the disastrous situation described in this opening chapter.[21] Equally hostile is the tone in 22:1-14, "The Valley of Vision," which describes ineffective measures taken in preparation for an attack, recalling measures taken by Hezekiah faced with the prospect of an Assyrian siege.[22]

Most recent commentators read the threats and predictions of disaster in Isaiah 28–33 against the background of Hezekiah's anti-Assyrian rebellion of 704-701 B.C.E. which the prophet fiercely opposed — unlike the

20. D. D. Luckenbill, *The Annals of Sennacherib*. OIP 2 (Chicago: University of Chicago Press, 1924), II 143; *ANET*, 288.

21. Brevard S. Childs, *Isaiah and the Assyrian Crisis*. SBT, 2nd ser. 3 (Naperville: Allenson, 1967), 20-22; J. A. Emerton, "The Historical Background of Isaiah 1:4-9," *ErIsr* 24 (1993): 34-40; Blenkinsopp, *Isaiah 1–39*, 176-88.

22. 2 Kgs 20:20; 2 Chr 32:27-30. Childs, *Isaiah and the Assyrian Crisis*, 22-27; Blenkinsopp, *Isaiah 1–39*, 330-35.

Historian, who applauds rulers who rebel against the imperial powers. The reciprocal hostility between the Judean leadership and the prophet which comes to expression in this section is implacable. The leaders both civic and religious are rebellious, cynical, lacking in judgment, and addicted to false cults.[23] Their schemes will end in defeat and death (28:18, 22; 29:4; 31:3) since Yahveh himself is responsible for the crisis in the shadow of which they are living (29:1-4). Hezekiah is not named, but he must be included among the leaders whose political activity is represented as making a covenant with death (28:14).[24] Furthermore, it is difficult to believe that negotiations with Egypt were going on without Hezekiah's knowledge and consent; in fact, we are told that *his* princes were en route to Egypt to conduct negotiations (30:4). Towards the end of the section we hear of an individual who violated the treaty and despised its witnesses (33:8). The individual in question is not named, but we must consider the possibility that the writer is condemning Hezekiah's violation of his vassal oath to the Assyrian king, an oath which would have been confirmed by appeal to Yahveh as witness. There is a close parallel in Ezekiel's condemnation of Zedekiah for violating the covenant and making light of the oaths sworn to Nebuchadrezzar in the name of Yahveh (Ezek 17:11-19).

The Prophetic Role Redefined

How are we to explain the presence in one and the same book of such strongly contrasted profiles of Isaiah as prophet and of the prophetic role vis-à-vis the ruler? I suggest some progress may be made by taking another look at another problem of long standing, that of the almost complete absence from the History of the prophets to whom books are attributed — the so-called *Prophetenschweigen* problem.[25] To put it in a nutshell: there is practically no overlap between the canonical 15 to whom books are attributed and prophets mentioned in the History. The Histo-

---

23. Isa 28:7-22; 29:1-4, 9-10, 13-16; 30:1-17; 31:1-3.

24. See my article, "Judah's Covenant with Death (Isaiah XXVIII 14-22)."

25. See Klaus Koch, "Das Prophetenschweigen des deuteronomistischen Geschichtswerks" in *Die Botschaft und die Boten: Festschrift für Hans Walther Wolff zum 70. Geburtstag,* ed. Jörg Jeremias and Lothar Perlitt (Neukirchen-Vluyn: Neukirchener, 1981), 115-28; Christopher Begg, "The Non-mention of Amos, Hosea and Micah in the Deuteronomistic History," *BN* 32 (1986): 41-53.

rian's "canon" consists in the following in order of appearance in 1–2 Samuel and 1–2 Kings: Ahijah of Shiloh, Shemaiah, Jehu ben Hanani, Elijah, Elisha, Micaiah ben Imlah, Jonah ben Amittai, Isaiah, and Huldah. Jeremiah is conspicuous by his absence even though the last chapter of the History serves as an appendix to the book of Jeremiah. There is also the fact noted above that this book has been extensively rewritten to align the prophet with Deuteronomistic ideas about the prophetic role. The first of several indications of this "makeover" of Jeremiah is his commissioning for a 40-year ministry, thus aligning him with Moses the protoprophet (Jer 1:1-3, corresponding to the period 627-587 B.C.E.). In terms of ideologically motivated scribal activity, therefore, Jeremiah and Isaiah are parallel case histories.

Amos is also an absentee from the History. I referred earlier to the one brief biographical passage in the book of Amos (7:10-17) in which he predicted the violent end of Jeroboam II. By contrast, in the Historian's account of the reign of this king (2 Kgs 14:23-29), Jeroboam is the savior of his people, and the only prophet mentioned is Jonah ben Amittai, who supported Jeroboam's military campaigns. But then, quite suddenly, the Historian insists that "Yahveh had not spoken to the effect that he would blot out Israel's name from under the sky" (2 Kgs 14:27). The statement is clearly polemical, the way it is introduced indicates polemic against a *prophetic* pronouncement of doom on Israel, and the only prophet known at that time to have made such a pronouncement was Amos.[26] It therefore seems that the biographical passage (Amos 7:10-17), which interrupts the series of visions (7:1–8:3), was introduced into the book in much the same way that the narrative passages were inserted into the book of Isaiah. This gives us two different versions of the reign of Jeroboam II: the one positive featuring a supportive prophet called Jonah but without Amos; the other decidedly negative featuring Amos. The former is aligned with the Historian's generally positive evaluation of the Jehu dynasty which initially had the benefit of prophetic approval (2 Kgs 9:1-13; 10:30; cf. 15:12) and which

---

26. "The end has come upon my people Israel" (Amos 8:2); "I will destroy it (Israel) from off the surface of the ground" (9:8a). That the Historian was not the only one to find this prediction unacceptable as it stood is evident from the scribal addition to the latter: "Except that I will not utterly destroy the house of Jacob" (9:8b). See Frank Crüsemann, "Kritik an Amos im deuteronomistischen Geschichtswerk: Erwägungen zu 2. Könige 14:27," in *Probleme biblischer Theologie: Gerhard von Rad zum 70. Geburtstag*, ed. Hans Walter Wolff (Munich: Kaiser, 1971), 57-63.

began with a violent anti-Baalist crusade (2 Kgs 9–10). Amos did not have the right message for that time, and therefore the Historian passed him over in favor of Jonah ben Amittai. Hosea also condemned the Jehu dynasty (Hos 1:4), which helps to explain why he too is omitted from the History.

Another absentee is Micah, who issued a categoric prediction of doom on Jerusalem, along the lines of the "back to nature" theme often heard in Isaiah: "Because of you, Zion will be a ploughed field, Jerusalem will be a heap of ruins, and the temple mount will become wooded heights" (Mic 3:12). About a century later, Jeremiah's life was saved by a timely citing of this prediction, no longer understood as an unconditional announcement of disaster, which it clearly was, but as a call to repentance addressed to Hezekiah, one which he accepted and acted on (Jer 26:16-19). The trial narrative in Jeremiah 26, in which the citing of this prediction played a major role, is the continuation of the temple sermon in 7:1–8:3, the Deuteronomistic character of which is unmistakable.[27] As the trial unfolds, we recognize the same hand at work in such expressions as "emend your ways and your deeds" and "obey the voice of Yahveh your God." The death penalty for what was considered Jeremiah's false prophesying is also in keeping with Deuteronomistic guidelines about prophecy (Jer 26:8-9, 11; Deut 18:20). This would therefore be a case of an unconditional prophecy of doom reinterpreted as conditional, not unlike Jonah's announcement of doom on Nineveh, which underwent a similar transformation. The incident also throws another sliver of light on what is emerging as an alternative account of Hezekiah's reign. Micah's prediction of the destruction of Hezekiah's Jerusalem follows immediately after condemnation of a corrupt ruling class which, while professing confidence in the protection of Yahveh, "build Zion with blood and Jerusalem with wrongdoing" (Mic 3:9-11). This must be the ruling class surrounding Hezekiah, one of the Historian's great heroes.

The argument may be summarized as follows. The Historian omitted mention of the prophets to whom books are attributed not because these prophets are the creation of Second Temple scribes and therefore nonexis-

---

27. A detailed analysis is given in W. Thiel, *Die deuteronomistische Redaktion von Jeremia 1–25.* WMANT 41 (Neukirchen-Vluyn: Neukirchener, 1973), 105-19; also Ernest W. Nicholson, *Preaching to the Exiles* (New York: Schocken, 1971), 52-55; F.-L. Hossfeld and I. Meyer, "Der Prophet vor dem Tribunal: Neuer Auslegungsversuch von Jer 26," *ZAW* 86 (1974): 30-50.

tent at the time the History was written,[28] and not because they were in existence then but unknown to the Historian,[29] but because they were not consonant with the ideology inscribed in the History. The message of unconditional doom proclaimed by Amos and Micah was unacceptable, so they were simply omitted. Jeremiah, regarded as the last of the prophets as Moses was the first, was brought into line with the Deuteronomistic *Weltanschauung* by substantial additions and possibly also subtractions. Isaiah's fierce denunciations had to be offset with an alternative prophetic profile, one which illustrated a different understanding of the prophet-ruler relation. In general, prophetic activity had to be aligned with the Historian's evaluation of the rulers of both kingdoms, which is perhaps the central concern of the History. The Jehu dynasty receives a relatively benign press since it postponed the judgment by its initial anti-Baalist zeal; hence, as we have seen, Amos and Hosea, who condemned the dynasty unconditionally, were passed over in silence. In the kingdom of Judah Ahaz was a reprobate because he submitted to Assyria and introduced reprehensible religious practices, while his successor Hezekiah was presented as a figure of heroic proportions who reformed public worship, frequented the temple, and revolted against Assyria. The Historian therefore ended up with a theologically-inspired alternation of bad and good rulers: Ahaz bad, Hezekiah good; Manasseh very bad, Josiah good, an alternation which incidentally served to illustrate the Deuteronomistic rejection of intergenerational accountability.[30]

It is consistent with this ideological redefinition and reformation of the prophetic role that the Historian attributes the fall of the two kingdoms to the addiction of most of their rulers to "pagan," that is, non-Yahvistic cults.[31] Nowhere is it said or even hinted at that the disaster came about as the result of violating the norms of social justice.

---

28. As we have them, the books are certainly postexilic, but that is a different matter.

29. This was the opinion of Martin Noth, *Überlieferungsgeschichtliche Studien*, 3rd ed. (Tübingen: Niemeyer, 1967), 97-98 = *The Deuteronomistic History.* JSOTSup 15 (Sheffield: JSOT, 1981), 86.

30. Deut 24:16; 2 Kgs 14:6; cf. Ezek 18:5-20.

31. The fall of the kingdom of Samaria was due to the worship of the Baal and Asherah at open-air shrines (the "high places"), astral cults, and sacrifices to Molek (2 Kgs 17:7-20). The same practices, together with the introduction of Asherah into the official temple cult, are explicitly stated to have brought about the destruction of Jerusalem and the ensuing deportations (2 Kgs 21:1-9; 22:16-17; 23:26; 24:3).

One final example of this ideological rereading of the past may be given: the account of the visit of ambassadors from Merodach-baladan of Babylon to the Judean court during Hezekiah's convalescence in which Isaiah played a prominent role (2 Kgs 20:12-19 = Isa 39:1-8). The bringing of gifts to Hezekiah and the latter's demonstration of his ability to return the favor suggest not a charitable sick visit but diplomatic overtures with the purpose of persuading the king to enter into an alliance. This was standard practice. King Asa of Judah attempted by similar means to persuade Ben-hadad of Syria to form an alliance (1 Kgs 15:18-19), and the Chaldean Mushezib-marduk even took treasure from the temple of Marduk to induce the Elamites to join an anti-Assyrian alliance.[32] The biblical account simply ignores the problem that Hezekiah had only recently handed over all his gold and silver to the Assyrians, even stripping the gold plate from the temple doors (2 Kgs 18:14-16), which would not have left him much for his "show and tell" display for the Babylonian envoys. Finally, diplomatic overtures from Merodach-baladan (Marduk-apla-iddina) in the aftermath of the invasion of 701 cannot be squared with information available in the Assyrian annals and the Babylonian Chronicle. This Chaldean chieftain became king of Babylon after the accession of Sargon II in 722 and succeeded in holding on to the throne until 710, when he was ousted by the Assyrians. He made a brief comeback in 703 but was then driven into the southern marshes and disappeared from the historical record. If, therefore, such a visit took place, it could only have been before 701, and Hezekiah's display of wealth could only have had the object of demonstrating that he was a credible and solvent coalition partner.

Here, then, we see a Deuteronomistic scribe engaged in exonerating Hezekiah from responsibility for an alliance with the detested Babylonians, thereby shifting responsibility from Hezekiah to Manasseh for the disasters which Babylon would eventually inflict on Judah.[33]

To focus more directly on the main point of the argument so far: the editorial history of the prophetic books provides an opening into the redefinition of prophecy inscribed in Deuteronomy, a redefinition brought about by redescription, reinterpretation, in some cases omission and, in

---

32. J. A. Brinkman, "Babylonia in the Shadow of Assyria (747–626 B.C.)," in *CAH*, 2nd ed., III/2, 37.

33. Note how redundantly the Historian blames Manasseh for the fall of Jerusalem and associated disasters (2 Kgs 21:10-15; 23:26-27; 24:3-4) and how, by contrast, the author of Chronicles partially restores the balance, perhaps without consciously intending to do so.

the case of Isaiah 1–39, neutralization by addition. This impetus to redefinition was no doubt instigated by the loss of prestige suffered by both the optimistic prophets and the prophets of doom following on the fall of Jerusalem and the liquidation of the Judean state. The results of this process were of the greatest significance. One outcome was a heightened interest in the person of the prophet and a corresponding diminution of interest in the sayings, especially sayings predicting disaster. This is especially apparent in expanded and edited version of the book of Jeremiah, in which Jeremiah is an object of biographical interest in a way which is not at all the case with earlier prophetic figures. In other words, the book of Jeremiah provides us with some of the basic elements for a prophetic biography. By that time we also have what is, in effect, a biography of Moses from cradle to grave in which, here too, as many contemporary interpreters argue, the dominant impulse comes from the Deuteronomists (Exod 2:1–Deut 34:8). To these examples we may add the figure of the Servant of Yahveh as presented in the later chapters of Isaiah.[34] We now go on to see some of the further developments in this alternative portrait of the Isaiah of the first 39 chapters of the book.

Isaiah in Chronicles and Jesus ben Sira

The alternative prophetic profile of the first 39 chapters of the book of Isaiah created its own interpretative trajectory. As always, we are at the mercy of our sources, which are few and, for the most part, uncooperative, allowing us to do no more than identify some points along the trajectory without being able to join the dots. We begin with Chronicles, written shortly before or shortly after the conquests of Alexander. A peculiarity of this history, noted earlier, is the author's practice of citing prophetic sources. Isaiah ben Amoz is cited as historian of Uzziah's reign (2 Chr 26:22); the prophet's connection with Uzziah could have been suggested by the chronological note in the title of the book, if present at the time of writing (Isa 1:1), combined with the notice about that ruler's death in 6:1. This is one of

---

34. On the turn to prophetic biography in the 7th and 6th centuries B.C.E., see Gerhard von Rad, *Old Testament Theology* 2 (New York: Harper and Row, 1965); Odil Hannes Steck, *Israel und das gewaltsame Geschick der Propheten* (Neukirchen-Vluyn: Neukirchener, 1967); Klaus Baltzer, *Die Biographie der Propheten* (Neukirchen-Vluyn: Neukirchener, 1975).

the earliest intimations of the transformation of the prophet into historian attested by Josephus, according to whom prophets "obtained their knowledge of the most remote and and ancient history through the inspiration which they owed to God" (*C. Ap.* 1:37).

In his version of the reign of Ahaz (2 Chr 28; cf. 2 Kgs 16), the author of Chronicles either was not familiar with the Isaianic account of the Syrian-Samarian attack on Jerusalem (Isa 6–8) or chose not to include it, more probably the latter. In the Chronicler's version of the reign, Judah was defeated by Israel with incredible slaughter, and the disaster was only prevented from being terminal by the intervention of a northern prophet named Oded who persuaded the victorious Israelites to send their 100,000 captives back to Judah (28:8-15). The appeal of Ahaz for assistance to Assyria is mentioned and deplored but explained differently (2 Chr 28:16-21). It resulted in Tiglath-pilneser (sic) oppressing rather than assisting his client.

The author's account of Hezekiah's reign (2 Chr 29–32) is in some respects puzzling. Hezekiah's cult reforms are rehearsed in mind-numbing detail to make the point that he was the restorer of the great days of David and Solomon. Two points are of interest here. The first is that in addressing priests and Levites at the outset of the reforms he speaks of political disaster and exile as if they were in the past, quoting almost verbatim Jeremiah's description of the disaster of 586 B.C.E. and its aftermath (29:8-9; Jer 29:18). The other is his insistence that the religious restoration program was carried out by prophetic authorization, though no prophet is named (2 Chr 29:15, 25; 30:12). In his account of the miraculous deliverance from Sennacherib, there is no intervention of Isaiah, either solicited or unsolicited. After the boastful harangue of the Assyrian officials, both the king and the prophet Isaiah ben Amoz pray, and their prayer leads to deliverance (32:20-23). The king's sickness is healed without the assistance of Isaiah (32:24-26), and the incident of the Babylonian envoys gets only the briefest mention, with no Isaiah and no prediction of the disaster lying in the future (32:31). But the main point of divergence from the parallel version in 2 Kings is that the author of Chronicles explains the eventual destruction of Jerusalem and the deportations as the result not of Manasseh's wickedness but of a prideful disposition on the part of Hezekiah. Punishment must follow, but since the king repented it is postponed into the future (32:24-26). The author, in fact, has Manasseh undergo a religious conversion, with the result that he ended his reign almost as a model ruler — prayerful, humble, and obedient to prophetic guidance (2 Chr 33:10-20).

For the author of Chronicles, therefore, Hezekiah is center-stage throughout, and Isaiah, mentioned only once in passing, is a marginal figure. He is compensated, however, by being assigned the role of the historian of the reign, in keeping with the author's practice of citing prophetic sources at the conclusion of the reigns of several Judean kings.[35] There is no allusion anywhere to Isaiah's indictments of his contemporaries.

A final observation: It is not clear what the author had in mind in referring to his source as "the Vision of Isaiah ben Amoz the prophet in (Heb. *'al*) the Book of the Kings of Judah and Israel." Several ancient versions (LXX, Vulgate, Targum) add the copula before *'al,* thus indicating reference to two sources, Isaiah and the corresponding passage in Kings. The same conclusion would follow if we translate *'al* "in addition to," and in fact there are two (biblical) sources for the reign of Hezekiah. If, however, we retain MT and read "in the Books of the Kings of Judah and Israel," it will imply either that the author was aware that 2 Kings 18–20 corresponds to a section of the "Vision of Isaiah" or it could be alluding to an annalistic work incorporating prophetic narratives.[36]

Rather more than a century after Chronicles, Jesus ben Sira or, to give him his full name, Jesus ben Eleazar ben Sira (Sir 50:27), composed a didactic work in Hebrew in which he had occasion to mention Isaiah.[37] The section of the work in which this reference occurs (chs. 44–50) carries the title "A Hymn of Praise of the Ancestors" *(paterōn humnos),* in which

---

35. For the reign of David the sources are Samuel, Nathan, and Gad (1 Chr 29:29); for Solomon: Nathan, Ahijah of Shiloh, and Iddo (2 Chr 9:29); for Rehoboam: Shemaiah and Iddo (2 Chr 12:15); for Abijah: Iddo (13:22); for Jehoshaphat: Jehu ben Hanani (20:34); for Uzziah: Isaiah ben Amoz (26:22) and for Hezekiah: "The Vision of Isaiah" (32:32); for Manasseh he depends on "the records of the seers," if this is the correct reading (33:19). The role of chronicler or historian is one of the transformations that prophecy underwent in the Second Temple period, hence the attribution of the official annals of Judaism to prophets in Josephus (*C. Ap.* 1:37-39, 41) and the inclusion of the historical books in the category of prophecy in the rabbinic canon.

36. On which point see Sara Japhet, *I and II Chronicles.* OTL (Louisville: Westminster/John Knox, 1993), 996-97.

37. According to the Prologue, the work was translated into Greek by ben Sira's grandson ca. 132 B.C.E. The Greek version remained the standard text until Solomon Schechter in the late 19th century discovered fragments of a Hebrew text in the geniza of the Karaite synagogue in Old Cairo. More recently, a substantial Hebrew fragment came to light at Masada, and several smaller portions of the text were discovered in caves 2 and 11 at Qumran. See Alexander A. Di Lella, "Wisdom of Ben Sira," *ABD* 6:931-45; and Patrick W. Skehan and Di Lella, *The Wisdom of Ben Sira.* AB 39 (New York: Doubleday, 1987).

the great figures of Israel's history are eulogized, beginning with Enoch and concluding with ben Sira's contemporary, the high priest Simon II (219-196 B.C.E.). Jesus ben Sira's focus throughout his work is on the priesthood, to the extent that Aaron is described at much greater length than Moses. His list includes several prophetic figures beginning with Samuel (46:13-20) and concluding with Isaiah, Jeremiah, Ezekiel, and the Twelve ("the bones of the twelve prophets," 49:10). This would suggest that the prophetic books were available in what is now their canonical order — if not in precisely the form in which we have them — by the early decades of the 2nd century B.C.E. In these notices about prophets their social criticism and their indictments of rulers, priests, and other prophets are passed over in silence. The emphasis is on the prophet as miracle worker, visionary, and foreteller of future events. The alternative Isaianic tradition seems therefore to be well established by the time ben Sira was writing.

In the encomium Isaiah is first mentioned in association with Hezekiah. This eminently good king followed the guidance of Isaiah, who was "great and trustworthy in his visions" (48:22). During the invasion of Sennacherib the Holy One delivered Hezekiah and his people by means of Isaiah (48:20). The brief eulogy of Isaiah which follows (48:23-25) mentions the miracle of the sundial (2 Kgs 20:8-11; Isa 38:7-8) and his healing the king and thus prolonging his life (2 Kgs 20:1-7; Isa 38:1-6). Reading on in the book of Isaiah without regard to divisions in the text, he praised Isaiah for predicting the future exile and return to the land (in Isa 40–55), for comforting the mourners in Zion (cf. Isa 61:2-3), and revealing the last things hidden from the view of others. This last could be a vague allusion to the apocalyptic scenarios of the final judgment and deliverance in the third part of the book of Isaiah (chs. 56–66). Here too, therefore, the profile is that of the "man of God" and saint (ṣaddîq) rather than the free prophet as a critical and often destabilizing force in society.

Isaiah in *The Lives of the Prophets* and Josephus

In writings from the roughly two centuries between Jesus ben Sira and *The Lives of the Prophets* there are many citations from and allusions to Isaiah, not least in the Qumran texts, but no biographical references. As its superscription states, *The Lives of the Prophets* deals with "the names of the prophets, where they are from, where and how they died, and where they lie." Composed in all probability in the early decades of the 1st century C.E., about two centuries after ben Sira, *The Lives of the Prophets* is a brief compendium of biographical notes on 23 prophets including the 15 to whom biblical books are attributed and eight others.[38] Of these 23, six (Isaiah, Jeremiah, Ezekiel, Micah, Amos, Zechariah ben Jehoiada) died a martyr's death. The text has been handed down in Christian circles in Syriac, Ethiopic, Latin, and Armenian, but was written by a Jewish author early in the 1st century C.E., probably in Greek.[39]

Hagiographers in antiquity were particularly interested in the circumstances, generally extraordinary and often miraculous, of the death and burial of their subjects, and the veneration of holy men and women is often associated with the place where they were thought to have been buried. Cult linked with the tomb of a prophet *(nābî')* or saint *(ṣaddîq)* was well-established in Palestine by the first century of the era and no doubt helped to generate edifying legends about the holy person in question. The Jesus of the Gospels speaks about Pharisees and scribes building the tombs of the prophets and decorating the graves of the righteous (Matt 23:29; Luke 11:47), and this no doubt was actually taking place at that time. Herod set the pace by building an imposing and extremely expensive monument in white marble at the entrance to David's tomb *(Ant. 16:182)*.

According to the author's notice on Isaiah, first in the series, he was killed by Manasseh and buried in Jerusalem under the Oak of Rogel (i.e., Fuller's Oak), appropriately near the spot where, accompanied by his son Shear-yashub, he had his meeting with King Ahaz. Two miracles are mentioned. First, during the Assyrian siege he caused the Gihon spring to flow when the besieged inhabitants came to draw water and to stop when the Assyrians approached. Second, in answer to his prayer for water *in articulo mortis*, the water of the Siloam spring began to flow. The miracle suggests that Isaiah was, so to speak, the patron of the spring and the supernatural guarantor of its availability to his devotees. Of the rest of Isaiah's life we learn nothing at all, but it is interesting that the author has preserved the alternative view of Hezekiah more hinted at than stated explicitly in Chronicles. We are told that Hezekiah was not only guilty of showing Gentiles the secret

---

38. Daniel, Nathan, Ahijah, Joad (the man of God from Judah in 1 Kgs 13), Azariah, Elijah, Elisha, Zechariah ben Jehoiada.

39. See D. R. A. Hare, "The Lives of the Prophets," in *The Old Testament Pseudepigrapha*, ed. James H. Charlesworth (Garden City: Doubleday, 1985), 2:379-99 with bibliography (384).

wealth of David and Solomon, but that he defiled the bones of his ancestors, perhaps referring to Hezekiah's excavation of the famous tunnel (2 Kgs 20:20; 2 Chr 32:30). In punishment, Hezekiah became impotent from that day, and God swore that his descendants would be enslaved by their enemies.

In short, this brief biographical sketch of Isaiah's life and death manifests the essential components of the *legendum* as described by André Jolles. In this respect it anticipates the *Acta Sanctorum* and the *Acta Martyrum* of early Christianity and the *Legenda Sanctorum* of the Christian Middle Ages.

Josephus's account of Isaiah is as interesting for what it omits as for what it includes. He reproduces none of the diatribe and denunciations, especially none directed against temple worship (Isa 1:10-17; 66:1-4). He passes over in silence the account of Isaiah's dealings with Ahaz, whose cultic innovations would have offended his (Josephus's) priestly susceptibilities. Isaiah's reputation also suffers by contrast with that of Hezekiah, of high repute in rabbinic tradition and even elevated to messianic status in a dictum of Hillel II (*b. Sanh.* 99a).[40] But the Josephus who defected to the Romans was, predictably, unenthusiastic about Hezekiah's resistance to the imperial power of that time, and he even goes so far as to accuse Hezekiah of cowardice for sending three officers to parley with the Assyrians instead of going himself (*Ant.* 10:5). Basically, Isaiah emerges in Josephus as an ambiguous figure, a "man of God" endowed with predictive, therapeutic, and thaumaturgical capacities, but not one to inspire boundless enthusiasm.[41] Josephus's concluding reflections deserve to be cited:

> As for the prophet, he was acknowledged to be a man of God (*theios,* "divine") and marvellously possessed of truth, and, as he was confident of never having spoken what is false, he wrote down in books all that he had prophesied and left them to be recognized as true from the event by men of future ages. And not alone this prophet, but also others, twelve in number, did the same, and whatever happens to us, whether good or ill, comes about in accordance with their prophecies. (*Ant.* 10:35)

40. Josephus deals with the reign of Ahaz in *Ant.* 9:243-57 and that of Hezekiah in *Ant.* 10:12-34.

41. See Christopher T. Begg, "The 'Classical Prophets' in Josephus' *Antiquities,*" LS 13 (1988): 348-51; Louis H. Feldman, "Josephus' Portrait of Isaiah" in *Writing and Reading the Scroll of Isaiah,* ed. Craig C. Broyles and Craig A. Evans. VTSup 70 (Leiden: Brill, 1997), 2:583-608.

The Martyrdom of Isaiah

Rabbinic attestations speak of Isaiah as the confidant of kings and himself of royal lineage since his father Amoz, also a prophet, was the brother of King Amaziah; the connection would have been suggested by the fact that the names are practically identical.[42] The rabbis have nothing good to say about Isaiah's frequent denunciations of Judah and Jerusalem. They take him to task for accusing the people, rather than just himself, of having unclean lips (Isa 6:5) and for comparing Jerusalem with Sodom (1:10; 3:9).[43] They accuse him of blasphemy in claiming to have seen God, contrary to the explicit declaration of Moses that no one can see God and live (6:1; Exod 33:20). Rather than answer the charge, Isaiah pronounced the ineffable divine name and was at once swallowed by a cedar tree, some say a carob tree. His presence in the tree being detected by his fringes hanging out, on Manasseh's orders the tree was cut down and Isaiah died when the saw reached his unclean lips.[44] These shards of fictional and for the most part fanciful biography, which illustrate the rabbinical genius for creating new narrative out of old, all pivot on one biblical verse, the statement that Manasseh shed much innocent blood in Jerusalem (2 Kgs 21:16).[45]

These and similar fragments of a martyrological tradition about Isaiah could have been in circulation orally for centuries before being committed to writing in the Talmuds. At any rate, they reappear in more cohesive and complete form in *The Martyrdom of Isaiah*, an account of the persecution and death of Isaiah at the hands of Manasseh which has been preserved in Christian circles as part of a larger work entitled *The Ascension of Isaiah*. This apocryphon, which has come down to us in Ethiopic, Coptic, Slavonic, and Latin versions, represents a combination of three different and originally independent sections: *The Vision of Isaiah* (chs. 6–11) and *The Testament of Hezekiah* (3:13–4:22), both composed in Greek and unquestionably of Christian origin, and *The Martyrdom of Isaiah* (1:1–3:12 + 5:1-16). While this last has undergone some minor elaboration at the

---

42. *Pirke deRav Eliezer* 11:8; *Lev R.* 6:6; *b. Meg.* 10b.

43. *Pirke deRav Eliezer* 14:4.

44. *R. Eliezer ben Jacob* in *b. Yev.* 49b; *b. Sanh.* 103b; *y. Sanh.* 10:2.

45. For more on these traditions, see Louis Ginzberg, *The Legends of the Jews* (1928; repr. Philadelphia: Jewish Publication Society, 1959), 6:370-76; Gary G. Porton, "Isaiah and the Kings: The Rabbis on the Prophet Isaiah" in Broyles and Evans, *Writing and Reading the Scroll of Isaiah*, 2:693-716.

hands of a Christian editor,[46] the subject matter and the language point unmistakably to a Jewish work composed in Hebrew, perhaps early in the 1st century c.e. The classic Hebrew narrative style is in evidence (see, e.g., *Mart Isa* 2:1 and 3:2), and it has been pointed out that the Greek translator misunderstood the original genitival construction in the Hebrew expression *maśśôr ʿēṣ*, which can mean either a saw for cutting wood or a saw made of wood. The former is the obvious meaning of the Hebrew, but the Greek translator perpetuated the gruesome image, popular in Christian art, of Isaiah being painfully and laboriously cut in two with a saw of wooden manufacture.

It is also difficult to imagine the rabbis picking up a tradition of this kind which had been handed down in Christian circles, as is clearly the case from its inclusion in *The Ascension of Isaiah*. This version of Isaiah's martyrdom was nevertheless familiar to Christians from late in the 1st century, as is apparent from Heb 11:37.[47] Since the tradition is certainly of Jewish origin, the *legendum* about Isaiah's violent death probably arose in the same context as the Maccabee martyrdom narratives in 2 Maccabees 6–7 and 4 Maccabees 4–18, and perhaps also Daniel 3 and 6.[48] On the other hand, while providing a description of the death as detailed as the account of the deaths of the seven sons and their mother in 2 Maccabees 7, *The Martyrdom of Isaiah* has its own distinctive character and tone and is lacking the extensive speeches and philosophizing *in articulo mortis* of the Maccabee martyrs.

The narrative opens with Isaiah in the presence of Hezekiah and his

46. *Mart Isa* 1:2b-6a, 13b and 5:15-16 refer to Jesus under the title "the Beloved," common in the *Ascension*.

47. Justin *Dialogue with Trypho* 120:5; Tertullian *De Patientia* 14; Origen *Homilies in Isaiah* 1:5; Baruch 9:21-22. Other references in Emil Schürer, *The History of the Jewish People in the Age of Jesus Christ* 3/1, rev. and ed. Geza Vermes, Fergus Millar, and Matthew Goodman (Edinburgh: T. & T. Clark, 1986), 337-40.

48. David Flusser's ingenious argument for the origin of *The Martyrdom* in the Qumran community, as a coded account of the relations between the Teacher of Righteousness, the Wicked Priest, and the Lying Teacher, has won little support. See his article "The Apocryphal Book of *Ascensio Isaiae* and the Dead Sea Sect," *IEJ* 3 (1953): 30-47. On *The Martyrdom* in general, see R. H. Charles, *The Apocrypha and Pseudepigrapha of the Old Testament in English*, vol. 2: *Pseudepigrapha* (Oxford: Clarendon, 1913), 155-62; *The Ascension of Isaiah translated from the Ethiopic Version* (London: SPCK, 1917); Schürer, 3/1:335-41; Michael E. Stone, "Isaiah, Martyrdom of," *EncJud* 9:71-72; M. A. Knibb, "Martyrdom and Ascension of Isaiah," in Charlesworth, *The Old Testament Pseudepigrapha*, 2:143-76.

son Manasseh. In the course of the encounter Isaiah predicted that Manasseh would become a follower of Beliar (Sammael or Satan) and would execute him (Isaiah) by sawing him in half. After the death of Hezekiah, Manasseh began to fulfil the prediction by abandoning the service of the God of his father. Possessed by Satan, he turned Jerusalem into a center of apostasy, sorcery, and all kinds of iniquity. The persecution of the righteous led Isaiah and his followers to retire to Bethlehem, but since the moral corruption had already spread to Bethlehem, they fled from there into a mountainous region in the wilderness, presumably the Judean wilderness. There they lived for two years in extreme poverty, clothed in sackcloth, and lamenting the moral corruption of Israel.

Meanwhile a Samaritan named Belkira, who resided in the Bethlehem region, discovered the place where Isaiah and his prophetic followers had retired. Belkira was a descendant of Zedekiah ben Chenaanah, the false prophet who opposed Micaiah ben Imlah (1 Kgs 22:11). He had fled to Judah after the fall of the northern kingdom, abandoned the Samaritan religion after arriving there, but then began prophesying falsely in Jerusalem. When Manasseh succeeded Hezekiah, Belkira accused Isaiah before the king of predicting the destruction of Jerusalem and the exile of the king together with all Judah and Benjamin. He also charged Isaiah with calling Jerusalem Sodom and its princes the people of Gomorrah and, worst of all, with blasphemy in claiming to be greater than Moses and to have seen God and lived. Isaiah was seized and the king, inspired by Beliar who dwelt in his heart, had him sawn in two with a wood saw. As Isaiah was dying, Belkira and the false prophets mocked him and invited him to renounce his errors. Belkira — here speaking as Satan himself — even promised that if he did so the king and all the people would worship him. After rejecting the offer, and pronouncing a curse on Belkira and his followers, Isaiah told his prophetic disciples to go to Tyre and Sidon, "because for me alone the Lord has mixed the cup." During his final agony he neither spoke nor wept but communed with the Holy Spirit.[49]

The Lives of the Prophets and *The Martyrdom of Isaiah* represent the furthest limits of the process which began with the introduction of prophetic *legenda* into the book of Isaiah by the Deuteronomists. How successfully the latter imposed their theory of prophecy can be gauged by the

---

49. There are indications of a conflation of two versions since both the sawing in half (5:1, 11) and the presence and activity of bystanders (5:2-10, 12) are repeated.

fact that the radical and deliberately destabilizing social criticism contained in the book remained to all intents and purposes dormant until the beginnings of critical scholarship on the prophetic literature in the early modern period. Prophecy became a phenomenon more of the past than the present, hence the biographical approach. In *The Martyrdom* Isaiah is a visonary, a foreteller of the future including his own death, a miracle worker, a holy man — in other words, a *ṣaddîq*. His story is the forerunner of many stories about holy men and (less commonly) holy women in the formative period of both Judaism and Christianity. It is also basically the story of his death — at least that is the only part of the Isaiah *legendum* which has found its way into this particular text. In that respect it may be compared with the gospel accounts of the death of Jesus, calling to mind the definition of a gospel as a passion narrative with a long introduction. The comparison does not end there, however, since *The Martyrdom* has a remarkable number of features and motifs in common with the gospel accounts of the death of Jesus. In the following section we will discuss these features as one of the ways, and perhaps not the least important one, in which the interpretation of the book of Isaiah has made its impact on the early Christian movement.

The Lure of Martyrdom: The Passion of Isaiah and the Passion of Jesus

While the canonical gospels have some features in common with ancient biographies — that is, lives of holy men and women and of heroes human and divine[50] — they are more the product of developments within the Jewish literary tradition of late antiquity, some aspects of which we have been discussing in this chapter. The development at issue here is towards a prophetic biography which emerges in rudimentary form in *The Lives of the Prophets* and *The Martyrdom of Isaiah*. Jesus was acknowledged to be a prophet by his followers (Luke 24:19) and by the common people.[51] He

50. Moses Hadas and Morton Smith, *Heroes and Gods: Spiritual Biographies in Antiquity* (New York: Harper & Row, 1965); Arnaldo Momigliano, *The Development of Greek Biography* (Cambridge, Mass: Harvard University Press, 1971); Charles H. Talbot, *What is a Gospel?* (Philadelphia: Fortress, 1977).

51. Matt 16:14 = Mark 8:28; Luke 9:19; Mark 6:15 = Luke 9:8; Matt 21:46; Luke 7:16; John 4:19; 6:14; 7:40; 9:17.

spoke of himself as a prophet (Matt 13:57; Mark 6:4; Luke 4:24; John 4:44) and seems to have located himself within a long series of prophets martyred by their own people, a series which no doubt included Isaiah.[52] This is especially in evidence in the saying in which Jesus states that he must be on his way since it is impossible for a prophet to die anywhere but in Jerusalem (Luke 13:33). The acceptance by Jesus of the designation "prophet" contrasts with the rejection of this title by Hanina ben Dosa, the Galilean *ḥasîd* and contemporary of Jesus, quoting Amos 7:14, "I am neither a prophet nor the son of a prophet."[53] We can therefore be reasonably sure that the gospel writers were aware of this biographical tradition.

The events of the life of Jesus, and most particularly the event of his death, are described as fulfilling prophecy, sometimes in the form of explicit citation of a text for the most part from a prophetic book or a psalm, sometimes by allusion. In many instances text and event correspond at a remarkable level of detail. While there may be cases where the biblical text in question is used to craft a corresponding narrative which the writer believed may have happened — or ought to have happened, but in fact did not happen — it should not be taken for granted that this is the inevitable outcome of the prophecy-fulfillment pattern in the gospels. We might think of the text, long known and reflected on, as interpenetrating the gospel writer's consciousness in the act of describing the event in question. This interpenetration of text (especially the Suffering Servant text in Isa 53) and narrative will occupy us in a later chapter. For the present, we direct out attention to the literary parallels between the gospel passion narrative and the *Martyrdom of Isaiah*.

Did *The Martyrdom* play a role, a supporting role, in the formation of the narrative of the passion and death of Jesus, in addition to Isaiah 53, Psalm 22, and other texts with which interpreters have long been familiar? Uncertainty about the dating of ancient texts, and of traditions embedded in them, is rarely completely dispelled, but we have seen that most (but not all) scholars who have given close attention to *The Martyrdom* have concluded that the traditions it contains are pre-Christian and that it is itself almost certainly a pre-Christian text. We have also seen that it was known in Christian circles in the 1st century C.E. The possibility that it has influ-

---

52. The tradition is referred to in Matt 23:34, 37; Luke 11:50; 13:34; Acts 7:52.

53. Geza Vermes, "Ḥanina ben Dosa: A Controversial Galilean Saint from the First Century of the Christian Era," *JJS* 23 (1972): 28-50; 24 (1973): 51-64.

enced the gospel passion narratives should therefore not be excluded. The parallels are, at any rate, impressive. Isaiah foretold both his death and the manner of his death as did the Jesus of the gospel tradition.[54] In *The Martyrdom* there is much emphasis on the conspiring and conniving of Isaiah's enemies led by Belkira, whereas in the gospels hostility comes from the chief priests, elders, and scribes.[55] In both texts Satan (Beliar) is malevolently active behind the scenes (3:11; 5:1, 15; cf. Luke 22:31, 53). The similarities are particularly close with regard to the accusations leading to execution. Isaiah is accused of comparing Jerusalem to Sodom (*Mart Isa* 3:10; Isa 1:10), and Jesus also denounces Jerusalem as the city that kills the prophets and stones those sent to it (Matt 23:37-38; Luke 13:34-35). Both are accused of predicting the destruction of Jerusalem (*Mart Isa* 3:6; Luke 19:41-44). Even more serious is the charge of blasphemy. Belkira accuses Isaiah of claiming superiority as a prophet to Moses (3:8), while Jesus makes a similar claim with regard to Abraham (John 8:52-59). Isaiah's claim to have seen God and lived (3:9; cf. Isa 6:5), contrary to the statement of Moses that no one can see God and live (Exod 33:20),[56] is paralleled by Jesus' assurance addressed to the high priest that they would see the Son of Man seated at the right hand of the Power (Matt 26:64), a statement judged to be blasphemous and worthy of death.

Several of the narrative details in the brief account of Isaiah's trial and execution are replicated in the gospel accounts of the death of Jesus. He is mocked by his enemies, Belkira and the false prophets, as he is being sawn in two (5:1-5, 12), as Jesus is by the priests, scribes, elders, and bandits (Matt 27:39-44). Belkira even urges Isaiah to recant and promises that he will be worshipped by all Jerusalem if he does, reminiscent of the temptation of Jesus in the wilderness (Matt 4:8-10; Luke 4:5-8). The silence of both Isaiah and Jesus during their sufferings is noted (5:14; cf. Matt 27:14; Mark 14:61; 15:5). The suffering and death is compared to a cup which is not to be shared with disciples (5:13; Matt 20:22; 26:39). These disciples are charged to leave Jerusalem and go to Tyre and Sidon (5:13) or to Galilee (Matt 26:32; 28:7, 10). One or other of these features might be considered characteristic hagiographical or martyrological topoi — for example, the

54. *Mart Isa* 1:7-9; Matt 16:21; 17:22-23; 26:1-2 and par.

55. Matt 26:3-5; Mark 14:1-2; Luke 22:1-2.

56. The accusation also appears in *4 Bar* 9:21-22, where Jeremiah's prophecies about Christ are compared by his hearers to what Isaiah had said, "I saw God and the Son of God." See also *b. Yeb.* 49b.

silent acceptance of suffering — but the cumulative effect leads to the conclusion that *The Martyrdom of Isaiah,* or at least the narrative tradition which it embodies, is a significant part of the narrative *arrière-plan* of the gospel story of the death of Jesus.

· CHAPTER 3 ·

Isaiah at the Beginnings of Jewish Sectarianism

Questions about Definition

All critical scholars today accept that the book of Isaiah as we have it is the end product of a literary history extending over several centuries. A cumulative process of interpretation and expansion of an initial core of material was going on throughout the period of the formation of the book, until the point was reached after which commentary could no longer be incorporated in it but had to be written up separately. The existence of the Qumran pesharim on Isaiah, the earliest commentaries on the book, is an indication that this point had been reached by the 1st century B.C.E., though we have to wait more than two more centuries for the first Christian commentaries. We have no independent information on the process by which the book of Isaiah, or for that matter any biblical book, achieved the shape in which we have it. All we can do is speculate on the basis of clues within the book itself. In the previous two chapters we noted one interpretative trajectory in which the putative author of the book becomes the object of biographical interest. We also noted one direction not taken in the early stages of interpretation, namely, the prophetic criticism of social mores and the fierce denunciation of corruption in high places in sayings attributed to Isaiah. We can now take up and pursue further the point made earlier about the book read as an apocalyptic text; about how the end-time scenarios of judgment for the many and salvation for the few which come to the fore in the latest stages of the formation of the book support the identification of the sealed book of Isa 29:11-12 with the book of Isaiah read from the perspective of the apocalyptic worldview.

To risk only a slight oversimplification, we can say that the line leading from prophecy to apocalyptic eschatology is one of the principal interpretative trajectories in the book.[1] The apocalyptic element is especially dense in the last two chapters of the book, which also provide evidence of the existence of an apocalyptically-minded, dissident group at odds with the temple authorities, namely, those hated and cast out by their brethren on account of their eschatological beliefs (Isa 66:5). This situation raises the possibility that such groups were involved in the final stages of the formation of the book, a conclusion which poses serious questions for the common perception of canonicity as expressing a normative judgment of the religious authorities. But we have already seen that this view of canonicity cannot be taken for granted. Normativity is not an unproblematically straightforward concept and does not necessarily entail a cohesive, self-consistent, and theologically unified corpus of writings. To repeat, we have no information bearing directly on the circumstances under which a book like Isaiah became "canonical" and must therefore be guided by indications in the book itself.

A trajectory leading in the same direction as the book of Isaiah has also been detected in the Book of the Twelve *(Dodekapropheton)* with which Isaiah has much in common. This collection of prophetic material, covering a span of time equal to that of Isaiah, concludes with a prediction of the final, fearful, and imminent Day of Yahveh to be preceded by the return of Elijah (Mal 3:19-24 [Eng. 4:1-6]). The same theme is prominent throughout the collection, with emphasis on the prophetic-eschatological motif of the Day of Yahveh.[2] In this respect, and in the variety of prophetic

---

1. On the link between prophecy and apocalyptic eschatology, see John J. Collins, "From Prophecy to Apocalypticism," *The Encyclopedia of Apocalypticism*, 1:129-61. Also Jacques Vermeylen, *Du prophète Isaïe à l'apocalyptique*. EBib. 2 vols. (Paris: Gabalda, 1977-78), the title of whose book encapsulates the point about the trajectory from prophecy to apocalyptic; Robert R. Wilson, "From Prophecy to Apocalyptic: Reflections on the Shape of Israelite Religion" in *Anthropological Perspectives on Old Testament Prophecy*, ed. Robert C. Culley and Thomas W. Overholt. Semeia 21 (Chico: Scholars, 1982), 79-95; Stephen L. Cook, *Prophecy and Apocalypticism* (Minneapolis: Fortress, 1995).

2. The theme appears in Joel 3:1–4:21 (Eng. 2:28–3:21); Amos 9:11-15; Obad 15–21; Zeph 3:11-20; Zech 14. See Rolf Rendtorff, "How to Read the Book of the Twelve as a Theological Unity" in *Reading and Hearing the Book of the Twelve*, ed. James D. Nogalski and Marvin A. Sweeney. SBLSymS 15 (Atlanta: SBL, 2000), 75-87. On Mal 3:23-24 (Eng. 4:5-6) as the conclusion to the Latter Prophets as a whole, see my *Prophecy and Canon*, 120-23.

material which it contains, Isaiah is much closer to the Twelve than to Jeremiah or Ezekiel.

Since in both ancient and modern times apocalyptic eschatology is a characteristic concern of sects, we can now go on to inquire whether the reading and interpretation of Isaiah from this perspective contributed to the development of sectarianism in the later Second Temple period.

The current opinion among scholars of Judaism in late antiquity is that sects made their first appearance on the scene in the 2nd century B.C.E. The assumption is that they came into existence as a result of the campaign of hellenization pursued by Antiochus IV and his supporters within the Jewish community and reached their full development in reaction to policies pursued by the Hasmoneans, especially their usurpation of the high priestly office. Josephus inserts his brief notice about the three Jewish "schools of thought" (Greek *haireseis*) abruptly into his account of the exploits of Jonathan Maccabee (161-142 B.C.E.), and some scholars have concluded that this is because he dates the existence of the sects from that time (*Ant.* 13:171-73). But those who hold this view would in any case admit that the sects named by Josephus do not represent a *creatio ex nihilo,* and that their emergence must have been prepared for during the preceding decades, perhaps even centuries.[3] In agreement with this opinion, I will argue in the present chapter that a type of sectarianism made its first appearance in the century following the destruction of Jerusalem in 586 B.C.E., that important aspects of the phenomenon are reflected in the book of Isaiah, and that the interpretation of the book of Isaiah was a significant factor in both the development towards sectarianism in early Judaism and the actual formation and self-understanding of the sects of the Greco-Roman period. The argument will involve presenting an outline of what is known or can reasonably be surmised about the development of sectarianism during the period of the Second Temple up to the emergence of the three sects named by Josephus. The survey is meant to prepare for a closer look at the decisive role played by the book of Isaiah in the formation and consolidation of the sects of the Hellenistic and Roman periods, especially the Qumran sects and early Christianity.

In this chapter and throughout our study, "sect" is used in a neutral and unprejudicial way. It is the accepted term in use in the sociological literature, and I know of no entirely acceptable alternative. It is also the com-

---

3. E.g., Collins, "From Prophecy to Apocalypticism," 130-34.

mon translation for *hairesis* in Josephus, the New Testament, and elsewhere. The negative associations of the term derive from its use in the context of Christian ecclesiastical history, whether with reference to heretical sects in the early church, or splinter groups from the mainline Reformation churches, or those contemporary apocalyptic subgroups or "cults" which live off a fundamentalist reading of biblical texts. While etymology is not necessarily a guide to meaning, the Latin word *secta*, from which the word in English and other European languages derives, occurs in Cicero, Livy, Tacitus, and other writers with reference to a philosophical school or, more generally, adherence to a particular way of life.

Two questions come to mind. What is peculiar to a sect as opposed to any other kind of subgroup in a particular society? Are some kinds of societies more favorable to the formation of sects than others? Judea and the Judean Diaspora generated sects while Greek-speaking lands apparently did not. It might therefore be worthwhile to ask why not. In presenting his three Jewish sects to a Greek-speaking public, Josephus compared them to philosophical schools, matching the Pharisees with the Stoics, the Essenes with the Pythagoreans, and, by implication, the Sadducees with the Epicureans. How far does such a comparison take us? In Athens philosophical schools were defined as religious associations and, as such, given legal status according to the laws of Solon. The Stoic school of the 3rd century B.C.E. has been compared to a church; Pythagoreans practiced community of property; and some schools expelled members who deviated from accepted teachings.[4] There are therefore features shared in common by religious sects and philosophical schools, but most scholars would not feel comfortable describing the Damascus covenanters, the Qumran *yaḥad,* and the early Christian church as philosophical schools. But apart from philosophical schools, a bewildering variety of associations *(thiasoi, collegia)* is attested in inscriptions and papyri from the Hellenistic period including clubs, burial societies, and guilds of different kinds both secular and religious, the latter under the aegis of or dedicated to the cult of a nonofficial deity or hero — Asklepios, Herakles, Dionysos. In Jewish communities the synagogue functioned in similar ways. Contact between Greek and Jew resulted, usually in outlying regions, in syncretistic associations such as the Sabbatistai, who worshipped a Sabbath deity, or the Hypsistarioi with their cult of a

---

4. See the remarks of J. B. Bury, *The Hellenistic Age,* 6-7, 16.

Most High God.⁵ Numerous other Jewish, Christian, and Jewish-
Christian sects are listed by early Christian heresiologists, especially
Epiphanius, Hegesippus, and Hippolytus.⁶ There is, therefore, a wide
range of associations with some features in common with sects, but in
what follows we will prudently stay within a narrower band for purposes
of comparison.

To begin much further back in time: the biblical record attests to the
existence of distinctive subgroups in northern Palestine in the 9th century
B.C.E. There were the "sons of the prophets" *(běnê hannĕbî'îm or nĕbî'îm,
tout court)* who lived a cenobitic-type existence in segregated settlements,
were recognizable by their attire and other distinctive features including
self-lacerations (1 Kgs 20:35-41; 2 Kgs 1:8, 13), and attained states of collective mental dissociation with the help of music, percussion, and perhaps
also psychotropic drugs. There were the Rechabites, an order of strict observance, whose members eschewed intoxicants and other amenities of ur-
ban existence;⁷ and there were the Nazirites, with their own rules, who in
this early period were closely associated with the *nĕbî'îm* (Amos 2:11-12).
Samuel is explicitly identified as a *nāzîr* in the 4QSamᵃ reading of 1 Sam
1:22, though the conception and birth narrative may have originally referred to Saul rather than Samuel. At any rate, at a later point in time we
find him presiding over a group of ecstatics in the manner of a *muḥaddam*
or sheik presiding over a Dervish *tawaf* (1 Sam 19:18-24).

We know practically nothing about the organization and internal dy-
namics of these subgroups, but we do know that they acknowledged the
leadership of a charismatic individual. Elijah (2 Kgs 2:12), Elisha (13:14),
and Jonadab founder of the Rechabite order (Jer 35:6) are all addressed as

5. These associations are classified and discussed by Philip A. Harland, *Associations,
Synagogues, and Congregations* (Minneapolis: Fortress, 2003), 25-53.

6. See Matthew Black, *The Scrolls and Christian Origins* (New York: Scribner's, 1961),
48-74; A. F. J. Klijn and G. T. Reinink, *Patristic Evidence for Jewish-Christian Sects.* NovTSup
36 (Leiden: Brill, 1973). On rabbinic sources, see Saul Lieberman, "Light on the Cave Scrolls
from Rabbinic Sources," *PAAJR* 20 (1951): 395-404; J. M. Baumgarten, "The Pharisaic-
Sadducean Controversies about Purity and the Qumran Texts," *JJS* 31 (1980): 157-70;
Shaye J. D. Cohen, *From the Maccabees to the Mishnah.* LEC 7 (Philadelphia: Westminster,
1987), 158-60.

7. For the view that Essene asceticism had its ultimate origin in the "nomadic" lifestyle
of the Rechabites and Kenites, see Black, *Scrolls and Christian Origins*, 15-16; and the critical
remarks of Chris H. Knights, "The Rechabites of Jeremiah 35: Forerunners of the Essenes?" in
Qumran Questions, ed. James H. Charlesworth (Sheffield: Sheffield Academic, 1995), 86-91.

"father" *('āb)*, and Elisha, like Samuel, presided over nebiistic seances.[8] In some respects these groups resemble the well-known sects of the Hasmonean and Roman periods, including the Qumran sects. They deviated from generally accepted social norms, some of them shared common space, and all of them obeyed a charismatic leader. They had a marked affinity for states of mental dissociation reinforced by group solidarity, generally solicited but sometimes spontaneous. They would fit comfortably into several of the sect-types listed in contemporary social theory, for example, the taxonomy proposed by Bryan Wilson.[9] Their members could be described as revolutionary and manipulationist, some were thaumaturgical, and all were to some degree conversionist. They also bear comparison in some respects with the shamanistic figures from archaic and classical Greece discussed by E. R. Dodds and, more recently, John Pairman Brown.[10] Nevertheless, we do not call these groups sects, and it may be helpful to ask why we are not justified in doing so.

I would argue that a crucial factor is the relation of the subgroup not just to the world in general outside the group (the common sociological criterion) but to the parent body or matrix from which it dissociates itself or is coercively dissociated. What is diagnostically important here are the claims which the subgroup either makes explicitly or which can be deduced from its activities. All three groups mentioned above belonged to a fanatical "Yahveh-alone" *Schwärmerei* in radical opposition to the syncretism promoted by successive dynasties in the northern kingdom of Israel, but it would not have occurred to them to think of their status *qua* Israelites as in any way problematic or to question the status of their fellow-Israelites. Or, to take a more recent example, religious orders in the Roman Catholic church — Benedictines, Cistercians, Dominicans, and many others — are subgroups which in different ways and to different degrees segregate themselves from "the world" including other Christians, follow a strict rule, make vows, and practice asceticism but see themselves as part of the church and its mission and are therefore in no way sectarian.

---

8. 2 Kgs 4:38; 6:1; 9:1. See my *History of Prophecy in Israel,* rev. ed. (Louisville: Westminster, 1996), 48-64.

9. Bryan Wilson, *Religion in Sociological Perspective* (Oxford: Oxford University Press, 1982), 103, 111-12.

10. E. R. Dodds, *The Greeks and the Irrational* (Berkeley: University of California Press, 1951), 64-101, 135-78; John Pairman Brown, *Ancient Israel and Ancient Greece: Religion, Politics, and Culture* (Minneapolis: Fortress, 2003), 81-117.

The Damascus covenanters, the Qumran *yaḥad,* and the early Christian community, on the other hand, in effect took over and appropriated for themselves the claims which, on their view, the parent group had forfeited. This position was activated and reinforced by establishing clearly defined ideological boundaries which set them apart from outsiders.[11]

The problem then arises as to the identity of the parent body, the level of tolerance (or intolerance) it had attained, and the extent to which it could be said to embody normativity. It was not enough that the Damascus group rejected the legitimacy and authority of the religious leaders; many have done this at different times, and continue to do it, without qualifying as sectarian. What sets the Qumran groups and the primitive Christian movement apart as sectarian is their radical reinterpretation of traditions and texts, especially halakhic traditions and texts, held in common, together with their conviction, based on this interpretative activity, about their own centrality in the plans of God and the great scheme of things in general. It is along these lines that the interpreted book of Isaiah came to play a crucial role in generating and consolidating the identity and self-understanding of these groups.

If this criterion is accepted, we can go on to explore the possibility that the phenomenon of sectarianism in Judaism can be traced back further than the Qumran sects and their immediate progenitors (*asidaioi* or whoever), and specifically to the dissolution of the Judean state and its primary institutions, political and religious, in the 6th century B.C.E. It is testimony to the vigor and cogency of Max Weber's thought that, in spite of the fact that he was not a specialist in the literature of the period, and notwithstanding the volume of criticism to which his conclusions have been subjected, he still provides the best point of departure for discussion of this issue. Weber argued that loss of political autonomy after the Babylonian conquest led to the emergence in Judah and the Diaspora of a confessional community *(Glaubensgemeinschaft, Bekenntnisgemeinde)* which sought to preserve its identity by means of ritual segregation — circumcision, dietary laws, sabbath, strictly enforced endogamy, the prohibition of commensality with outsiders, the complete incorporation into the cult

11. On the ideological boundaries of the Damascus sect, see Philip R. Davies, "The 'Damascus' sect and Judaism," in *Pursuing the Text: Studies in Honor of Ben Zion Wacholder on the Occasion of His Seventieth Birthday,* ed. John C. Reeves and John Kampen. JSOTSup 184 (Sheffield: Sheffield Academic, 1994), 70-80; also "Who Can Join the 'Damascus Covenant'?" *JJS* 46 (1995): 134-42.

community of resident aliens *(gērîm)* — and the enforcement of the physical and ethnic disqualifications for membership listed in Deut 23:2-9, all of which measures Weber dated to the exilic period.[12] Weber held that this process began with the destruction of the Judean state by the Babylonians in the 6th century and was completed by Ezra and Nehemiah about a century and a half later. Both Ezra and Nehemiah belonged to the economically and socially dominant Judeo-Babylonian party which had resettled in Judah during the early years of Persian rule and which segregated itself from the local population while remaining in principle open to proselytes, subject of course to certain conditions.

Though Weber went on to argue that sectarianism properly so called arose only with what he called the *Sektenreligiosität* of the Pharisee fellowships *(ḥăbûrôt),*[13] his description of the Judeo-Babylonian party at the time of Ezra and Nehemiah corresponds rather closely with his theoretical account of sectarianism.[14] Membership was no longer ascriptive as it was for Judeans under the monarchy. Certain qualifications now had to be met, ritual segregation was mandatory, and a strict moral code enforced. In general, a pervasive in-group, out-group mentality prevailed, together with a factionalism, reflected also in certain psalms, which prepared the ground for the eventual emergence of sects. This is so in spite of the social and economic predominance of the party to which both Ezra and Nehemiah belonged, a consideration which suggests caution in assuming that sects are always drawn from the deprived and marginalized sections of society. This is often the case — think of the "poor" *('ebyônîm, dallîm)* whose voice is heard frequently in psalms and prophetic texts and the *pauperes* of the Middle Ages — but deprivation theory does not cover all cases.

12. It should be noted that the notorious term *Pariavolk* was used by Weber in a precise technical sense and applied to both Judaism and Hinduism. He defined it as "a distinctive hereditary social group lacking autonomous political organization and characterized by internal prohibitions against commensality and intermarriage originally founded upon magical, tabooistic, and ritual injunctions"; *Economy and Society,* ed. Günther Roth and Claus Wittich (Berkeley: University of California Press, 1978), 1:493. See also his *Ancient Judaism* (Glencoe: Free Press, 1952), 336-55.

13. On our definition of sect, the Pharisee *ḥābēr* was not a sectarian since, while dissociating himself from the *'am hā'āreṣ* (e.g., *m. Demai* 2:2-3), he did not make exclusive claims implying ideological self-segregation.

14. *Economy and Society,* 1:492-500; 2:1204-10. Note that Weber did not regard the *asidaioi* of 1-2 Maccabees as forming a sect. He held that the *sunagōgē asidaiōn* of 1 Macc 2:42 are to be understood in the same generic sense as the *qĕhal ḥăsîdîm* of Ps 149:1.

The sociological study of sectarianism inevitably moved beyond the limitiations of the Troeltschian church-sect typology and the Weberian theory of charisma though, as it seems to an outsider, without making much progress in conceptual clarity.[15] Meanwhile, several biblical scholars were taking issue with one or another aspect of Weber's analysis. One of the critics from the biblical studies side was Frank Crüsemann, for whom Weber's *Glaubensgemeinschaft* model underestimates the *political* status of the province of Judah under Persian rule and overestimates the role of the priesthood, which achieved dominance only in the Hellenistic period — a common tendency in writing on the Persian period. Crüsemann also thought that Weber attached too much weight to the ritual over against the social legislation of the Pentateuch. In general, Crüsemann maintained, Weber's description of the situation in the province of Judah in the postdestruction period is oversimplifed.[16] Other scholars have raised similar objections, and it goes without saying that in several respects our understanding of the sociology of postdestruction Judah has broadened out since Weber's time.[17]

Sectarian Phenomena in the Early Persian Period

Criticisms notwithstanding, a growing body of scholarly opinion holds that Weber was on the right track in tracing the origins of Jewish sectarianism back to the century or so following the fall of Jerusalem and the dissolution

---

15. Peter Berger, "The Sociological Study of Sectarianism," *Social Research* 21 (1954): 467-71; Bryan Wilson, *Sects and Society* (Berkeley: University of California Press, 1961); "A Typology of Sects in a Dynamic and Comparative Perspective," *Archives de Sociologie de Religion* 16 (1963): 49-63; ed., *Patterns of Sectarianism: Organization and Ideology in Social and Religious Movements* (London: Heinemann, 1967); "The Sociology of Sects," *Religion in Sociological Perspective*, 89-120. On Weber's contribution to sectarianism in Judaism, see Jay A. Holstein, "Max Weber and Biblical Scholarship," *HUCA* 46 (1975): 159-79; David L. Petersen, "Max Weber and the Sociological Study of Ancient Israel" in *Religious Change and Continuity*, ed. Harry M. Johnson (San Francisco: Jossey-Bass, 1979), 129-43.

16. Frank Crüsemann, "Israel in der Perserzeit: Eine Skizze in Auseinandersetzung mit Max Weber," in *Max Webers Sicht des antiken Christentums: Interpretation und Kritik*, ed. Wolfgang Schluchter (Frankfurt: Suhrkamp, 1985), 205-32.

17. Apropos of which, see Shemaryahu Talmon, "The Internal Diversification of Judaism in the Early Second Temple Period" in *Jewish Civilization in the Hellenistic-Roman Period* (Philadelphia: Trinity, 1991), 16-43, esp. the works cited on pp. 16-17.

of the Judean kingdom. One of the first to entertain this possibility was none other than William Foxwell Albright, who observed that "the Babylonian exile, often described as the great watershed of Israel's history, may well have seen the first stirrings of classical Jewish sectarianism, and of this we get hints in the memoirs of Ezra and Nehemiah."[18] In his brilliant and controversial *Palestinian Parties and Politics that Shaped the Old Testament*, Morton Smith took a different but not incompatible line in arguing that the rise and changing fortunes of the syncretist element over against the "Yahveh-alone party," and the various parties or factions within it, generated a situation of conflict which intensified at the time of Nehemiah and prepared the way for the sects of the Greco-Roman period.[19]

Other students of the Second Temple period have taken similar approaches. After presenting some general criticisms of Weber, Shemaryahu Talmon went on to restate the Weberian thesis in terms of a change following on the fall of Jerusalem from monocentrism to pluricentrism. His point is that the in-group, out-group mentality developed in the Diaspora, especially the eastern Diaspora. After the return to the province of Judah of Judeo-Babylonian immigrants the same mentality was then internalized as *gôlâ*-group against the indigenous population, those who returned against those who remained. This situation is reflected in Ezra-Nehemiah and in prophetic texts from the first century of Persian rule. Talmon ended up with a three-tier model which was not essentially different from that of Weber: the *gôlâ*-group as a distinct entity within the Jewish ethnos, itself segregated from the Gentile world. The same pattern is basically replicated in the Qumran sect, which also combined strict legalism with prophetic charisma.[20]

This thesis can be filled out by a close reading of the biblical sources

18. William F. Albright and C. S. Mann, "Qumran and the Essenes: Geography, Chronology, and the Identification of the Sect" in *The Scrolls and Christianity*, ed. Matthew Black (London: SPCK, 1969), 16.

19. Morton Smith, *Palestinian Parties and Politics that Shaped the Old Testament* (New York: Columbia University Press, 1971), 144-47, 173-74.

20. Shemaryahu Talmon, "The Emergence of Jewish Sectarianism in the Early Second Temple Period" in *King, Cult and Calendar in Ancient Israel* (Jerusalem: Magnes, 1986), 165-201; also "The Internal Diversification of Judaism in the Early Second Temple Period." Much earlier, Talmon made the interesting if debatable proposal that the *gôlâ*-group referred to itself as a *yaḥad*, a term familiar from the Qumran texts, on the basis of his reading of Ezra 4:3, *kî 'ănaḥnû yaḥad nibneh*, translating "for we as a *yaḥad* shall build." See his article, "The Sectarian יחד — a Biblical Noun," *VT* 3 (1953): 133-40.

for the period in question. In the first place, the existence of the self-segregating immigrant, Diaspora, or Judeo-Babylonian element in the Persian province of Judah, referred to as *běnê haggôlâ* or simply *haggôlâ,* is fully in evidence in Ezra-Nehemiah.[21] This is not the case of a group which had severed itself from the parent body but rather of one party claiming legitimacy as the true inheritors of the traditions and rejecting other claimants, specifically those who remained, those who had never left the province of Judah. The radical nature of their claim can be seen in the way they appropriated for themselves such titles as "Judah and Benjamin" (Ezra 1:5; 4:1; 10:9), "the holy seed" (9:2), "the seed of Israel" (Neh 9:2), and spoke of their members as forming a *qāhāl,* an assembly, the term used in the biblical account of national origins for the assembly of Israel in the wilderness.[22] They preserved their distinct genealogical identity, forbade marriage with outsiders, made covenants among themselves, came together in plenary assembly, and reserved the right to exclude certain ethnic and ritually disqualified categories from membership (Neh 13:1-3). They also expelled those who transgressed or disobeyed the leaders (Ezra 10:8). While it is important to bear in mind that the information contained in Ezra-Nehemiah is of different kinds and that much of it comes from as much as two centuries after the events described, the situation as presented is, in its main lines, plausible. Since in this instance the winning side wrote the history, we know practically nothing about the claims advanced by the indigenous population described dismissively as "the people of the land."[23]

But there are also indications of a subgroup within the *běnê haggôlâ.* Those who supported Ezra's campaign to enforce endogamy within the Diaspora community, and to coerce those who had married outside the group to dismiss their wives and children, included what appears to be a

21. Ezra 1:11; 6:19-20; 8:35; 9:4; 10:7, 16; *běnê gālûtā*' in Aramaic (Ezra 6:16); Ezra 2:1 and Neh 7:6 refer to *šěbî haggôlâ,* "the captivity of the diaspora." These *šābîm* ("returnees") will play an important role in late Second Temple sectarian historiography; see pp. 82-83.

22. Ezra 2:64; 10:1, 8, 12, 14; Neh 5:13; 7:66; 8:2, 17. The gloss *zera*' *qodeš* at Isa 6:13 probably refers to the *běnê haggôlâ* as the prophetic remnant; the expression occurs only here and Ezra 9:2.

23. Heb. '*am hā*'*āreṣ* (Ezra 4:4; Neh 10:29 [Eng. 30]), sometimes used in the plural (Ezra 3:3; 9:1-2; 10:11). One of the very few allusions to the position adopted by those who remained in the land is Ezek 33:24, where they say that "Abraham was only one man yet he took possession of the land; we, however, are many, so the land is given to us as a possession." This argument, stated by a hostile witness, would not have impressed members of the immigrant group.

distinctive group referred to as "those who tremble at the word of the God of Israel" (Ezra 9:4) or "those who tremble at the commandment of our God" (10:3). The members of this group are presented as the prime movers in the campaign to force through a policy which must have been unpopular and was in any case doomed to failure. They insist that action be taken in accordance with the law (Ezra 10:3), but since there is no law mandating coercive divorce it was evidently a matter of a rigorous interpretation of law. The law in question would have been Deut 7:3 — not strictly a law in any case — according to which those about to enter Canaan under Joshua are forbidden to intermarry with the native population. But the title by which Ezra's support group was known, namely, *ḥărēdîm* ("Tremblers"), of a type well attested in the history of religions (Shakers, Quakers, etc.), suggests that a rigorist legalism was combined with an intensity of religious emotion characteristic of some forms of prophecy in Israel and elsewhere. This being so, "the word of the God of Israel" which occasioned the trembling could have insinuated the prophetic, revealed word as well as the legal word.

It is also possible that Ezra was regarded, and regarded himself, as one of the *ḥărēdîm*. We note his emotional reaction at hearing the news of transgressive marriages (Ezra 9:3-4), which included sitting on the ground in a trancelike stupor, a condition described in terms identical with that of Ezekiel's prophetic-catatonic state on his arrival among the Diaspora community at Tel Aviv in Babylon (*měšômēm*, Ezek 3:14-15). This would be in keeping with what we have already been told about Ezra, that "the hand of Yahveh was on him" (Ezra 7:6, 28), an expression indicating prophetic endowment, also used of Ezekiel.[24] We might say that the milieu in which Ezra operates at this junction is not far removed from that described at several points in Daniel: fasting (Ezra 9:5; 10:6), mourning (10:1, 6), penitential prayer, confession of sin (9:3, 5, 6-15), and keeping night vigil (10:6).[25]

Mention of this subgroup within the *gôlâ*-community brings us back to the book of Isaiah as a source for the emergence of an at least inchoate form of sectarianism in early Second Temple Judaism.[26] Isaiah 66:5 leaves

24. Ezek 1:3; 3:14, 22; 8:1; 33:22; 37:1; 40:1.

25. On the prophetic aspects of the Ezra profile, see Klaus Koch, "Ezra and the Origins of Judaism," *JSS* 19 (1974): 173-97.

26. The following exposé is a brief summary of arguments I have presented in several publications: "The 'Servants of the Lord' in Third Isaiah," *PIBA* 7 (1983): 1-23, repr. in *"The*

us in no doubt that, at the time of composition, a minority group within
the Jewish community known by the same designation had been forcibly
segregated or shunned by their fellow Jews:

> Hear the word of Yahveh, you who tremble at his word!
> Your brethren who hate you,
> who cast you out for my name's sake have said,
> "May Yahveh reveal his glory, that we may witness your joy!"
> But it is they who will be put to shame.

Who are these people and why are they hated and shunned by their "brethren," that is, their fellow Jews? The designation *ḥărēdîm* is not a title comparable to Pharisees and Essenes since it always appears with a qualifier —
they tremble "at his word," or "at the word of the God of Israel," or "at the
commandment of our God." But in this form, a participial substantive, the
word occurs only in Isaiah 66 (vv. 2 and 5) and in the account of the marriage crisis in Ezra 9–10 referred to above. The verbs in this passage clearly
imply coercive segregation: *niddāh* has much the same force as in classical
Jewish sources, where it refers to excommunication from the synagogue,[27]
while *śānē'* ("hate") connotes active dissociation, as in the divorce formula
"I hate my wife," "I hate my husband."[28] The occasion for this shunning or
excommunication is the eschatological doctrine of the group and especially the belief that they, and they alone, will have reason to rejoice while
their opponents will be put to shame on judgment day, when God would
finally intervene in human affairs, an event which they anticipated for the
near future. We recognize this idea of eschatological reversal as one of the
quintessential sectarian themes.

Place Is Too Small For Us": The Israelite Prophets in Recent Scholarship, ed. Robert P. Gordon
(Winona Lake: Eisenbrauns, 1995), 392-412; "A Jewish Sect of the Persian Period," *CBQ* 52
(1990): 5-20; "The Servant and the Servants in Isaiah and the Formation of the Book," in
Craig C. Broyles and Craig A. Evans, *Writing and Reading the Scroll of Isaiah*, 1:155-75; *Isaiah
56–66*, 51-54, 63-66, 266-317. For a different approach with special reference to Isa 66:1-4, see
Alexander Rofé, "Isaiah 66:1-4: Judean Sects in the Persian Period as Viewed by Trito-Isaiah,"
in *Biblical and Related Studies Presented to Samuel Iwry*, ed. Ann Kort and Scott Morschauser
(Winona Lake: Eisenbrauns, 1985), 205-17.

27. E.g., *b. Ber.* 19a; *b. Pes.* 52a. Compare the different formulas in the Priestly texts in
the Pentateuch, e.g., Lev 7:20; 17:4.

28. Examples in Abraham Cowley, *Aramaic Papyri of the Fifth Century B.C.*, 27, 45. In
one instance (p. 55) *dîn śin'āh* (lit., "a judgment of hatred") is the term for a deed of divorce.

Reading Isa 66:5 in the context of the last section of the book, chapters 65–66, we learn that those who tremble at God's word were not simply the object of official and general reprobation but had voluntarily segregated themselves from the official representatives of the community. The eschatological convictions of the group are echoed in an earlier passage which can be read either as the reply to the taunt of "the brethren" or as the claim which instigated the taunt:

> These therefore are the words of the Sovereign Lord Yahveh:
> "My servants will eat, while you go hungry;
> my servants will drink, while you go thirsty;
> my servants will rejoice, while you are put to shame;
> my servants will rejoice with heartfelt joy,
> while you cry out with heartache
> and wail with anguish of spirit." (65:13-14)

The close thematic and verbal link between 65:13-14 and 66:5 practically obliges us to conclude that "Servants of Yahveh" (*'ăbādîm, 'abdê YHVH*) and "Tremblers" (*ḥărēdîm*) are alternative designations for the same dissident, minority group. And as we read further in these last chapters of the book, we learn that these "Servants" are the one good bunch among the rotten grapes (65:8), they are the elect who form God's new people from the old stock of Jacob (v. 9), they are the ones whom Yahveh now recognizes as "my people who seek me" (v. 10). They are also associated with the poor, the afflicted in spirit, and those who mourn over Jerusalem (66:2, 10; cf. 61:3). They are certainly deprived, not only religiously on account of their exclusion from the temple cult — not surprisingly in light of the opinions expressed in 66:1-4 — but also socially and economically.[29] We learn from Ezra 10:8 that members of the *gôlâ* group who absented them-

---

29. In *Prophecy and Apocalypticism*, 35-54, Stephen L. Cook did well to question deprivation as the essential feature in the emergence of sects and to identify a type of apocalyptic discourse unrelated in any obvious way to sectarianism. There is no reason to doubt that learned priests and scribes, presumably not deprived, could have composed apocalyptic scenarios, including the authors of Ezek 38–39 (Gog and Magog), Zech 1–8, and Joel mentioned by Cook, to whom we may add some of the authors of the Enoch material and God's servant John, author of the Christian apocalypse. But there is plenty of evidence that deprivation and removal from the sources of power, privilege, and material resources constitute a powerful stimulus to the formation of sects and projections of a different future, and it would be difficult to explain the language of Isa 65:13-14 on any other supposition.

selves from the plenary gathering convoked to solve the marriage crisis were not only excluded from the group but forfeited their (presumably immovable) property. This would help to explain why those who tremble at God's word are listed with the poor and afflicted. YHVH's preferential option for the poor is clearly stated in 66:2:

> On these I look with favor, the poor, the afflicted in spirit, and those who tremble at my word.

If we take in the even broader context of Isaiah 40–66, and if we may assume some degree of coherence in this second major section of the book, we can draw the further conclusion that these "Tremblers" and "Servants of Yahveh" are associated in some way with the Servant of Yahveh to whom reference is made in Isaiah 40–55, no doubt as disciples in relation to a prophetic and charismatic leader and founder. In the last of the four so-called Servant Songs, the Servant is promised descendants (*zera'*, lit., "seed"), which, since the Servant has died a martyr's death, must refer to disciples who will continue his mission (Isa 53:10). We may compare this prophet-disciple link with the promise made to another anonymous prophet — or perhaps the same one — later in the book, using similar language:

> As for me, this is my covenant with them, declares Yahveh: my spirit that rests upon you and my words that I have put in your mouth will not be absent from your mouth or from the mouths of your descendants (*zera'*, "seed") or from those of the descendants of your descendants fom this day forward and for ever more. (59:21)

The language of spirit-endowment (cf. Isa 61:1-4) and words placed in the mouth (cf. Deut 18:18; Jer 1:9) are classical expressions of prophetic status. The prophetic gift with which the anonymous individual addressed is endowed will be passed on to his descendants, that is, his disciples, into the foreseeable future. The assurance is expressed in the form of a promissory covenant made with the prophet's public, recalling a previous passage in which the Servant is described as a "covenant to the people" (Isa 49:8). In the immediate context, however, those on whose behalf the prophet has been endowed with the spirit are "those who turn from transgression" of the previous verse, the penitents who are destined to encounter Yahveh's saving presence when he comes to Zion as Redeemer (59:20).

The connection made its impact on the sectarians of the Damascus

Document, who appropriated for themselves the designation "those who turn from transgression" (*šābê peša'*, CD II 5; XX 17). Though the pesher on Isa 59:21 has not survived, we can envisage a Qumranic reading according to which God's covenant with the members of the sect guaranteed them access to prophetic revelation mediated through the Teacher of Righteousness and other inspired leaders.

In a later text (Isa 65:8-10), Yahveh promises to bring forth descendants from Jacob for the sake of "my servants." These servants are represented as the good bunch of grapes, one of several metaphors expressive of the prophetic idea of the holy remnant of Israel, a major theme in the book. We will be looking more closely at this topic in a later chapter.

Since we hear of *ḥărēdîm* only in these two texts, Ezra 9–10 and Isaiah 66, it is at least possible that we are dealing with one and the same group. There is, of course, the problematic matter of dating this last chapter of Isaiah, but a date in the mid-5th or early 4th century is certainly possible, and in any case the *ḥărēdîm* of Ezra 9–10 need not be the exact contemporaries of those shunned by their fellow Jews in Isaiah 66.[30] The identification is not ruled out by the fact that in the Ezra text they are obviously playing a dominant role while in Isaiah they are excommunicated and impoverished. We may be observing one and the same group from different perspectives and at different points in a developing situation, with the excommunication of the *ḥărēdîm* either preceding or following a campaign to impose a sectarian understanding of law on the province which was almost certainly of short duration. In any event, it is difficult to see why these "Tremblers" and "Servants of Yahveh" may not be described as a sect, a sect at once prophetic and committed to a rigorist interpretation of the law.

As a title, *ḥărēdîm* is still in use among the ultraorthodox in Jerusalem, but it does not appear with reference to a distinctive group in postbiblical texts of the Hellenistic and Roman periods including the Qumran material. We therefore have no direct indication that the group in question continued in existence beyond the time of Ezra and that of the Isaianic texts we have been discussing. It is true that several major features of the sectarianism of the Hellenistic and Roman periods — periodization of history and a well-developed dualism in particular — do not appear in these earlier texts we have been discussing. But the sense of an imminent ending, the pervasive

---

30. On the wide variety of opinion on formation of Isa 56–66 and the dates assigned to successive strata, strands, or traditioning circles, see my *Isaiah 56–66*, 54-60.

insider-outsider mentality, and the acute prophetic consciousness combined with adherence to a strict interpretation of the laws, in evidence in Ezra 9–10 and Isaiah 65–66, have much in common with the ideology of dissident groups during a time of even greater crisis at a considerably later date.

Another indication of incipient sectarianism during the first century of Iranian rule is the tendency to form distinct associations bound by a pact, a covenant sealed with an oath, with named signatories and specific stipulations. This is definitely a new development. Ezra's campaign against exogamy was fortified by such a bĕrît (Ezra 10:3). Nehemiah's covenant was likewise confirmed by a curse and an oath which bound "those who had separated themselves from the peoples of the lands" to fulfill certain specific obligations stated in writing, principally concerned with support of the sanctuary (Neh 10:1-40 [Eng. 9:38–10:39]). This looks like a private cult group, not entirely dissimilar from some thiasoi in the Greek-speaking world, and certainly comparable to the group formed by covenant in the land of Damascus. Morton Smith brought Nehemiah's covenant closer to the Damascus covenant by suggesting that it derived from Levites in the early Hellenistic period. They entered into it in opposition to the assimilationist party, which was dominant at that time, and attributed it to their hero Nehemiah. It was thus "the first example of Jewish sectarianism."[31] There is nothing comparable in Isaiah, but Malachi, generally dated to the time of Ezra and Nehemiah, refers to God-fearers who confer together, whose names are written in a "book of remembrance," and who await the day of Yahveh's decisive intervention when the distinction between the righteous and the reprobate, those who serve God and those who do not, will be as manifest to the rest of the world as it is to those whom we hear pacting together (Mal 3:16-18).[32]

The Gap between the Fifth and the Second Centuries B.C.E.

Our information about what was happening in Judah (Yehud) and the Jewish Diaspora between the governorship of Nehemiah (445 to some time

31. Morton Smith, "The Dead Sea Sect in Relation to Ancient Judaism," NTS 7 (1960/61): 347-60. See also his Palestinian Parties and Politics, 173-74.
32. On this passage see Blenkinsopp, CBQ 52 (1990): 14-16. The Malachi passage is applied to members of the Damascus covenanting sect in CD XX 17-21.

after 433 B.C.E.) and the accession of the Seleucid Antiochus Epiphanes IV in 175 B.C.E. is not abundant. Josephus, our principal source apart from the biblical texts, is not well informed on the Persian period and makes things worse by a tendency to conflate the three rulers named Artaxerxes and the three named Darius. After his lengthy paraphrase of Esther (*Ant.* 11:184-296), which he regarded as chronologically the last biblical book, he ran out of source material almost completely. Josephus seems nevertheless to have had some information on the high priesthood. He gives an account of a crime of fratricide committed by the high priest Johanan during the reign of Artaxerxes II Mnemon (404-359) which provoked a strong reaction from the Persian authorities and resulted in seven years of oppression (*Ant.* 11:297-301). He records the marriage between Manasseh, brother of the high priest Jaddua, and Nikaso, daughter of Sanballat governor of Samaria, resulting in the erection of the sanctuary on Mount Gerizim and the appointment of Manasseh as a rival high priest to the one in Jerusalem (*Ant.* 11:302-47). Mention of Jaddua, last high priest under Persian rule, places this incident at the time of Darius III and Alexander, though some scholars suspect that his account is a garbled version of a similar incident recounted in Neh 13:28-29, especially since Samaritan tradition knows of no high priest with the name Manasseh.[33] At any rate, both Josephus (*Ant.* 11:322-34) and the Samaritan Chronicle state that Alexander gave permission for the construction of a sanctuary on Mount Gerizim, the sanctuary later destroyed by John Hyrcanus in 128 B.C.E. Conflict between Judean Jews and the inhabitants of the Samaria region continued long after the time of Nehemiah (e.g., *Ant.* 11:340-47). With good reason, the Samaritans have not been considered to be sectarians but rather as forming a schismatic branch of Judaism.

One conclusion we can draw from what Josephus does tell us is that the politicization and commercialization of the high priesthood, a signifi-

33. Josephus is presumed to have confused the Sanballat of this account with the opponent of Nehemiah who bears the same name (*Ant.* 11:302). However, the occurrence in the Samaria papyri of the name Sanballat, belonging to the father of a mid-4th century governor of Samaria, removes the problem of the Sanballat, opponent of Nehemiah, but does not thereby necessarily authenticate Josephus's account. See Emil Schürer, *The History of the Jewish People in the Age of Jesus Christ*, rev. ed., 2:17-19; and James C. VanderKam, *From Joshua to Caiaphas: High Priests after the Exile* (Minneapolis: Fortress, 2004), 63-85. For the older view, prior to the discovery of the Samaria papyri, see Victor Tcherikover, *Hellenistic Civilization and the Jews* (1959; repr. New York: Atheneum, 1970), 44-45, 419-20.

cant factor in the formation of dissident groups in the Seleucid period, was already underway in the 4th century. The fratricidal struggle between claimants to the office during the reign of Artaxerxes II was, to take one example, occasioned by the promise of the high priesthood to Joshua, brother of the current incumbent, made by the Persian general Bagohi (Bagōsēs in Josephus), a promise which led to murder, mayhem, and a long period of oppression by the Persian authorities (*Ant.* 11:297-301).

The Greek historians who cover the period, principally Diodorus Siculus, Xenophon (to 362), and Ctesias (to 382), are concerned in the first place with Greek-Persian relations. None of them so much as mentions Judah and the Jewish people. At the same time, the interminable military activity in the region which they record, occasioned by revolts in Egypt, Cyprus, and the Phoenician cities under Persian rule and incessant warfare between Ptolemies and Seleucids thereafter, must have had an impact on the social and religious situation in Judah. Josephus records the sufferings inflicted on the inhabitants of Judah in the years following Alexander's conquests. The country was devastated, Jerusalem was occupied more than once, and many Judean Jews were deported to Egypt (*Ant.* 12:1-10). The conquest and annexation of the country by Antiochus III in 198 B.C.E. also caused much hardship (*Ant.* 12:129-38).

Since bad social and economic conditions are often productive of strife and the formation of dissident groups, we should in this connection factor in the frequent allusions in biblical and postbiblical texts to poverty, chronic debt, indentured service, and the crippling burden of taxation.[34] The careers of the vastly wealthy Transjordanian Tobiads, Joseph and Hyrcanus, read against the background of the Zeno papyri, illustrate the extent of economic inequality and hardship while revealing the existence of a wealthy Jewish lay aristocracy not greatly concerned with either the Law or the Prophets (*Ant.* 12:160-236).[35] These are conditions calculated to encourage discontent, alienation, and dissidence, not necessarily confined to the poorest strata of the population.

The shortfall in source material means that, for the most part, we are dependent on the biblical texts, which are, almost without exception, no-

34. E.g. Job 22:1-11; 24:1-25; Eccl 4:1-8, and frequently in Psalms.
35. On the Zeno papyri, from the archives of the Ptolemaic finance minister Apollonius, see Tcherikover, 60-73; Martin Hengel, *Judaism and Hellenism* (Philadelphia: Fortress, 1974), 1:39-47.

toriously difficult to date. For the period in question the relevant texts are
Ezra-Nehemiah, Isaiah, and the Twelve. Debate about the date of Ezra's
mission, in the course of which he enjoyed the support of the *hărēdîm*, has
been going on for more than a century. It is said to have taken place in the
seventh year of Artaxerxes (Ezra 7:1, 8), but it remains uncertain whether
the reference is to Artaxerxes I, which would date the mission to 458 B.C.E.,
or Artaxerxes II, therefore 398.[36] The book was in any case put together
from diverse source material, including the first person account of the
marriage crisis, at a considerably later date, probably from the time and
milieu of the Chronicler, shortly before or shortly after the conquests of
Alexander.[37] There are also insertions from an even later period in both
Ezra and Nehemiah. A scribe active long after the time of Nehemiah has
inserted a list of high priests ending with Jaddua, a contemporary of Darius III and Alexander.[38] The name Joiarib, ancestor of the Maccabees, was
added to the list of priests in Neh 12:1-7 during the Hasmonean period
with the idea of tracing the family history back to the first return from the
exile (12:1; 1 Macc 2:1).[39] As I noted earlier, there are also grounds for dating
Nehemiah's covenant (Neh 10) to the 4th century. Together with Chronicles, Ezra-Nehemiah could therefore be expected to provide some information at least on the political, social, and religious situation at the time of
writing as favoring or discouraging sectarian tendencies.

The information gap would be significantly reduced if we could accept the late date of Isaiah 65–66 proposed by some commentators. Their
reasons have to do with the many end-time scenarios in these chapters —
new heaven and new earth, the coming of God in fiery judgment, rotting
corpses, worms, and inextinguishable fire — reminiscent of Daniel and
other late sectarian texts. Some scholars have also convinced themselves
that the "pagan" cults denounced in these chapters — sacrifices in gardens,
secret rituals in tombs, cult offered to the gods of good luck — are more

36. I argued for the earlier date, and therefore for the chronological priority of Ezra,
in *Ezra-Nehemiah*. OTL (Philadelphia: Westminster, 1988), 139-44.

37. Ezra 1–6 is especially close in theme and language to Chronicles. I agree with
Hugh G. M. Williamson, who assigns these chapters to the end of the 4th or the beginning of
the 3rd century; see his *Ezra, Nehemiah*. WBC (Waco: Word, 1985), xxxv-xxxvi; and "The
Composition of Ezra i–vi," *JTS* 34 (1983): 1-30.

38. Neh 12:10-11; cf. 12:22; *Ant.* 11:306.

39. See Wilhelm Rudolph, *Esra und Nehemia samt 3. Esra* (Tübingen: Mohr, 1949),
191; and on the lists, my *Ezra-Nehemiah*, 332-41.

characteristic of the Hellenistic than the Persian period.[40] There is no question that additions were made to Isaiah 56–66, and to the rest of the book, during the Hellenistic period, perhaps as late as the 2nd century B.C.E., but the cults assumed to be Hellenistic could as well be seen as continuous with reports from the cultic underground during the time of the late Judean monarchy.[41]

In brief, I would conclude that there is still much to be said for the view that a core component of Isaiah 56–66 was composed close to the time of the activity of Ezra and Nehemiah, that is to say, about the mid-5th century B.C.E. If the *ḥărēdîm* of Ezra 9–10 refer to the same group as those of Isaiah 66, the condition of the latter as a shunned and hated minority group would then have either preceded the arrival of Ezra or have come about as a result of the (predictable) failure of his mission and his disappearance from the scene. In either case, we have a situation of tension and conflict favorable to the development of sects. And since the increasing power of the temple priesthood throughout the second century of Persian rule and on into the Hellenistic period would, predictably, have intensified this situation of conflict, it is not beyond belief that a connection *of some kind* exists between this group and the *sunagōgē asidaiōn* ("the assembly of the devout") of 1 Macc 2:42, however one views the relation of these gatherings of the devout to the Qumran sects.

Several passages in the so-called Isaianic Apocalypse (chs. 24–27) would also not be out of place in a 2nd century B.C.E. setting. We noted earlier the remarkable passage in which a voice breaks in proclaiming a privileged revelation at odds with the prevailing religious euphoria — "I have my secret! I have my secret!" (24:16b-17). The exclamation is followed by a woe pronounced on traitors and the triple threat of "terror, the trap, the deep pit," a threat interpreted in terms of his own situation by the author of the Damascus Document (CD IV 14-21). There are passages in this section, and elsewhere in the book, where "Egypt" and "Assyria" served as code names for the Ptolemies and Seleucids, respectively,[42] not unlike the

40. Isa 65:1-7, 11-12, 17; 66:15-16, 17, 22, 24. Characteristic arguments for Hellenistic dates can be found in Paul Volz, *Jesaja II: Zweite Hälfte: Kapitel 40-66* (Leipzig: Deichert, 1932), 279-80; and Odil Hannes Steck, *Studien zu Tritojesaja* (Berlin: de Gruyter, 1991), 237-38. Steck read the lament in Isa 63:7–64:11 (Eng. 12) as a reaction to Ptolemy I's capture of Jerusalem in 301 B.C.E., on which see my *Isaiah 56–66*, 42-44, 58.

41. 2 Kgs 21:3-7; 23:4-14; Jer 7:30-31; Ezek 8:1-18.

42. Isa 27:13; 30:31; see also 10:12; 11:11, 16; 14:25; 19:23-25.

kind of cryptography attested occasionally in the Qumran texts and in the Targum where "Edom" stands for Rome (e.g., the Targum on Isa 34:9: "The streams of Rome shall be turned into pitch").

No less difficult is the task of dating in the second, pseudonymous section of Zechariah (chs. 9–14). Zechariah 9:1-8 is often read as a typically cryptic allusion to Alexander's campaigns, and Jewish hostility towards the early Ptolemies is thought to lie behind 9:11-13. In Zech 10:8-12 "Egypt" and "Assyria" are taken to refer to Ptolemies and Seleucids, respectively, in much the same way that the Qumran sectarians use the code-name Kittim for the Romans (e.g., 1QM I 2, 4). Some commentators refer the much-exegeted allusion to the Pierced One in Zech 12:10-14 to the murder of the high priest Onias III in 170 B.C.E., in spite of the fact that this identification is not easy to reconcile with the ritual mourning for a dying and rising god and the inclusion of the house of David among the mourners.

Bridging the Gap

While the lack of historical data remains a serious problem, we at least have continuity in interpretation, and interpretation is not a disembodied activity but is carried forward by specific individuals and groups; in other words, interpretation is a social, not just a literary phenomenon. The only question is whether it is possible, using the relevant biblical texts, to create a trajectory eventuating in apocalyptic sectarianism of which the book of Daniel is the premier example. Otto Plöger attempted to describe such an interpretative trajectory with Joel 3, Zechariah 12–14, and Isaiah 24–27 as points on the line. His argument assumed that the *asidaioi* of Maccabees had antecedents in the form of "Hasidic" conventicles reaching back into the Persian period. According to Plöger, it was among such groups of the devout that the prophecies in question were expanded in the direction of the apocalyptic worldview. He added the interesting proposal that these eschatological conventicles or *ecclesiolae* "paved the way for the understandable but fatal attempt to translate the dualistic world view into terms of their own situation, which was marked by opposition to the official community, and thus to convert cosmic dualism into an ecclesiastical and confessional dualism."[43] Surprisingly, Plöger found no place for Isaiah 65–66 on his parabola.

43. Otto Plöger, *Theocracy and Eschatology*, 2nd ed. (Richmond: John Knox, 1968), 44-

Another well-known attempt, that of Paul D. Hanson's *The Dawn of Apocalyptic,* is in some respects similar, especially in locating the emergence of the apocalyptic worldview in innercommunity conflict. His thesis sets up prophetic groups deprived of power allied with disenfranchised (and consequently unemployed) Levites over against the Zadokite hierocracy which came to power after the relocation of Babylonian Jews in Judah in the early Iranian period. The anti-eschatological ideology of the priestly faction is expressed in Haggai, Zechariah 1–8, and Ezekiel 40–48, while Isaiah 65–66 and Zechariah 9–14 represent the utopian perspective of the opposition. Progress from prophetic eschatology to protoapocalyptic, which would eventuate in full-blown apocalyptic, can be gauged, so Hanson claimed, by the application of a precisely calibrated prosodic theory combined with an assessment of the increasing prevalence of mythic representations reflected in the texts. The movement in the direction of apocalyptic is fueled by the resentment of those deprived of power and kept in subjection by the priestly elite with their power base in the Jerusalem temple with its considerable religious resources and economic perquisites.[44]

Hanson's essay has provoked a good amount of discussion and helped to move the issue of the origins of apocalyptic away from the rather sterile debate pitting wisdom against prophecy as its progenitors, a debate associated with the name of Gerhard von Rad. It has also been subject to criticism on several counts. The prosodic typology criterion has been thought to be too precise and the remythologizing criterion too vague and diffuse to establish a chronological sequence. Some have found Hanson's use of sociological theory problematic, not least the heavy emphasis on deprivation theory. More importantly, the bipolar analysis of Second Temple society is oversimplified and leads to questionable results. The visionary and utopian author of Ezekiel 40–48 is represented as anti-prophetic, as is Haggai in spite of his prediction of the violent overthrow of the Persian Empire. The author of the visions in Zechariah 1–8 is also placed on the hierocratic and anti-eschatological side of the balance sheet. The fact that Zadokite priests form an important element, perhaps even the core, of the Damascus sect would call for an explanation if

52 (48); first published as *Theokratie und Eschatologie.* WMANT 2 (Neukirchen-Vluyn: Neukirchener, 1959).

44. Paul D. Hanson, *The Dawn of Apocalyptic,* rev. ed. (Philadelphia: Fortress, 1979); *Old Testament Apocalyptic* (Nashville: Abingdon, 1987).

Hanson's profiling of the Zadokite, anti-prophetic, anti-eschatological faction were to be accepted. Hanson seems to be working with rather depassé stereotypes according to which the priest is by definition anti-prophetic and anti-eschatological and the prophet is the priest's antithesis and reverse image.[45]

For both Plöger and Hanson texts from the Twelve served as important points on the trajectory from prophetic eschatology to apocalyptic eschatology and, since apocalyptic eschatology is essentially a group phenomenon, to sectarianism. We know from Jesus ben Sira's allusion to "the bones of the twelve prophets" that this compilation was in existence by the early 2nd century B.C.E. In anticipating Elijah's return before "the great and terrible day of Yahveh," the final paragraph of the Twelve recapitulates one of its central themes, the old prophetic topos of "the Day of Yahveh."[46] The earliest interpretation of Elijah's return, in Sir 48:10, understands his function to be that of gathering in dispersed Israel, a role which is stated in terms of the Isaianic Servant's mission: "to restore Jacob to him, so that Israel may be gathered to him . . . to raise up the tribes of Jacob, to bring back the survivors of Israel" (Isa 49:5-6). The apocalyptic language in which the central theme is often expressed throughout the collection comes from the late biblical period. Bernhard Duhm went even further in deriving the expansions to Joel from synagogue preaching during the Maccabean period,[47] though a sectarian origin would seem to be much more probable.[48] The Day of Yahveh is also prominent in Zephaniah. A core group of sayings directed against both Judah and hostile nations is preceded and followed by the threat of universal judgment (Zeph 1:2-6; 3:9-10), from which only a small remnant, "the humble of the land," will

45. Among the critics of Hanson's theses are Robert P. Carroll, "Twilight of Prophecy or Dawn of Apocalyptic?" *JSOT* 14 (1979): 3-35; Lester L. Grabbe, *Judaism from Cyrus to Herod* (Minneapolis: Fortress, 1992), 1:104-10; B. Schramm, *The Opponents of Third Isaiah.* JSOTSup 193 (Sheffield: Sheffield Academic, 1995); Cook, *Prophecy and Apocalypticism.*

46. The proposal that the Day of Yahveh is the central theme of the Twelve was argued by Rolland Emerson Wolfe, "The Editing of the Book of the Twelve," *ZAW* 53 (1935): 103-4; and, more recently, by Rendtorff, "How to Read the Book of the Twelve as a Theological Unity."

47. Bernhard Duhm, "Anmerkungen zu den Zwölf Propheten," *ZAW* 31 (1911): 161-204.

48. Plöger, *Theocracy and Eschatology,* 96-105, derived the expansions to Joel from eschatological conventicles during the 4th century; similarly Paul L. Redditt, "The Book of Joel and Peripheral Prophecy," *CBQ* 48 (1986): 225-40.

emerge unscathed (2:3; 3:12-13). This, too, presupposes a similar origin, though of uncertain date.[49]

The diverse material in Zechariah 9–14 has proved difficult to contextualize historically and socially. From the time of Eichhorn's celebrated *Einleitung* (4th ed., 1824) most commentators have opted for the period from Alexander's conquests to the Maccabees. The sayings against Syrian, Phoenician, and Philistines cities (Zech 9:1-8), for example, are often interpreted against the background of Alexander's progress down the Mediterranean coast after the battle of Issus, and "I will arouse your sons, O Zion, against your sons, O Greece" (9:13) has been read as a prediction of the defeat of Alexander by divine intervention. In one way or another, much of Zechariah 9–12 has been read as sectarian literature. Hanson assigned these chapters to his dissident prophetic-Levitical party in the first half of the 5th century, but in fact these chapters betray little evidence of the kind of dissidence postulated by Hanson.[50] Though much earlier (the usual date is the mid-5th century), Malachi is more promising in this respect since it presents an eschatologically-oriented covenanting group of God-fearers whose names are recorded in writing and who have segregated themselves from the arrogant evildoers who put God to the test (Mal 3:16-18).

Returning to Isaiah, most critical scholars since Duhm assume that the material in chapters 56–66 is too diverse to permit of unity in regard to either date or authorship and that the original core, however identified or whenever dated, was progressively augmented well into the Hellenistic period. In numerous studies on these 11 chapters, Odil Hannes Steck argued for a theory of cumulative expansive comment *(Fortschreibung)* covering an extensive period from the 6th to the 3rd century B.C.E. An initial edition of the entire book concluded with the anticipated salvation of Jerusalem in 62:10-12. This first edition was expanded with the execution of judgment on Edom (63:1-6), followed by the community lament in 63:7–64:11 (Eng.

49. Louise Pettibone Smith and Ernest R. Lacheman, "The Authorship of the Book of Zephaniah," *JNES* 9 (1950): 137-42, dated the book as late as the early 2nd century B.C.E.

50. *The Dawn of Apocalyptic,* 280-401. Hanson's reference to "attacks against the dominant temple cult in Zechariah 10,11,12, and 14" (p. 283) is puzzling since (1) neither the temple nor its cult is mentioned in these chapters, and (2) the only allusions to the temple in Zechariah 9–14 are positive: Yahveh will guard it (9:8), in the end time it will serve all the survivors of the nations (14:16-19), and its holiness will be maintained and enhanced (14:20-21).

12), which Steck believed was a reaction to the capture of Jerusalem by Ptolemy I in the last year of the 4th century B.C.E. This penultimate redaction was then further expanded with the addition of chapters 65–66 sometime early in the 3rd century.[51]

Steck is one of a number of scholars over the last few decades who have plotted the process by which the book, or at least this last part of the book, was transformed into something resembling an apocalyptic manual throughout the later Persian and Hellenistic periods.[52] Steck was not much interested in identifying the social coordinates of this redactional process, but it seems safe to say that the prophetic-apocalyptic worldview which comes increasingly into view in chapters 56–66, and in other parts of the book — conspicuously chapters 24–27, as we have seen — presupposes a group phenomenon. If this is admitted, it does not seem far-fetched to suppose continuity of some kind between the *ḥărēdîm* and *'ăbādîm* of the third section of the book and the *ḥăsîdîm* of the early 2nd century B.C.E.

If prophetic texts are difficult to date, psalms provide even fewer clues to their even approximate time of composition. But since we will have occasion in the course of our study to note thematic links between Isaiah and Psalms, the possibility of a date even as late as the Maccabean period for some psalms, especially those which refer to or are addressed to *ḥăsîdîm* ("the devout"), should at least be mentioned. So, for example, Ps 50:5 speaks of a covenant with the devout *(ḥăsîdîm)*, in Ps 149:1 the devout form an assembly *(qĕhal ḥăsîdîm)*, and Ps 116:15 speaks of their (probably violent) death. The apocryphal Psalm 154 is similarly "Hasidic" (11QPs[a] XVIII 1-16), and the Qumran sectarians are often described as *ḥăsîdîm*. The old issue of Maccabean psalms has been revived recently, in a somewhat different form, by Christoph Levin, who argues that the final edition of Psalms had its *Sitz im Leben* not in the temple liturgy but in "Hasidic" conventicles of the

51. Odil Hannes Steck, "Beobachtungen zu Jesaja 56-59," *BZ* 31 (1987), 228-46. Steck provides a diagram setting out these stages in *Studien zu Tritojesaja*. BZAW 203 (Berlin: de Gruyter, 1991), 278-79.

52. Claus Westermann, *Isaiah 40–66*. OTL (Philadelphia: Westminster, 1967), commented on a number of *Zusätze* from the final stages of redaction, including 60:19-20; 65:17; 66:22; 65:25; 66:18-19, 21; Vermeylen, *Du prophète Isaïe à l'apocalyptique*, 2:471-89, laid out six stages of formation ending in the 3rd century with some final apocalyptic *retouches;* Wolfgang Lau, *Schriftgelehrte Prophetie in Jes. 56–66*. BZAW 225 (Berlin: de Gruyter, 1994), traced the development of three circles of tradition *(Tradentenkreise)* around chs. 60–62, the center of Trito-Isaiah. Other examples in my *Isaiah 56–66*, 54-60.

Greco-Roman period, where it served as a book of prayer, study, and reflection. At this point, Psalm 1 was added as an introduction to the collection and several psalms were reformulated to emphasize the polarity between the righteous and evildoers (e.g., Ps 26:4-5). At the same time, foreign enemies were reinterpreted as internal to the Jewish community.[53]

Taking all this material into account, we can conclude that the sectarian or, to speak more cautiously, quasi-sectarian character of the Judeo-Babylonian settlers in Judah, the *běnê haggôlâ*, whose activities are described in Ezra-Nehemiah, provides the clearest ideological link with the sectarians of the late Second Temple period, in the first place the sect which produced the Damascus Document. They were a self-segregating group composed of "those who had separated themselves from the peoples of the land" (Neh 10:29 [Eng. 28]), and they could refer to themselves as "the holy seed" (Ezra 9:2; cf. Isa 6:13b) and the "remnant of the people" (Neh 7:72; 10:29 [28]; 11:1, 20). The much debated expression *šābê yiśrā'ēl* in the Damascus Document (CD VI 5; VIII 16 = XIX 29), an expression borrowed from Isaiah (1:27; 59:20), can be translated either "those (Israelites) who returned (from exile)" or "the penitents of Israel," and there is no reason to doubt that the author was aware of the ambiguity. But the expression can also be parsed as *šěbî yiśrā'ēl*, "the captivity of Israel," which is the preferred self-designation for the dominant Judeo-Babylonian group in Ezra-Nehemiah.[54] In using this language the Damascus sectarians aligned themselves with those who first returned from exile in Babylonia and therefore, in effect, with the *běnê haggôlâ*. The Damascus Document refers to a list containing the names of the "founding fathers" *(hāri'šônîm)* of the group and "those who entered after them" (CD IV 6-8). The actual list is unfortunately not included, or has subsequently been removed, but it will inevitably bring to mind Nehemiah's list of the first immigrants, similarly described *(hā'ôlîm bāri'šônāh)*, those who had come up from captivity in the Diaspora *(miššěbî haggôlâ)*, a list with which the Nehemiah memoir reaches its climax. We have the impression that this list, repeated deliberately at this point (cf. Ezra 2:1-70), marks the completion of the founding of a new society and encodes a kind of realized eschatology, as if present-

53. Christoph Levin, "Das Gebetbuch der Gerechten: Literargeschichtliche Beobachtungen am Psalter," *ZTK* 90 (1993): 355-81 = *Fortschreibungen: Gesammelte Studien zum Alten Testament.* BZAW 316 (Berlin: de Gruyter, 2003), 291-313.

54. Ezra 2:1; 3:8; 6:21; 8:35; Neh 1:2-3; 7:6; 8:17.

ing a profile of the saved community comparable to the absent list of the Damascus text.

One further point requires mention. All commentators agree that this list cannot be what it purports to be but must include later immigrants from the parent community in Babylon, corresponding therefore to "those who entered after them" of CD IV 6-8. This would be consonant with the evidence for later rewriting, additions, and updatings in Ezra-Nehemiah noted earlier. A date for Nehemiah's covenant in the late 4th century, which finds support in the way the Chronicler describes covenant-making,[55] brings it closer both chronologically and formally to the sectarian covenant-making of the Damascus sect and the Qumran *yaḥad*. Beyond this we cannot safely proceed, but it does not seem out of place to conclude that the texts we have discussed not only formed the essential *interpretandum* for the sectarians of the late Second Temple period but testify to some measure of continuity at the level of social realities as well.

A different approach to closing or at least narrowing the chronological gap is to track backwards from the time of the *asidaioi* into the 3rd and possibly even the 4th century B.C.E. While we can hardly take on faith Pliny's assertion that the Essenes had lived beside the Dead Sea for thousands of ages,[56] the suggestion that their presumed antecedents, whether in Judah or Babylon, whether the kind of "Hasidic" group known to us from 1-2 Maccabees or others unknown, were themselves part of a history reaching back before the Maccabean revolt is entirely credible. A link of some kind with the *ḥăsîdîm* ("devout") whose voice is heard in several of the Psalms and whose death is lamented in Isa 57:1-2 cannot be ruled out, even if one does not subscribe to the thesis about Maccabean psalms. There must have been several "Hasidic" groups of the kind identified in

---

55. Like Ezra's covenant, that of Asa involved a public gathering, attendance at which was enforced with severe penalties. The penalty imposed by Ezra's faction was expulsion from the *qāhāl* with confiscation of property (Ezra 10:8), while absentees were threatened by Asa with the death penalty (2 Chr 15:12-15). On the late date of Neh 10, in addition to Smith, *NTS* 7 (1960/61): 347-60; and *Palestinian Parties and Politics*, 173-74, see L. W. Batten, *A Critical and Exegetical Commentary on the Books of Ezra and Nehemiah*. ICC (Edinburgh: T. & T. Clark, 1913), 2-3, who claims that "it is quite impossible to place the work (i.e., Chronicles-Ezra-Nehemiah) earlier than 300 B.C."; more soberly, Rudolph, *Esra und Nehemia samt 3. Esra*, XXIV-XXV, opts for a date early in the 4th century.

56. *Naturalis historia* V 17.73.

1 Macc 2:42 as a *sunagōgē*, a congregation. They are described as volunteers and warriors,[57] and while they were willing to fight for their religious freedom they did not support the political agenda of the Maccabees (see 1 Macc 7:12-17). It is probably correct to think of these *asidaioi* as providing a promising seedbed for the development of sects rather than being themselves sectarian.[58]

It is also generally accepted that elements of the Enoch and Daniel cycles originated in the 3rd century if not earlier. The Book of the Watchers (*1 En* 1–36) and the Astronomical Book (*1 En* 72–82), in particular, betray intriguing affinities with Priestly traditions about the early history of humanity in Genesis 1–5 and Priestly speculation about the divine throne (Ezek 1 and 10). These traditions seem to have matured in the eastern Diaspora.[59] There is much that is esoteric about this material, but whether it should be described as sectarian may for the moment be left an open question.

The Final and Decisive Phase in the Formation of Sects

In order to contextualize adequately the appropriation and interpretation of Isaiah in the sects of the late Second Temple period it will be useful to survey briefly the final phase when the documentation becomes rather more abundant. After the conquests of Alexander (332 B.C.E.) the tensions within Palestinian Judaism, of which the biblical texts from the Persian period afford glimpses, became more severe with the spread of the dominant Greek culture and the attraction it exercised on the Jewish political and religious elites. The situation is hinted at in the traditionalist Jesus ben Sira's denunciation of the "assembly of sinners" (Sir 16:6). Both the books of Maccabees and Josephus refer often to conflict between faithful Jews and renegades *(anomoi, paranomoi)* but, apart from Oniads and Tobiads, they provide no solid information on factions or sects until Josephus abruptly introduces his three "schools of thought" into his account of Jonathan Maccabee's exploits (*Ant.* 13:171-73). By that time, however, the formation of associations of the devout, including but not limited to the *sunagōgē*

57. The language is borrowed from the account of Jehoshaphat's militia in 2 Chr 17:16.
58. In agreement with Philip R. Davies, "Hasidim in the Maccabean Period," *JJS* 28 (1977): 127-40.
59. Michael E. Stone, "The Book of Enoch and Judaism in the Third Century B.C.E.," *CBQ* 40 (1978): 479-92; *Scriptures, Sects and Visions* (Philadelphia: Fortress, 1980), 27-47.

asidaiōn of 1 Macc 2:42 and the *sunagōgai hosiōn* of *Pss Sol* 17:16, must have been well under way. The information on these groups is too sparse to permit confident conclusions, but it suggests that, while they were socially visible, and some more in sympathy with the Maccabee cause than others, they were not ideologically self-segregating and therefore should not be thought of as sectarian in the strict sense.

With the accession of the Seleucid Antiochus IV in 175 B.C.E. and his deposition of the high priest Onias in favor of the hellenized Jason (formerly Jesus) shortly thereafter,[60] the situation entered a critical phase. According to 2 Macc 4:10, it was Jason who introduced *ton hellēnikon charactēra* ("the Hellenistic way of life") into Judaism, and he is no doubt the *huios paranomos* ("the lawless man") of 1 Macc 1:11 in the Alexandrine codex.[61] This was the beginning of the secularization of the high priesthood, an office which Antiochus was content to auction out to the highest bidder. But Jason was at least in the legitimate line of the high priesthood, being the son of the high priest Simon II, and according to Josephus (*Ant.* 12:238) Menelaus, who outbid him for the office, was also.[62] A complete break with the past came about only two decades later when Jonathan Maccabee, who had no claim to the office whatever, appointed himself high priest in 152 B.C.E. after the office had lain vacant for seven years (1 Macc 10:18-21). Hence, the period of greatest crisis for Palestinian Judaism must have been the roughly two decades from the deposition of Onias III and his subsequent murder early in the reign of Antiochus to the assumption of the high priesthood by Jonathan following the by now notorious seven-year intersacerdotium.

The issue was not, however, just the legitimacy of the high priesthood. The high priest had been transformed into a political functionary comparable to priests in the Greek-speaking world, the temple cult was re-

---

60. 2 Macc 4:7-10; *Ant.* 12:237.

61. Codex Sinaiticus has the plural. There is some doubt about this information, since according to Josephus (*Ant.* 12:240) Menelaus and the Tobiad faction were responsible for introducing the *hellēnikē politeia*.

62. Menelaus may have been descended from a cadet branch of the Oniads, which would explain the statement in 2 Macc 4:23 (cf. 3:4) that he was the brother of Simon, the temple superintendent. But it is also possible that Josephus confused this Simon with the high priest of the same name. The Zadokite status of Alcimus, who succeeded Menelaus as high priest, is not attested, but he was acknowledged to belong to the Aaronid line (1 Macc 7:14-16; *Ant.* 12:387; 20:235).

duced to the status of accessory to the political functioning of the Jerusalemite polis ("Antioch in Jerusalem"), and the law of Moses was subordinated to the laws and customs governing life in the polis. In short, the usurpation of the office implied the abolition of the "covenant of the fathers" and a new constitution for the Jewish ethnos. This was the situation prior to the success of the Maccabean rebellion, but even after that point the abolition of the legitimate Zadokite-Oniad high priesthood must have been a decisive factor in precipitating schism and the formation of sects.

The importance of the legitimacy of the high priesthood, and consequently the validity of the temple cult, is reinforced by the cryptic historiography of the book of Daniel. The Anointed Prince at the beginning of the 62 weeks of years and the Anointed One at the end are generally understood to be priests — Joshua ben Jehozadak and Onias III, respectively (Dan 9:24-27). In Daniel's vision beside the Tigris, the Prince of the Covenant is likewise taken by most scholars to be Onias III, murdered at the instigation of Menelaus in or about 170 B.C.E. (Dan 11:22). The Lamb that is Slain in the dream-visions of Enoch is also, in all probability, a veiled allusion to Onias (1 En 90:8). The Zadokite element in the Damascus covenant sect and the yaḥad is therefore entirely compatible with the situation in Judah during those two decades.[63]

The same critical period is also the point of convergence for several attempts to trace the predetermined course of historical events in the form of *vaticinia ex eventu,* a familiar kind of sectarian activity in times of crisis in ancient as in modern times. The last of the seven weeks of years of Dan 9:24-27 corresponds to the period from the murder of Onias III to the restoration of the temple cult. At the corresponding point in the Enochian "Apocalypse of Weeks" (1 En 93:1-14; 91:12-17), the entire postexilic period, seen as a time of apostasy, gives way to "an eternal plant of righteousness," a close parallel to the 390 years followed by "the plant root" in the Damascus Document (CD I 5-8). The same schema is filled out symbolically in the Enochian "Animal Apocalypse," which also alludes to the fate of Onias (1 En 90). In the Testament of Levi (*T Levi* 16–18) the 70 weeks of Daniel are restated as seven jubilees, each lasting 49 or 50 years. The last jubilee will witness the total corruption of the priesthood, but there will follow

---

63. For the status of the běnê ṣādôq in the yaḥad, see 1QS V 2, 9; 1QSa I 2, 24; II 3; 1QSb III 22-23; and for the central role of Zadokites in the Damascus sect, see the midrash on Ezek 44:15 in CD III 21–IV 6.

the coming of an eschatological priest who will bring with him a blessed epoch described for the most part in terms taken from Isaiah. Noteworthy, finally, is the hypothesis according to which the overall biblical chronology is based on a 4000-year cycle of Zoroastrian inspiration, a "Great Year," inserted into the biblical narrative calculating backwards from the same point in time, namely, the purification of the temple and the restoration of the temple cult in 164 B.C.E.[64]

The "sense of an ending" induced by the events of those two crucial decades provides a plausible setting for the emergence of the Damascus sect around the middle of the 2nd century B.C.E., the splintering off of the Qumran *yaḥad* from the Damascus sect, and eventually for the emergence of the Jesus group, which began its existence as a Palestinian Jewish sect. The debate about the origins of the Damascus covenanting sect, whether Palestinian or Babylonian, seems at this writing to be unresolved and will no doubt continue.[65] However we configure these groups and relate them

64. For details, see my *The Pentateuch: An Introduction to the First Five Books of the Bible* (New York: Doubleday, 1992), 47-50. For the Zoroastrian 4000-year cycle, see Mary Boyce, *Zoroastrians: Their Religious Beliefs and Practices* (London: Routledge, 2001), 74-75.

65. The hypothesis of Babylonian origins for the Damascus sect was first proposed, to the best of my knowledge, by William Foxwell Albright in *From the Stone Age to Christianity*, 2nd ed. (Garden City: Doubleday, 1957), 19-22, 374-78; and in Albright and Mann, "Qumran and the Essenes," 19. Albright and Mann dated the origins of the sect in relation to the Parthian invasion of Babylon in 140 B.C.E., but in the earlier publication Albright proposed that the sectarians came to Judah following on the success of the Maccabee resistance some two decades later. See also Samuel Iwry, "Was There a Migration to Damascus? The Problem of שבי ישראל," *ErIsr* 9 (1969): 80-88; and the many publications of Jerome Murphy-O'Connor in which he has defended the Babylonian origins of the sect. The arguments are summed up in "The Essenes and Their History," *RB* 81 (1974): 215-44; "The *Damascus Document* Revisited," *RB* 92 (1985): 224-30; and, most recently, "Damascus," *EDSS* 1:165-66. Philip Davies has also supported the hypothesis in *The Damascus Covenant: An Interpretation of the "Damascus Document."* JSOTSup 25 (Sheffield: JSOT, 1983), 90-104; and "The Birthplace of the Essenes: Where is 'Damascus'?" *RevQ* 14 (1990): 503-19 = *Sects and Scrolls: Essays on Qumran and Related Topics* (Atlanta: Scholars, 1996), 95-111. An obvious problem with the hypothesis is that we know practically nothing about the Babylonian diaspora under Seleucid rule, though we can be sure that the close contacts with Judah in evidence during the Persian period continued; see, e.g., Josephus: *Ant.* 12:138; 17:26. No Jewish names have come to light in cuneiform texts from Hellenistic Babylon, on which see T. Boiy, *Late Achaemenid and Hellenistic Babylon.* OLA 136 (Leuven: Peeters, 2004), 295 and *passim.* On the other hand, the intense interest in the Babylonian exile and the sectarian identification with those who survived it and returned to Judah would be consistent with a Babylonian origin for the parent group of the sect that settled at Qumran.

to one another, they all found in the interpretation of the book of Isaiah one of the most convincing sources of legitimacy and one of the most powerful resources for understanding and expressing their own identity and agenda. To demonstrate this will be the principal goal of the following chapters.

CHAPTER 4

Reading Isaiah at Qumran

The Source Material: Scrolls and Scraps

Speaking of the source material available for reconstructing the history of ancient Greece, George Grote, one of the great 19th-century historians, lamented that "we possess only what has drifted ashore from the wreck of a stranded vessel."[1] In spite of the enthusiasm generated by the discovery of ancient manuscript material at Qumran and the surrounding region, something of the same can be said for the history of the last two or three centuries of Second Temple Judaism. But while we acknowledge our poverty, we have to do the best we can with what we have. In the present chapter and the one following we will be dealing with only one aspect of the religious and intellectual history of that time. Our aim will be to get an idea as adequate as the available sources permit as to how the book of Isaiah was read and interpreted at Qumran and in early Christianity and what were the consequences of this interpretative activity. We begin with Qumran, and the first stage will be to state what source material is available for our study.

Two copies of the book of Isaiah were discovered in Cave 1. One of these (1QIsa[a]) was carefully deposited in a jar and in consequence is virtually complete. It is one of the longest of the Qumran scrolls, measuring 7.34 meters and containing 54 columns. It has been judged on paleographic grounds to be the oldest of the 22 manuscripts of the book discov-

---

1. *A History of Greece* (New York: Harper & Brothers, 1879), vii.

ered at or near Qumran, having been copied about the mid-2nd century B.C.E. It is therefore roughly a thousand years older than the oldest Hebrew copies of Isaiah previously available, namely, the Leningrad Codex of the Latter Prophets from the late 9th century and the Aleppo Codex from the early 10th century C.E.[2] It was written by two scribes whose respective contributions are indicated by a three-line gap at the midpoint of the book, therefore between chapters 33 and 34, at the bottom of column 27.[3] There are also a few additions from a later hand (e.g., in Isa 40:6-8).

This premier Isaiah scroll has the normal amount of scribal errors and its own characteristic orthographic conventions, including generous use of vowel letters, longer pronominal suffixes, and frequent use of the copula. According to one count, it has 1,480 textual variants vis-à-vis the Masoretic text (hereafter MT), none of which is of a clearly sectarian nature. The substitution of *tôb* ("good") for *šālôm* ("well-being") in Isa 45:7 ("I form light and create darkness, I bring about good and create woe") may indicate that the scribe wished to make the dualism more explicit, but other explanations are possible. The same can be said for the expression *yōṣēr 'ōtôt* ("creator of signs") with reference to astrology in Isa 45:11, bearing in mind the astrological texts discovered at Qumran including four copies of the Astrological Book of Enoch (4Q208-211, 335-336). Some scholars have suggested that the shift from the first to the third person singular here and there in the scroll (e.g., "*his* arm will govern the peoples," 1QIsa[a] 51:5) may have been intended as a messianic allusion, but there is no way to be sure.[4] Only a few of these variants contain readings superior to MT. In 21:8 1QIsa[a] reads *hārō'eh* ("the seer") for MT *'aryēh* ("lion"), which is obviously correct, as is *'ārîṣ* ("tyrant") for *ṣaddîq* ("righteous") in 49:24,

2. The Aleppo Codex serves as the basis for the Hebrew University Bible Project, in which the first volume to appear was *The Book of Isaiah* edited by the late Moshe Goshen-Gottstein and published by Magnes Press, Jerusalem in 1995.

3. William H. Brownlee, *The Meaning of the Qumrân Scrolls for the Bible, with Special Attention to the Book of Isaiah* (New York: Oxford University Press, 1964), 247-59, argued that the gap supported the thesis of Charles C. Torrey that chs. 34 and 35 are part of Deutero-Isaiah and that the editors of the book, belonging to the school of the prophet Isaiah, divided it into two parallel parts of equal length, following a well-attested procedure visible also in Ezekiel (chs. 1–24, 25–48). I argued against Torrey's hypothesis in *Isaiah 40–55*. AB 19A (New York: Doubleday, 2002), 44-46.

4. Eugene Ulrich, "Our Sharper Focus on the Bible and Theology thanks to the Dead Sea Scrolls," *CBQ* 66 (2004), 3, 12. On the textual characteristics of the Qumran Isaianic corpus in general see his article "Isaiah, Book of" in *EDSS* 1:384-88.

while in 49:12 the substitution of *swnyym*, "people of Syene" (Aswan in Upper Egypt), for *sînîm* of MT, equally correct, eliminates China from the Hebrew Bible (*sînîm* means "Chinese" in Modern Hebrew). An example from the last part of the book would be Isa 65:3, which occurs in the context of a denunciation of "pagan" cults, where it seems that MT ("they burn incense upon bricks") is an attempt to avoid mentioning an obscene cult practice, the reading preserved in 1QIsaᵃ.[5] There are also some additions or pluses. In the passage about the coming of the herald of good tidings in 52:7-12, the 1QIsaᵃ scribe adds that Yahveh will return to Zion "with compassion" and adds at the end of the pericope, "He is called the God of all the earth." But, in general, 1QIsaᵃ provides no basis for a distinctive and consistent approach to the interpretation of the book.

Also from Cave 1 is an incomplete scroll of Isaiah together with some broken-off fragments. Designated 1QIsaᵇ, this copy, from the Herodian period, contains parts of 46 chapters of the book. It is practically identical with MT, and almost without exception its textual variants are of minor import.[6] One exception appears in 53:11, where the addition of the word *'ôr* ("light"), absent from MT, provides that after his painful life the Servant "will see light and be satisfied." But this superior reading is also present in 1QIsaᵃ, 4QIsaᵈ, and LXX.

Parts of 18 manuscripts of Isaiah were identified among the thousands of fragments recovered from Cave 4. Three of these (4QIsaᵃ ᵇ ᶜ) are fairly substantial, containing several hundred verses, often fragmentary, from as many as 36 chapters. The rest are mostly scraps, one of which, 4QIsaʳ, has only one complete word. We therefore cannot be sure that all 18 belonged to complete scrolls of Isaiah. There are no indications that any of them belonged to a pesher on the book. The longest, 4QIsaᵇ, certainly comes from a complete copy, since it has preserved the first and the last verse of Isaiah (1:1; 66:24). These copies are dated within a time span from the early 1st century B.C.E. to the mid-1st century C.E., with 4QIsaᶜ and 4QIsaᵈ being the most recent. While of obvious importance for the text critic, they provide disappointingly few variants of genuine interpretative interest and provide no evidence for a distinct Isaianic literary or textual

---

5. The consonantal text of MT reads *wmqṭrym 'l hlbnym*; cf. 1QIsaᵃ *wynqw ydym 'l h'bnym*, ("they suck hands on the stones"); see my *Isaiah 56–66*, 266-67, 271.

6. Variant readings are listed and categorized by Bleddyn J. Roberts, *The Second Isaiah Scroll from Qumrân (1QIsb);* repr. from *BJRL* 42 (1959/60): 132-44.

tradition, a conclusion which holds for the Qumran Isaianic textual material as a whole. To quote the editor of the Isaiah fragments: "After all the thousand-plus variants in the Isaiah manuscript corpus are reviewed, no evidence appears that would ground a pattern of intentional change according to consistent principles which would constitute evidence for variant literary editions of the book."[7]

Several of the nonbiblical manuscripts, the rules in particular, either cite or allude to texts from Isaiah, and in some few cases the citations or allusions provide significant clues to the way the book was interpreted at Qumran. The following examples are by no means exhaustive. The metaphorical descriptions of the community in the Community Rule *(serek hayyaḥad)* often draw on Isaiah. The community council is "an everlasting plantation" *(maṭṭāʿat ʿôlām,* 1QS VIII 5), a figure which draws on Isa 60:21, where the Israel of the future, identified with the *yaḥad,* is described as "the shoot that I myself planted" (see also 61:11).[8] Paraphrasing Isa 28:16, it is also described as a well-tested wall and a precious cornerstone *(ḥômat habbōḥan, pinnat yāqār,* 1QS VIII 7-8[9]):

> I will lay in Zion a stone, a foundation stone for a tower,
> a precious cornerstone set firmly in place.

Later in the same part of the rule (VIII 12-16), the seminal text Isa 40:3, about preparing the way in the wilderness, is applied to the admission of postulants who must be set apart for the study of the law *(midrāš hattôrâ),* a curriculum which, since it has to do with all that the prophets have revealed through the Holy Spirit of God, must in the context include both Law and Prophets. These figurative representations of the sect are reproduced in the New Testament with reference to the Christian church. So, for example, the Corinthian community was planted by Paul, watered by Apollos, but only God makes it grow (1 Cor 3: 6, 9). The *ekklēsia* is often compared to a building, and 1 Pet 2:4-8 parallels the Community Rule in citing Isa 28:16 together with other texts in presenting it as a spiritual temple built of living stones.

The book of Isaiah therefore served as a major resource for the lan-

---

7. Eugene C. Ulrich, "Isaiah, Book of," *EDSS* 1:387. For the 4Q fragments, see Ulrich et al., *Qumran Cave 4.X: The Prophets. DJD* 15 (Oxford: Clarendon, 1997): 7-143.

8. See below pp. 248-49.

9. Also 1QHᵃ XIV 26; XV 9; 4Q259 11.16.

guage in which both the Qumran sectarians and the first Christians articulated their self-understanding. The Damascus Document in particular
makes generous use of Isaiah, sometimes in allusive and indirect ways.
When the opponents of the sect are described as "those who light their
own fire and kindle their own firebrands" (CD V 13), the description is
taken verbatim from a condemnation of the opponents of the Servant of
Yahveh in Isa 50:11. When the same opponents are compared to spiders and
vipers (CD V 13-14), the unflattering comparison draws on Isa 59:5-6
("They hatch vipers' eggs, they spin spiders' webs"). In the historical introduction to the Admonitions, the 20 years of disorientation prior to the appearance of the Teacher of Righteousness is said to be a time when "they
recognized their iniquity and acknowledged that they were guilty
(ăšîmîm); they were like the blind, and like those who grope for the way"
(CD I 8-9). Here the image derives from Isa 59:10:

> We grope like the blind along a wall,
> we feel our way like the sightless;
> we stumble at midday as at twilight,
> like the walking dead among the healthy.[10]

Shortly afterwards the writer goes on to speak of the appearance on the
scene of an opponent and former member of the sect referred to as "the
Scoffer" (*'îš hallāṣôn* CD I 14), elsewhere given such uncomplimentary
nicknames as "the Driveller" *(mēṭîf)*[11] and Zaw (CD IV 19). The principal
source for the latter is the MT of Hos 5:11 which speaks of Ephraim determined to go after Zaw, especially since "Ephraim" would have been an obvious designation for rival sectarians, and in fact the opponents of the Damascus sect are so designated.[12] But we can be reasonably sure that the
writer also had in mind the prophet's mimicking of the unintelligible

10. Reading *mĕgaššĕšîm* ("those who grope") with 4Q268 1.16 and 4Q306 2.4. It looks
as if *ăšîmîm* ("guilty") is an attempt to extract a contextually suitable meaning from the
hapax legomenon *'ašmannîm* in Isa 59:10b, which I translate "the healthy"; see my *Isaiah 56–
66*, 190.

11. The normal translation of the verb *hēṭip* would be "to preach," according to the
biblical texts a characteristically prophetic activity (Amos 7:16; Mic 2:6, 11; Ezek 21:2, 7 [Eng.
20:46]). The pejorative sense "to drivel," suggested by the root meaning of *nṭp* (Qal, "drip"),
is illustrated by Mic 2:11, where the (false) prophet says, "I will preach to you about wine and
strong drink."

12. See p. 112.

drivel of the inebriated prophets and priests in Jerusalem *(ṣaw lāṣaw, qaw lāqaw)* in Isa 28:10, 13, and it is the same people who immediately afterwards are addressed as "you scoffers *('anšê lāṣôn)* who rule this people in Jerusalem" (28:14). To complete this cluster of allusions, the name Zaw occurs in the context of a kind of midrash[13] on Isa 24:17:

> Terror, the trap, the deep pit
> await you who dwell on the earth!
> If you flee from the sound of the terror
> you will fall into the pit;
> if you get out of the pit,
> you will be caught in the trap.

These are interpreted as the three nets of Belial, respectively, fornication, wealth, and desecration of the temple, and it is at this point that Zaw and his followers are accused of fornication by taking two wives (CD IV 12-21).

A more complex kind of midrashic procedure is exemplified by CD VII 10-20. This part of the text reads as follows:

> As for all those who reject (the law): when God visits the earth to render retribution on the reprobate; when the word written in the sayings of the prophet Isaiah ben Amoz is fulfilled where he says, "There will come upon you, your people, and your ancestral house a time such has not been since Ephraim departed from Judah" (Isa 7:17) . . . When the two houses of Israel went their separate ways, Ephraim departed from Judah, and all the renegades were delivered up to the sword, whereas those who remained firm escaped to the land of the north . . . as he (God? Amos?) says, "I will send into exile the Sikkuth of your king *(sikkût malkěkem)* and the Kiyyun *(kiyyûn* = base?) of your images from my tent Damascus" (an adaptation of Amos 5:26-27). The books of the law are the booth of the king *(sukkat hammelek)* as he says, "I will raise up the booth of David *(sukkat dāwîd)* which is falling" (Amos 9:11). The king is the assembly *(qāhāl)* and the bases of the images are the books of the prophets whose utterances Israel despised. The "star" is the Interpreter of the Law who came (is coming? is about to come?) to Damascus, as it is written, "A star comes forth from Jacob

13. A more developed example of this kind of innertextual midrash starts out from Num 21:18, the Song of the Well, and cites Isa 54:16 (CD VI 3-11).

and a scepter arises from Israel" (Num 24:17). The scepter is the Prince of the entire congregation, and when he comes forth he will destroy all the sons of Seth (Num 24:17).[14]

The division of the kingdoms is here seen as foreshadowing schism within the sect between those who seceded (i.e., Ephraim) and those who remained faithful to the Teacher of Righteousness (i.e., Judah), and the fate of Ephraim is seen to foreshadow what will happen to the recidivists in the coming judgment. The congregation of the exile, that is, the authentic Judah, will restore observance of the law and the prophets under the guidance of their interpreter and teacher. Meanwhile, they await the final reckoning when the Prince of the Congregation, identified with the Davidic messiah, will destroy their enemies. This seems to be the drift of the midrash, but for our purposes it is less important to decode this exegetical *catena* in terms of personalities and events in the history of the sects than it is to note how, starting with Isa 7:17, several biblical texts are linked by a certain train of thought. The linkage is suggested by the author's understanding of the place of the sect in the history of Israel helped out with verbal associations, for example using the word *sukkâ* ("booth") in Amos 5:26 and 9:11. Everything in the law and the prophets coheres; everywhere there is interconnection and intercommunication, but everything is written in coded language awaiting inspired decryption. The author of the passage is clearly convinced that he is authorized to crack the code.

We come across a different kind of exegetical procedure in 4QFlorilegium (fr. 1. I 14-17) which cites Isa 8:11:

> For thus Yahveh addressed me, with his hand strong upon me, warning me against following the lead of this people.

As the name suggests, the Florilegium is not formally a pesher but an anthology (the precise Greek equivalent of the Latin word), a collection of commented and thematically interconnected biblical texts. This text has interested scholars primarily because of its concept of a human temple *(miqdāš 'ādām)* along the same lines as the architectural metaphor in 1QS VIII, where the building is identified by the author with the community to which he belonged. The passage from the Florilegium also provides an in-

---

14. The alternative version of the midrash in MS B (CD XIX 5-6) cites Zech 13:7; 11:11; Ezek 9:4; and Hos 5:10 instead of Isa 7:17; Amos 5:26-27; and Num 24:17.

teresting perspective on Qumranic exegetical method. After citing Ps 1:1: "Blessed is the one who does not walk in the council of the wicked," the text continues as follows: "The pesher of the text (refers to) those who turn away from the path of the wicked, as is written in the book of the prophet Isaiah with reference to the last days: 'With his hand strong upon me, he warned me against following the lead of this people' (Isa 8:11)."[15] It then continues: "These are the ones of whom it is written in the book of the prophet Ezekiel: 'They must not defile themselves any longer with all their idols.' These are the sons of Zadok and the men of their council, those who seek justice, (together with) their successors in the council of the community." We see, then, how, employing a thematic rather than a sequential, verse-by-verse exegetical approach, the three texts (Ps 1:1; Isa 8:11; Ezek 44:10) are linked so as to provide biblical warranty for the segregation of the community, living through the last days, from their fellow Jews and from the world beyond Judaism.[16]

Different again is the Melchizedek text discovered in Cave 11 (11QMelchizedek = 11Q13), which can be described as an eschatological midrash with its point of departure in the biblical texts dealing with the Jubilee Year (Lev 25:13; Deut 15:2). The text unfortunately has many lacunae, so the line of thought leading to Melchizedek as an eschatological figure, identified with the archangel Michael, is unclear. In the 10th and final Jubilee Melchizedek/Michael will take up arms and execute God's judgment on the forces of Belial, freedom will be proclaimed, and there will be a final atoning for sin. The figure of Melchizedek at Qumran and in early Christian writings is the subject of a considerable amount of commentary, and its overall interpretation exceeds the limits of our present agenda. It calls for comment at this point only because it incorporates several Isaianic texts into its eschatological scenario, chiefly 52:7 and 61:1-3. The first of these reads as follows:

> How welcome on the mountains are the footsteps of the herald, announcing well-being, bringing good tidings, announcing victory, declaring to Zion: "Your God reigns as king!"

15. Lit., "he warned me against following in the path of this people." I read *wĕyissranî* verbal stem *ysr* ("warn") rather than *wayĕsirēnî sûr* ("turn aside") in spite of 1QIsaᵃ, which supports the latter.
16. On the Florilegium, see George J. Brooke, *Exegesis at Qumran: 4QFlorilegium in its Jewish Context* (1985; repr. Atlanta: SBL, 2006); Annette Steudel, *Der Midrasch zur Eschatologie aus der Qumrangemeinde (4QMidrEschatᵃ,ᵇ)*. STDJ 13 (Leiden: Brill, 1994).

This text, seminal for early Christianity, combining as it does the idea of gospel with that of the kingdom of God, is given its own pesher in which each item in the text is assigned its correspondent as antitype to type. The mountains are the prophets. The herald is the one anointed with the spirit, in which connection the pesher cites the cryptic allusion to an anointed prince in Dan 9:25, probably a priestly figure. The text is defective at this point, but it seems that the midrashist identifies the one in the Isaianic text who announces well-being and brings good tidings in the second verse with an individual distinct from the herald in the first verse. This person appears to be identified with the prophet whose voice is heard in Isa 61:1-3:

> The spirit of the Sovereign Lord Yahveh is upon me,
> because Yahveh has anointed me.
> He has sent me to announce good news to the poor,
> to bind up the wounds of those broken in spirit;
> to proclaim freedom to captives,
> release to those in prison;
> to proclaim the year of Yahveh's good pleasure,
> a day of vindication for our God;
> to comfort all those who mourn,
> to give to those who mourn over Zion
> a turban in place of ashes,
> festive oil in place of a mournful appearance,
> a splendid garment in place of a drooping spirit.

This same text, which in Luke's gospel provides the keynote to the public activity of Jesus (Luke 4:18-19), is alluded to earlier in the midrash where it speaks of the proclamation of freedom and the year of the Lord's good pleasure (II 6, 9). The interpretation of the third and last verse of the quotation is also defective. It is possible that the scribe identified "Zion" with the community and thought of Melchizedek, the final liberator from the power of Belial, as a divine or quasi-divine eschatological figure; as one of the ʾĕlohîm attendant on Yahveh, he is in some way within the sphere of divinity though not presented in the text as a hypostasis of Yahveh. 11QMelchizedek also alludes to Isa 30:20-21, the passage about the hidden teacher (teachers), and 8:11, the warning against walking in the way of this people discussed earlier. It therefore illustrates the availability of the book of Isaiah for the creation of end-time scenarios, while providing a good example of a kind of interpretation which finds points of interconnection and convergence between different biblical texts based on a conviction of the essential inner coherence and unity of the prophetic corpus as a whole.

The Qumran Pesher Commentaries

With the exception of Psalms and Deuteronomy, the book of Isaiah enjoyed the greatest prestige and popularity among biblical books at Qumran, as also in early Christianity. One important reason, not the only one to be sure, would be that throughout its transmission and redaction it was being nudged in the direction of the apocalyptic worldview which animated the Qumran sectarians. While it would be anachronistic to speak of the book of Isaiah as belonging to a Qumran biblical canon, it clearly enjoyed a high level of authority. Isa 24:7 is cited as word of God communicated through the prophet Isaiah (CD IV 13-14). The War Scroll (1QM XI 11-12) predicts the end of Roman rule on the basis of the prophecy in Isa 31:8 which it attributes directly to God: "From of old you (God) announced to us the appointed time of your demonstration of power against the Kittim (i.e., Romans), saying: 'Assyria will fall by no human sword, no human sword will consume him.'"

We have seen some indications of the book as a fundamental resource while surveying the textual material preserved in the Qumran caves and the Wadi Murabbaʿat, most of it fragmentary with the exception of 1QIsaᵃ. But of greater interest for the history of interpretation are the remaining fragments of commentaries on the book, the product of a close and assiduous reading of the text. These are the earliest extant commentaries on any biblical book. The closest parallel from early Christian times would be the series of fulfillment sayings drawn up in formulaic manner in Matthew's gospel, to be considered in due course. But for chapter-by-chapter and verse-by-verse commentaries similar to those of Qumran from a Christian source, we must wait until the early 3rd century with the commentary on Daniel of Hippolytus of Rome and the 30-volume commentary on Isaiah from Origen, now lost.

What is a pesher? The term itself, usually translated "interpretation" or "meaning," makes only one appearance in the Hebrew Bible where

Qoheleth, the critic of those who claim to know and understand too much, asks "Who knows the meaning of anything?" (*mî yôdēaʿ pēšer dābār?* Eccl 8:1). The Aramaic equivalent, *pĕšar,* is used frequently in Daniel, and to this we shall turn in due course. In the Qumran texts, *pēšer* (*pĕšārîm* in the plural) describes a type of line-by-line commentary which, at Qumran, is limited to psalms and prophetic books, including Isaiah. Less frequently it is applied to collections of texts drawn from different biblical books organized around a theme, for example the temple or the Davidic dynasty.[17] These two types have come to be known, respectively, as continuous and thematic pesharim. There are also one or two brief commentaries on biblical texts embedded in the rule books in which the term occurs. An Isaianic example mentioned earlier is the identification of the alliterative *paḥad wāpaḥat wāpaḥ* (roughly "terror, the trap, the deep pit") of Isa 24:17 with the three nets of Belial in the Damascus Document. Other embedded pesharim occur in the the rule books and the War Scroll.[18]

The associated verbal stem *pšr* occurs only twice in the Qumran texts (1QpHab II 8 and 1Q22 1 I 3) and not at all in the Hebrew Bible, while the corresponding Aramaic verb *(pĕšar)* appears twice in Daniel with the meaning of interpreting or explaining (Dan 5:12, 16).

In addition to the five line-by-line pesharim on Isaiah, there are pesharim on six of the so-called minor prophets (Hosea, Micah, Nahum, Habakkuk, Zephaniah, and Malachi), among which the Habakkuk pesher, discovered in the first Qumran cave, is the best preserved and the most informative. While we have to keep reminding ourselves that survival under the circumstances in which these fragile texts were preserved was extremely fortuitous, it is interesting that no commentaries or fragments of commentaries on either Jeremiah or Ezekiel have come to light, which reinforces the point made earlier about the close affinity between Isaiah and the Twelve. On paleographical grounds helped out with spectrometry, the pesharim texts have been dated within a time period of about three centuries, from the middle of the 3rd century B.C.E. to the last decades of the Qumran settlement (roughly 250 B.C.E. to 50 C.E.). Within this range, the Isaiah pesharim have been dated from about 100 B.C.E. (4QIsaᶜ) to the mid-1st century C.E. (4QIsaᵃ).

---

17. 4Q176 Florilegium; 4Q177 Catena A; 11Q13 Melchizedek.
18. CD III 20-44; VI 3-11; VII 10-21; VIII 8-15; XIX 7-13; 1QS VIII 14-16; 1QM XI 11-12.

The pesharim therefore represent a stage in the evolution of an exegetical tradition which goes back well before the founding of the Qumran sects and links up with the interpretative activity in evidence in the prophetic books themselves, including Isaiah. The latter contains many examples of similar though less formulaic contemporizing addenda. At the end of the Throne Room Vision passage (6:13), a Second Temple scribe has added a comment on the word *maṣṣebet* ("tree stump"), identifying it with the *zeraʿ qōdeš* ("the holy seed"). The only other place where the expression occurs is Ezra 9:2 with reference to Ezra's *gôlâ*-community in which he exercized temporary leadership. The same referent is assumed for Isa 4:3, which declares holy those who are left in Zion and who remain in Jerusalem. In an Isaianic poem on the divine anger, the statement that Yahveh has cut off from Israel both head and tail (9:13-14) inspired a gloss identifying the tail with "the prophet, the teacher of falsehood," which, again, is almost certainly from the Second Temple period and is in keeping with the low opinion of a certain type of prophecy familiar at that time. The same unfavorable opinion is expressed in Zech 13:2-6, which also refers to the prophet who teaches falsehood. These and similar small-scale examples could have been set out in a more formulaic manner characteristic of the Qumran pesharim, or for that matter as marginal or end notes, but the book had not yet reached the point at which commentary could no longer be included in the text. In general, a critical reading of the book reveals an incremental and cumulative process of interpretation, of rereading *(Fortschreibung, relecture)* covering a period of several centuries.

The form specific to the Qumran pesher could have developed out of the study sessions of the community members. According to the Community Rule, the final coming of God, the parousia, was to be prepared for by "the study of the law which He commanded through Moses, acting in accord with all that is revealed from one age to the next and according to what the prophets have revealed through His Holy Spirit" (1QS VIII 15-16). Study was communal, under the direction of a master-interpreter, and was carried on round the clock, during the night as well as during the daylight hours (1QS VI 6-7). As in the series of formulaic quotations in Matthew's gospel, most of them from Isaiah, the biblical text is cited and the pesher is introduced with one of several standard formulae. One of the most frequent of these is *pēšer haddābār ʿal . . .* ("The pesher of the text concerns . . ."), followed by the application of the text to a contemporaneous person, event, or situation. It may be questioned whether this practice of simply linking prophetic passages with personalities, events, and situations of interest to the sectarians — still widely practiced — can be called interpretation. The issue will confront us throughout our study; for the moment we will take the broad view and continue to speak of the pesher as a form of commentary.[19] While all the pesharim are written from an end-time perspective, several deal with situations and events of concern to the community at the time of writing, which the authors were convinced was the end time. The formula occurring frequently in the commentaries on Isaiah, *pēšer haddābār lĕ'ăḥărît hayyāmîm* (lit., "the interpretation of the text for the last days"), explicitly designates the interpretations as eschatological.[20]

The pesher-type commentary proceeds verse by verse in sequence, though there are instances of nonsequential comment; for example, 4QpIsa[b] omits Isa 5:15-24 and 4QpPs[a] goes from Psalm 37 to Psalm 45. In deriving meanings from texts, the accepted critical axioms governing interpretation, that context determines meaning and that the unit of meaning is the sentence, are completely ignored. The pesher proceeds on the basis of wholesale decontextualization. Occasionally other biblical citations form part of the pesher. In 4QpIsa[c] fr. 8-10.8-9, for example, a text from Zechariah (3:9) is cited in confirmation of the decree of Yahveh in Isa 14:26-27, in defiance of the fact that the latter refers to something completely different.[21]

Since the authors of the pesharim interpret contemporary events in the light of the biblical texts as they affect themselves and their communities, their commentaries could be expected to provide information about the groups to which they belong and the religious situation in the late Second Temple period in general. For the most part, however, individuals are

19. For a comparison with exegetical procedures in early Christian texts, see Joseph A. Fitzmyer, "The Use of Explicit Old Testament Quotations in Qumran Literature and in the New Testament," *NTS* 7 (1961/62): 297-333.

20. In biblical texts the expression *lĕ'ăḥărît hayyāmîm* can refer to future events in general, and therefore should be translated "in days to come," "in time to come," or something of the sort depending on the context (e.g., Gen 49:1; Num 24:14; Deut 4:30; 31:29; Jer 48:47; 49:39). But it also occurs in eschatological contexts (e.g., Isa 2:2 = Mic 4:1; Jer 23:20; Hos 3:5; Ezek 38:16; Dan 10:14), and in the Qumran pesharim (4QpIsa[a] fr. 2-6 II 22; 4QpIsa[b] II 1; 4QpIsa[c] fr. 4-6 II 12; fr. 23 II 10) the context is undoubtedly eschatological.

21. On the genre of *pēšer*, see Maurya P. Horgan, *Pesharim: Qumran Interpretations of Biblical Books.* CBQMS 8 (Washington: Catholic Biblical Association, 1979), 229-59; and, more recently, Shani L. Berrin, "Pesharim," *EDSS* 2:644-47; and Timothy H. Lim, *Pesharim* (London: Sheffield Academic, 2002). As Lim points out (p. 14), "the scholarly publications on the pesharim alone can fill a small library."

referred to by sobriquets rather than by their real names (e.g., Teacher of Righteousness, Wicked Priest, Liar, Driveller, Wrathful Lion), and the same is true at the level of collectivities (e.g., Kittim, House of Absalom, House of Peleg, Seekers after Smooth Things). This circumstance continues to keep Qumran scholars busy debating how these allusions fit into what is known of late Second Temple history. Few direct historical references are to be found.[22]

The pesher involves a highly distinctive way of reading texts. It differs from the targum, which is basically a translation, though the targum often contemporizes in the manner of the pesharim, as when Targum Jonathan substitutes Rome for Edom in Isa 34:9 ("The streams of Rome will be turned into pitch"). The targums, moreover, are essentially liturgical while the pesharim are the products of learned, scribal activity. The distinctive form of the pesharim will be apparent if we compare them with the Qumran targums on Job (11QtgJob; 4QtgJob) and Leviticus 16 (4QtgLev). By the same token, the pesher differs from such biblical paraphrases or rewritings as the Genesis Apocryphon (1Q20), the Temple Scroll (11Q19), and the Book of Jubilees. There has been some discussion about classifying the pesher as a type or *sous-genre* of midrash. This seems to be acceptable so long as midrash is given the broad sense of the investigation of the meaning and contemporary relevance of authoritative texts. But it entails the danger of overextending the scope of what is, in the first place, a rabbinic genre, one attributed typically to named authors, one which is noneschatological and concerned with Torah rather than prophecy.[23]

While the authors of the pesharim betray some acquaintance with

22. Demetrius, probably Demetrius III (95-88 B.C.E.), and Antiochus, probably Antiochus IV Epiphanes (175-164 B.C.E.), are named in the Nahum pesher (4QpNah fr. 3-4 I 2-3). The names of Shelomzion, i.e., queen Alexandra-Salome (76-67 B.C.E.), and her son Hyrcanus appear in 4Q332 fr. 2 4.6. These historical issues are not a major concern in this study.

23. The category of midrash pesher is defended by George Brooke, "Qumran Pesher: Towards the Redefinition of a Genre," *RevQ* 10 (1979/81): 483-503, following William H. Brownlee, "Biblical Interpretation among the Sectarians of the Dead Sea Scrolls," *BA* 14 (1951): 54-76; *The Midrash Pesher of Habakkuk*. SBLMS 24 (Missoula: Scholars, 1979). The contrary position was defended by Karl Elliger, *Studien zum Habakuk-Kommentar vom Toten Meer*. BHT 15 (Tübingen: Mohr, 1953), 163-64, on the grounds that in the pesher the interpretation is derived not from anything in the text but from a private revelation. For recent summary accounts of midrash, with bibliography, see Merrill P. Miller, "Midrash" in *IDBSup* 593-97; Gary G. Porton, "Midrash," *ABD* 4:818-22.

exegetical procedures known from the classical Jewish sources,[24] they claim to arrive at the true meaning of the text by direct access to the source, namely, the deity who is "the revealer of mysteries" (Dan 2:28-29, 47). The assumption is that God dictated a coded message to the original prophetic author, one which is to be decoded only in the final epoch of history: "God told Habakkuk to write what was to happen to the last generation, but he did not make known to him the end of the age" (1QpHab VII 1-2). The key to crack the code, to open up the true meaning of the text, will be revealed to a chosen intermediary, one living through the final countdown to the end. In the case of Habakkuk, and possibly other prophetic texts, the recipient is the Teacher of Righteousness as inspired interpreter of prophecy.[25] The Qumran sectarians believed that the inspired interpretation of prophecy comes about through the agency of the Holy Spirit (*bĕrûaḥ haqqodeš*, e.g., 1QS VIII 13-16), but they did not produce a theory of inspiration. The frequency with which the author of the *Hodayot* ("Hymns of Thanksgiving") speaks of the presence of the Holy Spirit within him and of himself as the Servant of God, therefore as a prophetic figure, provides some support for identifying him with the Teacher of Righteousness. He is privy to secret knowledge which comes to him through the Spirit with which he is endowed (1QH^a V 24-25; XX 11-12), the Holy Spirit has been spread over him (IV 26; XV 6-7), and he has been favored with the spirit of knowledge (VI 25). In a later chapter we will have to return to this prophetic profile of the Qumran Teacher.[26]

Text Interpretation and Dream Interpretation

The Akkadian cognate of the Hebrew *pēšer* is *pišru* and its corresponding verb is *pašāru*. The verb denotes the narration or explanation of dreams or the healing of the effects of a bad dream by therapeutic magic. The interpretation of dreams was an activity of great importance in Mesopotamian religion and in ancient cultures in general.[27] Dream interpretation also af-

24. Some of these procedures are listed and briefly discussed by Elieser Slomovic, "Toward an Understanding of the Exegesis in the Dead Sea Scrolls," *RevQ* 7 (1969): 3-15.

25. 1QpHab II 6-10; VI 15–VII 5.

26. See pp. 268-85.

27. See A. Leo Oppenheim, *The Interpretation of Dreams in the Ancient Near East: With a Translation of an Assyrian Dream-Book.* Transactions of the American Philological Society N.S. 46/3 (Philadelphia: American Philological Society, 1956): 179-373.

fords an interesting analogy to the interpretation of texts. A. Leo
Oppenheim's *Assyrian Dream-Book* provides a key to translating the symbolic language of dreams in the form of a long list of point-by-point correspondences between things seen in dream and their respective "meanings,"
reminiscent of the atomized approach of the Qumran pesharim; perhaps
we can think of this approach as a distant predecessor of Freudian dream
analysis (e.g., house = body).[28] The correspondence could be established
in a variety of ways including simple verbal similarity, assonance, or the
existence of homonyms, a phenomenon also attested in the pesharim. Interesting rabbinic parallels are available. If, for example, you see an ele-
phant (Heb. *pîl*) in your dream it presages a miracle *(pele')*; if you see a
reed *(qāneh)* you may hope to acquire wisdom on the basis of Prov 4:5
(*qĕnēh ḥokmâ*, "get wisdom").[29] This will no doubt appear irrational, even
bizarre, to our educated Western sensitivity. But the chance sequence of
events in real time also has its irrationalities and inconsequentialities, and
there may well be a kind of wisdom in seeking a way out of dead ends and
the paralysis of the will by such means.

In Mesopotamia and Egypt mantic dreams presaging future events,
being of supernatural origin, called for direct or indirect appeal to a deity,
and the repetition of the same dream, by the same person or by two different persons, confirmed its supernatural origin and the assurance of its
eventual fulfillment. This, too, is a well-attested feature of ancient dream
interpretation, instances of which can be found in the Mari letters from
the 18th century B.C.E., the Gilgamesh poem, the Hebrew Bible, and the
New Testament.

The association between dreams and the mantic interpretation of
texts is especially in evidence in Daniel. The stories and visions in Daniel
are located in Mesopotamia, the great heartland of interpretation by
dreams and omens, and in the Aramaic sections they use essentially the
same vocabulary and formulae as at Qumran.[30] In Nebuchadnezzar's
dreams of the statue and the great tree (Dan 2 and 4) the texts to be decoded are dreams in the head of a mad king, one of which he cannot even

28. Oppenheim, *Interpretation of Dreams*, 256-373.
29. Asher Finkel, "The Pesher of Dreams and Scriptures," *RevQ* 4 (1963/64): 357-70.
30. The principal formulae are: "This is the interpretation" (*dĕnâ pišrā'*, Dan 4:21)
and "this is the interpretation of the matter" (*dĕnâ pĕšar-millĕtā'*, 5:26; cf. 5:15; 7:16). Where a
dream presages an eschatological event, we find the phrase "in the last days" (*bĕ'aḥărît
yômāyyā'*, Dan 2:28; cf. *bĕ'aḥărît hayyāmîm* frequently in the pesharim).

remember. Both these dream narratives sound surrealistic, as dreams often do. They must mean something, but the meaning is not apparent since it is a mystery *(rāz)* awaiting elucidation. As the "revealer of mysteries" *(gālē' rāzayyā',* Dan 2:28-29), God can choose to communicate the meaning of such coded messages through a heavenly intermediary, as when Gabriel interpreted Daniel's dream of the four beasts (Dan 7:16-27). It could also be channeled through a privileged human intermediary, usually in the context of prayer, fasting, penitential exercises, and converse with angelic beings. In this way the symbolism is spelled out, text and interpretation are brought together, and the mystery is resolved.

Characteristic of all such resolutions, in Daniel as in Qumran, is the revelation of future events otherwise unknowable, and in a particular way events of the end time. In the story of Belshazzar's feast (Dan 5), the text consists in cryptic writing which appears mysteriously on the wall of the royal dining room. It consists in four words written in code (5:5-9, 25) which only the Jewish sage is able to decipher (5:26-28). At a later point we observe the seer poring over the book of Jeremiah, and we realize that the biblical text to be interpreted is a cryptogram no less resistant to decipherment by noninitiates than the words written on the dining room wall. The text in question is Jer 25:11-12 or, more probably, 29:10, predicting 70 years of exile, but it does not mean what it seems to mean and it does not mean what its author thought it meant either. It is a coded message awaiting its true interpretation, perhaps many years later. The author of the Habakkuk pesher understands the text he is interpreting in precisely the same way: "God told Habakkuk to write down what would happen to the final generation, but did not make known to him the consummation of the end time" (1QpHab VII 1).

The story of Joseph "the dream master" *(ba'al haḥălomôt,* Gen 37:19) reinforces the analogy between dream interpretation and the interpretation of texts. Each dream, like each textual cryptogram, has its own interpretation *(pittārôn,* Gen 40:5; 41:11-12) which deals invariably with the course of future events otherwise unknowable. The events in question can occupy a period as short as three days or as long as 14 years. In a way somewhat similar to allegory, each item in the dream has its correspondent in real time and space: the 11 sheaves are Joseph's 11 brothers (37:5-7), the sun, moon, and 11 stars are Jacob, Rachel, and the brothers (37:9), and the three vine branches and the three baskets are the three days which will elapse prior to fulfillment (40:9-11, 16-17). The interpretation is expressed in formulaic manner: first, "this is its interpretation" (*zeh pitrōnô*, 40:12, 18), similar to the Qumran formulas (*pišrô, pišrô 'ăšer*, etc.), then the principal elements in the dream are elucidated (sheaves, heavenly bodies, cows, ears of wheat), and finally the event predicted in symbolic fashion is clearly stated. In keeping with ancient beliefs about predictive dreams, the fulfillment of a dream that is repeated, with or without variations, is more clearly predetermined by God and therefore its fulfillment is that much more certain (Gen 41:32). The same conclusion can be inferred from the close parallelism between the dreams of the Pharaoh's cupbearer and chief baker, emphasized by the deadly ambiguity latent in the allusion to Pharaoh "lifting up their heads." It was also significant that their dreams occurred on the same night. The statement that each dream was in keeping with its interpretation (*'îš kĕpitrôn ḥălōmô*, 40:5) emphasizes the essential priority of the event to the dream which prefigures it. By the same token, it illustrates the fundamentally deterministic view of time, and the succession of events in time, of this prophetic-apocalyptic worldview.

The Qumran pesharim therefore represent a highly distinctive way of reading texts. Superficially similar to rabbinic gematria or even to such modern curiosities as *The Bible Code*,[31] they differ by requiring close reading of the texts themselves and by presupposing a coherent view of history as directed by God to a predetermined end. The conviction of their authors that they were living in the last phase of history gives to their readings a seriousness and narrative coherence that these other approaches lack.

The Isaiah Pesharim

While the Qumran sectarians may have produced a pesher-type commentary on all 66 chapters of Isaiah, the five surviving Isaiah pesharim (six including 3QpIsa in which the word *pēšer* does not occur[32]) do not amount to anything like a commentary on the book as a whole. The database consists in some 85 fragments, about half of which contain no more than a

31. Michael Drosnin, *The Bible Code,* 2 vols. (New York: Simon & Schuster, 1997-2002).

32. On 3QpIsa, see Maurice Baillet et al., *Les 'petites grottes' de Qumrân.* DJD 3 (Oxford: Clarendon, 1962), 95-96; Horgan, *Pesharim,* 260-61.

word or two. As few as about a hundred verses out of a total of 1,291 in the book are cited, drawn from only 14 of the 66 chapters, and the pesharim on many of these are either completely lost or too fragmentary to render consecutive meaning. In spite of these severe limitations, a review of the surviving pesharim can serve as an entry to the religious world of the Qumran dissident groups and to the different ways in which their reading of Isaiah helped to give shape and substance to that world. The material will be presented in the order in which the texts occur in Isaiah rather than according to the numbered pesharim or the presumed chronological order of composition. Translations of pesharim and biblical texts are my own; the translation of the biblical texts is reproduced from my three-volume Anchor Bible commentary on Isaiah. Only major variants in the biblical texts quoted will be mentioned; for others, the reader may consult the notes in Maurya P. Horgan, *Pesharim*, and the Anchor Bible Isaiah commentary. Where the extent of the biblical text cited in the pesharim is not seriously in doubt, lacunae are not indicated by brackets as in the critical editions.

1:1-2a (3QpIsa = 3Q4)

The vision of Isaiah ben Amoz which he saw concerning Judah and Jerusalem in the days of Uzziah, Jotham, Ahaz, and Hezekiah, kings of Judah.
Hear, heaven, earth, give heed, for Yahveh speaks!

These opening verses are also reproduced in the Great Isaiah Scroll (1QIsa^a) and in two of the Isaiah fragments (4Q55 = 4QIsa^a and 4Q56 = 4QIsa^b). After verse 1, which is the superscription to the book as a whole, there is a gap in this first pesher followed by the words "Isaiah prophesied concerning (or, against) . . . the king of Judah," and after the opening invocation all that remains is the phrase "the day of judgment" *(yôm hammišpāṭ)*. But with the help of formulaic language in other pesharim,[33] the pesher following verse 1 can be reconstructed as follows: "Its interpretation concerns all that will happen which Isaiah prophesied concerning (or, against) Judah and Jerusalem to Uzziah king of Judah." "The day of judgment" would then belong to a pesher on the invocation to the heaven and earth (v. 2a) and would suggest that Isaiah's prophesying to the Judean

---

33. 1QpHab II 10; VII 1.

kings named in the title of the book presages the final judgment. We do
not know whether this first comment was intended as the beginning of a
pesher-type commentary on the book as a whole, but it provides the first
of many pointers to a reading of the book as eschatological from beginning to end. The expression *yôm hammišpāṭ* does not occur in the Hebrew
Bible and very rarely in the Qumran texts,[34] but the Greek equivalent
(hēmera kriseōs) is quite frequent in the New Testament, especially in the
gospel according to Saint Matthew.[35]

5:5-6 (4QpIsa[b] I 1-6 = 4Q162)

So now, I give you notice
as to what I will do with my vineyard:
deprived of its hedge, it will be open for grazing,
its fence breached and broken, it will be trampled down;
I will turn it into a wasteland,
it will be neither pruned nor hoed,
thorns and weeds will spring up,
I will give command to the clouds
to send down no rain upon it.

Together with the following verse, which identifies the vineyard as the
house of Israel, this is the conclusion to the Vineyard Song (Isa 5:1-7) in
which judgment is passed on the unproductive vineyard, a familiar figure
for Israel. Only a fragment of the pesher has survived, and its meaning is
ambiguous. The sentence *pēšer haddābār 'ăšer 'ăzābām* could be translated
"The interpretation of the text (is) that he (God) has abandoned them,"
but the verb *'zb*, "abandon," occurs more often in Isaiah with reference to
the people abandoning God, or the covenant,[36] and with equal frequency
it shows up with this connotation in the Scrolls as, for example, in the
phrase *bĕ'ăzābām 'et-bĕrît*, "when they abandoned the covenant" (CD III
11). The sense in which the author of the pesher would have understood
the verdict on the vineyard can be seen more clearly in the light of another
Qumran text. 4Q433a (4QHodayot-like text B) uses language reminiscent
of Eden in speaking of God's delightful plantation in his garden and vineyard. The vine planted by God will bring forth no rotten grapes *(bĕ'ûš)* and

---

34. 1QpHab XII 14; XIII 3.
35. Matt 10:15; 11:22-24; 12:36; also 2 Pet 3:7; 1 John 4:17.
36. Isa 1:4, 28; 58:2; 65:11.

no thorns and weeds *(šāmîr wāšāyit)*. This is precisely the language used in the verdict on the vineyard in Isaiah which produced rotten grapes and therefore will be given over to thorns and weeds (Isa 5:4, 6). The Isaianic poem concludes:

> For the vineyard of Yahveh of the hosts is the house of Israel,
> and the people of Judah the plantation in which he delighted.
> He looked for justice and instead there was bloodshed,
> for righteousness, and instead a cry of distress. (5:7)

The community in whose name the commentator writes understands itself to be God's true vineyard, one which, unlike the Israel taken to task in Isa 5:1-7, will not disappoint. In this respect, the vineyard *(kerem)* motif links up with the motif of the community as God's planting *(maṭṭāʿ,* CD I 7), and, as was noted earlier,[37] this too is an Isaianic theme:

> Your people, righteous one and all,
> will possess the land forever,
> the shoot that I myself planted,
> the work of my hands so that I might be glorified. (60:21)

This figurative retrospect on the history of Israel, drawing on the Isaianic text, suggests comparison with the parable of the Neglected Vineyard in Matt 21:33-41, which opens by citing Isa 5:1 LXX. It also brings to mind the saying of Jesus that "every planting *(phyteia = maṭṭāʿ)* that my heavenly Father has not planted will be rooted out" (Matt 15:13).

5:9-10 (4QpIsa^b II 1-2)

Yahveh of the hosts has sworn in my hearing:
"many houses will be turned into ruins,
houses splendid and spacious left without occupants;
a vineyard of ten hectares will yield but one barrel of wine,
a homer of seed will produce but one bushel."

This second column of the pesher begins with a comment on the text cited at the end of the previous column but now lost. Since the pesharim are usually continuous, the text may have been 5:8-10, but in any case the

---

37. See above ch. 3, p. 92.

pesher refers more directly to verses 9-10 quoted above. It may be translated as follows: "The eschatological interpretation of the text concerns the punishment of the land by means of sword and famine. This will happen at the time when punishment is visited on the land." The citation formula *pēšer haddābār lĕʾaḥărît hayyāmîm,* literally, "the interpretation of the word with reference to the end of the days" and here translated "the eschatological interpretation of the text," is peculiar to the Isaiah pesharim, where it occurs fairly frequently.[38] The word translated "punishment" in the phrase "the punishment of the land" *(ḥôbâ)* is attested neither elsewhere in the Scrolls nor in Biblical Hebrew, but a related verb in Dan 1:10 and CD III 10 has the meaning of incurring guilt. In Mishnaic Hebrew *ḥôbā'* means "debt" or "sin," a meaning reflected in the prayer for forgiveness of "debts" *(opheilēmata)* in the Lord's Prayer (Matt 6:12). Since famine and the sword are frequently linked in the prophetic books as agents of divine punishment,[39] it required no effort to locate them in the end time. "The visitation of the land" — or, perhaps, "the visitation of the earth" *(pĕqūdat hāʾāreṣ)* — is synonymous with the final judgment, and the final judgment is prefigured in the Babylonian exile which the Damascus Document refers to as "the first visitation."[40] Exile and end time are the two poles around which the thinking of the Qumran sectarians revolves.

5:11-14 (4QpIsa^b II 2-6)

Woe to them who rise early in the morning
in pursuit of strong drink,
who stay up late in the evening
that wine may inflame them;
Lyre and harp, timbrel and flute,
and wine are not lacking at their feasts.
They pay no heed to the work of Yahveh,
they regard not the operation of his hands.
Therefore: bereft of understanding, my people is exiled,
their nobles are famished,
their commoners parched with thirst.
Therefore: Sheol stretches wide its gullet,

38. 4QpIsa^a 2-6 II 26 has the slight variation *pēšer happitgām lĕʾaḥărît hayyāmîm,* "the eschatological interpretation of the message."
39. Isa 51:19; Jer 5:12; 14:15; 32:24; Ezek 14:21.
40. CD VII 21; VIII 3; XIX 10-11.

> its mouth opens wide beyond measure,
> down go her nobles and commoners,
> her throng in the midst of their revels.

This long citation gets only a short comment: "These are the Scoffers *('anšê hallāṣôn)* who are in Jerusalem." But then the commentator introduces a citation of Isa 5:24-25 internal to the pesher which calls for a further comment:

> They are the ones who — here begins the quotation — "have rejected the instruction of Yahveh and despised the word of Israel's Holy God. So Yahveh's anger was roused against his people; he stretched out his hand against them and struck them down. The mountains quaked, their corpses lay like refuse in the streets. Yet his anger did not abate, still was his hand outstretched." This refers to the congregation of the Scoffers who are in Jerusalem.

In the Damascus Document these "Scoffers" are defectors who have rejected the teachings of the group and the covenant made in "the land of Damascus" (CD I 10-12). They are followers of a leader known to his opponents as "the Scoffer" (*'îš hallāṣôn*, CD I 14), who is accused of lying, leading Israel astray, and abandoning traditional teachings (CD I 14-18). He is probably to be identified with the "Lying Preacher" (*mētîp hakkāzāb*, CD VIII 12-13; 1QpMic 8-10), or the Liar *tout court* (*'îš hakkāzāb*, CD XX 15), who opposed the Teacher of Righteousness and went on to build a city with blood.[41] He broke with the Teacher of Righteousness, which, given the nature of internecine sectarian polemics, may mean that the Teacher of Righteousness broke with him (CD XX 15). He then went on to found his own congregation.[42]

For our present purpose it is not necessary to enter the debate about the identity of this much-reviled individual. We will content ourselves with noting that the expression *'anšê hallāṣôn* derives from Isa 28:14: "Hear the word of Yahveh, you scoffers who rule this people in Jerusalem." The reference is to the Judean counterparts to the political and religious elite in Samaria who, in the same discourse, are accused by the prophet of indulging in drunken bouts as are those castigated in 5:11-14 (28:1-13). This would

---

41. 1QpHab II 1-4; V 9-12; X 9-10.
42. CD II 1; XIX 26; 1QpHab X 9-10.

strengthen the position of those who identify the Scoffer and Liar, whatever his origins, with a prominent political figure, the most likely candidates being either Jonathan or Simon Maccabee. More to our present concern, it provides a good illustration of the exegetical method of explaining one text by referring to another, the rabbinic technique of *gezera shava* much in use in the pesharim.[43] A further indication may be the rather cryptic sobriquet Ṣaw attached to the Lying Preacher in CD IV 19. As was noted earlier, this title brings to mind the *ṣaw lāṣāw, ṣaw lāṣāw* of Isa 28:10, 13, reproducing either gibberish uttered during a drunken bout or unintelligible foreign speech.[44]

5:29-30 (4QpIsa[b] III)

Their roaring is like a lion,
they roar like lion cubs;
snarling, they seize their prey;
when they carry it off, none can rescue it.
He will growl over it on that day like the growling of the sea,
If one looks to the earth there is only darkness and distress,
the light is obscured by the clouds.

The roaring and snarling lions are the Assyrians whom Yahveh is deliberately "siccing" on Israel as instruments of divine punishment; we are told that he will whistle for them from the ends of the earth (5:26). Only a few words of this passage have survived in the first two lines of the column, but enough to indicate that they were part of a longer citation. The pesher is completely lost, but we may suppose that the Assyrians of this passage would have stood for the Kittim, that is, the Romans — similar, therefore, to the pesher on Isa 10:33-34 in 4QpIsa[a].

8:5-8 (4Qpap pIsa[c] 2.1-7 = 4Q163)

Once again Yahveh addressed me, "Since this people has rejected the waters of Shiloah that flow so softly, rejoicing with Rezin and the son of Remaliah, therefore the Sovereign Lord is about to bring up against them the waters of the River, mighty and abundant [the king of Assyria in all his splendor]. It will crest over all its channels and overflow

---

43. Examples in Slomovic, *RevQ* 7 (1969): 3-15.
44. For attempts to explain this passage, see my *Isaiah 1–39*, 389-90. There may also be an intent to bring to mind the similar ṣōʾâ, ṣāw, "excrement" (4Q472a 2; 11Q19 XLVI 15).

all its banks, sweeping on into Judah in a flood, reaching up to the
neck. Its branches will be spread far and wide, filling the breadth of
your land, Immanuel."

Since Rezin and ben Remaliah are mentioned in the pesher, now almost
completely lost, the citation would have begun at verse 5 rather than verse
7 as it does in this papyrus fragment. The text itself is generally understood
to reflect the predictable outcome of the foreign policy of Ahaz of Judah in
the 8th century B.C.E. Under threat from a coalition of Syria under Rezin
and Israel under Pekah ben Remaliah, Ahaz sought protection in an alliance with Assyria, the superpower of that day. From the few words of the
pesher that are still readable, we would suppose that Rezin and ben
Remaliah represent opponents of the group and, depending on the date,
the Assyrians would, as elsewhere in the Scrolls, stand for the Romans
who, under Pompey, did sweep into Judah in a flood in 63 B.C.E. So what
happened during the reign of Ahaz would have served as a predictive analogy to Judah coming under direct Roman rule following on requests for
assistance from both Aristobulus II and Hyrcanus II (*Ant.* 14:34-79).

The fragmentary]*m htrh hbˀ rṣyn wbn* [*rmlyhw*] in line 4, which
speaks of the Torah and mentions Rezin and the son of Remaliah, could
imply a symbolic correspondence between the waters of Shiloah rejected
by "this people" and the Torah rejected by the opponents of the sect represented by the two foes of Ahaz. In that case we would suspect a cross-
reference to Isa 5:24, where the pesher identifies those who "have rejected
the instruction of Yahveh of the hosts" *(māˀăsû ˀēt tôrat YHVH ṣĕbāˀôt)*
with the Scoffers *(ˀanšê hallāṣôn)* in Jerusalem (4QpIsa^b II 6-8).

9:11, 13-16, 17-20 (4Qpap pIsa^c 4-7 I)

Fragments from 9:7-20, a poem about the wrath of God. Nothing of
the pesher has survived.

10:15-19 (4Qpap pIsa^c 6-7 II 1-9)

Should the axe vaunt itself over the one wielding it?
Should the saw flaunt itself over the one handling it?
As if a rod should brandish the one wielding it!
As if a wooden stick should wield one not made of wood!
Therefore the Sovereign Lord, Yahveh of the hosts,
will send wasting disease among the most prosperous of his people,

under his most distinguished folk a fire will be kindled.
The Light of Israel will become a fire,
the Holy One of Israel will become a flame;
it will burn up and consume in a single day
his land choked with thorns and weeds.
The best of his woodlands and orchards will be destroyed root
   and branch
as a sick person faints and falls;
the remnant of the trees of his forest will be so few
that a child can count them and write them down.

There is considerable uncertainty about the fit between fragments 6 and 7, and therefore about the extent of the citation.[45] In fact, the only legible portion of the citation, and the only part for which a pesher has survived, is the last couplet corresponding to Isa 10:19. In the context of the book of Isaiah, the passage is a response to the imperial hubris of Assyria (10:5-11). Only disjointed phrases survive from the beginning of the pesher, then Isa 10:19, referring to the few surviving trees of the forest, is repeated, and its pesher is given as "the reduction (diminution?) of humanity" *(mĕ'ût hā'ādām)*. The significance of this expression will be discussed in the next passage, where it is repeated.

10:20-23 (4QpIsa^a 2-6 II 1-9; 4Qpap pIsa^c II 10-21)

On that day the residue of Israel and the survivors of the household of Jacob will no longer rely on the one who struck them, but they will rely in truth on Yahveh the Holy One of Israel. A residue will return, the residue of Jacob, to the God of Might, for even if your people Israel were as numerous as the sand of the sea, only a residue of them will return. Destruction is decreed, with vindication abounding; for the Sovereign Lord, Yahveh of the hosts, will bring about the destruction that is decreed in the midst of the earth.

This passage, which is itself a variation on the theme of Shear-yashub ("a remnant will return"), the name of Isaiah's son (7:3), must have had strong appeal to the Qumranites, with its emphasis on the holy remnant of Israel

---

45. See Horgan, *Pesharim*, 97-98, 110-12; and cf. *The Dead Sea Scrolls Study Edition*, ed. Florentino García Martínez and Eibert J. C. Tigchelaar (Grand Rapids: Wm. B. Eerdmans, 1997), 1:320-21.

with which they identified themselves and the predestined divine decree of final destruction with which it concludes. It seems that verse 22a ("Even if your people Israel were as numerous as the sand of the sea only a remnant of them will return") was repeated within the pesher and given an eschatological interpretation (*pēšer haddābār lĕʾaḥărît hayyāmîm*). The interpretation refers to the exile, from which only a few will return.[46] This in its turn suggested the application to Israel of the universal eschatological depopulation and diminution in the pesher on the previous section, in which respect the commentator aligned himself quite closely with the Isaianic passage which applies the previous passage about Assyria to the postexilic community, the few who survived the exile with their faith intact. The belief that only a few will attain salvation is not confined to the Qumran sectarians; it occurs frequently in Jewish and Christian texts in late antiquity.[47] It was axiomatic for the author of the Damascus Document that the Zadokite priests formed the nucleus, or at least a major component, of this new community (CD III 21–IV 6), a conviction hinted at in the 4QFlorilegium text mentioned earlier.

The people numerous as the sand of the sea is a fairly explicit allusion to the Abrahamic promise of progeny, the "great nation" theme.[48] It seems that both the Isaianic author and his Qumran interpreter have subjected this promise to drastic revision. An allusion to the diminution brought about by the great deluge which resulted in a new humanity, small in number, is also present below the surface.

The pesher in 4QpIsaᵃ is too fragmentary to be of much help in reconstructing the Qumran understanding of the passage. The phrases which have survived from the pesher on 10:20-21, *ʾanšê ḥêlô* ("the men of his army") and *hakkôhănîm* ("the priests"), could indicate the military aspects of the sect, in the service of the "Mighty God" (*ʾēl gibbôr*, 10:21), and its priestly-Zadokite character, respectively, but are not very informative. A reconstructed sentence from the pesher on verse 22 speaks of destruction on the day of slaughter when many will perish. Apart from Jer 12:3, the expression "the day of slaughter" (*yôm hărēgâ* or *yôm hereg*) occurs only once

---

46. The phrase *yēlkû baššĕbî* should be translated "they will go into captivity" rather than "they will walk among the returnees of Israel" (Horgan, *Pesharim*, 98). The verb *hlk* is routinely paired with *šĕbî* in biblical texts (e.g., Deut 28:41; Isa 46:2; Jer 20:6; 22:22; 30:16; Ezek 12:11; Amos 9:4; Nah 3:10).

47. E.g., 4 Esd 8:1, 3; Matt 22:14; *Gos Thom* 23.

48. Gen 12:1-3; 22:17; 32:13 (Eng. 13); cf. Isa 48:19.

elsewhere, in a passage clearly apocalyptic in character which anticipates "a day of great slaughter when the towers come crashing down" (Isa 30:25). This would provide one more example of the kind of cross-referencing exegesis practiced by the members of the group.[49]

The predetermined, final, and annihilating act of judgment (*killāyôn ḥārûṣ . . . kālâ wĕneḥĕrāṣâ*, vv. 22-23), which is to follow after the time of wrath has come to an end (*kālâ za'am*, v. 25), is taken up in Daniel where the reader is assured that the tyrant Antiochus will continue on his godless and boastful way "until the time of wrath is fulfilled, for what is decreed must be accomplished" (*'ad-kālâ za'am kî neḥĕrāṣâ ne'ĕśātâ*, Dan 11:36). The same Isaianic text, the pesharim to which are unfortunately lost, is also behind allusions in the Scrolls to the predetermined final judgment.[50]

10:24-27a (4QpIsaᵃ 2-6 II 10-19)

Therefore, thus says the Sovereign Lord, Yahveh of the hosts: "O my people who dwell in Zion, do not be afraid of the Assyrians when they beat you with a rod and wield their stick over you as the Egyptians did. In a very short while the time of wrath will be over and my anger will be directed at their destruction." Yahveh of the hosts will wield a whip against them as when he struck Midian at the rock of Oreb. His staff will be extended [over the sea,] and he will wield it as the Egyptians did. On that day his burden will be removed from your shoulder, and his yoke broken off from your neck.

The passage is commented on in both 4QpIsaᵃ and 4QpIsaᶜ, but fragments of the commentary have survived only in the former. What is left of the pesher is disjointed but can be reconstructed as follows: "The interpretation of the text concerns . . . when they return from the wilderness of the peoples . . . the Prince of the Congregation, and afterwards it will be removed from off them." The strange expression "the wilderness of the peoples" draws on Ezek 20:35, where it indicates a place intermediate between the land of exile and the homeland, a place where judgment will take place,

---

49. The restoration of 4QpIsaᵃ 2-6 II 7 [. . . *whm ym*]*lṭw lmṭ*['*m b*] '*rṣ b'mt*, "but they will be rescued by being planted in the land in truth," is possible and could have been suggested by *ṣĕdāqâ* in v. 22 as it would have been interpreted at that time. God's planting represents a major *topos* in the Qumranic understanding of the history or prehistory of the group (cf. CD I 7-8; 1QS VIII 5; XI 8; 1QHᵃ XIV 15; XVI 6, 9-10).

50. 1QS IV 20, 25; 1QHᵃ XI 36.

where a covenant will be made, and transgressors will be weeded out (Ezek 20:33-38). This passage would have provided important clues for the Qumranites concerning their place in the divine plan for Israel, and they would have found solace in the assurance that the turning point would come "in a very short while." They could also have found in the Ezekiel passage verbal links with the Isaianic text. The Assyrian rod *(šēbeṭ)* and Yahveh's staff *(maṭṭēh)* in Isaiah would have brought to mind the rod of Yahveh in Ezekiel under which those returning from exile will have to pass in the wilderness of the nations. This location is mentioned elsewhere at Qumran only in the War Scroll (1QM I 3), where it is intermediate between the place of exile and "the wilderness of Jerusalem." The same text speaks of the war between the exiled community of the desert *(gôlat hammidbār)* and the sons of darkness including "the Kittim of Assyria." The Assyrians of the Isaianic text are therefore identified with the Kittim, namely, the Romans, as are the Chaldeans of the Habakkuk pesher.[51]

In the War Scroll, the Prince of the Congregation *(nĕśî' ha'ēdâ)* has an important military role in the final battle,[52] and in the Damascus Document he is identified as the scepter of the Balaam oracle that will arise and destroy all the sons of Seth (CD VII 19-20 on Num 24:17). The scepter *(šēbeṭ)* of this text probably accounts for associating the Prince of the Congregation, a Qumranic title for the Davidic Messiah, with the prospect of the final defeat of the Assyrians in Isa 10:24-27a, therefore by inference that of the Romans, and the removal of their yoke from the neck of those oppressed by them. This I take to be the meaning of the last sentence of the pesher, which can be translated "and afterwards it will be removed from them," with reference to the Assyrian yoke.[53]

10:27b-32 (4QpIsa[a] 2-6 II 21-29)

They have gone up from . . .
they have come upon Ayyath,
passed by Migron,
left their baggage at Michmash;
they have crossed the ravine,

51. 1QpHab II 12-14; VI 10-12.
52. 1QM III 16; V 1; cf. CD VII 19-21.
53. In 4QSefer ha-Milḥamah (4Q285) fr. 5, the Prince of the Congregation is identified with the *ṣemaḥ dāwîd,* "the shoot of David," who will be victorious over the Kittim. See Craig A. Evans, "Prince of the Congregation," *EDSS* 2:693-94.

bivouacked at Geba.
Ramah is racked with fear,
Gibeah of Saul has fled;
cry aloud, Bath-Gallim,
hear it, Laish!
Answer her, Anathoth!
Madmenah is in flight,
the people of Gebim take cover.
This very day they halt at Nob,
they shake their fist at the mount of the daughter of Zion,
the hill of Jerusalem.

The pesher to this passage, a vivid description of an Assyrian advance on Jerusalem from the north,[54] is explicitly eschatological *(pēšer happitgām lĕ'aḥărît hayyāmîm)*. It seems to read into the text the advance of an unnamed individual from the Valley of Akko (Ptolemais) to Jerusalem to fight against the Philistines, who are already threatening the city. Since the Philistines, together with other traditional enemies such as Edomites, Moabites, and Ammonites, formed the evil axis opposing the Sons of Light in the final battle,[55] the main part of the citation was taken to describe the advance of a messianic figure towards the final reckoning in Jerusalem, while those making threatening gestures in the final verse 32 would be the eschatological forces of evil.

10:33-34 (4QpIsaᵃ 7-10 III 1-14)

See, the Sovereign Lord Yahveh of the hosts
will lop off the branches with frightening force,
the tallest of them will be hewn down, the lofty ones laid low;
the thickets of the forest will be cut down with an axe,
Lebanon in its majesty will fall.

These two verses conclude a section predicting the defeat of the Assyrians, here represented as the destruction of the Lebanon forest, and not inappropriately since the Assyrians had done their best to deforest the region in their quest for the much-prized cedarwood. The pesher is defective, but the

---

54. On the textual problems and exegetical issues in this passage, see Horgan, *Pesharim*, 79-80; and my *Isaiah 1–39*, 259-62.

55. 1QM I 1-2; cf. 4Q223-224 2 IV 22-25.

basic correspondence is between the Assyrians and the Kittim, i.e., Romans. The thickets of the forest are "the Kittim (Kittiyyim), who will be delivered into the hand of Israel," the tallest trees are the Kittim warriors, and Lebanon stands for the commanders of the Kittim.[56] The background is provided by the War Scroll, in which "the Sons of Light" engage in the final war against a coalition of enemies under the command of Belial including "the Kittim of Assyria."[57] The anti-Assyrian polemic in Isaiah has provided a rich source of assurance for the pesharists about the ultimate downfall of Rome. The War Scroll, for example, cites the prediction of the defeat of Assyria by divine intervention in Isa 31:8 as predictive of the outcome of the final war against the contemporary evil empire (1QM XI 11-12).

Isaiah 10:34–11:1 is also cited in the equally fragmentary 4QSefer ha-Milḥamah ("The Book of War"), which may have belonged to the missing conclusion to the War Scroll. It seems to present the eschatological Davidic Messiah, also known as the Prince of the Congregation, engaging in the final battle against the Kittim with the cooperation of the High Priest.

11:1-5 (4QpIsa^a 7.11-25)

A branch will grow from Jesse's stock,
a shoot will spring from its roots.
Yahveh's spirit will rest on him,
a spirit of wisdom and understanding,
a spirit of counsel and strength,
a spirit of knowledge and the fear of Yahveh.
[His delight will be in the fear of Yahveh.]
He will not judge by appearances,
he will not decide by hearsay,
but with righteous judgment he will judge the poor,
and with equity defend the lowly of the earth.

---

56. 4QpNah (4Q169) 1-2.7 appears to identify Lebanon with the commanders of the Kittim *(lĕmôšĕlâw)*, but this section of the pesher is defective and the syntax uncertain. Unfortunately, pesharim containing other references to Lebanon in Isaiah are lost, i.e., 4Q163 (4Qpap pIsa^c) 8-10.1-4 and 21.1-3 on Isa 14:8 and 29:17, respectively. In 1QpHab XII 3-4, Lebanon is identified with the Council of the Community, on which see Geza Vermes, "'Car le Liban, c'est le conseil de la communauté': Note sur le pésher d'Hab 12,3-4," in *Mélanges bibliques rédigés en l'honneur de André Robert*. Travaux de l'Institut Catholique de Paris 4 (Paris: Bloud & Gay, 1957), 316-25.

57. 1QM I 1-2; XVIII 2; XIX 10.

He will strike the violent with the rod of his mouth,
with the breath of his lips he will kill the wicked.
Justice will be the belt around his waist,
Truth will be the band around his middle.

This first half of the messianic poem in Isa 11:1-9, with its description of
the ideal, charismatically-endowed Davidic ruler of the future, is different
enough from the second half (vv. 6-9), which presents the ideal of a return
to the first creation, to have suggested to several scholars a conflation of
two originally distinct poems. The Qumran commentator no doubt noticed the difference and would have limited his comments to the first half
in any case, since the following verses would have made a somewhat awk-
ward fit with the common Qumran eschatological scenario of warfare,
judgment, slaughter, and the display of annihilating divine power.[58] The
reconstructed pesher speaks of the "sprout of David" (ṣemaḥ dāwîd), a
designation for the future Davidic dynast in Jeremiah (23:5; 33:15) and attached to Zerubbabel, grandson of Jehoiachin, in Zech 3:8; 6:12. In the
pesher he is the one who is to arise in the latter days and who will be sustained by God with a spirit of strength. The commentator fills out the picture in the poem by assigning to the messianic ruler a throne of glory, a
holy crown, and many-colored vestments.[59] He will rule over all the nations and will either defeat or annihilate the Magog of Ezekiel 38–39, here
understood to be a people, as in Rev 20:8 (cf. 1QM XI 16).

The one distinctive and characteristic addition which the commentator makes to the Isaianic portrait of the once and future king is stated in
a separate pesher on the judicial role of the ruler — "He will not judge by
appearances, he will not decide by hearsay" (11:3b). In discharging this all-
important function the ruler, according to the pesharist, must act in accordance with the instructions of the priests. The pesher (very lacunous, as
will be obvious) runs as follows: "Its interpretation is that . . . as they instruct him, so he must judge, and on their authority . . . with him will

58. Interestingly, the blessing on the Prince of the Congregation in 1Q28b (1QSb)
draws heavily only on the first part of the Isa 11:1-9 poem. It provides clear proof that the
Prince of the Congregation is identical with the "Sprout of David," the Davidic once and future king.

59. Or vestments made of different materials, or perhaps embroided vestments, but
in any case suitable for those of high estate; see Ezek 26:16; 17:3; Ps 45:15 (Eng. 14). Also for
priests according to 1QM VII 11.

function (lit., "go out") one of the distinguished priests holding in his hand the garments of . . ." The irreplaceable role of the priesthood in the dispensing of justice is based on the Deuteronomistic understanding of state offices, according to which the Levitical priests play a decisive role as interpreters of Torah and serve an important function in limiting the exercise of royal power (Deut 17:18-20; cf. Zech 6:13). It corresponds with the predominant role of the priesthood in the War Scroll and the so-called Messianic Rule (1QSa). A close parallel is the reference in 4QFlorilegium (4Q174) 1.10-13 to the *ṣemaḥ dāwîd* who will arise in the last days with the (priestly) Interpreter of the Law.

Unfortunately, most of the commentary on the remaining chapters of Isaiah 1–39 is written on the papyrus copy 4QpIsa^c and has been almost entirely lost. Papyrus has a hard time surviving the wet Palestinian winter, and in fact only one paleo-Hebrew papyrus text has survived from the biblical period from that region, the palimpsest from Wadi Murabbaʿat generally dated to the 7th century B.C.E. The list of passages commented on is as follows:

14:8 (4Qpap pIsa^c 8-10) The pesher on the cypresses and cedars of Lebanon (14:8a) has not survived.

14:19 (4QpIsa^c 3) "Those gone down to the stones[60] of the pit like a corpse trampled underfoot"; from the poem on the King of Babylon in the Underworld (14:3-23). No pesher.

14:26-27 (4QpIsa^c 8-10) Yahveh's plan dealing with the overthrow of the Assyrians. A passage from Zechariah is quoted in the pesher, but both the passage and the pesher itself are lost.

14:28-30 (4QpIsa^c 8-10) From an oracle about the Philistines predicting the destruction of their remnant (*šĕʾērît*) to the advantage of "the poor" (*ʾebyônîm*). The latter term is used at Qumran for the members of the group, while "Philistia" is one of the opponents of the Sons of Light in the eschatological war (see 4QpIsa^a 2-6 II 27), but the pesher is lost.

15:4-5 (4QpIsa^e 4) From the oracle about Moab. No pesher.

19:9-12 (4QpIsa^c 11 II) From a series of poems on the fate of Egypt. No pesher.

---

60. The citation reads *ʾabnê bôr* with MT, but should probably be emended to *ʾadnê bôr*, "the foundations of the pit"; see my *Isaiah 1–39*, 285.

21:10-15 (4QpIsa^e 5) The text includes the last verse of the prophetic announcement of the fall of Babylon (21:1-10) and the Dumah oracle immediately following. No pesher.

29:10-12 (4QpIsa^c 15-16) The loss of the pesher on this passage is particularly unfortunate; it refers to "the vision of all these things," perhaps with reference to the book of Isaiah, as a sealed book and to those who are unable to read it, that is, decode its true meaning.[61]

29:15-16 (4QpIsa^c 17) The allusion to those who oppose the plans of Yahveh would no doubt have been connected with the opponents of the sect, but the pesher is lost.

29:17-23 (4QpIsa^c 21, 18-19) The pesher on 29:17 (fr. 21) contains the word *môreh*, "teacher," and is followed by a citation of Zech 11:11, which speaks of "the poor of the flock who were observing me and who acknowledged on that day that it was the word of Yahveh." Perhaps the prediction of a blessed future in Isa 29:17, as interpreted by the Teacher of Righteousness, was accepted as the revealed word of God by the community. The following passage about a reversal of fortune for the deaf, the blind, and lowly is also without a pesher.

30:1-5 (4QpIsa^c 21) A denunciation of making treaties with Egypt. No pesher.

30:23 (4QpIsa^c 22) Contains a pesher on an unidentified text which speaks of "the sons of Zadok" and cites part of this verse: "grain for bread, the produce of the soil."

30:30b, 32b (4QpIsa^c 25) Some words from these verses in this fragment indicate the existence of a pesher on 30:29-33, describing the final punishment of Assyria. Mention of "the king of Babylon" at the beginning of this fragment and in 4QpIsa^e 8.1 seems to imply that the interpreter confused or conflated Assyria and Babylon on the basis of some biblical reference, perhaps Isa 23:12-13, which refers to the Kittim, the Chaldeans, and Assyria.

31:1 (4QpIsa^c 25) Perhaps part of a citation of and pesher on 31:1-3, a condemnation of making alliances with Egypt. Only the beginning of a pesher has survived: "They are the people who trust . . ."

---

61. On the Isaianic sealed book, see above, pp. 11-14.

32:5-7 (4QpIsa^e 1-2) The biblical text (32:1-8) anticipates a righteous kingdom in which villains and fools will no longer be tolerated. Only two or three words of the pesher have survived.

30:15-21 (4QpIsa^c 23 II)

This is what the Sovereign Lord Yahveh, the Holy One of Israel, has said:

> "In turning back and staying still you will be safe,
> in quiet confidence your strength will lie"
> — but you did not want it.
> "No," you said, "we can always flee on horseback."
> "All right, then, flee you shall!"
> "Swiftly will we ride."
> Then those who pursue you will swiftly follow.
> [A thousand will flee when threatened by one.]
> You will flee when threatened by five,
> until you are left
> like a flagpole on top of a mountain,
> like a lookout post on a hill.
>
> Therefore Yahveh waits to show you favor,
> therefore he bestirs himself to have compassion on you;
> for Yahveh is a God of justice,
> blessed are all those who wait for him!

You people in Zion, you who dwell in Jerusalem, you shall weep no more. He will surely show you favor when you cry for help, and he will answer you when he hears you. The Sovereign Lord may give you the bread of adversity and the water of affliction, yet your teacher will no longer remain hidden. Your eyes will see your teacher, and whenever you turn aside either to the right or to the left your ears will hear a word spoken behind you: "This is the way, keep to it."

Though little has survived of the commentary on this passage, it deserves our attention. The lively altercation in the first section (30:15-17) was in all probability addressed to the Judean political establishment contemplating high-risk military adventures during the reign of Hezekiah. This leads to the blessing on those who wait for God, a recurring motif in Isaiah (v. 18), the assurance that the time of affliction, adversity, and weeping will pass, and the promise of guidance in the vicissitudes that lie ahead (vv. 19-21).[62]

On the first two passages (30:15-18) the pesher begins: "The eschatological interpretation of the text *(pēšer haddābār lĕ'ăḥărît hayyāmîm)* concerns the Seekers after Smooth Things who are in Jerusalem." After some disconnected words, the commentator cites Hos 6:9a: "As robbers lie in wait for a man, a company of priests. . . ." Inclusion of this text may have been triggered by the occurrence in it of the same verb *ḥkh* ("wait") as in Isa 30:18 ("Yahveh waits to show you favor . . . blessed are all those who wait for him"), and the robbers are no doubt identified with the Seekers after Smooth Things. The pesher adds that these opponents have despised the law, an accusation which is directed against "the Scoffers who are in Jerusalem" in 4QpIsa[b] II 6-7 and against the "House of Absalom" in the Habakkuk pesher (1QpHab I 11; V 11-12). It is widely accepted that both sobriquets — Seekers after Smooth Things and House of Absalom — refer to Pharisees. The Seekers after Smooth Things will die by the swords of Gentiles (4QpNah 3-4 II 4-5), their evil deeds will be made known in the end time (3-4 III 3), their council will perish and their congregation will be scattered (3-4 III 6-7), and they have turned Jerusalem into a city of bloodshed (3-4 II 1-2).[63]

It is especially unfortunate that only two words of the pesher on 30:19-21 have survived (*'al 'āwôn*, "concerning the iniquity . . ."). It would have been interesting to know whether the commentary identified the teacher *(môreh)* of this text with Yahveh God, as did the Targum ("Your eyes will see the Shekinah in the sanctuary") or with a specific teacher known and revered in the sect. There must have been a strong temptation for the commentator to think of the Teacher of Righteousness, then hidden but to be revealed in the future, who will continue to give guidance to his followers posthumously (from behind them). But this is one of very many questions which must remain unanswered. Matthew 10:24-26 may send back an echo of the same text, where, in the context of a discussion about the relation between disciple and teacher *(didaskalos)*, Jesus gives an

---

62. On the text, see Horgan, *Pesharim*, 119-21; and my *Isaiah 1–39*, 417-22. "Blessed are all those who wait for him" (v. 18) renders, by gematria, a reference to the topos of the 36 righteous who sustain the world in existence — "Blessed are all those who wait for the thirty-six" — since 36 is the numerical value of לו = "for him."

63. Albert I. Baumgarten, "Seekers after Smooth Things," *EDSS* 2:857-59.

assurance that "nothing is covered up which will not be revealed, nothing is hidden which will not be known."

40:3 (1QS VIII 12-16)

Clear in the wilderness a way for Yahveh,
level in the desert a highway for our God!

This most seminal of texts for the Qumran *yaḥad* provided biblical warranty for the self-segregation of the group in the Judean wilderness by the Dead Sea. It is cited in the Community Rule (1QS VIII 12-16), and, though not strictly in the pesher formulation, the citation is referred directly to separation from sinners and segregation in the wilderness. Alluding to the same text, the Damascus Document speaks of the Teacher of Righteousness who guided them in the way of his heart (*lĕhadrîkām bĕderek libbô*, CD I 10-11), which would have included leading them into the wilderness. In the Community Rule, the clearing and leveling are identified with the study of the law (*midrāš hattôrâ*) commanded by God through Moses, to be practiced according to what has been revealed from age to age by prophets inspired by the Holy Spirit. In the gospel account of the appearance of John the Baptist, on the contrary, preparing the way involves *metanoia*, repentance, in view of the imminent breaking in of the kingdom of God (Matt 3:3 and par.). We will discuss this Isaianic text more fully in a later chapter.[64]

40:11-12 (4QpIsa^e 1-2 = 4Q165)

Like a shepherd he tends his flock,
he gathers them together with his arm,
the lambs he lifts into his lap,
the ewes he gently leads on.

Who has measured out the waters with the hollow of his hand
or marked off the sky by handbreadths
and enclosed the earth's dust in small measure?
Who has weighed the mountains in a balance,
the hills on the scales?

The critical reader will recognize these two verses as belonging to distinct passages with distinct themes, but the Qumran interpreter followed the text

---

64. See below pp. 182-84.

sequentially without making such distinctions. Only the last part of a pesher on 40:9-11 has survived. The citation, introduced with the familiar formula "and as for what is written," has been lost, but it is very likely the first part of verse 11a: "Like a shepherd he tends his flock." The reconstructed pesher reads: "The interpretation of the text concerns the Teacher of Righteousness (*môreh haṣṣedeq*) who revealed the Torah of righteousness (*tôrâ haṣṣedeq*)." This last expression, chosen to match the title of the Teacher, occurs only here in the Scrolls. It doubtless refers to the legal interpretation, the *midrash halakha,* of the Teacher as the basis for the life of the community founded by him. It may also carry the meaning of legitimate Torah teaching, to distinguish it from the halakha of the Teacher's opponents.

> 54:11-12 (4QpIsa^d 1 = 4Q164)
>
> City in distress, battered by storms,
> with no one to comfort!
> I will lay your stones with the finest mortar,
> your foundations with lapis;
> I will set up your shields with rubies,
> your gates with beryl.

The biblical text is part of an apostrophe to Zion holding out the prospect of a glorious future for the city (54:1-17). The commentary, from the early Herodian period, begins *in medias res* with the first of four brief comments on sections of text. The first, only partially preserved, covers the first half of verse 11b, the MT of which reads "I will lay your stones with the finest mortar" (*hinnēh ʾānokî marbîṣ bappûk ʾăbānayik*). The commentary, the first word of which is damaged, reads as follows: "[He will arrange/place?] all Israel as eyeliner around the eye." The oddity of this reading rests on the exploitation by the interpreter of the double meaning of the relatively rare word *pûk,* meaning a finely ground powder which can be used either as mortar (1 Chr 29:2) or, suitably processed, as kohl or mascara (2 Kgs 9:30; Jer 4:30).[65] The image is somewhat arcane, but the

---

65. The ambiguity may also have led him to read *ʿynyk* ("your eyes") for *ʾbnyk* ("your stones"). The interpreter may not have deemed it appropriate to refer mascara (kohl, eyeliner) directly to Jerusalem personified as a woman, as in Jer 4:30 (cf. 2 Kgs 9:30, where it is employed by Jezebel), but *pûk* was an indispensable item of toilette for upper-class women in general. Implements for applying it have been found at Masada and Ein Gedi from about the time of the pesher.

idea may be that Israelites will serve as adornment surrounding the new Jerusalem.

The second half of verse 11b reads *wîsadtîk bāssappîrîm,* "and (I will lay) your foundations with blocks of lapis."[66] The pesher follows: "Its interpretation (is) that they founded the council of the community, the priests and the laity . . . the congregation of his elect like a lapis stone in the midst of the stones." The basic idea is clear. The community *(yaḥad)* is a surrogate Jerusalem, Jerusalem in exile. The ordinary members are the stones with which this other Jerusalem is constructed, and the council is the lapis stone in the center, which also serves as its foundation. This body is composed of 12 laymen and three priests (1QS VIII 1), expressive of the community's conviction that it represents the authentic Israel in its lay and priestly character — the 12 tribes and the three Levitical families.[67] It is described in exalted language as an everlasting plantation, a holy house for Israel and, following Isa 28:16, a true and tried rampart and a precious cornerstone (1QS VIII 5-8). If the community is a temple, the community council is its inner sanctum, a "holy of holies for Aaron" (1QS VIII 8-9). The pesher inevitably brings to mind the duodecimal organization of the disciples of both John the Baptist (Acts 19:7) and Jesus (Mark 3:14, etc.), as well as the metaphor of the Christian church as a building or temple[68] and the individual Christians as living stones of which the temple is built (1 Pet 2:5).[69]

The pesher on the next element of the miraculously restored city, "I will set up your shields with rubies" (the first half of v. 12a), draws its main point from the obscure Hebrew word *šimšôt* (plural), which, whatever its precise meaning,[70] brings to mind the light of the sun *(šemeš)*. It is most

66. In MT *wîsadtîk* is a verbal form ("I will lay your foundations") rather than a substantive as in 1QIsa[d] *(wisôdôtayik).* It is impossible to conclude from the consonantal text how the interpreter read it.

67. On the significance of the three priests, see Frank Moore Cross, *The Ancient Library of Qumran,* 3rd ed. (Sheffield: Sheffield Academic, 1995), 166, who attributes this understanding of the three priests in the community council to Jósef T. Milik.

68. 1 Cor 3:16-17; Eph 2:20-22; Heb 12:22-23.

69. See Bertil Gärtner, *The Temple and the Community in Qumran and the New Testament.* SNTSMS 1 (Cambridge: Cambridge University Press, 1965); David Flusser, "Qumran und die Zwölf," in *Initiation,* ed. C. J. Bleeker. Studies in the History of Religions. NumenSup 10 (Leiden: Brill, 1965), 134-46; Joseph M. Baumgarten, "The Duodecimal Courts of Qumran, Revelation, and the Sanhedrin," *JBL* 95 (1976): 59-78.

70. Often translated "battlements" or "ramparts," but here "shields" suspended over

probably to be restored as follows: "Its interpretation concerns the twelve [chiefs of the priests who] enlighten by the decision of Urim and Thummim . . . [none] of them fails to appear, like the sun in all its light." The allusion must be to priests rather than the 12 lay members of the council, since the Urim and Thummim, a kind of dice used for divination, were manipulated exclusively by priests[71] and giving enlightenment by means of instruction was a priestly prerogative. In the last sentence the antecedent of "none of them" is not apparent; it could be the 12 shields, and the phrasing could depend on a reminiscence of Isa 40:26, which states that none of the heavenly bodies fails to appear when summoned by God.

The last half of verse 12a, "(I will set up) your gates with beryl," refers according to the pesher to "the heads of the tribes of Israel for the last days." This is another aspect of the new Jerusalem which goes back to the vision of Ezekiel in which the names of the tribes, therefore the names of the tribal eponyms or heads, are inscribed on the 12 city gates (Ezek 48:30-34). In the longest of the fragmentary Qumran texts on the theme of the new Jerusalem, the city appears to have 12 gates (5Q15 1 I 10), but the author is too concerned with detailed town planning to contribute much to the symbolism. Another text, 2QNew Jerusalem (2Q24, in Aramaic), mentions a gate made of sapphire or lapis. The heavenly building seen by the visionary Enoch was constructed of white marble with floors of crystal and gates of fire (1 En 14). The new Jerusalem of John of Patmos, the Christian visionary, also has 12 gates, each one a single pearl (Rev 21:21). The image of the new Jerusalem will continue to haunt the apocalyptic imagination throughout the subsequent history of Christianity, whether attached to the site of the old Jerusalem, as for many at the present time, or relocated elsewhere — Pepuza of the Montanists, Münster of the Anabaptists, or England's green and pleasant land of William Blake.

---

the walls which reflect the light of the sun, as in Ps 84:12 (Eng. 11); cf. Ezek 27:11; Cant 4:4. Ibn Ezra rendered it as "windows."

71. Esp. in view of the 12 precious stones set in the high priest's bib, in which the Urim and Thummim were kept (Exod 28:30; Lev 8:8). See also Num 27:21; Deut 33:8 (cited in 4QTest 14), Ezra 2:63 = Neh 7:65.

CHAPTER 5

Reading Isaiah in Early Christianity, with Special Reference to Matthew's Gospel

The Gospel according to Isaiah

In this chapter I want to suggest that the interpretation of the book of Isaiah played a unique role in shaping the identity, religious orientation, and agenda of early Christianity. One could get a rough idea of its importance by checking the marginal cross-references in the Nestle-Aland Greek New Testament. Another indication is that Justin Martyr's *Dialogue with Trypho*, composed ca. 160 C.E., contains more than twice the number of proof texts from Isaiah than from all other prophetic books taken together. The conviction of the centrality of the book of Isaiah also pervades Jerome's commentary on it written in the early 5th century and is stated in summary fashion in the prologue. He justifies the length of his commentary on the grounds that "Isaiah contains the totality of the mysteries of the Lord: Immanuel born of a virgin, worker of famous deeds and signs, his death, burial, and resurrection from the lower regions, together with the proclamation of the Savior to all the nations."[1] The first and, for Trypho and his Jewish contemporaries, the most impenetrable of these "mysteries of the Lord" was the ignominious death by crucifixion of one believed to be the Messiah. In the context of beliefs and expectations in Judaism at that time, the idea of a messiah who dies may not have been com-

---

1. "Cum universa domini sacramenta praesens scriptura contineat, et tam natus de virgine Emmanuhel quam illustrium patrator operum atque signorum, mortuus ac sepultus et resurgens ab inferis et salvator universarum gentium praedicetur"; *PL* 24:18-21.

pletely absent, and Justin's Jewish interlocutor was willing to concede the possibility. There were also well-established traditions about God's providence for the righteous sufferer and the suffering and death of martyrs, but there was no tradition about a messiah dying a death by violence, least of all by crucifixion.[2]

If the death of Jesus as messiah was not to remain beyond belief, it had to be shown: first, that his messianic identity was not in keeping with current expectations; second, that Jesus anticipated and freely accepted his death at the hands of others; and third, that such a death was foretold in the Scriptures and was therefore part of a history divinely preordained and predetermined. Hence the the gospels insist on the noncontingency of the death. Armed resistance to the arrest of Jesus by the authorities was excluded, since "how then could the Scriptures be fulfilled that thus it must come about?" (Matt 26:54). It is at this point, as the narrative of the death of Jesus begins to unfold, that the author of the gospel summarizes by saying that "all this came about in order that the prophetic writings might be fulfilled" (Matt 26:56).

The only Scripture text which fulfilled the conditions stated above was the panegyric on the Servant of the Lord in Isa 52:13–53:12 (hereafter, for convenience, Isa 53), which uses sacrificial language in speaking of his death at the hands of his enemies and concludes with his eventual vindication by God. It is not surprising therefore that it assumed a central place in the earliest Christian profession of faith (e.g., 1 Cor 15:3-4; Rom 4:25) and is reflected in early Christian liturgy, as in the hymn preserved in Phil 2:6-11 about Jesus taking on the form of a servant. The account in Acts of the earliest Christian assemblies in Jerusalem is quite explicit that "the Servant of God" *(pais theou)* was one of the most common designations of Jesus in the earliest period (Acts 3:13, 26; 4:27, 30).

The presentation of Jesus as the Servant of Isaiah 53, and of his death as replicating the pattern of the sacrificial and substitutionary death of the Servant, also dominates the gospel story, more explicitly in Matthew and Mark than in Luke. The identification in the gospels of Jesus, Servant of the Lord, with the Son of Man might suggest that the Servant figure has been medi-

---

2. Trypho's objection was based on Deut 21:23, "The one hanged on a tree is under God's curse" *(Dial. Tr.* 89:2; 90:1). There was never any evidence that the Qumranic Teacher of Righteousness was crucified, as was at one time suggested. On the misnamed "Dying Messiah" text (4Q285), see John J. Collins, *The Scepter and the Star: The Messiahs of the Dead Sea Scrolls and Other Ancient Literature* (New York: Doubleday, 1995), 58-59.

ated through Daniel 7 and perhaps also through the Similitudes of Enoch (*1 En* 37–71), in both of which a heavenly figure called the Son of Man appears. Daniel has certainly borrowed from Isaiah, and the Similitudes have certainly borrowed from Daniel, and less overtly from Isaiah,[3] but neither Daniel 7 nor *1 Enoch* 37–71 says anything about the death or resurrection of a Son of Man. It therefore appears more likely that the two figures were conflated for the first time in early Christian circles, probably by Jesus himself.

That the Servant figure is less explicit in Luke than in Matthew and Mark may be due to its being folded into Luke's presentation of Jesus as persecuted and martyred prophet (Luke 4:24; 13:33), the culmination of a long history of prophets rejected, persecuted, and put to death.[4] Luke's narrative of the public ministry begins with the rejection of Jesus in Nazareth after he had read the *haftara* from Isa 61:1-2 in the synagogue and explained it with reference to himself:

> The spirit of the Lord is upon me,
> on which account he has anointed me;
> to announce good news to the poor he has sent me,
> to proclaim freedom to captives and light to the blind,
> to set free the oppressed,
> to proclaim the year of the Lord's good pleasure. (Luke 4:18-19)[5]

We cannot say that Luke associated this passage with the four acknowledged Isaianic Servant texts, as some commentators in the modern period have done, and that he therefore identified the speaker with the Servant whose voice is heard in Isa 49:1-6 and 50:4-11. He may well have done, but what is certain is that he found in the book of Isaiah the model for and recapitulation of the prophetic career of Jesus.

The death of Jesus, and the manner of his death, were no doubt the most crucial issues, but there were others in which the interpretation of

---

3. For dependence on Isaiah, see esp. *1 En* 62. In *1 En* 48:4 the Son of Man is "the light of the nations," following Isa 42:6; 49:6.

4. Luke 6:23; 11:49-50; 13:28, 34; 16:31.

5. On the Lucan use of this passage, see James A. Sanders, "From Isaiah 61 to Luke 4," in *Christianity, Judaism and Other Greco-Roman Cults*, ed. Jacob Neusner. SJLA 12 (Leiden: Brill, 1975), 1:75-106; "Isaiah in Luke," *Int* 36 (1982): 144-55; Jack T. Sanders, "The Prophetic Use of the Scriptures in Luke-Acts," in *Early Jewish and Christian Exegesis: Studies in Memory of William Hugh Brownlee*, ed. Craig A. Evans and W. F. Stinespring (Atlanta: Scholars, 1987), 191-98.

Isaianic texts played a defining role. One of these has to do with the aims of Jesus and his first followers. Was a mission to the Gentile world in view from the outset, or was it undertaken only at a later point in time? The latter alternative is suggested by the injunction of Jesus to the Twelve to go only to "the lost sheep of the house of Israel," an injunction which, however, is recorded only in Matthew's gospel (Matt 10:5-6). In his missionary activity Paul began by addressing Jewish communities in local synagogues until opposition led to a change of strategy. This seems to have taken place in the course of a visit to Antioch in Pisidia when he and Barnabas his companion declared their intention to "turn to the Gentiles" (Acts 13:46). But here, too, early Christian interpretation of Isaiah should be taken into account. In the second of the four Servant passages the mission of the Servant is to take on a broader scope, even though he complains that up to that point his mission to Jacob/Israel, his own people, had not been successful:

> Is it too light a task for you to be my servant,
> to establish the tribes of Jacob and restore the survivors of Israel?
> I appoint you a light to the nations
> that my salvation may reach to the ends of the earth. (Isa 49:6)

A dual mission, first to the Jewish people, then to the Gentiles, was therefore mandated by prophecy, a point which could hardly have escaped the attention of an assiduous reader of Scripture like Paul or, for that matter, Jesus. There is the further point that, read within the Isaianic tradition as a whole, the Servant's mission to the Gentiles is postulated on the basis of the eschatological expectations which course strongly through the book. In other words, a universal mission is an essential precondition for the final, decisive intervention of God in history, inaugurated in early Christian writings with the second coming of Christ, the Parousia:

> I am coming to gather together nations of every tongue, so that they can come and witness my glory. I shall place a sign among them, and I shall send some of them, the survivors, to the nations . . . those who have neither heard about me nor seen my glory. (Isa 66:18-19)[6]

---

6. With Claus Westermann, *Isaiah 40–66*, I argue that 66:20, which limits the role of the Gentiles to repatriating Diaspora Jews, is inconsistent with the context and has been interpolated by a scribe disturbed by the claim that priests and Levites may be recruited from among Gentile converts to Judaism. See my *Isaiah 56–66*, 311-17.

The survivors, the remnant of Israel, are therefore to take their message out into the world so that all peoples can participate in the final revelation of the glory of God.

Though not cited in the New Testament, Isa 66:18-19 may have helped to shape the understanding of mission among the first generation of Christians.

However the Matthean version of the mission of the Twelve is interpreted, it soon became apparent that the gospel was to be offered to all peoples as an essential precondition for the final consummation: "This gospel of the Kingdom will be proclaimed throughout the whole world as a testimony to all peoples; and then will come the end" (Matt 24:14). That the gospel message is addressed to all, Jew and Gentile alike, is, of course, one of the great themes in Paul's letters. Paul even found confirmation of the necessity of a Gentile mission in his own idiosyncratic reading of the LXX version of the last Servant passage: "Those who have not been told about him shall see, and those who have never heard [about him] shall understand" (Rom 15:21; Isa 52:15b).[7]

Quite apart from the Servant passages, the book of Isaiah would have provided abundant warranty for a universalist perspective on the Christian mission. While the invitations in Second Isaiah to "turn to Yahveh and be saved" (44:3-5; 45:20-25) may signify no more than an openness to accepting proselytes,[8] these texts remained open to a broader interpretation. It would be difficult to find a more inclusive view than Isa 19:24-25, the remarkable benediction pronounced over Israel flanked by the two evil empires of Israel's historical experience:

> In that day Israel will make up one third of a whole together with Egypt and Assyria, a blessing in the midst of the world. Yahveh of the hosts will pronounce this blessing over them, "Blessed be my people Egypt, Assyria the work of my hands, Israel my possession."

7. Justin Martyr makes the same point by citing the same verse but combines it with 53:1a, "Who has believed what we have heard?" to make the additional point about the rejection of Jesus by the Jewish people (*Dial.* 118:4).

8. See my remarks in "Second Isaiah — Prophet of Universalism?" *JSOT* 41 (1988): 83-103; repr. in *The Prophets,* ed. Philip R. Davies. Biblical Seminar 42 (Sheffield: Sheffield Academic, 1996), 186-206. Note that the interrogative mark in the title was unaccountably omitted from both versions.

Another issue concerns the relation between Jesus and his disciples. If the Isaianic Servant of the Lord (ʿebed YHVH) had disciples, it would not be surprising if they were known by the designation "Servants" (ʿăbādîm). Since the Servant was certainly put to death, the assurance that he will "see offspring" (53:10b) would most naturally refer to disciples, and of these servant-disciples we hear in the last two chapters of the book. The Servant titulary carried over into the New Testament with respect to Jesus but not to his disciples, not directly at any rate. The first disciples of Jesus are not explicitly designated as "servants" in the Gospels, but the incident in which Jesus settles the issue of precedence among them in the coming kingdom associates the status of the disciple as servant (in this instance *doulos*) with Jesus as the Servant of Isaiah 53:

> Whoever among you wishes to be first must be your servant; just as the Son of Man did not come to be served but to serve, and to give his life as a ransom for many. (Matt 20:27-28 = Mark 10:44-45)

The teacher-disciple relationship is also reflected in the beatitudes addressed to the disciples (Matt 5:1-12; Luke 6:20-26). The archetype or pattern for the gospel Beatitudes is to be found in the assurance addressed to the Isaianic Servants of the Lord that in the age to come their current situation of destitution, oppression, and marginality would come to an end. This assurance embodies the typically sectarian theme of eschatological reversal and is addressed to their opponents; there will be a new order in which the present distribution of honor and shame, well-being and destitution will be reversed (Isa 65:13-14). The theme of hatred, persecution, and shunning for the sake of the name of Jesus, which is most clearly expressed in Luke's version of the Beatitudes (Luke 6:22-23), echoes the assurance addressed to those who, in Isa 66:5, tremble at the word of God. There can be no doubt that these are identical with the Servants of the Lord to whom the promised reversal of 65:13-14 is addressed.

So much for the messengers; what of the message? Paul begins and ends his Letter to the Romans by speaking of his message encapsulated in the gospel as validated by prophecy. The gospel is the revelation of a mystery announced in the prophetic writings and now disclosed (Rom 1:2; 16:25-27). The Hebrew word for "gospel" or "good news" (*bĕśorâ* or *bĕśorâ tôbâ*) does not occur in Isaiah, but in the second major section of the book a herald of good news is promised to Jerusalem (Isa 41:27), and somewhat later we are told what the good news is:

> How welcome on the mountains are the footsteps of the herald
> announcing well-being, bringing good tidings, announcing victory,
> declaring to Zion: "Your God reigns!" (52:7)

Here we have Paul's gospel and that of the evangelists proclaimed in advance together with its essential content, since "the kingdom of God" *(basileia tou theou)* is simply an abstract formulation of the statement "Your God reigns." Furthermore, the miracles of healing and resuscitation performed by Jesus and his disciples are diagnostic "signs" *(sēmeia)* of the new dispensation, this too with reference to Isaiah. To John the Baptist's disciples, sent to find out whether Jesus really was the One to Come, Jesus answered by pointing to the miracles. John's emissaries were invited to consider how these miracles were to be understood prophetically: "The blind see, the lame walk, lepers are cleansed, the deaf hear, the dead are raised, and the poor have the good news proclaimed to them" (Matt 11:5). The Isaianic echoes are unmistakable:

> Then (in the new age) the eyes of the blind will be opened,
> the ears of the deaf unstopped;
> then the cripple will leap like the deer,
> and the tongue of the dumb shout for joy. (Isa 35:5-6)

also:

> Your dead will live,
> their corpses will rise from the dead;
> you that lie in the dust, awake and sing for joy! (26:19)

and finally:

> The spirit of the Sovereign Lord is upon me,
> because the Lord has anointed me;
> he has sent me to announce good news to the poor. (61:1)

One of the principal sources of the eschatological worldview in which the Christian movement developed was the prophetic concept of the remnant of Israel. While the relevant terminology and the concept are by no means confined to the book of Isaiah, it is the Isaianic tradition which moves the prophetic idea of the remnant of Israel, first clearly articulated in Amos, in the direction of a new community, a community which originated with those who survived the Babylonian exile. The seeds of this development are already present in the symbolic name of the prophet's son Shear-yashub (Isa 7:3) — "a remnant will return." The meaning is made explicit in the earliest interpretation of the name later in the book: "A remnant will return, the remnant of Jacob to the God of might; for even if your people Israel were as numerous as the sand of the sea, only a remnant of them will return" (10:21-22). The Greek version of the relevant Hebrew terminology (*šĕʾār, šĕʾērît*, etc.) does not appear in early Christian writings, but is subsumed metaphorically in the Gospels. The disciples form the nucleus of the saved community of the end time; they are the "little flock" to which the kingdom is promised (Luke 12:32). Other figurative expressions include the wheat separated out from the tares (Matt 13:24-30), the few who enter through the narrow gate (Matt 7:13-14; Luke 13:22-24), the few who are chosen as against the many who are called (Matt 20:16; 22:14).[9] In a later chapter we shall see some of the broader implications of this seminal prophetic and Isaianic concept.[10]

In the Prologue to his translation of Isaiah, Jerome represents Isaiah as more evangelist than prophet, and the description of the book of Isaiah as "the Fifth Gospel" has often been repeated.[11] My contention in this opening section is that it is not just a matter of certain Isaianic texts which have played a key role in the Gospels, in Christian teachings, and in Christian-Jewish polemic, among which texts Isa 7:14 ("A virgin will conceive and bear a son . . .") is perhaps the most familiar. It is rather the case that, as appropriated and interpreted by the first generation of Christians, the book of Isaiah came to serve as a grid or cognitive map by means of which they could articulate their sense of the unique character of their founder and chart the direction in which their destiny was leading them. I see no more reason to doubt that this dependence on Isaiah goes back in

9. Joachim Jeremias, "Der Gedanke des 'Heiligen Restes' im Spätjudentum und in der Verkündigung Jesu," *ZNW* 42 (1949): 184-94; Ben F. Meyer, "Jesus and the Remnant of Israel," *JBL* 84 (1965): 123-30.

10. See below pp. 222-25.

11. It provides the title for John F. A. Sawyer, *The Fifth Gospel: Isaiah in the History of Christianity* (Cambridge: Cambridge University Press, 1996). I have not been able to find the origin of this description of the book.

its essential lines to Jesus himself than to doubt the essential role of the Teacher of Righteousness in shaping the identity of the Qumran *yaḥad* with reference to the interpretation of biblical texts.

Mention of the Qumran Union or Community *(yaḥad)* reminds us that the first Christians were part of a history, the history of Judaism and, more specifically, the history of Jewish sectarianism in the late Second Temple period, which we now know much better after the discovery and publication of the Qumran texts. The availability of this new material puts the historian of early Christianity under obligation to reread early Christian texts and rethink taken-for-granted assumptions in the field of New Testament studies. It has become much clearer, for example, that the origins of Christianity are to be understood in the context, not just of Second Temple Judaism in general, but of late Second Temple *sectarian* Judaism. Both early Christianity and rabbinic Judaism, which developed out of an originally sectarian Pharisaism, evolved beyond their sectarian origins, of course, but neither can be adequately understood without reference to their respective origins — hence the need for a comparative study of biblical interpretation in this formative period, in the context of the present work the interpretation of Isaiah in particular, as an aspect of Christian sectarian origins. Since surveying the entire spectrum of early Christian writings, or even a significant part of them, is for practical purposes not an option, I propose to take a cross-section by concentrating on the gospel according to Matthew (hereafter "Matthew" *tout court,* leaving aside questions of authorship). My proposal is to read this gospel as a sectarian text comparable to those of the Qumran sects, and in doing so to focus on the author's use of citations from and allusions to Isaiah. It seems to me that Matthew lends itself more readily to such a task than the others, not excluding the Fourth Gospel. At any rate, my expectation is that a reading of Matthew from this angle will throw another sliver of light on Christian origins by underlining similarities and differences, lines of continuity and discontinuity, between Qumran and one late 1st-century Christian community. And since both the Qumran sects and early Christians drew largely on the prophetic writings, it may also contribute eventually to a comparative hermeneutics as an important aspect of the religious and intellectual history of the late Second Temple period.

The Jesus Sect and the Sect of John the Baptist

We begin by repeating an observation made earlier, that historically and phenomenologically considered the first Christians, disciples of Jesus, formed a Palestinian-Jewish sect and emerged out of a broad and widespread segment of nonconformist, sectarian Judaism by no means confined to the Qumran sectarians.[12] On the assumption that the excavated site at Qumran is connected with the scrolls and scraps discovered in the caves nearby, accepted by most but not all Qumran specialists, we can conclude that this settlement on the northwest shore of the Dead Sea was flourishing at the same time as the public activity of Jesus and the formation of the first group of his disciples. Though the disciples of Jesus and the Qumran sectarians could in that case hardly not have been aware of each other, contemporaneity and physical proximity do not necessarily entail close association, and the fact that the primitive Jesus group was for the most part itinerant is one obvious contrast with the sedentary Qumranites. But the situation might look different if we were to consider the possibility of a connection effected through a mediating link, and that John the Baptist and his disciples constituted such a link has long been suspected. John emerged on the scene as an apostle of religious regeneration to Jews in Judea and beyond. He preached a call to repentance in view of the imminent, final intervention of God in history. In Matthew this eschatological event is presented metaphorically as "the kingdom of heaven." Both John and Jesus use this expression, though its attribution to John may be due to the author of the gospel (Matt 3:1-6).

There may have existed "Baptist" writings from an early period, perhaps even as early as the gospels, but as it is we are dependent exclusively on the not always friendly information available in early Christian writings and the brief notice about John in Josephus.[13] Of John's antecedents and

---

12. See, *inter alia*, Matthew Black's discussion of the pre-Christian Nasorean sect, based principally on Epiphanius, in *The Scrolls and Christian Origins*, 66-74, 81-83, 88.

13. *Ant.* 18:116-19. The biographical account in the Slavonic version of Josephus's *War*, exploited by Robert Eisler, *The Messiah Jesus and John the Baptist according to Flavius Josephus' Recently Discovered 'Capture of Jerusalem' and Other Jewish and Christian Sources* (New York: Dial, 1931); and accepted by S. G. F. Brandon, *The Fall of Jerusalem and the Christian Church*, 2nd ed. (London: SPCK, 1968), 114-25; and *Jesus and the Zealots* (New York: Scribner's, 1967), 364-68, cannot be used as a source of reliable historical information. The same goes for references to the Baptist in Mandaean writings. After a survey of this litera-

early years we have some information, of uncertain historical value, in the Lukan version of the infancy and early years of Jesus. John was born into a priestly family, and was therefore himself a priest, being the son of a certain Zechariah who belonged to the eighth of the 24 priestly "houses," that of Abijah (Luke 1:5). John's priestly status is alluded to in the *Gospel of the Ebionites,* but there is no reference to it in the canonical gospels. He was dedicated at birth as a Nazirite and, as such, was filled with the Holy Spirit from the womb (Luke 1:15). He was related to Jesus through his mother Elizabeth, who was a relative *(sungenis)*[14] of Mary (Miriam), Jesus' mother (1:36), a circumstance which may help to explain the close association between John and Jesus in their public careers. Unlike the infant Jesus, he was not presented after birth in the temple but passed his early years up to the time of his public appearance in a wilderness region (*en tais erēmois,* Luke 1:80). This last piece of information does not create a necessary link with the Qumran sect, which was not the only location in the wilderness region on either side of the Jordan where John could have passed his early years. In his autobiography Josephus claims to have spent his late teens in the same location with a certain Bannus, a John the Baptist-like figure whom he describes as "wearing only such clothing as trees provided, feeding on such things as grew of themselves, and using frequent ablutions of cold water, by day and by night, for purity's sake" (*Life* 11-12). There was plenty of room in the wilderness for many such ascetics and their disciples, not to mention the pseudoprophets and messianic pretenders of whom Josephus speaks.[15] But for those who identify Qumran as an Essene settlement, an association of some kind with Qumran would be consistent with Josephus's notice that the Essenes, having no children of their own, adopted other people's children and molded them according to their own principles.[16]

---

ture, Charles H. H. Scobie concluded that "Mandaeism is of no value in providing source material for the life and teaching of John the Baptist"; *John the Baptist* (Philadelphia: Fortress, 1964), 23-31. On the hypothesis that Luke 1:68-79, the prophecy of Zechariah (the *Benedictus*), is an adaptation of a "Baptist" psalm, see Carl H. Kraeling, *John the Baptist* (New York: Scribner's, 1951), 16-17, 166-69.

14. *Sungenis* is identical in meaning with *sungenēs,* a generic term for "relative," or even "compatriot" (Rom 9:3; 16:21). It would include cousins but is distinguished from parents and siblings (Luke 14:12; 21:16).

15. *Ant.* 20:97-98, 169-72, 188; cf. Matt 24:26.

16. *War* 2:120. The Messianic Rule (1Q28a I 6-8) regulates the education of children from the age of 10, but since the sectarians addressed are not celibate, the children in question may have belonged to the members.

Caution is in order, as always, but the Qumran settlement was certainly flourishing in the Judean wilderness during John the Baptist's minority, and the many points of overlap between John's preaching and the practice of his disciples on the one hand and the teachings and practices of the Damascus sect and the Qumran *yaḥad* on the other have been seen by many scholars to create a presumption in favor of a connection. The parallels include the call to repentance in view of the "wrath to come,"[17] corresponding to the Qumranites' self-description as "the penitents of Israel" or "those who have repented of sin."[18] Moreover, both the Qumran sectarians and John justify their sojourn in the wilderness with reference to the same text of Isaiah (40:3).[19] Both refer to their opponents, or the unregenerate in general, as vipers,[20] here too drawing on an Isaianic image (59:5), and the animus of both Qumranites and John the Baptist is directed with special force against the Pharisees, as we shall see shortly. John's rejection of the claim of his fellow Jews to exclusive descent from Abraham (Matt 3:9) was anticipated in the sectarian commentary on Isa 10:22, according to which the promise of a people as numerous as the sand of the seashore will be subject to drastic revision in the last days.[21] The identity of the children of Abraham will continue to be a major issue in early Christian-Jewish polemic.[22]

It has also been noted that none of the traditions about John the Baptist associates him in any way with the Jerusalem temple. The silence of the traditions on this point is not in itself decisive, but it is consistent with the Qumran sectarians' attitude to the temple, its services, and officiants (e.g., CD VI 11-14).[23] The temple was at all times a major cause of dispute and schism.

The gospel references to the baptism administered by John[24] provide

17. Matt 3:7; cf. *qēṣ ḥārôn*, CD I 5; 1QHᵃ VII 17; XI 28; XXII 5; *ḥārôn 'ap*, CD X 9; 1QpHab I 12; 4Q169 1-2.11.

18. *šābê yiśrā'ēl, šābê pešaʿ*, based on Isa 1:27-28 and 59:20.

19. Matt 3:3 and par.; 1QS VIII 12-16; IX 19-20.

20. Matt 3:7; the same expression is used by Jesus in Matt 12:34; 23:33. Cf. CD V 13-14 = 4Q266 3 II 2.

21. 4QpIsaᵃ 2-6 II 1-9; 4QpIsaᶜ II 10-21.

22. See esp. Rom 4; Gal 3; Matt 8:11-12; Luke 3:8; also Justin, *Dial.* 25:2-5.

23. Hostility between the temple priestly aristocracy and the generally impoverished rural clergy, to which John's family belonged, may have been an additional factor, as suggested by Kraeling, *John the Baptist*, 23-27.

24. Matt 3:1-6 = Mark 1:2-6 = Luke 3:2-6.

a more credible account of the rite than Josephus, who limits its function to purification of the body (*Ant.* 18:117). It was a "baptism of repentance for the remission of sins" and, as such, resembled the baptismal rite practiced at Qumran in requiring a complete break with the past by means of repentance. It also resembled the Qumran rite by signifying entrance into the eschatological Israel.[25] Since John certainly had disciples, it would also have served as a rite of initiation into the company of his followers who, like the Qumran sectarians, would have thought of themselves as the core of the "penitents of Israel" constituting the true Israel of the last days.[26]

If these indications, certainly not exhaustive, justify us in postulating some kind of connection between John the Baptist and Qumran, the most likely explanation would be either that John had previously belonged to a less strict branch of the sect or that he had decided to go his own way, taking the eschatological teaching of the sect and the message of repentance out into the world to anyone who would listen. But, as is always the case, we are at the mercy of our sources. Qumran is only a part, perhaps only a small part, of a larger picture of sectarian activity around the turn of the eras, including the ascetical, nonconformist, and baptizing kind, of which the early Christian heresiologists and the few rabbinical sources represent a somewhat blurred reproduction.

What, then, of the relation between the disciples of John and those of Jesus? According to the gospel record, Jesus began his public career in association with the Baptist and his disciples and took over both the mission and the message from the Baptist after the latter was arrested and removed from the scene (Mark 1:14-15). Behind the Baptist's allusion to "the one who comes after me" we can detect a covert reference to Jesus as initially, and for an indeterminate length of time, a disciple of the Baptist, one of those who "came after him" as a disciple follows in the footsteps of the

---

25. 1QS II 25–III 12; IV 20-22; V 8-23.

26. The comparison is between John's baptism and the rite which accompanied the acceptance of the postulant into the *yaḥad* after a period of probation, rather than the ritual lustrations carried out by the members on a routine basis. The objections of Hartmut Stegemann, *Die Essener, Qumran, Johannes der Täufer und Jesus* (Freiburg/Breisgau: Herder, 1993), 318-19, in addition to overlooking this distinction, seem to rely on an exaggerated view of the "sacramentality" of John's baptism, his role as priestly mediator, and the symbolic importance of his performing the rite in the Jordan. This last point is in any case dubious in view of John 3:23 and Stegemann's questionable identification of Bethany and Aenon, where the baptizing is said to have taken place.

master both literally and metaphorically. This may be deduced from John's allusion to "the one who comes after me" (Matt 3:11 and par.).[27]

Jesus therefore began his public activity as a disciple of John the Baptist and continued to be closely associated with him until John's arrest put an end to his public activity. The Fourth Gospel, a particularly important source of information on the Baptist, has Jesus with his disciples baptizing in Judah while John was engaged in the same mission in Ainon near Salim in Samaria further to the north.[28] The same gospel also reports that Jesus was making *and baptizing* more disciples than John (John 4:1-2). Disciples were therefore initiated into the group by means of a baptismal rite, but even if the baptism of Jesus by John was not originally a rite of initiation into John's discipleship, here too following practice in the Qumran *yaḥad* (1QS III 4-5, 8-9), Jesus was in fact a disciple of John and recruited his first disciples from among John's followers (John 1:35-42). Moreover, he apparently did so after John's arrest, thus reinforcing the conclusion that Jesus took over and carried further John's mission (Mark 1:14-20; Matt 4:18-20).

After John was eventually executed by Herod Antipas,[29] Jesus retired once again into a desert region, and it is at this point that he spoke of the multitude as "sheep without a shepherd" (Mark 6:17-34), in the narrative

27. Elsewhere in the New Testament the preposition *opisō* in *opisō mou* ("after me") occurs invariably with a spatial connotation, esp. with reference to discipleship; e.g., "If anyone wishes to come after me *(opisō mou elthein),* let him deny himself, take up his cross, and follow me" (Matt 16:24; see also 4:19; 10:38 = Mark 8:34 = Luke 9:23, etc.). For the temporal sense we would expect *meta,* as in Acts 5:37, where both *meta* and *opisō* occur in connection with Judah the Galilean. The counterarguments of Knut Backhaus, *Die "Jüngerkreise" des Täufers Johannes* (Paderborn: Ferdinand Schöningh, 1991), 38-41, based on the context of Matt 3:11 and par., are not persuasive. With Matt 3:11, *ho de opisō mou erchomenos* ("he who is to come after me") cf. 4:19, where Jesus says to Simon and Andrew, *deute opisō mou* ("come after me"), where the context is clearly about discipleship.

28. There is some doubt about the location of Ainon, but it is probably the town of that name in northern Samaria; see the convincing argument of Raymond E. Brown, *The Gospel accordng to John I-XII.* AB 29 (Garden City: Doubleday, 1966), 151. On the somewhat speculative connections between the disciples of the Baptist, Simon the Samaritan magus, and Simonian gnosis, see Ethelbert Stauffer, *Jesus and His Story* (London: SCM, 1960), 64-65; *Jerusalem und Rom im Zeitalter Jesu Christi* (Bern: Francke, 1957), 101.

29. According to Josephus *(Ant.* 18:116-19), John's success as a preacher was the reason for his execution by Herod Antipas, due to fear that his antiauthoritarian message combined with his popularity could lead to insurrection *(stasis).* A similar point is made in Mark 1:5. Josephus adds that Herod's defeat at the hands of the Nabatean Aretas IV was, in the popular view, divine punishment for the execution of John.

context alluding to John's death. Even more significant is the fact that it was only after John's execution that Jesus began to speak about his own inevitable and inevitably violent death (Matt 16:21-23; Mark 8:31-33). This close association between John and Jesus appears to have been commonly acknowledged. Though no miracles of the Baptist are recorded, and we are told that those who followed him knew of none (John 10:41), Herod Antipas concluded that the miracles of Jesus could best be explained on the supposition that he was a reincarnation of the Baptist (Matt 14:1-2). This opinion seems to have been widely shared (Mark 6:14-16). The same belief may have contributed to the accusation of Satanism (i.e., necromancy) directed at Jesus by his opponents.[30] Taking all of this into account, it is impossible to ignore how first the arrest, then the execution of John mark decisive turning points in the life of Jesus.

The fact that the Jesus group was in its origins so intimately connected with the Baptist's group in no way implies that its practices and way of life were identical. John's disciples had their own form of prayer, which, according to Luke 11:1, led the disciples of Jesus to request him to teach them to pray too. But the difference was most clearly in evidence in the rejection of rigorous asceticism on the part of the Jesus group. In the matter of fasting and prayer, John's followers appear to have been closer to the Pharisees than to the disciples of Jesus (Matt 9:14-17; 11:18-19; Luke 5:33). It would be interesting to know whether they also differed in Sabbath observance and the laws of clean and unclean, but we are not told. The Baptist's group would presumably have taken a more conservative line than the more liberal approach that the Gospels record of Jesus and his disciples with respect to Sabbath (Matt 12:1-14), dietary prescriptions (Matt 15:10-20), table fellowship (Matt 9:10-13), and the laws of clean and unclean.

As it emerged as a distinctively Christian rite, baptism came to be understood in a way which differed from the understanding of the same immersion rite among John and his disciples. So much is clear from the case of the "Baptist" Apollos (Acts 18:25-26; 19:1-7), who acknowledged only the baptism of John and whose followers professed ignorance about the Holy Spirit. But in the beginning, before the break between the two groups, immersion could have had the same meaning for both, namely,

---

30. Matt 10:25; 12:22-30; Mark 3:22; Luke 11:14-22. See Carl H. Kraeling, "Was Jesus Accused of Necromancy?" *JBL* 59 (1940): 147-57.

passing through judgment and entry into the eschatological community of the saved, whether as a disciple or a member of the public whose immersion signified the renunciation of a sinful way of life.

The break between the disciples of Jesus and those of John seems to have occurred some time prior to the composition of the Fourth Gospel. Undertones or rumblings of a muted hostility can be detected beneath the surface of the biblical texts. The author of the Fourth Gospel goes out of his way to deny that John the Baptist was the light that was to come into the world (John 1:8), which would imply that this claim was being made about John from within the Baptist's following, as it was much later among the Mandaeans. When John sent a delegation from prison to inquire whether Jesus really was the One to Come, Jesus authenticated his own status by referring to the miracles promised for the last age by Isaiah,[31] and he rounded it off by issuing what sounds like a reproach — "Blessed is the one who will not take scandal at me" (Matt 11:2-6 = Luke 7:18-23). In spite of his greatness, John the Baptist belonged to a dispensation preparatory to and completely different from the one inaugurated by Jesus (Matt 11:11-15).

Tension between the disciples of John and those of Jesus reflected in the gospels was still in evidence as John's disciples spread abroad from Judah and Samaria into Egypt, Asia Minor, and no doubt elsewhere. The author of Acts records the case of Apollos, a missionary for Christ, knowledgeable in the Scriptures, and a powerful speaker (Acts 18:24), but familiar only with the baptism of John. A native of Alexandria, he arrived in Ephesus, where he received more accurate instruction in "the Way" from Priscilla and Aquila. Their catechesis seems not to have been entirely successful, however, since after leaving for Corinth Apollos left behind a "cell" composed of 12 disciples[32] who acknowledged only the baptism of John (Acts 18:24–19:7). In Corinth, meanwhile, in spite of the efforts of Priscilla and Aquila, Apollos seems to have had his own faction, and his

31. Isa 26:19; 29:18; 35:5-6; 61:1.

32. Lit., "about twelve in number," but since Luke routinely gives approximate numbers, with *hōsei* ("about") preceding the numeral (Luke 3:23; 9:14, 28; 22:59; 23:44; Acts 1:15; 4:4; 10:3; 19:34), we may take it that the John the Baptist group had organizational features in common with the Qumran *yaḥad* in which the community council was composed of either 12 members three of whom were priests or 12 lay persons and three priests (1QS VIII 1). This could be seen as a significant clue to the John the Baptist group mediating between Qumran and the Twelve who formed the core of the discipleship of Jesus.

preaching of a more rarified, perhaps gnosticizing type of Christian faith merited a sharp rebuke from Paul (1 Cor 1:12, 18-20).[33]

Opposition to the Pharisees is one feature that Qumran, John the Baptist, and Jesus shared in common. A straightforward comparison is hardly possible given the inadequacy of the sources, especially for John's group, not to mention the late date of Matthew's gospel, composed at a time when the Pharisees could no longer be considered a sect comparable to the Qumran sects. At the same time, a consideration of the respective attitudes of the three entities, using what we know about the Pharisees as a *tertium comparationis,* may help to bring out certain similarities and differences. Space permits only the briefest consideration of what is obviously a complex set of issues. The Qumran commentaries on Nahum and Hosea provide some information about the Pharisees' attempt to depose Alexander Jannaeus in 88 B.C.E., an attempt which ended with a mass execution of 800 Pharisees by crucifixion.[34] Neither these commentaries nor any other Qumran text refers to Pharisees by name, but there is broad agreement that the sobriquets "Seekers after Smooth Things" *(dôrĕšê ḥălāqôt)* and "Ephraim" refer to the Pharisees. Both occur together in the Nahum pesher in connection with the independently attested events referred to above.[35] This faction had its own congregation *('ēdâ)* under a leader referred to as the Scoffer *('îš hallāṣôn).* Its members seem to have broken with the Qumran sectarians at some point, or perhaps the Qumran sectarians broke with them, and they are represented as opponents of the Teacher of Righteousness and his associates.[36]

The accusation of seeking "smooth things" draws on Isa 30:10, where the Judean leadership insists that the prophets and seers "tell us smooth things, see seductive visions" — another example of the pervasive influence of Isaiah among the sectarians. The sobriquet involves the accusation of coming up with accomodating and self-interested interpretations, no doubt principally legal interpretations. The expression may perhaps involve a punning double entendre between *dôrĕšê ḥălāqôt* ("seekers of

---

33. Note the punning allusion to the name of Apollos in Paul's citation of Isa 29:14 LXX, *apolō tēn sophian tōn sophōn,* "I will destroy the wisdom of the wise," 1 Cor 1:19. The gnostic element is fully in evidence among the Mandaeans, who claimed continuity with these first disciples of John.

34. 4QpNah (4Q169) 3-4 I and II; 4QpHos (4Q167) V 13-14.

35. 4QpNah 3-4 II 2; III 5; IV 5.

36. In addition to 4QpNah, see 1QHᵃ X 15, 32; XII 10; CD I 18; XIV 1; 4Q171 II 1-2.

smooth things") and *dôrĕšê hălākôt* ("seekers after legal rulings"), meaning legal interpretations of which the opponents of the Pharisees did not approve.[37] The relation between the Jesus of Matthew's gospel and the Pharisees is, at least on the surface, somewhat similar. They accuse Jesus of laxity in consorting with sinners (Matt 9:10-13), in the matter of Sabbath observance (12:1-14), and the laws of clean and unclean (15:1-20). They present themselves as more diligent in fasting (9:14-17), praying (23:14), and tithing (23:23). Yet Jesus tells his disciples that their righteousness must exceed that of the scribes and Pharisees (5:20) and warns them against the Pharisaic "commandments of human origin" (15:8-9) and Pharisee teaching (*didachē*, 16:6, 11-12) in general. It becomes clear from the catalogue of woes pronounced against the Pharisees in Matthew 23 that their teaching was seen to consist in legal interpretations which served their own interests, not unlike the "smooth things" referred to in the Qumran texts. To what extent these accusations were justified is, of course, another matter.

John the Baptist excoriated Pharisees and Sadducees coming to him for his ritual of immersion in a manner resembling that of the prophets of old denouncing the powers that be (Matt 3:7-12), notwithstanding which the religious practices of John's disciples, including fasting and regular prayers (Matt 9:14-17; 11:16-19), probably had much in common with those of the Pharisees. But here too we must bear in mind that by the time John the Baptist appeared on the scene, a fortiori by the time Matthew's gospel was written, the Pharisees belonged to the religious and intellectual leadership and could no longer be considered sectarian.

To summarize: with respect to the first Christians, John the Baptist and his disciples represented in several respects a link if not directly with Qumran, at least with the broader sectarian phenomenon in late Second Temple Judaism for which the Qumran scrolls provide the best available evidence. Together with his disciples, the Jesus of Matthew's gospel retains some of the features characteristic of that alternative form of Jewish life and thought. Far from being an advocate of "family values" as many suppose,

---

37. Suggested by Albert I. Baumgarten, "Seekers after Smooth Things," 857-59. In his speech before Herod Agrippa II Paul found it convenient to present the Pharisees in a more positive light as the most meticulous Jewish sect (*akribestatē hairesis*, Acts 26:5). He betrays no embarrassment or misgiving in declaring his Pharisaic background (Acts 23:6), and may be referring to it obliquely in a punning reference in Rom 1:1, *aphōrismenos eis evangelion theou*, "set aside for the gospel of God," where *aphōrismenos* reproduces the consonants of *pĕrûš*, "Pharisee."

Jesus identifies the circle of his disciples as his family, his real brothers, sisters, and mother (Matt 12:46-50). He tells a candidate for discipleship who wishes first to bury his father to let the dead bury the dead (8:22). His first disciples saw themselves as the few who, though hated and persecuted in this age (5:11-12; 10:22), would survive the future judgment and enter through the narrow gate into salvation (7:13-14). And wherever we turn, in Matthew and early Christian writings in general, the sectlike configuration of the first Christians follows lines laid down in the book of Isaiah.

On the subject of organizational features and practices of the first Christians which resemble those of Qumran, so much has been and continues to be written as to practically defy documentation. For our present purpose it is more relevant to note that the first disciples had their own esoteric teachings, "dark sayings from of old" (Ps 78:2), confided to those capable of reaching to the inner meaning of the parables and denied to those outside, who, following Isa 6:9-10, look without seeing and listen without hearing (Matt 13:10-15). But it is precisely at this point that the basic difference between the Qumran sects and the Jesus movement appears. For the latter, the mysteries of the kingdom are, in spite of their inner, esoteric meaning, not to be confined to those within the group as are the Essene mysteries.[38] They are available for all who are willing to accept them and live by them. "Nothing is hidden that will not be revealed, nothing concealed that will not be known. What I say to you in the dark, say in the light; what you hear whispered, announce on the rooftops" (Matt 10:27). The first followers of Jesus were a sect which opened out to the world.

The Matthean Commentaries

The interpretation of the book of Isaiah in Qumran and early Christianity is a prime example of the power of a textual tradition to move the course of

---

38. Josephus *War* 2:141-42: The Essenes bind themselves "to report none of their secrets to others, even though tortured to death . . . to preserve the books of the sect and the names of the angels." This longest of Josephus's reports on the Essenes (2:119-61) lists several characteristics shared with the first followers of Jesus: they have a deterrent attitude to wealth and (with respect to the first Jerusalemite cell) practice community of property; they travel light; they partake of sacred meals together; they avoid oaths, as Jesus enjoins in the Sermon on the Mount (Matt 5:33-37); and they value prophecy. But anyone reading this little treatise with Matthew's gospel in mind will be much more aware of the differences than the similarities.

history in certain directions and thus to effect change, change in this instance of great import, in the "real world." For both Qumran and early Christianity the interpretation of the prophetic writings was a major constitutive part of their identity and raison-d'être, and among these writings the book of Isaiah had a uniquely important role. This statement can be checked against a reading of the First Gospel. Matthew contains about 60 explicit citations from the Old Testament including 16 from Isaiah. Of these 16, seven are introduced by the author of the gospel rather than by the actors in the narrative and are of the formulaic type to be discussed shortly, The others are spoken by Jesus, with the exception of the *bat qol* (heavenly voice) at the baptism and transfiguration (Matt 3:17; 17:5).[39] It is to be expected that the authorial citations would be more directly indicative of the way Matthew has shaped the narrative of the life and death of Jesus against the *arrière-fond* of the prophecies. This is indeed the case, but there are also many allusions to Isaiah in this gospel which could have a no less significant part to play. In one way or another, all these references, direct or indirect, serve to bring out the depth dimension of the gospel narrative.

Matthew is also concerned to present Jesus as himself insistent on prophetic fulfillment, especially in the course of events leading to his death, hence the rejection of the offer of armed resistance to his arrest since events had to unfold according to a pattern laid down in the Scriptures (Matt 26:54). At this point Jesus alludes to his own prophetically predetermined destiny as the self-designated Son of Man — "the Son of Man goes as it is written of him" (26:24). Where it is written is not stated. Some commentators have suspected a reference to a nonbiblical text, but there is no allusion to the death of the "Son of Man" either in Daniel 7 or the Similitudes of Enoch (1 *En* 37–71), both of which present a mysterious figure known by that title. In the Hebrew Bible the verb *hālak* ("go," "walk") serves as a simple and natural euphemism for dying, which carries over into the rabbinic expression *hālak lô* ("he died").[40] Since in the Gospels the figure of the Son of Man

39. For the formulaic citations, see the list below. Isaiah 42:1 is the text cited by the voice from heaven at the baptism and transfiguration, while Jesus quotes from Isa 61:1 (Matt 11:5); 14:13, 15 (Matt 11:23); 6:9-10 (Matt 13:14-15); 29:13-14 (Matt 15:8-9); 56:7 (Matt 21:13); and 5:1-2 (Matt 21:33).

40. Job 14:20; 16:22; Eccl 3:20; 5:14-15; *Sifre Num.* 148. A connection with usage in John's gospel, where Jesus speaks of going to the Father (e.g., John 13:33; 14:4 with *hupagein*), as suggested by Ulrich Luz, *Das Evangelium nach Matthäus*. EKK (Düsseldorf: Benzinger, 2002), 4:89, does not seem likely.

is combined with that of the Isaianic Servant, the reference must be to the death of the Servant alluded to in Isaiah 53. It is at this stage of Matthew's narrative that the author provides his own summary of events leading to the death of Jesus, where he reminds the reader that "all this came about in order that the writings of the prophets might be fulfilled" (Matt 26:56).

The 11 Matthean citation formulas which constitute a special category of commentary are presented according to a simple but distinctive pattern consisting in the narration of an event or circumstance in the life of Jesus linked with an explicit biblical citation by means of a formula.[41] The function of the formula is to indicate that the event or circumstance fulfills what is said in the citation. The formula therefore performs the important function of linkage. The following texts belong to this series of Matthean formula quotations:

1. 1:22-23   *event:* The virgin birth of Jesus
formula: All this came about in order that what was spoken by the Lord through the prophet might be fulfilled.
text: Isa 7:14, mostly LXX

2. 2:14-15   *event:* The flight into Egypt
formula: In order that what was spoken by the Lord through the prophet might be fulfilled.
text: Hos 11:1

3. 2:16-18   *event:* The slaughter of children by Herod
formula: Then what was spoken through Jeremiah the prophet was fulfilled.
text: Jer 31:15

4. 2:23   *event:* Jesus came to live in Nazareth
formula: In order that what was spoken through the prophets might be fulfilled.
text: "He will be called a Nazorean" — Isa 11:1?

5. 3:3   *event:* John the Baptist's appearance in the wilderness
formula: This is the one who was spoken of through Isaiah the prophet
text: Isa 40:3

---

41. I have included Matt 3:3 in spite of the slightly different formula; several scholars omit it, e.g., Graham Stanton, "Matthew," in *It Is Written: Scripture Citing Scripture. Essays in Honour of Barnabas Lindars, SSF,* ed. D. A. Carson and Hugh G. M. Williamson (Cambridge: Cambridge University Press, 1988), 205-19.

6. 4:12-16   *event:* Jesus settles in Capharnaum
                  formula: In order that what was spoken through Isaiah the
                  prophet might be fulfilled.
                  text: Isa 8:23–9:1 (Eng. 9:1-2)

7. 8:17   *event:* Healings and exorcisms of Jesus in Capharnaum
                  formula: In order that what was spoken through Isaiah the
                  prophet might be fulfilled.
                  text: Isa 53:4

8. 12:15-21 *event:* Jesus heals and enjoins silence
                  formula: In order that what was spoken through Isaiah the
                  prophet might be fulfilled.
                  text: Isa 42:1-4

9. 13:34-35 *event:* Jesus teaching by means of parables
                  formula: In order that what was spoken through the
                  prophet might be fulfilled.
                  text: Ps 78:2

10. 21:1-5   *event:* Jesus enters Jerusalem riding on a donkey
                  formula: This came about in order that what was spoken
                  through the prophet might be fulfilled.
                  text: Isa 62:11 + Zech 9:9

11. 27:9-10 *event:* Payment made to Judas for betraying Jesus
                  formula: Then what was spoken through Jeremiah the
                  prophet was fulfilled.
                  text: Zech 11:13; Jer 18:2; 32:8

The following observations are in order:

1. All 11 formulaic sayings contain the verb *plēroō* ("fulfill") except
Matt 3:3 (5), which is nevertheless included since John the Baptist in the
wilderness is identified as the one whose voice is heard in Isa 40:3. It is
therefore functionally similar in this respect to the Qumran Habakkuk
commentary (1QpHab I 12-13), in which the anonymous evildoer and the
righteous man of Hab 1:4 are identified, respectively, with the Wicked
Priest and the Teacher of Righteousness.

2. Unlike the text quoted by the chief priests and scribes in Matt 2:5-6,
or the Psalms text quoted by Satan in 4:6, or the many texts cited by Jesus
throughout the gospel, none of these formulaic sayings is spoken by a character in the narrative. Therefore Jesus' explanation for teaching in parables
(13:14-15), which looks similar, is not included, nor is 26:54, his rejection of

armed resistance to his arrest, since there is no text and therefore no linking formula. The statement that follows after the arrest, "All this came about in order that the writings of the prophets might be fulfilled" (26:56), is more likely a recapitulation by the author of the significance of events leading to Jesus' death rather than words spoken by Jesus himself — there are of course no inverted commas — but here too a text is lacking. While all use of biblical texts, no matter by whom spoken, are indicative of authorial intention, we should attach special significance to those instances where the author's voice is heard commenting on what is happening.

3. All 11 citations are from prophetic texts except 13:34-35 (9) from Ps 78:2, and possibly 2:23 (4), the source of which is unknown. Classifying a psalm as prophetic is not surprising, since in both early Christianity and Qumran the psalms, composed by David under divine inspiration, were regarded as prophetic and predictive. Their mantic character is particularly in evidence in the early chapters of the Acts of the Apostles, and the Qumran Psalms Scroll has a note to the effect that David composed 3,600 psalms and 450 other liturgical compositions, all of which he uttered through the spirit of prophecy.[42]

4. In two cases (3 and 11) the linking formula simply states that the event marked the fulfillment of the text. In all other instances it is stated that the event in question took place *in order to* fulfill a prophecy of divine origin communicated centuries earlier through a prophetic intermediary.[43] The event or circumstance in the life of Jesus therefore, in some way, activates for the first time a meaning or reference latent in a text written centuries earlier, in precisely the same way as the circumstances of the life of the Qumranic Teacher of Righteousness activate meanings latent in Habakkuk.

5. The question inevitably arises whether these 11 citation formulas belonged originally to an independent series utilized by the author of the First Gospel, comparable to the Qumran pesharim or Testimonia (4Q Test).[44] Their uneven distribution throughout the gospel (four in the first

42. Acts 2:25-28 (Ps 16:8-11), 2:34 (Ps 110:1), 4:11 (Ps 118:22), 4:25-26 (Ps 2:1-2); 11QPs^a = 11Q5 XXVII 2-11.

43. The prepositions used are *hina* (1, 2, 6, 8, 10) and *hopōs* (4, 7, 9). The word spoken by God is communicated *through (dia)* the prophet.

44. The case is argued in detail by Krister Stendahl, *The School of St. Matthew, and Its Use of the Old Testament*. ASNU 20 (Uppsala: Gleerup, 1954), 195-96; also Stanton, "Matthew," 208.

two chapters) would not exclude this possibility, since the author could have selected texts according to the requirements of his narrative. Moreover, the preference in the citations for the Hebrew text, or at least a mixed text, over LXX would favor the hypothesis of an independent series, and it has also been claimed that the citations contain a significant percentage of non-Matthean vocabulary.[45] It would not be surprising if such compilations of *dicta probantia* were in use in early Christian churches to meet the needs of catechesis or polemics, and the Matthean formulaic type is certainly not the only example. Other indications of a systematic and quasi-scholastic use of scriptural texts include citations introduced with the rubric *gegraptai* ("it is written"), abundant in Matthew,[46] and in John the fulfillment of prophecy is marked with the equally formulaic *kathōs estin gegrammenon* ("as it is written") or *hina hē graphē plērōthō* ("in order that the scripture text might be fulfilled").[47]

6. There is unfortunately little overlap between the Matthean citation formulas from Isaiah and the Qumran Isaiah pesharim. Isaiah 40:3 is commented on in the Community Rule (1QS VIII 12-16), but its pesher in 4QpIsa[b] is lost. If the title *nazōraios* in Matt 2:23 derives from *nēṣer* ("shoot") in Isa 11:1 (on which see below), the interpretation would be identical with 4QpIsa[a], which identifies the branch and shoot from Jesse's stock as *ṣemaḥ dāwîd*, "the branch of David." The Matthean formula citation differs from the Qumran pesher in several fairly obvious respects.[48] While both link event with text by means of a formula, the pesher moves from the text to the event, circumstance, or person in the affairs of the sect while the Matthean type moves in the opposite direction. The extant pesharim on six prophetic books and five psalms deal with the texts continuously, verse by verse, while the Matthean citation formulas, drawing on four prophetic books and one psalm, are integrated into an existing narrative. However, these formal features specific to each make the same point in different ways: the text cited becomes fully intelligible now, for the first time, in the contemporary event, circumstance, or person to

45. Georg Strecker, *Der Weg der Gerechtigkeit*, 3rd ed. FRLANT 82 (Göttingen: Vandenhoeck & Ruprecht, 1971), 83.

46. Matt 2:5; 4:4, 6, 7, 10; 11:10; 21:13; 26:24, 31.

47. John 12:14, 38, 40; 19:24, 36, 37.

48. Stendahl, *The School of St. Matthew*, 183-202, was one of the first to suggest the comparison, but at a time when the Habakkuk pesher was the only exegetical text available for comparison.

whom it is referred. The significant contemporary event, person, or circumstance in some way activates a meaning latent in the text cited, which then only remains to be spelled out or decrypted by an interpreter endowed with divine inspiration comparable with that of the original prophetic author.

In early Christianity as at Qumran, this close and systematic reading of biblical texts would seem to presuppose an institutional, scribal setting of some kind. One of the Qumran rule books stipulates round-the-clock study of *tôrâ* under the direction of a skilled interpreter: "Let there not be missing one to interpret the law day and night in the place where the Ten assemble . . . and the Many (the rank and file) shall keep vigil together for a third of every night of the year to read the book" (1QS VI 6-7). Whatever biblical texts were included in this *tôrâ*, the existence of the pesharim suggests that these communal study sessions would have included the prophetic books. The central panel of the Matthean pentad (see below) concludes by referring to scribes learned in the kingdom of heaven (Matt 13:52), a category which surely included the author himself. A saying attributed to Jesus includes, in its Matthean form, sages and scribes together with prophets among those sent on a mission and rejected (Matt 23:34), whereas the Lucan version has prophets and apostles (Luke 11:49). For the Christian movement in the first two generations the evidence is much less abundant than for Qumran, but what inferences can be drawn from the First Gospel suggest that Stendahl's postulation of a "school of St. Matthew" is by no means far-fetched.[49] The exegetical activity which went into these formulaic sayings also presupposes a claim to inspiration analogous to the inspiration attributed to the original prophetic authors. This is explicitly stated in the Qumran Habakkuk pesher, where we read that the Priest (i.e., the Teacher of Righteousness) has been put in the congregation by God in order to interpret all the words of his servants the prophets (1QpHab II 7-10). While we have nothing quite so explicit in early Christian sources, it raises the possibility of a role for early Christian prophets in the production of the gospels, or at least of the material incorporated in the gospels.

---

49. Stendahl, *The School of St. Matthew,* 35, suggests that the *hupēretai tou logou* to whom Luke refers in the preface to his gospel (Luke 1:2) could have functioned as instructors, but this is quite uncertain. See Karl Heinrich Rengstorf, "ὑπηρέτης, ὑπηρετέω," *TDNT* 8:530-44.

Isaiah according to Matthew's Gospel

The character of Matthew's gospel as a manual for disciples, a book of instruction comparable to the Qumran rule books, a new *tôrâ* containing, like the Pentateuch, both law and narrative, is expressed through its fivefold structure clearly indicated by the repetition of a similar *excipit* at the end of each section. The central panel of the pentad ends with the somewhat enigmatic statement referred to earlier: "Every scribe learned in the kingdom of heaven is like the head of a household drawing from his treasure things new and old" (Matt 13:52). This sounds distinctly self-referential and would lead us to think of it as the signature of the author of the gospel. Each section contains either narrative or debate between Jesus and his opponents followed by a discourse, the main purpose of which is instruction in discipleship. This results in the following arrangement with the *excipits* in parentheses:

Preamble	1–2	
I	3–7	(7:28-29)
II	8:1–10:42	(11:1)
III	11:2–13:52	(13:53)
IV	13:54–18:35	(19:1)
V	19:2–25:46	(26:1-2)
Epilogue	26:3–28:20	

This structure provides an appropriate frame of reference for exploring the contribution of Isaiah to the total picture of master-teacher and disciples viewed from the Matthean perspective. The brief survey which follows will take account of indirect but unmistakable allusions to Isaianic texts and texts cited by actors in the narrative in addition to the authorial formula citations listed above.[50]

---

50. On Matthean exegesis in general, in addition to the commentaries, see Bertil Gärtner, "The Habakkuk Commentary (DSH) and the Gospel of Matthew," *ST* 8 (1954): 1-24; Joseph A. Fitzmyer, *NTS* 7 (1960/61): 297-333; Robert H. Gundry, *The Use of the Old Testament in St. Matthew's Gospel: With a Special Reference to the Messianic Hope.* NovTSup 18 (Leiden: Brill, 1967); Strecker, *Der Weg der Gerechtichkeit;* O. Lamar Cope, *Matthew: A Scribe Trained for the Kingdom of Heaven.* CBQMS 5 (Washington: Catholic Biblical Association, 1976); R. T. France, "The Formula-Quotations of Matthew 2 and the Problem of Communication," *NTS* 27 (1980/81): 233-51; Stanton, "Matthew." George Dunbar Kilpatrick, *The Origins of the Gospel*

Preamble: Matthew 1–2

The preamble is also arranged as a pentad, each of the five sections organized around a prophetic text as follows (texts in parentheses):

I	1:16-24	The virgin birth	(1:23)
II	2:1-12	The visit of the Magi	(2:6)
III	2:13-15	The flight into Egypt	(2:15)
IV	2:16-18	Slaughter of the innocents	(2:18)
V	2:19-23	Jesus moves to Nazareth	(2:23)

The infancy of Jesus as recorded by Matthew is deliberately gridded on to the story of the infancy and early years of Moses in Exodus, with a subsidiary theme suggested by the story about the patriarch Joseph, the "dreammaster," featuring the homonymous husband of Mary mother of Jesus. The parallelism is at times practically verbatim, as when Joseph is instructed in a dream to leave Egypt "for those who sought the life of the child have died" (Matt 2:20), echoing Yahveh's command to Moses to return to Egypt (see Exod 4:19). The influence of Isaiah is in evidence throughout. The virgin birth of Jesus is established in 1:22-23 by citing Isa 7:14 in the Old Greek version, which translates the Hebrew ʿalmâ (a young woman either married or of marriageable age) with *parthenos* (which can mean "virgin"), as in LXX, rather than with *neanis* ("young woman"), which would be a more apt translation of ʿalmâ.[51]

The other (possibly) Isaianic citation formula in this section, in which Jesus takes up residence in Nazareth thereby fulfilling the prophetic text "he will be called a Nazorean" (*nazōraios*, 2:23), is famously obscure. Matthew clearly wishes to associate *nazōraios* with Nazareth, so much is certain, and Jesus is often referred to as *iēsous nazōraios*, usually translated "Jesus of Nazareth," in the Gospels and Acts.[52] Christians of the first generation are

---

According to St. Matthew (Oxford: Clarendon, 1946), emphasizes the rabbinic character of Matthew's use of the Old Testament and the liturgical use of the formula citations.

51. The identity of the young woman and her son in Isa 7:14 is a major point of dispute between Justin and Trypho (*Dial.* 43:4-8; 66:1-3; 71:3; 84:1-4). On the text, see Gundry, *The Use of the Old Testament in St. Matthew's Gospel*, 89-91.

52. Matt 26:71; Luke 18:37; John 18:5, 7; 19:19; Acts 2:22; 3:6; 4:10; 6:14; 22:8; 26:9. Mark uses only the alternative *nazarēnos* (Mark 1:24; 10:47; 16:6), once by itself with reference to Jesus (14:67).

referred to in Acts 24:5 as "the sect *(hairesis)* of the Nazoreans *(nazōraioi)*," and a sect so called, associated with the Mandaeans who claimed descent from John the Baptist, is mentioned by early Christian heresiologists.[53] This has encouraged the speculation that the title in Matt 2:23 originally signified Jesus's affiliation with John the Baptist. Some have suggested an allusion to Judg 13:5, in which an angel tells Samson's mother that her child is to be consecrated to God as a Nazirite. However, Judges 13 is not a prophetic text, the LXX translates "Nazirite" with *naziraios* not *nazōraios,* and, most importantly, there is no evidence that Jesus was destined to be a *nāzîr,* as was the case with John the Baptist (Luke 1:15). While substantial doubts remain, the best candidate would appear to be Isa 11:1, which speaks of the "shoot" *(nēṣer)* from Jesse's stock, in other words, the Davidic messiah.[54]

The Davidic-messianic theme is also latent in the story of the magi. There seems to be a deliberate ambiguity in the notice about the star seen "in the east" (*en tē anatolē,* 2:2, 9). In addition to indicating a point of the compass, *anatolē* serves as a technical astronomical term for the ascendancy of a star or planet, hence the possibility of the translation "we have seen his star in its rising." The same term, or the corresponding verb *anatolein,* occurs often in the LXX version of Isaiah with reference not to a star ascending in the sky but to a plant springing up from the ground, or to new and portentous events about to unfold.[55] Moreover, the corresponding Hebrew substantive *ṣemaḥ* ("sprout," "shoot"), translated *anatolē* in the Old Greek version (LXX), occurs in prophetic texts as a code name for "the shoot of David," the Davidic dynast or the future Davidic ruler, the once and future king.[56] Used as a title, *anatolē* appears in Zechariah's psalm (the *Benedictus*), where Zechariah looks forward to the coming of "the Day Star from on high" (*anatolē ex hupsous,* Luke 1:78), certainly a messianic designation. Prophetic interpretation in this instance, therefore, entailed a shift from a plant rising from the ground to a star rising in the sky.[57]

---

53. For details, see Matthew Black, *The Scrolls and Christian Origins,* 66-74, 81-83, 88.

54. Cf. 4QpIsaᵃ 8-10.11-18 (4Q161), where "the branch" and "the shoot" of Isa 11:1 are identified with "the shoot of David which will arise in the end time." The Targum and rabbinic texts also interpret this text with reference to the Messiah.

55. Isa 42:9; 43:19; 44:4; 45:8; 58:8; 61:11, with the verb *ṣmḥ* in Qal and Hiphil.

56. Jer 23:5; 33:15; Zech 3:8; 6:12. The expression *ṣemaḥ dāwîd* occurs as an eschatological figure in the restored text of 4QpIsaᵃ fr. 7, commenting on Isa 11:1-5.

57. See Heinrich Schlier, "ἀνατέλλω, ἀνατολή," *TDNT* 1:351-53. Justin understands *Anatolē* in Zech 6:12 LXX to be a messianic title (*Dial.* 100:4; 106:4; 121:2).

The star of Balaam's prophecy which will arise *(anatelei)* from Jacob (Num 24:17) is also part of the *arrière-fond* of the magi story. From early times this star which is to arise from Jacob was understood, usually in a political and military sense, as the messiah who would come forth from the Jewish people. As a messianic and eschatological symbol, it occupied a prominent place among the Qumran sectarians and in Judaism in general. There is the well-known incident when Rabbi Akiva greeted Simon bar Kosiba (Kokhba) with this text, and the "ambiguous oracle" mentioned by Josephus, according to which one from Judea would become world ruler, probably refers to Num 24:17 rather than Gen 49:10. In naming the messianic figure entitled *Oriens* (= *Anatolē*), Tacitus (*Hist.* 5:13) is probably referring to the same oracle.[58]

Before leaving the story of the magi, we note that the characteristically oriental gifts of gold and frankincense brought to the newborn child correspond to, and may have been suggested by, the tribute which, according to Isa 60:6, will come to the future Jerusalem from the east:

> All these from Sheba will come
> bearing gifts of gold and incense,
> proclaiming the praise of the Lord.

I. Matthew 3–7

The first of the five sections records the appearance of John the Baptist and the scriptural duel between Jesus and Satan in the wilderness followed by the "Sermon on the Mount" (chs. 5–7). The importance of Isa 40:3, the fifth of the Matthean citation formulas (Matt 3:3), for the origins of Qumran, the mission of John the Baptist, and that of Jesus was noted earlier, as also the frequent occurrence of Isaianic themes and turns of phrase in John's preaching.[59] The proclamation that the kingdom of heaven is near at hand reproduces a theme expressed with increasing urgency in the later stages of the Isaianic tradition:

58. In the midrash on Num 24:17 in CD VII 13–VIII 1, the Star is identified with the Interpreter of the Law; see in addition 4Q269 5.2-3 and 4QpIsaᵃ fr. 2-6 II 19. The text is also cited in 1QM XI 5-7 and 4QTest 12 (4Q175). For other references, see Collins, *The Scepter and the Star*, 201-4. Josephus, of course, referred it to Vespasian.

59. See pp. 138-47. The Baptist's allusion to "inextinguishable fire" (Matt 3:12) is also Isaianic (Isa 66:24).

I bring my deliverance near, it is not far off,
my salvation will not be delayed. (Isa 46:13)

And we have seen that this kingdom, the kingdom of God, is encapsulated in the acclamation "Your God reigns!" (Isa 52:7). In this first section each new beginning is signaled by a quotation from Isaiah: the appearance of John the Baptist in the wilderness (3:3 citing Isa 40:3), the voice from heaven at the baptism of Jesus identifying him as both Servant and Son (3:17 citing Isa 42:1),[60] and the inauguration of the public ministry of Jesus after John's arrest (4:15-16 citing Isa 8:23–9:1 (Eng. 9:1-2), the sixth of the citation formulas).

The parallel but much shorter version of Matthew 5–7, the Sermon on the Mount, in Luke 6:20-49 alerts us to the existence of a common source. The Lucan version unfolds on a level place, and many from as far away as the Phoenician cities were present in addition to the disciples (Luke 6:17). Luke's more direct reference to the poor and hungry, the despised and shunned, reflects the words addressed to or about the Servants of the Lord in Isa 65:13-16; 66:5 — those who tremble at God's word and are hated and cast out by their "brethren." The Matthean version, on the other hand, reproduces more clearly the theme of eschatological reversal expressed in the same texts. By separating the disciples from the crowds below, Matthew emphasizes the location of the disciples as occupying a different symbolic space, since they and they alone are the recipients of the teaching to be imparted. Rather than reproducing a local tradition known to the author, the mountain is probably a deliberate allusion to the scene in Exodus 19 where the people at Sinai are forbidden even to touch the mountain of revelation. We might think of this section not so much as a sermon, the traditional designation, as rather a manual of discipline in some respects comparable to the Qumran rule books. Its didactic character is further reinforced by Jesus sitting while delivering it, since this is the posture traditionally adopted by the teacher (Matt 5:1-2). Parallels with Qumran in the substance of the teaching are not lacking. The disciples address each other as broth-

---

60. This comes about as a result of combining an adaptation of the opening verse of the first of the Isaianic Servant passages (Isa 42:1: "This is my servant whom I sustain/my chosen one in whom I take delight") with Ps 2:7 ("You are my son, today I have begotten you"). Matt 3:17 has substituted "son" *(huios)* for "servant" *('ebed, pais)*. According to Acts, early Christian assemblies referred to Jesus as "Servant of God" *(pais theou,* Acts 3:13, 26; 4:27, 30), but the title seems not to have stayed in use after the first generations.

ers,[61] they are to have their own practices of almsgiving, prayer, and fasting,[62] their observance of the law is differentiated from that of the Pharisees,[63] they are to avoid taking oaths,[64] and they are to strive for perfection.[65] While these analogies might suggest a common praxis in which Qumran sectarians and early Christians shared, the contrast between the injunction to hate all the sons of darkness in the Manual of Discipline (1QS I 10) and the command to love one's enemies in Matt 5:43-44 will suffice to remind us of the gap which existed between the two groups.

II. Matthew 8:1–11:1

The one citation formula in this section (8:16-17) relates the healings and exorcisms to Jesus as the Servant of the Lord who "took on himself our infirmities and bore our diseases" (Isa 53:4). The incident in question, the healing of Peter's mother-in-law followed that evening by exorcisms and other healings, is recorded in all three Synoptics (Mark 1:32-34; Luke 4:40-41), but only Matthew adds the citation. Like most of the other citation formulas, it is closer to the Hebrew than the LXX, which has the Servant taking sin upon himself rather than infirmities. This would not have served Matthew's purpose at this point. The healings therefore correspond to one aspect of the Servant profile and prepare for the principal point of correspondence, namely, persecution, suffering, and violent death. The same point is made more obliquely in other summarizing statements in Matthew dealing with the healing activity of Jesus and his disciples (Matt 4:23; 9:35; 10:1).

The Matthean profile of Jesus superimposed on that of the Servant parallels the correspondence between the disciples of Jesus and those of the Servant, the "Servants of the Lord" mentioned in the last chapters of

---

61. Matt 5:22-24, 47; 7:1-5; cf. 1QS VI 10, 22; 1QSa I 18; CD VII 1-2; XIV 5; also VI 20-21, where each is to love his brother like himself.

62. Matt 6:1-18; cf. the form of prayer and fasting peculiar to the disciples of John the Baptist (Luke 11:1; Matt 9:14-17 and par.). The instructions to the disciples of Jesus about fasting appear to be influenced by Isa 58:1-9.

63. Matt 5:20. On the "Seekers of Smooth Things," see above, pp. 145-46.

64. Josephus *War* 2:141-42. Swearing an oath by the earth as God's footstool is reminiscent of Isa 66:1.

65. Matt 5:48; cf. the description of the members of the Damascus covenant community as "the perfect" or "the perfected" (*'anšê tāmîm*) in CD XX 2, 5, 7; cf. 1QS IX 2, 5-6, 8-9.

Isaiah.[66] In his instructions to the Twelve about to embark on their mission, Jesus warns them that they will be hated, excommunicated, and persecuted "for my name's sake" (Matt 10:17-23). This is precisely the destiny of the Servant's disciples who are hated and shunned by their "brethren," and for the same reason (Isa 66:5). The association between Servant-master and Servant-disciples is strikingly confirmed in the saying which follows: "The disciple is not above the teacher, nor is the servant above his master" (Matt 10:24). The disciples are then told that the teachings which have been imparted to them alone, things hidden and concealed, are to be proclaimed from the rooftops (Matt 10:26-27 and par.). This makes for a striking contrast with the Qumran sectarians, whose teachings were destined for them and for them alone. The Qumran attitude to unregenerate humanity is expressed unequivocally in the Community Rule (1QS V 17) by means of another text from Isaiah: "Leave the rest of humanity alone; doomed to perish as they are, of what value are they?" (Isa 2:22).

III. Matthew 11:2–13:53

The miracles of healing and resuscitation worked by Jesus which, in the previous section, fulfilled the role of the Isaianic Servant are now presented as diagnostic of the new and final age of the world, a sign that the decisive intervention of God in human affairs is at hand (Matt 11:2-6). The incident which precipitated this saying about the function of the miracles was the delegation sent by John the Baptist to inquire whether Jesus was the One To Come, namely, the Messiah. In replying, Jesus pointed to the miracles of healing and resuscitation as signifying that the new age predicted by Isaiah was at hand. Several prophetic texts predict the eschatological abolition of common human disabilities, but the inclusion of good news announced to the poor in the list of eschatological benefits listed by Jesus establishes that the reference must be to Isa 61:1, where an unnamed prophet is commissioned to proclaim good news to the poor. All the other works of mercy mentioned in reply to John's emissaries, with the exception of leprosy, correspond to conditions which, in Isaiah, will be removed in the new age: blindness and deafness (Isa 29:18; 35:5), lameness (33:23; 35:6), and death itself (26:19).

66. Isa 65:13-16; 66:1-5.

The incident leading to the longest of the citation formulas is the retirement of Jesus from Capharnaum, or wherever he happened to be, after hearing about plans to kill him (12:15-21). In this new location he continued to heal but admonished those healed not to spread the word. The hiddenness of Jesus is seen to fulfill the first of the Isaianic Servant passages, though the citation also answers the question why Jesus did not attract more followers during his lifetime:

> This is my servant whom I have chosen,
> my beloved in whom I take delight;
> I will put my spirit upon him,
> he will proclaim justice to the nations.
> He will not dispute or raise his voice,
> his voice will not be heard in the streets.
> A broken reed he will not crush,
> a dimly smoldering wick he will not quench
> until he makes justice victorious,
> and in his name the nations will hope.

This is the Matthean version of Isa 42:1-4. Matthew has adapted the citation to the context in a manner analogous to the Targum. It is much closer to the Hebrew than the LXX, with which it has little in common. It omits Isa 42:3b-4a, "He will truly establish justice for the nations, he will not grow faint or be discouraged," and it substitutes "in his name the nations will hope" for 42:4b, "the islands wait for his instruction." The second verse ("my beloved in whom I take delight") is practically identical with the wording used at the baptism (3:17), though *pais*, "servant" is retained rather than *huios*, "son," the more appropriate option in the baptism and transfiguration scenes (Matt 3:17; 17:5).[67] In keeping with the Targum on Isaiah, which renders 'abdî ("my servant") with 'abdî měšîḥâ ("my servant Messiah"), the Matthean context presents Jesus as the hidden and unacknowledged Servant-Messiah.

The location of this citation at the center of the Matthean pentad reads like a summary of the activity of Jesus viewed in prophetic and specifically Isaianic perspective. As such, it can be seen as the Matthean parallel to the Lucan recapitulation of the gospel story spoken by Jesus himself at the beginning of his public activity (Luke 4:16-21), this too based on a

---

67. The term *pais* can mean either "child" or "servant," but the Hebrew *'ebed* can mean only "servant."

quotation from Isaiah (61:1-2). It seems likely that both Matthew and Luke would have identified Isa 61:1-2 as a Servant passage, and therefore the anonymous prophetic speaker with the Servant of Isa 42:1-4 and 53:1-12.[68] Nothing could bring into sharper focus the creative role played by the interpretation of Isaiah in the process by which the first followers of Jesus came to grasp the significance of his person and mission.

Isaiah 6:9-10, in which the prophet is sent on a mission to make his fellow-Judeans hard of hearing and sight impaired, is used elsewhere in the New Testament to reflect the attitude of those who refused to accept the Christian message (John 12:40; Acts 28:26-27). In this midsection it is cited by Jesus (and is therefore not in the series) to explain why he taught by means of parables. Those outside this circle hear the stories but do not grasp the hidden meanings. Matthew avoids the problem confronting the reader of Isa 6:9-10, which seems to be saying that the mission was intended from the outset to make it impossible for the hearers to understand, and therefore to be healed. He does so by citing from the LXX, which, no doubt deliberately, sidestepped the problem:

> The heart of this people has grown dull,
> they have become hard of hearing and have closed their eyes,
> lest they might somehow see with their eyes, hear with their ears,
> understand with their hearts and be converted,
> so that I might heal them. (Matt 13:15)

The people themselves are therefore responsible for their spiritual lack of understanding. The distinction between disciples initiated into mysteries and the uncomprehending multitude is one more example of a kind of sectarian esotericism in this gospel, a contrast between insiders and outsiders familiar from Qumran, yet juxtaposed with an affirmation of a mission to those outside affirmed throughout the gospel and stated definitively at its conclusion (Matt 28:16-20).[69]

---

68. Cf. *thēsō* (LXX *edōka*) *to pneuma mou ep'auton* (Isa 42:1) with *pneuma kuriou ep'eme* (61:1). Several commentators in the early 19th century, and a few still today, read Isa 61:1-4 as a displaced Servant passage; see my *Isaiah 56–66*, 221.

69. Two other Isaianic allusions or echoes in this section should be mentioned: Jesus condemns Capharnaum (Matt 11:23) in terms borrowed from the poem on the King of Babylon in the Underworld (Isa 14:13-15); the analogy of entering a strong man's house and taking his property (Matt 12:29) is reminiscent of Isa 49:24, "Can prey be taken from a warrior?"

IV. Matthew 13:54–19:1

The theme of incomprehension and obduracy which runs through Matthew's gospel is expressed once more in Matt 15:8-9 in the course of a dispute about Pharisee legal traditions which Jesus concludes by citing Isa 29:13:

> This people honors me with their lips
> but their heart is far from me.
> They worship me in vain,
> teaching doctrines (which are) human commandments.

The quotation, here and in the Markan parallel (7:6-7), is closer to LXX than MT in order to allow for a reference to Pharisee teachings *(didaskaliai)* and commandments which are of human not divine origin *(entalmata anthrōpōn)*. The LXX version is used in much the same way and to much the same purpose by Justin (*Dial.* 78:11). It can therefore serve to address the dispute about clean and unclean and the broader issue about how God is to be honored. The verdict that Jesus passes on the Pharisees is also expressed in terms taken from Isaiah: "Every plant which my heavenly Father has not planted will be uprooted" (15:13). Isaiah 60:21 describes the righteous Israel envisaged for the future with the organic metaphor of a seed or shoot planted by Yahveh, a figure which was taken up both at Qumran and in early Christianity.[70]

The first of three predictions by Jesus of his sufferings, death, and resurrection emphasizes the element of prophetic predestination; events must follow a course laid down in the prophetic writings and spelled out there, at times in some detail (Matt 16:21). The fact that the three predictions are present in all three Synoptic Gospels shows how deeply embedded in the tradition is the idea of prophetic predestination.[71] The predictions become more detailed as the drama moves towards its climax, taking in a broader spectrum of texts deemed to be prophetic, conspicuously Psalm 22. But the primary source in all these predictive statements and wherever prophetic inevitability is mentioned is the panegyric on the Servant of the Lord in Isaiah 53. This must also include the prediction of the resurrection of Jesus. Once the death of the Servant was seen as predictive of the death of Jesus,

---

70. CD I 7-8; 1QS VIII 5; cf. 1 Cor 3:6.

71. Matt 16:21 = Mark 8:31 = Luke 9:22; Matt 17:22-23 = Mark 9:30-31 = Luke 9:43-44; Matt 20:17-19 = Mark 10:32-34 = Luke 18:31-33.

attention would have inevitably fixed on the assurance that the Servant would be vindicated by God and see light (Isa 53:10-11). Peter's second sermon in Acts 3:12-26 speaks of the God of the fathers glorifying his child (i.e., servant) Jesus (*edoxasen ton paida autou,* v. 13), reproducing the language of the LXX version of the Suffering Servant text, in which a major theme is the passage from the absence of glory and honor to glory (Isa 52:13-14; 53:2 LXX). Isaiah 53 does not say when this would happen, but since the Scriptures are one and indivisible the interpreter could have found a clue in Hos 6:2, the expectation that "on the third day he (God) will raise us up."

V. *Matthew 19:2–26:2*

In this section Matthew records three parables of Jesus (20:1-16; 21:28-32; 21:33-41), only the last of which has parallel versions in Mark and Luke, which draw on the Isaianic theme of Israel as God's vineyard (Isa 5:1-7). The third parable begins by quoting almost verbatim from Isa 5:2 and continues by telling a story about an absentee landlord who sends his servants and, finally, his own son to collect the fruits of his vineyard. After the tenants have abused and killed them, he comes himself to pass judgment on the guilty and hand care of the vineyard over to others. This symbolic history does not require an explanation since the explanation is already present in Isaiah:

> The vineyard of the Lord of hosts is the house of Israel,
> and the people of Judah the plantation in which he delighted.
> He looked for justice, and instead there was bloodshed,
> for righteousness, and instead a cry of distress. (Isa 5:7)

The parable peculiar to Matthew is, in effect, a symbolic history similar to those in Enoch, Jubilees, and the Damascus Document discussed earlier.

The one citation formula in this section (21:1-5) draws primarily on Zech 9:9, but this text is conflated with Isa 62:11b which serves to introduce it. We shall see that it contains other fainter but still audible biblical resonances:

> Say to daughter Zion:
> "Look, your king is coming to you,

humble, riding on a donkey,
on a colt, the foal of a donkey."

Approaching Jerusalem, Jesus and his disciples reach the village of Bethphage on the Mount of Olives. There is an atmosphere of secrecy and danger as Jesus sends two disciples to find and bring back a donkey and its foal which are tethered in the village. The mission of the disciples looks like an action deliberately calculated to fulfil a prophecy, in this instance literally and at the cost of the implausible spectacle of Jesus entering Jerusalem riding on both animals. This is Matthew's doing, deliberately ignoring the verse parallelism in the text, since the other three gospels all speak of one animal only.[72] Matthew has substituted Isa 62:11b ("Say to daughter Zion") for the opening verse of the Zechariah text ("Rejoice greatly, daughter Zion, shout out aloud, daughter Jerusalem"), the substitution facilitated by the frequent apostrophes to "daughter Zion" in Isaiah[73] and the no less frequent calls in the same book to rejoice over Zion/Jerusalem.[74] The messianic implications of the scene, with the acclamations to the son of David, the One Who Is to Come (Matt 21:9), could hardly have failed to bring to the writer's mind Jacob's oracle on Judah in Gen 49:8-12. This characteristically cryptic deathbed prediction also speaks, in *parallelismus membrorum*, of Judah's foal and the foal of a donkey tethered and waiting to be mounted by the one who is to come. If this is so, it would seem to imply that Matthew understood Gen 49:10b to read "until he comes to whom it belongs," in keeping with one of several interpretations of the enigmatic term *šiloh*.[75]

A typically Matthean use of Scripture is the combination of texts which accompany the scene generally referred to, following Mal 3:1-4, as the cleansing of the temple (Matt 21:12-13 with the par. Luke 19:45-46). The

72. Mark 11:2 and Luke 19:30: "a foal tethered on which no one has yet sat"; John 12:14: "a young donkey."

73. The expression *bat ṣiyyôn* is characteristic of Isaiah (1:8; 10:32; 16:1; 37:22; 52:2; 62:11) and the closely related Micah (1:13; 4:8, 10, 13), and rare elsewhere (Jer 6:2, 23; Zeph 3:14; Zech 2:14; 9:9).

74. Isa 62:5; 65:18-19; 66:10, 14.

75. Shiloh is a name for Messiah in Targum Onkelos; cf. *Gen. Rabbah* 98:8; *b. Sanh.* 98b. One might suspect that the Matthean "their owner needs them" (*ho kurios autōn chreian echei*), instead of "the Lord has need of it" (*ho kurios autou chreian echei*) of Mark and Luke was suggested by an association with *šiloh* of Gen 49:10b understood as "to whom it belongs."

saying of Jesus, "My house shall be called a house of prayer but you have turned it into a den of thieves," combines Isa 56:7 with Jer 7:11. The Isaiah text is addressed to members threatened with expulsion on grounds of physical or ethnic disqualification (Isa 56:1-8). They are assured of their good standing and right of access to the liturgical life of the community. It suggests that, not unlike the Qumran sectarians, Jesus had regard for what the temple stood for together with rejection of what it had become.

Several other echoes of Isaiah can be heard in this section. The cosmic upheaval predicted in the Matthean version of the eschatological discourse, the sun and moon darkened and the stars falling from the sky (24:29), draws on a broad textual repertoire including Isaiah (13:10; 34:4). Only in Matthew does Jesus speak of the sequel to these catastrophic events as a *palingenesia*, a rebirth of the world, a world regenerated (Matt 19:28). The word occurs neither elsewhere in the New Testament nor in the Septuagint, but the closest parallel is the Isaianic vision of new heavens and new earth (Isa 65:17; 66:22), a topos which entered early into the Christian apocalyptic imagination (2 Pet 3:13; Rev 21:1) and has remained as a constant feature in apocalyptic scenarios ever since.

Finally, the scene of judgment presented in the symbolism of the Enochian Animal Apocalypse, the sheep separated from the goats (Matt 25:31-46), reproduces the works of mercy enumerated in Isa 58:6-7 — directed towards the confined, hungry, homeless, and naked — and has been described as a targumic adaptation of this passage in Isaiah.[76]

Epilogue: Matthew 26:3–28:20

The idea of prophetic predestination casts a long shadow over this final and climactic section of the narrative. We saw at the beginning of the chapter that the most intractable problem for the early Christian apologist was the death of the founder by crucifixion. This was the crucial issue in the disputation between Justin and Trypho (*Dial.* 89-96), one which the Christian interlocutor had some difficulty in resolving. Trypho accepted the possibility of a suffering and dying Messiah but balked at the idea of crucifixion since "the one hanged on a tree is under God's curse" (Deut 21:23). This forced his partner in dialogue to retreat into typology: Moses'

---

76. Gundry, *The Use of the Old Testament in St. Matthew's Gospel,* 142.

hands raised in the sign of a cross during the battle against Amalek (Exod 17:9-12), the horns of the unicorn similarly configured in the Blessing of Joseph (Deut 33:17), and the serpent lifted up in the wilderness (Num 21:8-9). If this was basically unsatisfactory, Paul dealt with the issue in a theologically more direct, if paradoxical, way by linking the curse in Deut 21:23 with the curse in Deut 27:26 on those who did not adhere to the law, and then claiming that Christ took the curse of the law on himself (Gal 3:13).

The only citation formula in this last section establishes a basis in prophecy for the purchase of the Potter's Field with the 30 silver shekels paid to Judas (27:9-10). The incident is presented as the fulfillment of Zech 11:12-13, but the citation is attributed to Jeremiah, no doubt by association with the prophet's visit to the potter's workshop (Jer 18:1-4) and his purchase of a field for 17 silver shekels (32:9). This is one of only four, or possibly five, of the citation formulas which do not refer to a text from Isaiah.

Several incidents in the narrative of the death of Jesus (27:27-66) draw on the panegyric on the Suffering Servant linked with the complaint of the sufferer in Psalm 22. Combined appeal to these two texts leads us to suspect that the author of the gospel may have read Psalm 22 as referring to the Isaianic Servant. The psalm not only describes one despised by the public and ostensibly abandoned by God, but it concludes, as far as the corrupt state of the text of verses 30-32 (Eng. 29-31) allows, with the assurance of deliverance from death and posterity (*zeraʿ*, "seed"; cf. Isa 53:10-11). Some of the detailed correspondences between text and incident suggest the possibility that the latter owes its place in the narrative to the former. This would be especially the case with incidents as specific as the dividing of the garments among the executioners of Jesus (Matt 27:35; Ps 22:19 [Eng. 18]) and the role assigned to a wealthy individual in his burial (Matt 27:57; Isa 53:9).[77] Other details are less consequential — including the silence of Jesus during his trial (Matt 26:63 and 27:12, 14; Isa 53:7) and the mockery (Matt 27:39-44; Ps 22:9 [Eng. 8]). It was noted earlier that similar descriptive detail is to be found in the account of the martyrdom of Isaiah.[78]

The introduction to the story of the death of Jesus is centered on the betrayal by the disciple Judas (Matt 26:2b–27:26). The sequence of events is

---

77. The MT of Isa 53:9, *wěʾet-ʿāšîr běmotayw*, "and with a wealthy man in his deaths," is unintelligible as it stands, but survived in the Peshitta, the Vulgate, the Targum, and, most importantly, in LXX (*dōsō . . . tous plousious anti tou thanatou autou*).

78. See above, p. 51.

as follows. First, the chief priests and elders decide on Jesus' death (26:3-5). The incident which follows in the house of a certain Simon in the village of Bethany, in which an anonymous woman anoints the head of Jesus with precious ointment, served as a proleptic funerary rite; it was so understood by Jesus and almost certainly by the woman herself (26:6-13).[79] It leads to Judas contracting with the chief priests to hand Jesus over to them. Only the Johannine version (John 12:1-8) identifies the one who objects with Judas, but it may be that the betrayal was the outcome of Judas understanding the significance of the act as stated by Jesus. The Passover meal of Jesus and his disciples follows (26:17-29). In the course of the meal Judas is identified as the one who, by his betrayal, activates the fulfillment of Scripture. "The Son of Man goes, as it is written of him; but woe to that man by whom the Son of Man is betrayed" (v. 24). The enigmatic allusion to the Son of Man "going" is a euphemism for death, as we have seen, and the Scripture in question can be none other than Isaiah 53. The same reference is implied in the proleptic celebration of the shedding of blood "on behalf of (the) many for the remission of sins" (cf. Isa 53:11-12). The element of prophetic predestination is stated even more strongly in the delivery of Jesus to his enemies in Gethsemane (26:30-56), which concludes with the author's comment: "All this came about in order that the prophetic writings might be fulfilled" (v. 56). There follows the trial and the suicide of Judas (26:57–27:26).

79. The account in Mark 14:3-9 is closely parallel, but in Luke 7:36-50 the event takes place in the house of a Pharisee, the woman is a prostitute, and she anoints not his head but his feet. In John 12:1-8 it takes place in Bethany, but in the house of the resuscitated Lazarus, and the woman is now Mary who anoints his feet. Only in this version is the one who objects to the waste of good perfume identified as Judas, who has been stealing from the common fund.

CHAPTER 6

Isaianic Titles in Qumran and Early Christianity

Titles, Rubrics, and Self-descriptions in General

A dictionary or encyclopedia would seem to be the proper place for titles, and, in fact, most of the titles to be discussed in this chapter can be found in theological and biblical lexicons and such well-known manuals as *The Anchor Bible Dictionary*. The justification for taking them out of their more customary habitat is to show how the book of Isaiah served as a re-source for the self-understanding of the Qumran sects and early Christianity. For both Qumran and early Christianity, and for self-segregating groups in general, self-descriptive titles serve to define those who use them over against "the others," or "the world," or the parent group from which the sect has splintered off. Names reinforce identities and promote group cohesion. Study of the titles assigned to Jesus has always been an important part of the agenda of early Christian studies, and there has always been an assumption of a correspondence of some kind between what is predicated of Jesus and what is predicated of his followers.[1] With Qumran and early Christianity it was to be expected that the terms in which they described themselves would draw primarily and perhaps exclusively on biblical texts. Tracing these self-descriptive rubrics back to their biblical sources, Isaiah in the first place, should tell us something about the fea-

---

1. For an older example, see Vincent Taylor, *The Names of Jesus* (New York: St. Martin's, 1953); and, more recently, Gerd Theissen, *Sociology of Early Palestinian Christianity* (Philadelphia: Fortress, 1978), 24-30, with regard to the title "the Son of Man."

tures common to Qumran sectarianism and early Christianity respectively and in what ways they differed.

In the present chapter I want to focus on the book of Isaiah as a major source for these self-descriptive titles while taking into account other potential source material against which the significance of the Isaianic examples can be more clearly grasped. To clarify and limit the scope of our inquiry: I do not propose to deal with the common phenomenon of titles or designations pinned on a movement by outsiders, titles such as the Ranters of the 17th century or the Quakers of the 18th century, irrespective of whether the titles in question were accepted or rejected. Our aim will be rather to get some idea of the self-understanding of these groups generated from within.

The Qumran sectarian writings contain a superabundance of appellatives, but none analogous to *christianoi* or *nazōraioi* which came into use in primitive Christianity. The absence of any reference to Essenes in these texts (or, for that matter, in the New Testament) has, in particular, been a source of frustration to Qumran scholars, except perhaps those who reject the connection between Qumran and Essenism. If the Qumran sect had survived the war with Rome it may have come to be known by a more specific and informative title, as did the Jesus movement, but this did not happen. The generic and abstract term "Christianity" *(christianismos)* appears for the first time in the correspondence of Ignatius bishop of Antioch in Syria — incidentally, the city in which the term "Christian" was first coined according to Acts 11:26 — and the context in which the term occurs suggests that it was modeled on the similar formation "Judaism" *(ioudaismos)* already in existence.[2] Its use indicates that the Christian movement had begun to achieve social visibility as a religion, an achievement denied to Qumran. The titles "Christian" and "Nazorean" are first encountered in Acts (11:26; 24:5; 26:28). They are not pejorative terms, though probably bestowed by outsiders in an attempt to identify the followers of Jesus as one of several Jewish schools or factions *(haireseis).*[3] The term *Christianoi* (Lat. *Christiani*) is of a type in common use for a group or movement formed around an individual, as, for example, *Augustiani,*

2. *Phil.* VI 1; *Magn.* X 3. Ignatius died a martyr during the reign of Trajan (98-117 C.E.).

3. The term *hairesis* (party, faction, sect) is applied to the Jesus group by outsiders (Acts 24:5, 14; 28:22) but disavowed by Paul (Acts 24:14). In the *Testimonium Flavianum* Josephus — or Pseudo-Josephus — refers to Christians as a tribe *(phulon tōn christianōn, Ant.* 18:64).

Caesariani in early imperial Rome. By the late 1st century, at any rate, the title "Christian" was familiar both within the church and in society in general. Tacitus, for example, reports that in his day the term *Christiani* was widely recognized.[4]

A further point of clarification about titles is in order. There are rubrics indicative of social organization which could, in principle, be applied to several groups, rubrics such as "congregation," "assembly," "community," or even "church" and "synagogue." In the Greco-Roman world in which the Christian movement emerged, and in Greek cities before that time, the "church" *(ekklēsia)* was the assembly of adult, male citizens called together in an open space — in Athens on the hill called the Pnyx — to deliberate on matters of public interest. Used in this secular sense, the term occurs in the New Testament only in the account of a riot in Ephesus instigated by Paul's preaching against the cult of Artemis (Acts 19:32, 39-41). Private associations were known under one or other of numerous titles, including *koinon, thiasos, synodos, collegium.* But there are also self-referential terms which reflect different aspects of a group's understanding of what it is or what it is meant to be, what qualities it aspires to embody, its way of being in the world in general. To this category belong such terms as "the righteous," "the poor," "the elect," "the saints," and it is this kind of title which will concern us in the present chapter. In the biblical texts these are not usually titles in the strict sense, especially where they are accompanied by a qualification as, for example, "the poor in spirit" (Matt 5:3) or "those who tremble at his (God's) word" (Isa 66:5). They can, however, become quasi-titular by being appropriated and applied to itself by a specific group. The history of religious minority movements provides many examples: the *pauperes* at the time of the Crusades, the Cathar *perfecti,* Thomas Müntzer's Anabaptist *elect,* the *ḥărēdîm* ("Tremblers") in contemporary Jerusalem. This would be the case with the Essenes if the derivation of the name from *ḥăsayyā*', the Aramaic equivalent of Hebrew *ḥăsîdîm* ("devout"), is correct. One of the goals of this chapter is to examine the Isaianic

---

4. *Annals* XV 44 (*quos . . . vulgus Christianos appellabat*). For the title, see Ignatius *Rom.* III 2; *Magn.* X 3; *Pol.* VII 3; Pliny *Epistles* X 96; Suetonius *Nero* XVI 2. Those Corinthians who claimed adherence to Christ rather than Apollos or Cephas ("I belong to Christ," 1 Cor 1:12) may have called themselves Christians, but it is unlikely that the title originated in this way. See the interesting observations in Jan M. Bremmer, *The Rise and Fall of the Afterlife,* Appendix I: "Why Did Jesus' Followers Call Themselves 'Christians'?" (London: Routledge, 2002), 103-8.

contribution to some of the more frequently used examples of this kind of appellation.

Little need be said about the principal functional-organizational appellations in use at Qumran and in early Christian writings since they do not derive from Isaiah. In the Christian context, the most common term is, of course, *ekklēsia*, which should be traced to the LXX translation of the Hebrew *qāhāl* ("assembly") rather than to secular usage. The term *qāhāl* is one of two terms, the other being *'ēdâ* (usually translated "congregation"), used of Israel as a whole, and both occur at maximum density in the paradigmatic narratives about Israel's sojourn in the wilderness. Without entering into a detailed linguistic study, and making due allowance for inconsistency in usage, we can say that, where they occur together, *qāhāl* indicates more the actual, physical assembly, the concrete expression and embodiment of the abstract idea of "Israel." Hence the prescriptions for Passover are addressed to "the entire assembly of the congregation of Israel" or, put more succinctly, "the congregation of Israel assembled in plenary session."[5]

The Priestly sections of the Pentateuch (P) present Israel in the wilderness as a well-organized congregation *('ēdâ)* under civil and religious rule, whereas in Deuteronomy and related writings Israel is almost invariably called an assembly *(qāhāl).*[6] This distinctive usage is acknowledged in LXX, which adopts the translation word *ekklēsia* in preference to *sunagōgē* in these passages, reserving the latter term for the wilderness narratives elsewhere in the Pentateuch.[7] Early Christian emphasis on the individual community as actualized in its periodic assemblies may help to explain the adoption of *ekklēsia-qāhāl* rather than some other designation. In the Qumran sectarian writings, however, *'ēdâ* occurs with much greater frequency than *qāhāl*, no doubt reflecting the predominantly priestly character of the Qumran sects with priests of Zadokite origin, mentioned in all the major rule books, occupying prominent leadership positions.[8] By con-

---

5. *kol qĕhal 'ădat-yiśrā'ēl*, Exod 12:6.

6. The only exceptions occur in three passages in Joshua (9:15-21; 20:1-9; 22:13-34) in which *'ēdâ* and not *qāhāl* appears. However, indications of Priestly vocabulary in these passages have led several commentators to assign them to a Priestly source.

7. The designation *ekklēsia*, which does not appear in Genesis through Numbers, occurs often in Deuteronomy (9:10; 18:16; 23:2-9; 31:30), in the related History (1 Kgs 8:14, 55, 65), and in texts of Deuteronomistic inspiration, esp. in Psalms.

8. For the references, see Philip R. Davies, "Zadok, Sons of," *EDSS* 2:1005-7.

trast, early Christian communities were essentially lay in character. Acts 6:7 reports that a number of priests joined the movement, but there is no indication that they continued to function as such. In any case, the first Christians described themselves in traditional biblical terms in the conviction, shared with Qumran, that they represented the authentic inheritors of the ancient traditions, the true Israel.

Of the other titles of a more formal nature in use in the Qumran texts, the most common is *yaḥad,* usually translated "community."[9] It appears frequently in the Community Rule (1QS) and the so-called Messianic Rule, occasionally in the *Hodayot,* and rarely elsewhere. It is often accompanied by a qualifier as, for example, "the community of God" (1QS I 12; II 22), "the community of truth" (1QS II 24, 26), "the holy community" (1QS VIII 2). There has been considerable discussion about its origins. The thesis that the Qumran *yaḥad* took its form and structure as well as its title from the Hellenistic *koinon* was defended by Martin Hengel but has not won much support.[10] A biblical origin is much more likely, with a preference for the Blessings of Moses, in which Israel as a totality is described as *yaḥad šibṭê yiśrāʾēl,* "the union of the tribes of Israel" or, more idiomatically, "the united tribes of Israel" (Deut 33:5).[11] If this is so, *yaḥad* would be another way of expressing the conviction of the group that they alone constitute the authentic Israel of which the traditions speak. Use of this designation would also embody the idea of ideological and physical proximity — living in common and sharing material goods.

There is no expression in early Christian writings corresponding to the Qumran *yaḥad,*[12] though the earliest Jerusalem Christians imple-

---

9. Other terms for the community occuring in the Qumran texts, which do not call for discussion, are *sôd* ("council," "secret council"), *ḥeber* ("association"), *kěnesset* ("assembly").

10. Martin Hengel, *Judaism and Hellenism,* 243-47, based in part on B. W. Dombrowski, "היחד in 1QS and τό κοινόν: An Instance of Early Greek and Jewish Synthesis," *HTR* 59 (1966): 293-307.

11. As a substantive, *yaḥad* also appears in 1 Chr 12:18, where David declares himself to be in harmony with the Benjaminites and Judahites who approach him. Shemaryahu Talmon claimed to discover another occurrence in Ezra 4:3, where the *běnê haggôlâ* rebuff an offer to help in rebuilding the Jerusalem temple with the assertion that *ʾănaḥnû yaḥad nibneh,* which he translates as "we as a community will build"; *VT* 3 (1953): 133-40.

12. On the view of Joseph A. Fitzmyer that *koinōnia* in Acts 2:42 is the equivalent of *yaḥad,* see the critical remarks of Richard Bauckham, "The Early Jerusalem Church, Qumran, and the Essenes," in *The Dead Sea Scrolls as Background to Postbiblical Judaism and*

mented what is implied in the expression by commensality and community of property.

The Many

This designation (*hārabbîm*, "The Many") is used in both the Community Rule (1QS; *serek hayyahad*) and the Damascus Document (CD) for the members of the group as a whole, especially the group in plenary assembly.[13] The term has practically the same connotation as *yahad*, except that while the primary scope of the latter indicates communal living in pursuit of a common purpose, *hārabbîm* expresses a totality, but one within clearly defined limits. This is close to those biblical contexts where the word appears as a collective noun with the meaning of a majority, especially in a legal sense, with or without the article (Exod 23:2; 1 Kgs 18:25). In the Damascus Document, *hārabbîm* is limited to the sections dealing with procedural and judicial matters and the responsibilities of the Overseer *(mĕbaqqēr)* (CD XIII–XV). Elsewhere in that text the usual term is *'ēdâ*, as we saw earlier. Absent from the Damascus Document is the term *yahad*, which is standard in 1QS, whereas in the latter *hārabbîm* is for the most part confined to the sections dealing with the conduct of the plenary assemblies (1QS VI–VIII).

In both 1QS and CD the Many are under the direction of a supervisor *(hammĕbaqqēr 'al hārabbîm)* drawn from the ranks of the priesthood, whose relationship to his charges is described in paternal (or paternalistic) and pastoral terms.[14] The Community Rule had a procedure for a member to be recognized and given the floor during the plenary gathering: he had

---

Early Christianity, ed. James R. Davila, STDJ 46 (Leiden: Brill, 2003), 85-89. As Bauckham points out, in the context of Acts 2:42 *koinōnia* has to be something that happens, like the apostles' teaching and the breaking of bread, not the community itself. If *yahad* had been in use in early Christianity, we would have expected to come across a term such as *koinon*, but that does not happen. However, the phrase *epi to auto* ("together") translates *yahad* (*yahdâw*) in LXX — see, e.g., the citation of Ps 2:2 in Acts 4:26. It is used several times in Acts with reference to the Christian assembly as a united body, but it is an adverbial phrase not a title or self-designation (1:15; 2:1, 44; 4:26). Cf. 1 Cor 11:20 with reference to the eucharistic meal; also Ignatius *Eph.* V 3 with reference to absentees from the common assembly.

13. *môsab hārabbîm*: 1QS VI 8, 11-12; VII 10, 13; 4Q259 (4QSᵉ).

14. CD XIII 9; XIV 8-9; XV 5; 1QS VI 11-12, 14, 19-20.

to stand up and say, "I have a matter to present to the Many" (1QS VI 12-13). The responsibilities of this body included testing postulants for membership, the periodic review of their status, and the disposal of their property (1QS VI 15-21). The Many also made the final decision about the expulsion of members, and in discharging this function this body showed concern to safeguard the sacrosanct nature of its own authority; those who rejected its rulings or showed contempt for its decisions were to be expelled without the possibility of returning.[15]

Procedures set out in the Community Rule Book for the resolution of conflicts between members provide an interesting parallel between the Qumran *rabbîm* and the early Christian *ekklēsia*. 1QS VI 1 reads:

> Let no one bring an action against his fellow-member before the Many except when issuing a reproof in the presence of witnesses.

This regulation can be compared with the more detailed instruction in Matt 18:15-17:

> If your brother offends you, go and reprove him when you and he are alone together. If he heeds you, you have won over your brother. If he will not heed you, take along one or two others with you so that "on the evidence of one or two witnesses the charge may be sustained" (Deut 19:15). If he will not heed them, report it to the assembly *(tē ekklēsia)*. If he refuses to heed even the assembly, let him be to you as a Gentile and a tax collector.

Four stages, therefore: settle the issue without arbitration; if that is unsuccessful, bring an accusation in the presence of witnesses according to the law; if that does not work, bring the issue before the plenary assembly of church members; if, finally, the decision of the assembly is rejected, the offending individual is to be shunned.

Equivalence in function between the Qumran *rabbîm* and the Christian *ekklēsia* leads us to inquire whether the expression *rabbîm* in the Qumran sense, or something like it, occurs elsewhere. It appears occasionally in rabbinic texts with reference to an assembly gathered together for

---

15. 1QS VII 16, 23-24; VIII 21–IX 2. The procedures for reintegrating less serious offenders into the sect, also at the discretion of the Many, are laid out in 1QS VIII 18-19; cf. VIII 26 and IX 2.

some specific purpose. The phrase "in the presence of the company of the Many" *(bipĕnê ḥăbûrat hārabbîm)* is attested, and the expression "the prayer of the Many" *(tĕpillat hārabbîm)* stands for congregational prayer.[16] Whether *rabbîm* (Aram. *śaggî'în*) has this meaning in biblical texts is less clear. It occurs as a collective noun with the meaning "the majority" (Exod 23:2; 1 Kgs 18:25), and, more to the present purpose, it appears in psalms where the psalmist vows to praise God *bĕtôk rabbîm* (Ps 109:30: "in the midst of many"). In these instances it seems that the vow is to be fulfilled in the liturgical assembly, elsewhere in Psalms referred to as "the great assembly" *(qāhāl rab,* Ps 22:26; cf. *bĕtôk qāhāl,* v. 23). While these observations are inconclusive, they suggest the possibility that in this context the *rabbîm* are those qualified to participate in the plenary liturgical assembly, the *qāhāl rab.*[17]

To come finally to Isaiah: A case of particular interest occurs towards the end of the panegyric on the Servant of the Lord, the fourth of Bernhard Duhm's *Ebed-Jahwe-Lieder,* which speaks enigmatically of the Servant vindicating and atoning for "many" or "the Many" (Isa 53:11b, 12c). The first half of verse 11b may be restored as follows:

bĕda'tô yaṣdîq 'abdî lārabbîm
"By his knowledge my servant will vindicate (or: render righteous) the Many."[18]

It is at least clear that in this verse (though not in v. 12c) the Masoretes read *rabbîm* in the determined state, with the article. They were not the first to do so. In the fourth and final vision of Daniel (chs. 10–12), we hear that the people who acknowledge their God will stand firm and take action (this is during the persecution of Antiochus IV) and that those who instruct the

16. For the former, see *t. Dem.* 2:14, and for the latter, *Sifre Debarim* on Deut 3:24; see also *m. Kidd.* 4:5 and *b. Yeb.* 86b.

17. Psalm 22 speaks of the poor *('ănāwîm),* "those who seek God" *(dōrĕšāyw),* and those who fear or revere God *(yĕrēš'āyw)* as associates of the one making the vow. These are expressions appropriated and applied to themselves by the conventicles and sects. Worship in the *qāhāl rab* is also referred to in Ps 35:18 and 40:10-11 (Eng. 9-10), with which compare the *qĕhal ḥăsîdîm* of 149:1. This last phrase also occurs in the apocryphal Psalm 154 (11QPsᵃ XVIII 12).

18. Prosody and syntax suggest that *ṣaddîq* ("righteous," "innocent") was added, perhaps to make a connection with the *ṣaddîq* of Isa 57:1-2 whose death at the hands of evildoers went unregarded. For this reading of Isa 53:11, see my *Isaiah 40–55,* 348-500.

people will confer understanding on the Many (Dan 11:33). Towards the conclusion of the vision, the heavenly interlocutor promises that "the *maśkîlîm* will shine like the brightness of the firmament, and the *maṣdîqê hārabbîm* (those who vindicate/lead to righteousness the Many) like the stars for ever" (12:3). The language is clearly intended to evoke the Servant of Isaiah 53, who imparts knowledge, vindicates or renders righteous the Many, is himself assured of ultimate vindication, and will see light (Isa 52:13; 53:11) as the Danielic *maśkîlîm* are promised astral immortality.

There are too many gaps in our knowledge to permit the conclusion that these allusions in Daniel to the martyred Servant of Isaiah 53 belong on an unbroken exegetical continuum extending through the latter part of the Second Temple period. But it is not unreasonable to make a connection between the *rabbîm* associated with the Servant in Isa 53:11 and the *rabbîm* associated with the *maśkîlîm* in the book of Daniel, as also between the latter and the Qumran *rabbîm*. This is one strand of a powerful interpretative trajectory from Isaiah to Daniel, and then to the Enoch cycle, Qumran, and early Christianity which will call for further discussion.

The question now arises whether the same expression was taken over in early Christianity. In one of the gospel logia, Jesus speaks to the issue of precedence among his followers by insisting that whoever wishes to be first must be a servant *(doulos)*, and he goes on to state that the Son of Man came to give his life "a ransom for many" or "a ransom for the Many" *(lutron anti pollōn,* Matt 20:28 = Mark 10:45). Since the context is clearly reminiscent of the panegyric on the Servant in Isaiah 53, the use of *lutron* can be understood as one of several attempts to reproduce the idea of the Servant as an *'āšām,* a guilt offering or reparation sacrifice (Isa 53:10), which would suggest the more specific and determined meaning for *polloi.* In the New Testament, reference to "the Many" is restricted to contexts dealing with the sacrificial interpretation of the death of Jesus (e.g., Rom 5:15, 19; Heb 9:28). The eucharistic words announce that the body of Jesus is broken and his blood is shed "on behalf of the Many" (Matt 26:28 and par.). While the inclusive sense of *polloi* certainly came to be accepted on theological grounds, that is, the doctrine of the universal efficacy of the sacrificial death of Jesus, the Many *(hoi polloi)* of this primary statement would have indicated *in the first place* the group which owed allegiance to Jesus and was present with him on that occasion.[19]

19. The inclusive sense ("the many who cannot be counted") is argued by Joachim

To summarize: what the few texts at our disposal permit is a glimpse here and there of an exegetical continuum grounded in the great panegyric of Isaiah 53, taken further by the group to which the author of the Danielic visions belonged, and appropriated by the first generation of Christians in their task of understanding and articulating the identity of their founder and the significance of his life and death. There is also a Qumran link, though of a different kind, with this early Christian language about "the Many." In the Community Rule, the term *hārabbîm* stands not just for the sect doing business in its plenary sessions but for the sectarians as initiates gathered together for their sacred meal. Only full members in good standing were admitted to "the pure food of the Many" and "the drink of the Many."[20] On this specific point of usage, namely *hārabbîm* as a variant of *qāhāl / ekklēsia*, it appears quite possible that early Palestinian Christianity was influenced by Qumran.

The Way

One of the most common and yet most telling of biblical metaphors, "the way" (Heb. *derek*) evokes the image of life as a journey towards a goal, always threatened with the possibility of deviation, "turning aside from the way,"[21] or choosing a way of one's own rather than the God-ward way, a theme prevalent in the last section of Isaiah,[22] or being reduced to groping along the way like the blind,[23] or just losing one's way.[24] In the biblical

---

Jeremias, "πολλοί," *TDNT* 6:536-45. The problem for the medieval schoolmen, and for theologians in general, was to reconcile this form of words with the doctrine of the universal efficacy of the death of Jesus. Aquinas, e.g., conflates the Matthew-Mark version with that of Luke-1 Corinthians to give the meaning "for you the Jews, and for many, the Gentiles"; see *Summa Theologiae* III qu. 78 art. 3 ad. 8.

20. *tohorat hārabbîm* (1QS VI 16-17, 25; VII 3, 16, 20; also referred to as "the pure food of the men of holiness" (1QS VIII 17). For "the drink of the Many," see 1QS VII 20; 4Q284ª (4Q Harvesting) fr. 1.3.

21. With the verb *sûr*, e.g., Isa 30:11; very frequent in the Qumran texts: CD I 13; II 6; VIII 4; 4QFlorilegium fr. 1 I 14, etc.

22. Isa 53:6; 56:11; 57:10, 18; 58:13; 65:2; 66:3.

23. Isa 59:10; cf. CD I 8-10 based on this Isaian text. In CD I 9 *'ăšēmîm* ("guilty people") looks like a deliberate alteration of the difficult hapax legomenon *'ašmannîm* ("healthy"?) in Isa 59:10. See my *Isaiah 56–66*, 189-90.

24. With the verb *t*ʿ*h*: Isa 16:8; also Ps 107:4, 40; Job 12:24; also CD I 15; IV 1.

context "the way," together with the associated verb "to walk," evokes a mode of existing and acting proper to human beings in the most general sense, including following one's instincts and inclinations ("the way of the heart"),[25] sexuality ("the way of a man with a maiden," Prov 30:19),[26] and death ("the way of all the earth," Josh 23:14; 1 Kgs 2:2). In the biblical context the word is almost always qualified. It is the way of something, the way of somebody, the way to somewhere.

But more often than not "the way" has an ethical and religious import and as such features often in didactic and aphoristic writings. One's way can be sinful, foolish, false, corrupted, crooked, the way of darkness rather than light, and so on. It can also, but less commonly, be the good way (1 Kgs 8:25; Ps 119:1), the way of life (Prov 6:23), the way of wisdom (Prov 4:11), or the way of peace and well-being (Isa 59:8). There is also a way that looks good but leads to death (Prov 14:12). The biblical authors are not unaware of moral ambiguity and not slow to stress the limitations of moral capacity. One sometimes gets the impression that deviation is the norm, that "the way of humanity" is irremediably prone to evil: "The inclination of the human heart is evil from youth" (Gen 6:5; 8:21). In the Qumran sectarian writings this conviction will be expressed in sharper and starker tones.

God also has his *derek*,[27] which, while totally and inscrutably other than and removed from that of humanity (Isa 55:6-9; cf. Rom 11:33), at the same time provides an ideal towards which humanity is to strive, the spiritual discipline of *imitatio dei*. Hence people are said to walk, or more often not to walk, in God's ways — a theme of frequent occurrence in Psalms and much in evidence in the Qumran sectarian texts.

The capacity of the metaphor for expressing the basic ethical orientation of a human life is expressed most clearly in the formulation of the Two Ways, a familiar feature of philosophical and moralistic writings in many cultures, for example, in the fable of Herakles at the crossroads.[28] In

---

25. *derek lēb, derek libbô*: Isa 57:17; also Eccl 10:3; 11:9. Often in Qumran: CD I 11; 1QH XII 18, 21, 24; XIV 6, 21; 4Q434 (4Q "Bless O My Soul!") fr. 1 I 11. At 1QS III 6-10 "the ways of a man" *(darkê ʾîš)* are contrasted with "the ways of God" *(darkê ʾēl)*.

26. Reinforced by the secondary meaning of *derek* as "strength," "sexual vigor," as in Isa 57:10; also Jer 3:13; Prov 31:3.

27. Often in the plural, *dĕrākîm*, e.g., Isa 42:24, and often in Qumran: CD II 15-16; III 15; XX 18; 1QH XII 31; 4Q511 2 I 6.

28. Wilhelm Michaelis, "ὁδός," *TDNT* 5:42-96.

biblical texts it is exemplified in the contrast between the way of the righteous and that of the unrighteous in Psalm 1 and in the Deuteronomistic alternative of blessing or curse, life or death (Deut 11:26-28; 30:19). The formulation is also represented at Qumran (4Q473) and in other postbiblical writings (e.g., 2 En 30:15). In early Christian texts it is expressed equivalently in certain gospel logia — the contrast between the broad and the narrow gate, the hard and the easy road (Matt 7:13-14) — and explicitly in the *Didache* (1-6) and the *Epistle of Barnabas* (17).

The most striking use of the metaphor of the Way in early Christian writings is to be found in Acts, where it serves as an appellative for the Christian movement. The choice of this title to underline the distinctiveness of the Christian movement can be observed in Paul's trial before Felix in Caesarea. The prosecuting attorney Tertullus identified Paul as a ringleader of the sect of the Nazoreans (*prōtostatēn te tēs tōn nazōraiōn hairesiōs*, Acts 24:5), but in refuting the charge Paul provided his own terminological clarification: "According to the Way *(hodos)*, which *they* call a sect *(hairesis)*, I worship the ancestral deity, believing everything in keeping with the Law and those things written in the Prophets" (24:14). Paul seems to be declaring his allegiance to a movement with deep roots in Judaism but at the same time of a different order from Pharisees, Sadducees, and others to whom the term *hairesis* could be and was applied.[29] The author of Acts adds that the governor himself was well informed about the Way (24:22). Paul also spoke of the Christian movement as the Way in requesting authorization from the high priest to make arrests in Damascus (9:2), and he recalled later on that he had persecuted "this Way" (22:4). We hear of opposition to "the Way" from the Jewish community in Ephesus (19:9, 23), a situation which was to be expected and was no doubt replicated in many other places.

What is implied in the use of this title is not immediately self-evident. The Way *(hodos)* would be appropriate for a philosophical school or the teaching of an individual philosopher or sage, e.g., "the Way of Truth" of Parmenides or the "Tao Te Ching" ("Dao De Jing") of ancient China.[30] A much closer parallel may be found in the enigmatic allusion, in

29. In early Christian writings, *hairesis* and the corresponding adjective *hairetikos* refer in the first place to parties or factions within Judaism, in this respect no different from Josephus (*Ant.* 13:171-72); see Acts 5:17 (Sadducees); 15:5; 26:5 (Pharisees); 24:5 (Nazoreans). The term also applies to dissentions or factions within Christian churches: 1 Cor 11:19; Gal 5:20; Titus 3:10; 2 Pet 2:1.

30. Michaelis, "ὁδός," 88-91; Georg Sauer, "דֶּרֶךְ *derek* way," *TLOT* 1:343-46. For com-

a late text in Isaiah, to an unnamed teacher and his "way" which his disciples must continue to follow after the master has been removed from the scene:

> Your teacher will no longer remain hidden, but your eyes will see your teacher, and whenever you turn aside to the right or to the left your ears will hear a word spoken behind you, "This is the way; keep to it." (Isa 30:20-21)[31]

If we stay within the context of Acts we would most readily understand "the Way" to be an abbreviation of "the Way of the Lord," in the sense of a specifically Christian body of teaching. We hear, for example, that Apollos had been instructed in "the Way of the Lord" but required more accurate instruction in "the Way of God" (Acts 18:25-26). According to the Synoptic Gospels, the substance of the teaching of Jesus is encapsulated in the same expression: he taught the way of God (Matt 22:16; Mark 12:14; Luke 20:21). A connection is to be expected since it is normal for parties, sects, denominations, and religions to form around specific teachings enunciated by the founder of the group in question.

But "the Way of the Lord" or "the Way of God," understood purely as a teaching about God and the moral life, seems to be too unspecific to designate a group distinctive enough to be recognized as a sect, and it therefore seems mistaken to limit the meaning of *hodos*, as it occurs in Acts, to a doctrine or way of life and to deny that it serves to identify the earliest Christian community as a social reality.[32] We should therefore look for

---

parative material in general, Klaus Koch, Jan Bergman, Alfred Haldar, and Helmer Ringgren, "*derek [derekh]*," *TDOT* 3:270-93.

31. See further pp. 254-57.

32. As Kirsopp Lake and H. J. Cadbury, *The Acts of the Apostles: English Translation and Commentary*, vol. 4 of *The Beginnings of Christianity*, pt. 1, ed. F. J. Foakes-Jackson and Lake (London: Macmillan, 1933), 100; C. K. Barrett, *A Critical and Exegetical Commentary on the Acts of the Apostles*. ICC (Edinburgh: T. & T. Clark, 1994), 1:448. Most scholars agree that where *hodos* occurs in Acts without further qualification it refers to Christians as a social reality. See, e.g., S. Vernon McCasland, "The Way," *JBL* 77 (1958): 222-30; Ernst Haenchen, *The Acts of the Apostles* (Philadelphia: Westminster, 1971), 320; Ben Witherington III, *The Acts of the Apostles: A Socio-Rhetorical Commentary* (Grand Rapids: Wm. B. Eerdmans, 1998), 316, 711; Joseph A. Fitzmyer, *The Acts of the Apostles*. AB 31 (New York: Doubleday, 1998), 423-24, 638. I have seen only a summary of Eero Repo, *Der "Weg" als Selbstbezeichnung des Urchristentums*. AASF, B, 132/2 (Helsinki: Suomalainen Tiedeakademia, 1964).

some further connection which would endow the expression with a more specific content. Since the first Christians turned so often to the book of Isaiah in their attempt to understand and articulate their own identity and mission, it would be natural to think of the call to prepare the way of the Lord, citing Isa 40:3, with which the gospel accounts of the public activity of Jesus open (Matt 3:3 and par.). In order to relate the Isaianic text more closely to the activity of John the Baptist, it is cited according to LXX, which departs from the parsing of the Masoretic Text. The latter reads as follows:

> A voice proclaims:
> "Clear in the wilderness a way for YHVH,
> level in the desert a highway for our God."

The gospel citation differs from the Masoretic Text in locating the voice and the speaker in the wilderness in order to create a more direct reference to the Baptist, who was in fact in the wilderness: "The voice of one proclaiming in the wilderness: 'Prepare the way of the Lord. . . .'" John's proclamation encapsulates the eschatological message common to both Qumran and Jesus. Those who respond to the proclamation form a discipleship of believers, first around John, then around Jesus. The call to prepare the way of the Lord provides these disciples with their *raison d'être* and, as it seems, provided both with an appropriately self-descriptive title.

The citation of Isa 40:3 as the keynote for the gospel is one link in an exegetical chain, one moment in an interpretative continuum, the first stages of which must be recovered from the book of Isaiah itself, especially the latter part of the book (chs. 40–66) in which "the way through the wilderness" is a major theme. This is a large subject which cannot be dealt with adequately here; one or two indications must suffice. Isaiah 62:10-12 uses the same language as 40:3-5 in describing the future, and 35:8-10 presents a more ample scenario with a *via sacra (derek haqqodeš)* along which the redeemed will return to Zion. In these and other places, "the way" is removed from the historical particularities of Isa 40:3, which has in mind the return of the deportees or their descendants from exile and nudges the metaphor in the direction of the end-time perspective of judgment and salvation, the destruction and re-formation of Israel most explicitly formulated in the last two chapters of Isaiah and more definitively in Qumran and early Christianity.

The sectarian texts from Qumran are also part of this exegetical continuum starting out from Isa 40:3. The author of the *serek hayyaḥad*, the Community Rule, adapts the same text, this time in the Masoretic form, to the situation of the group he is addressing. He does so by omitting the voice of the one proclaiming and presenting a command of divine origin to prepare the way of the Lord in the wilderness: "In the wilderness prepare the way of the Lord, in the desert level a highway for our God." This section of the Rule runs as a follows:

> When these have become a community *(yaḥad)* in Israel, in keeping with these prescriptions they must segregate themselves from the dwellings of sinners by going into the wilderness to prepare his way there, as it is written: "In the wilderness prepare the way of the Lord, in the desert level a highway for our God." This stands for the study of the Law in order (for us) to act in accordance with all that has been revealed from age to age, and in accordance with what the prophets have revealed through his Holy Spirit. (1QS VIII 12-16)[33]

Whether the Qumran *yaḥad* was actually motivated by this text to segregate itself in the Judean wilderness at Qumran, or whether it read the text post factum as warranty for the move, there can be no questioning its crucial significance for the identity and mission of the group.

The question now arises whether, inspired by this text, the Qumran sectarians anticipated the first Christians in applying the designation "the Way" to themselves as the ones who were to prepare for the final coming of God, thus bringing the text of Isaiah to fulfillment. At a later point in the Rule (1QS IX 12-26), the members who are to be instructed by the *maśkîl* (Master? Guardian? Instructor?) are referred to as "the elect of the way" *(běḥîrê derek)*. This expression should not be translated "those who have chosen the way," since the substantive *bāḥîr, běḥîrîm* occurs frequently, with different modifiers, with reference to members of the sect. The term *derek* would then appear to be used in the absolute sense, referring to the community and its way of life, in much the same way as in Acts.[34] This in-

---

33. Also in two recensions: 4Q258 (4QS^d) VI 6-7 and 4Q259 (4QS^e) III 3-6. In 4Q176 (4Q Tanhumim) 1-2 I 4-9, Isa 40:1-5 is cited without comment.

34. The members are referred to as *běḥîrê yiśrā'ēl*, "the elect of Israel" (CD IV 3; 1Q37 1.3; 4Q165 6.1; 4Q171 11.2; 4Q174 1-2 I 19); *běḥîrê 'ēl*, "the elect of God" (1QpHab X 13; 1Q14 8-10.7); *běḥîrê sedeq*, "the righteous elect" (1QH^a X 13; 4Q215^a 1 II 3); *běḥîrê 'emet*, "the true

struction of the *maśkîl* is to be imparted "according to the determination of the appointed time" (*kĕtikkûn hā'ēt,* IX 18),[35] and the Rule goes on to state that the appointed time in question is the time for preparing the way in the wilderness. At that time, preordained by God, they are to segregate themselves from those who refuse the call, and they must do so by literally retiring into the wilderness.[36] Retirement into the wilderness was seen to be the first, necessary step towards the final consummation.

The disclosure of the true meaning of Isa 40:3, now that the appointed time had arrived, was therefore fundamental for the identity and mission of the Qumran *yaḥad.* The parallel with the beginning of the gospel narrative is striking. Isaiah 40:3 validates the message of the Baptist delivered in the Judean wilderness, and after John is removed from the scene Jesus proclaims the same message now that the appointed time *(kairos)* has arrived (Mark 1:1-15).

The use of *derek* as a group designation is admittedly not so clear in Qumran as *hodos* is in Acts, but usage in the various rules favors that conclusion: the members are "the elect of the way" (1QS IX 17-18) and "the perfect of the way" (1QM XIV 7), while recidivists are those who "deviate from the way" (CD I 13; II 6). It is arguable that this designation was taken over by the first generation of Palestinian Christians from Qumran, perhaps mediated through John the Baptist and his disciples including Apollos. Apollos is described as a formidable biblical exegete *(dunatos en tais graphais)* who came to the Jesus movement from that of John the Baptist but needed further instruction in "the way of God" (Acts 18:24-28). But

elect" (4Q418 69 II 10). The absence of the article is not significant; cf. *bĕḥîrê 'am,* "the elect of the people" (1QM XII 1; 4Q491 5-6.1), and *bĕḥîrê šāmayim,* "the heavenly elect" (1QM XII 5), both without the article.

35. The substantive *tikkûn* has different meanings in different contexts in the Scrolls, including rank among members and liturgical arrangements, but the context of 1QS IX 18-20 strongly suggests a prophetically predetermined time, an appointed time (Gk. *kairos*). Cf. 1QpHab VII 10-14, which refers to "the men of truth who observe the Law, who will not weaken in the service of the truth when the final age comes upon them; for all the ages of God come according to their established order *(lĕtikkûnām)* as he decreed."

36. That the Qumran sectarians identified the *midbār* of Isa 40:3 with the Qumran region is supported by the fact that Qumran really is in *midbar yĕhûdâ* ("the desert of Judah") as pointed out by McCasland, *JBL* 77 (1958): 228. The identification can also be deduced from the texts themselves as noted by George J. Brooke, "Isaiah 40:3 and the Wilderness Community," in *New Qumran Texts and Studies,* ed. Brooke and Florentino García Martínez. STDJ 15 (Leiden: Brill, 1994), 117-32.

if this is so, we would have to add that, given the basic differences between early Christianity and Qumran, and for that matter between early Christianity and the followers of John the Baptist, the borrowing would necessarily have been polemical.[37]

The Righteous

We can now turn to titles more directly denoting moral and religious qualities rather than structural and organizational features. In the sectarian context they serve to define the members over against those outside the group, and especially opponents of the group, and are therefore often paired with their respective antonyms (e.g., the righteous/the reprobate). This is, in fact, one of the principal reasons for the adoption of these self-descriptive rubrics, namely, to signify segregation from those outside, to define and set them apart over against "the others," to stake out boundaries. It is also the case that sects and movements often establish degrees of belonging, comparable to the distinction between professed members of a religious order and members of the third order, or, with the Cathars, the distinction between the perfect and the rank and file. The Damascus Rule distinguishes between "those who walk according to these instructions in the perfection of holiness" and those who have families and live in "camps" (CD VII 4-7). If the rich young man in the gospel of Matthew (19:16-22) wishes to move beyond normal observance and be perfect *(teleios),* he must get rid of his possessions and become a disciple. There are many more of these gradations and qualifications in both Qumranic and early Christian texts than can be usefully included in our list, and it will come as no surprise that several of them are gender-specific — "brethren," "men of truth," "men of the covenant," and so on. We shall focus on those which are more frequently used and which owe a special debt to Isaiah.

The first to be considered illustrates the traps and pitfalls of translation. Righteousness is easily confused with self-righteousness, lending itself readily to irony, as when we use such expressions as "the righteous empire." To begin at the beginning, Hebrew *ṣaddîq* (plural *ṣaddîqîm*) has a

---

37. A point emphasized by Bauckham, "The Early Jerusalem Church, Qumran, and the Essenes," 75-78.

broad semantic range including being right as opposed to being wrong,[38] or being innocent as opposed to being guilty.[39] It can also connote legitimacy, as in the expression ṣemaḥ ṣaddîq, a code name for a present or future Davidic ruler, which should be translated "legitimate branch" rather than "righteous branch" (Jer 23:5 NRSV). A less common meaning is illustrated by Zech 9:9, where the prophet bids Jerusalem rejoice at the coming of her king, ṣaddîq wĕnôšāʿ ("triumphant and victorious").[40] Most frequently attested, however, is the meaning "just" or "righteous," which expresses a general orientation of life and is said of a person whose life embodies the quality of justice in the broadest sense and who lives in accordance with God's law. Certain individuals in Israel's tradition came to serve as models of righteousness — the three ancient worthies Noah, Daniel, and Job in Ezek 14:12-20 — while the destruction of Sodom and Gomorrah came to be seen as a paradigm of judgment on the unrighteous but also of the fate of the righteous caught in the destructive flow of events (Gen 18:22-33). Not coincidentally, this incident also raised the question in what ways and with what consequences the qualification "righteous" may properly be attributed to the God of Israel.

The contrast between the righteous and unrighteous is thematic in different kinds of biblical material. The first Solomonic compilation in the book of Proverbs (Prov 10:1–15:33), for example, draws on its entire vocabulary of the moral life in contrasting the righteous person with the reprobate, the sinner, the fool, the one who trusts in material goods, and so on.[41] The contrast is equally in evidence in Psalms.[42] In the course of our study we will have occasion to note many close parallels, analogies, and points of contact between Psalms and the book of Isaiah. By the time of Qumran and early Christianity, David as author of Psalms had been co-opted into the ranks of the prophets, with the result that psalms could be read as predictive of contemporary situations and events no less than prophetic texts. The Cave 11 Psalms Scroll (11QPs XXVII 11) informs us that David com-

38. Exod 9:27; Prov 18:17.
39. Exod 23:7-8; Deut 16:19.
40. The corresponding abstract noun ṣĕdāqâ, usually translated "righteousness," occurs often in Isaiah with the meaning "vindication," "victory," "triumph." See Isa 1:27; 51:6, 8; 56:1; 59:9, 16-17; 61:10-11; 63:1.
41. E.g., Prov 10:21; 11:28; 13:21.
42. Ps 7:10 (Eng. 9); 11:5; 31:18-19 (17-18); 34:22 (21); 58:11-12 (10-11); 68:3-4 (2-3); 75:11 (10); and esp. Ps 37, where the epithet ṣaddîq occurs nine times.

posed 4,050 psalms "through (the gift of) prophecy given to him from the Most High." Psalms is the only biblical text apart from prophetic books which received a pesher, and it will be recalled that Acts cites psalms as predictive in the same way and to the same degree as prophetic texts.[43]

The contrast between the righteous and the unrighteous is stated programmatically in Psalm 1, which serves as a proem for the collection as a whole. The following points deserve our attention:

1. The righteous person on whom the blessing is invoked is described as deliberately segregating himself from the unrighteous. The absolute nature of this separation is expressed by the sequence of three verbs: he neither walks, stands, nor sits with them, and the righteous/unrighteous polarity is recapitulated in the final verse in the contrast between the two ways, that of the righteous *(ṣaddîqîm)* and that of the wicked *(rĕšā'îm)*.

2. The self-segregation is further emphasized by the exclusion of sinners from the congregation of the righteous (*'ădat ṣaddîqîm*, v. 5). Similar "congregational" language occurs throughout the collection wherever the righteous/unrighteous polarity comes to expression. Thus, after release from oppression and persecution, the psalmist promises to praise God or fulfill a vow in "the great assembly" (*qāhāl rab*, 22:26, etc.). We also hear of an "assembly of the saints" (*qĕhal qĕdōšîm*, 89:6) and an "assembly of the devout" (*qĕhal ḥăsîdîm*, 149:1).[44] Psalms are practically impossible to date with certainty, but this last phrase is the Hebrew equivalent of the *sunagōgē Asidaiōn* ("assembly of the Devout") of 1 Macc 2:42. In another psalm the author praises God "in the company of the upright and the congregation" (Ps 111:1), and yet another expresses the assurance that God is with "the righteous company" (*dôr ṣaddîq*, 14:5).[45] We have no direct clues to the social setting of these psalms, but the kind of language used in them is characteristic of self-segregating religious conventicles and sects of the kind that come fully into view in the late Second Temple period.

3. The irregular meter of Ps 1:2 ("his pleasure is rather in the law of Yahveh, and on his law he meditates day and night") has persuaded several commentators that this verse has been inserted into the composition to complement the negatively stated point about the segregation of the righ-

43. Acts 1:20; 2:25-31, 34-35; 4:11, 25-26, etc.

44. See also 11QPs[a] XVIII 12.

45. See also Ps 24:6; 73:15. On this meaning of *dôr*, see David Noel Freedman and Jack Lundbom, "dôr," *TDOT* 3:174-75.

teous with a more positive mention of their devotion to the law. If this is the case, the insertion would have been made at a very late date, and while the reading and study of the law by night as well as day could be simply a hyperbolic way of expressing fidelity and commitment to the law, it could also be intended literally. Nocturnal devotions carried out in the temple are referred to in Psalm 134 and hinted at in one or two other psalms (88:2 [Eng. 1]; 92:3 [2]; 119:55, 62). According to the Qumran Community Rule, the Many are to engage in the study of the law and in prayer for one third of the night (1QS VI 7-8), while in the *Hodayot* prayer is to be offered *lĕmô'ēd laylâ*, at the appointed time of night (1QH^a XVIII 14-15; XX 6). In Ps 1:2, the word translated "meditate" (verbal stem *hgh*, "murmur," "speak sotto voce") is used in other psalms with reference to study of the law and prayer, including nocturnal prayer (Ps 63:7 [6]). This usage may explain why the Qumran sectarians refer to the Book of the Torah as "the Book of Hagu" (vocalization uncertain), perhaps best translated as "the Book of Meditation."[46]

These considerations support the argument that at a late point in the evolution of the Psalter it came to serve as the prayer book of self-segregating conventicles of the devout. This thesis, argued or at least hinted at by scholars of an earlier generation, has been restated recently by Christoph Levin.[47] Levin argues that the reworked Psalms compilation had its social setting not in the temple cult but in "Hasidic" conventicles of the Greco-Roman period, and that at this stage of its development it served not as the "Hymns Ancient and Modern" of the Second Temple, as it were, but as a book of personal prayer, instruction, study, and meditation in use among the conventicles at that time. In keeping with this function, a redactor prefaced the collection with Psalm 1 as a way of setting the tone for the entire compilation. This process of "deliturgizing" the psalms involved reinterpreting in a collective sense psalms originally spoken by or addressed to an individual. Other psalms were reformulated, or a few verses added, to emphasize the theme of the segregation of the righteous few from the reprobate many. This would be the case with the strongly-worded dissociation from hypocrites and evildoers in Ps 26:4-5, where we

46. CD X 6; XIII 2-3; XIV 8 restored; 1Q28^a I 7. Some scholars identify this book differently; see Steven D. Fraude, "Hagu, Book Of," *EDSS* 1:327.

47. Christoph Levin, "Das Gebetbuch der Gerechten," repr. in *Fortschreibungen*, 291-313 (page references are to the republished edition).

find the same polarity (righteous/reprobate) as in Psalm 1. In these psalms the unrighteous are no longer foreigners but fellow Jews, no different therefore from the "brethren" who shun those who tremble at God's word in Isa 66:5. At this stage, then, we are well on the way to, or have actually arrived at, the situation in the Hellenistic period which witnessed the formation of the separatist groups mentioned in sources from that time.

Moving along parallel lines is Otto Plöger's hypothesis about the so-called Isian Apocalypse (chs. 24–27). This section of the book contains prophetic sayings of a marked eschatological character interspersed with brief psalms in which the contrast between the innocent and the guilty, the righteous and the wicked, is no less marked than in the psalms just referred to (Isa 25:1-5, 9; 26:1-6). The date of composition of these somewhat fragmentary psalms, and of the section as a whole, has long been the subject of debate. Bernhard Duhm proposed a date in the 1st century B.C.E.[48] Moving more cautiously, Plöger opted for the century of Ptolemaic rule and argued that it was composed to serve as "a prayer-book for the eschatological groups."[49] It is at least apparent that characteristically sectarian language occurs in these chapters, in the first place the polarity between "a righteous people" (*gôy-ṣaddîq*, 26:2) on the one hand and "the world" (*tēbēl*, 26:9) on the other, combined with an unforgiving attitude to the latter (26:10-11), a disposition to forgive not being a distinguishing mark of sects. It is hardly surprising that Isa 24:17, with its alliterative *paḥad wāpaḥat wāpaḥ* ("terror, the trap, the deep pit"), caught the eye of the author of the Damascus Document (CD IV 14-19). The previous verse (24:16), in which the verb *bgd* ("to betray," "to be unfaithful") occurs five times, is probably also behind the expression "the congregation of traitors" (*ʿădat bōgĕdîm*), a standard way of referring to defectors from the sect.[50]

The epithet *ṣaddîq*, which describes Yahveh's Servant in Isa 53:11 (*yaṣdîq ṣaddîq ʿabdî lārabbîm*, "my righteous Servant will vindicate/lead to righteousness the many"), is of particular interest. The text of these final verses in the panegyric on the Servant is obscure. Some commentators excise *ṣaddîq* since it overloads the verse and the adjective exceptionally pre-

---

48. Bernhard Duhm, *Das Buch Jesaja*, 172. On the section in general, see my *Isaiah 1–39*, 346-79.

49. Otto Plöger, *Theocracy and Eschatology*, 66.

50. CD I 12; cf. VIII 5; XIX 17, 34.

cedes the noun it governs. But it is there in the text, and its presence calls
for an explanation. It may have been added on account of the similar word
yaṣdîq ("will vindicate") immediately preceding, but if it was added it was
presumably because it was thought to contribute to the total meaning of
the poem. The solution to this exegetical problem may involve an equally
enigmatic passage in the last section of the book (57:1):

> The righteous one perished, and no one took it to heart;
> the devout are "gathered," and no one gives it a thought.
> It was on account of evildoing that the righteous one
>   was "gathered."

While *haṣṣadîq* in the first and last line could be understood as a collective
noun, its location at the beginning and end of the statement, with the article, leaves open the possibility that it refers in cryptic fashion to an individual *ṣaddîq* together with his followers described as *'anšê-ḥesed*, the equivalent of *ḥăsîdîm*, "devout." If this is so, *ṣaddîq* may have been added to 53:11
to create an intertextual link between Isaiah 53 and 57:1-2. In spite of the
obvious differences between 53:1-12 and 57:1-2, the similarities are not difficult to detect. The Servant was "taken away" (53:8a) as the Righteous One
of Isa 57:1-2 "perished" and was "gathered," and in neither case did anyone
take it to heart (53:8a; 57:1). After death and burial (53:9a), the Servant will
"see light" while the Righteous One will "enter into peace" (53:11a; 57:2). If
the Servant's "seed" *(zera')* refers to his disciples among whom the example of his life and message live on, there would also be a parallel with the
devout associated with the Righteous One in 57:1-2.[51]

The intertextual link between the Isaianic Servant and the Isaianic
Righteous One was at any rate not lost on readers of prophecy in late antiquity. In *The Wisdom of Solomon* (Wis 2:12-20), the persecution and violent death of a righteous one *(dikaios)* who calls himself the servant or
child of God *(pais theou)* is followed by a meditation on the contrasting
destinies of the righteous and the ungodly (3:1–4:19). The righteous who
have died before their time have been removed from evil and are at rest.
No one takes their death to heart, but they have entered into peace (3:1-3;

---

51. The connection between the two texts is argued more fully in my "Who Is the
Ṣaddiq of Isaiah 57:1-2?" in *Studies in the Hebrew Bible, Qumran, and the Septuagint Pres-
ented to Eugene Ulrich*, ed. Peter W. Flint, Emanuel Tov, and James C. VanderKam (Leiden:
Brill, 2006), 109-20.

4:7, 11, 14-15). The language is too close to Isa 57:1-2 to be coincidental, and there are other indications in this first part of *The Wisdom of Solomon* that the author had both the Servant poem in Isaiah 53 and this section of the book (chs. 56–57) in mind when writing.

The Damascus Document also seems to have had Isa 57:1-2 in mind in speaking of the death of the Teacher of Righteousness (or perhaps in this instance "the Unique Teacher," *môreh hayyahîd*, CD XIX 35; XX 13-14), since it speaks of him being "gathered," an abbreviated form of "gathered to his people," using the same verb *('sp)* as in Isa 57:1-2.[52] This would be consonant with the identification of the Teacher in the pesharim as "the Righteous One" *(hassadîq)*.[53]

The Qumran sectarian texts also identify members as "the righteous ones" *(saddîqîm)* and make much of the polarity between the righteous and the reprobate, as we would expect.[54] In one of the fragments of a sectarian commentary on Psalms (4QPs^b fr. 5), the first half of Ps 118:20 ("this is the gate of God" or "this is the gate to God") is written in cryptic characters and is followed by "the righteous will enter through it" written in plain text. As Levin has noted,[55] though without referring to the Qumran *pesher*, Ps 118:20 can be construed as a reinterpretation of the previous verse, "open to me the gates of righteousness." In the original context of this psalm of praise the reference would have been to the gates of the temple, but the cryptic Qumran script alerts the reader to a less overt meaning. The point would be that the righteous community, the community of the elect, has now taken the place of the temple; the gates of righteousness are no longer the gates leading into the temple but the community into which only the righteous have admittance.

In early Christian texts the righteous *(dikaioi)* include but are not limited to the disciples of Jesus. In fact, the mission of Jesus to sinners rather than the righteous would set early Christianity off against the Qumran sectarians and may have been directed against both them and the Pharisees (Matt 9:13 and par.). Prophetic, and especially Isaianic, teaching on the final, eschatological separation of the righteous from sinners is emphasized. While in the present age the Heavenly Father sends rain on the righteous and the unrighteous

---

52. The connection was noted by Chaim Rabin, *The Zadokite Document*, 2nd ed. (Oxford: Clarendon, 1958), 39-40.

53. 4QpPs IV 7-10 on Ps 37:32; 1QpHab I 12-13 on Hab 1:4b (reading supplied); V 8-12 on Hab 1:13b.

54. E.g., CD XX 20-21; 1QH^a XII 38; XV 12; 4QMessianic Apocalypse (4Q521) 14.2.

55. *Fortschreibungen*, 301.

(Matt 5:45), at the end of the age the angels will separate out the former from the latter or, using an Enochian image, the sheep from the goats (Matt 13:49; 25:31-46). Following the promise of astral immortality in Dan 12:3, the righteous will be raised up and shine like the sun (Matt 13:43; Luke 14:14).

Like the high priest Simon II, the Teacher of Righteousness, and James the brother of Jesus ("James the Just"), Jesus himself was known as The Righteous One *(ho dikaios, haṣṣadîq)*.[56] In this instance, as elsewhere, righteousness is associated with prophetic status; the righteous one is the prophet *par excellence*. On setting out on their mission the disciples are told that the one who welcomes a prophet *in the name of a prophet* (i.e., in the name of Jesus) will receive a prophet's reward, and the one who welcomes a righteous one *in the name of a righteous one* (i.e., in the name of Jesus) will receive the reward of a righteous one (Matt 10:40-41). The disciples are assured that many prophets and righteous ones longed to see what they see and did not see it (Matt 13:17). In another logion, the Pharisees are taken to task for disingenuously building the tombs of the prophets and decorating the monuments of the righteous (Matt 23:29), and the same discourse speaks of the "righteous blood" of the prophets (v. 35). The *dikaios/prophētēs* association, one example of the semantic expansion of the idea of prophecy in the Second Temple period, is therefore clearly in view in the New Testament, more so than in Qumran.[57]

After making all due allowance for the uncertainties endemic to this kind of investigation where the source material is uneven and sporadic, we can conclude that both the Qumran sectarians and the first generation of Christians referred to themselves as "the righteous ones," at least in the sense of striving after righteousness and as separating themselves ideologically and, in different ways and to different extents, physically from an unrighteous world. Each group also venerated its founder as "The Righteous One" *(haṣṣaddîq, ho dikaios),* thus illustrating the homology between founder or leader and members referred to earlier. As in many other respects, the interpretative impulse for this aspect of their self-understanding was supplied by psalms and prophecy, in the first place the book of Isaiah. The model is the Servant of the Lord, also the Righteous

---

56. Matt 27:19, 24; Luke 23:47; Acts 3:14; 7:52; 22:14; Jas 5:6.

57. In 4QApocryphon of Moses[a] (4Q375 I 6-7), a prophet accused of preaching apostasy is defended on the grounds that he is notwithstanding a righteous man, a trustworthy prophet *(ṣaddîq hû'â nābî' ne'ĕman).*

One, whose death is recorded in Isaiah 53 and 57:1-2 and whose disciples perpetuated his example and message.

The Elect

Divine election has always been considered one of the key biblical themes. It has also been one of the most influential throughout Jewish and Christian history, often in problematic ways. It therefore merits close attention both in its biblical essence and in the transformations it underwent during the period with which we are concerned. One way of tracking developments and transformations in the language of divine election is through successive stages in the formation of Isaiah and the subsequent history of its interpretation. Before attempting to do this, a word about the vocabulary of divine election in the Hebrew Bible is in order.[58]

In Hebrew the concept is expressed primarily by different forms of the verbal stem *bḥr* ("choose") and the corresponding substantive *bāḥîr*, plural *bĕḥîrîm* ("chosen"). The alternative form *bāḥûr*, passive participle of the same verb, therefore also "chosen," is restricted almost completely to the sphere of warfare, perhaps on account of the homonymous *bāḥûr* meaning "youth," specifically a youth fit for military service. The idea of divine election, in the sense of the antecedent choice by God of a people or an individual (king, leader, priest, prophet),[59] always threatens to shade off into a doctrine of divine predestination, as in fact it does in the Damascus Document. According to this text, those who defect from the sect reveal themselves not to have been chosen in the first place and therefore to have been predestined to act in this way from the beginning of time (CD II 7). Somewhat similar, though in a positive sense, is the assurance given to Ephesian Christians that "He (God) chose us in him before the foundation of the world that we might be holy and spotless in his sight" (Eph 1:4). A strong sense of predestination also pervades the Johannine writings, perhaps the most sectarian-sounding among early Christian texts.

This language of divine election is not evenly distributed over the

58. Jan Bergman, Helmer Ringgren, and Horst Seebass, "*bāḥar [bāchar]*," *TDOT* 2:73-87; Hans Wildberger, "בחר *bḥr* to choose," *TLOT* 1:209-26; Dale Patrick, "Election: Old Testament," *ABD* 2:434-41.

59. I leave aside the divine choice of a place (country, city, temple) prominent in Deuteronomistic texts; on which, see Bergman *et al.*, *TDOT* 2:79-82.

range of biblical books and is entirely absent from some of them. Qoheleth, for example, betrays no interest in ideas about divinely guaranteed national or ethnic destiny. Nor are these ideas of divine election and the manifest destiny of a people confined to the Hebrew Bible and writings dependent on it. Jupiter, for example, reminds the Romans of their divinely appointed mandate to rule the nations with the scepter, to spare those who accept its rule, and beat down the proud who refuse to do so.[60]

Israelite tradition commemorates outstanding individuals as the objects of God's choosing, among them Abraham, Levi, Aaron, Moses, Jacob, and Judah. According to the royal ideology in the days of the kingdoms, the authority of the ruler was sustained by a doctrine of divine election, this idea too by no means confined to Israel and Judah. Those in the early Iranian period who advocated restoration of the native dynasty in the person of Zerubbabel hailed him as God's chosen one (Hag 2:23). But all these individuals could be so designated only by virtue of God's antecedent choice of a people. Though the expression "God's chosen people" occurs only once in the Hebrew Bible (Isa 43:20), the divine election of Israel is a recurring theme, appearing most programmatically and insistently in Deuteronomistic writings and in the later sections of the book of Isaiah. It is here that we pick up the interpretative trajectories leading to the divisions and sects which came out into the open in the last two centuries before the Common Era.

This is a point of prime importance. One of the clearest indications in biblical texts of incipient sectarianism is a referential shift in the language of election from the people as a whole to a minority within it. We can take the related language about the people as Yahveh's "treasured possession" (*sĕgullâ*, a key theological term) as an instructive parallel. Israel as *'am sĕgullâ* ("a people which is Yahveh's treasured possession") is closely associated with ideas of divine election, as when a psalmist rejoices that "Yahveh has chosen Israel for his treasured possession"(Ps 135:4). In a late prophetic text, however, Yahveh's *sĕgullâ* is no longer the people as a whole but a group of the devout who pact together, whose names are written in God's book, and who await the day when the distinction between God's true servants and those who are such only in name will be as clearly acknowledged by all and sundry as it is to them (Mal 3:13-18).

---

60. "Tu regere imperio populos, Romane, memento . . . parcere subiectis et debellare superbos" (*Aeneid* VI 847-53), quoted by Augustine, *Civ. Dei* V xii).

The problematization of the language of divine election can also be traced through successive stages in the formation of the book of Isaiah. The vocabulary of election, noted earlier, is with one exception confined to the second part of the book (chs. 40–66). The exception (Isa 14:1-2), which all critical commentators date to the postdestruction period, is of interest for our theme. By speaking of a *second* election of Israel ("Yahveh will take pity on Jacob and will *once again* choose Israel"), it combines the sense of a failed history now at its terminus with the prospect of a new history. The identity of the bearers of this new history is already an issue in the book of Isaiah and will be a central concern for both the Qumran sectarians and the first generation of Christians.

Some of the stages leading to this point can be traced throughout Isaiah 40–66. In Deutero-Isaiah (to use the conventional title for chs. 40–55) the elect are also the Servants of Yahveh, election and service being closely related concepts.[61] In the final section of the book, the so-called Trito-Isaiah (chs. 56–66), however, the identity of these chosen Servants is no longer self-evident. In the communal lament in 63:7–64:11 (Eng. 12), Israel as a whole, though conscious of a history of infidelity, is still unproblematically God's people and can plead with God as such ("Consider, we are your people," 64:8 [9]). But the sequel describes a people alienated from its traditional religious allegiances and practices, and we have the impression that this somber description, immediately following the lament, is meant to explain why the lament went unheeded (65:1-7). As we read on, we see that the elect who will inherit the land and the servants who will dwell there are no longer identified with Israel as a whole but with a remnant which is to form the core of a new people:

These are Yahveh's words:
"When there is still some juice in a bunch of grapes,
people say, 'Don't destroy it, there's a blessing in it.'
So shall I do for the sake of my servants,
so as not to destroy all the people.
I shall bring forth descendants from Jacob,
from Judah heirs to inherit my mountains.
My chosen ones will inherit the land,
my servants will have their abode there." (65:8-9)

---

61. Isa 41:8-9; 43:10; 44:1-2; 45:4.

Occupation and usufruct of the land are now limited to "my people who seek me," meaning "those among my people who seek me" (65:10). The servants of Yahveh, those who tremble at his word and have been rejected by their "brethren," including the religious authorities (65:13-16; 66:5), see themselves as the true elect of God, the beginnings of a new people. An invisible line has been drawn through the community.

It seems entirely possible, though unprovable in the present state of our knowledge, that those whose voices we are hearing in these last chapters of Isaiah, the Servants of Yahveh and those who tremble at his word, originated a movement which continued on into the Hellenistic period when the existence of sects is explicitly attested. It is at any rate the case that the book of Isaiah as a whole, and chapters 40–66 in particular, are prominent in both the Qumran and early Christian texts to the point of conferring a distinctively Isaianic character on both.

The Qumran texts, sectarian and nonsectarian alike, refer often to the election of Israel more or less in the Deuteronomistic manner but with a stronger emphasis on predestination.[62] In the rule books only community members qualify as God's chosen people: they are "the Elect of the Way" *(běhîrê derek)*[63] and "the Perfect of the Way" *(těmîmê derek)*,[64] chosen out of all humanity (1QS XI 17). By virtue of their election they are united to the angels, "the sons of heaven" and "the holy ones" (1QS IX 7). As in the late Isaianic texts we have been discussing, so in the Qumran texts the idea of election and of the elect as a privileged minority goes hand in hand with an eschatological orientation. That the Instructor *(maśkîl)* is to admonish "the Elect of the Way" according to "the regulation of the time" (1QS IX 12-19) implies the belief that the members of the sect occupied an axial position in a series of divinely preordained and prophetically revealed moments in the history of Israel and therefore of the world.[65] For the Qumran *yaḥad,* the last of these epochs was ushered in with their retreat into the wilderness dictated by the interpretation of Isa 40:3 with its injunction to "clear in the wilderness a way for Yahveh, level in the desert a highway for our God" (1QS IX 5-6, 19-20). They were therefore

---

62. 1QM X 9; 4Q266 11.11; 4Q393 3.6; 4Q503 (4QDaily Prayers[a]) 24-25.4; 4Q504 (4QWords of the Luminaries[a]) 1-2 III 9).

63. 1QS IX 17-18; also 4Q258 VIII 2; 4Q259 III 16.

64. 1QS IV 22; cf. 1QS[b] I 2.

65. 1QS VIII 15; IX 13; cf. CD I 13; XVI 3-4.

living in the last age, with its climax in the final judgment over which they, the elect, would preside (1QpHab V 3-4).

The first Christians also referred to themselves as "the elect of God" *(eklektoi theou).*[66] Paul, in particular, manifests a strong sense of election as apostle to the Gentiles (Acts 15:7) and constantly reminds his readers of their election. Combining election with the metaphor of the community as a temple, and adding another figure, that of the cornerstone, borrowed from Isa 28:16, 1 Pet 2:1-10 addresses the readers as an "elect race" or "chosen people" *(genos eklekton),* deliberately echoing the Greek version of Isa 43:20, *genos mou to eklekton* ("my chosen people"). The Synoptic Gospels also evince a strong sense of Christians as chosen by God in view of the final consummation of history towards which the world was rapidly moving. The first disciples are the few chosen *(eklektoi)* among the many called *(klētoi,* Matt 20:16b). The tribulations of the last age will be abbreviated on account of the elect (Matt 24:22), and there will follow the ingathering of the elect from the four corners of the earth (v. 31). The gospel of John, with its strong contrast between insiders and outsiders, speaks of the disciples chosen out of the world (John 15:19), and the same contrast is stated even more strongly in Revelation (e.g., Rev 17:14). Much of this language, and the perspective on history and Israel's place in history which it expresses, can be read as a further development of the apocalyptic view of history which comes to expression in the later stages of the Isaianic literary tradition.

The Servants of the Lord

Throughout Isaiah 40–48 Israel as the Chosen, the Elect, is also addressed repeatedly as the Servant of Yahveh.[67] The association between election and servanthood is one of several precipitates of Deuteronomistic theology in this section of the book. In the Deuteronomistic scheme of things Moses is the prototypical servant, the one who offers service to God of unique value,[68] and it is a major theme in Deuteronomistic writings that

---

66. Rom 8:33; Col 3:12; Titus 1:1. On the language of election in general, esp. in the New Testament, see Gottlob Schrenk and Gotffried Quell, "ἐκλέγομαι," *TDNT* 4:144-68; Jost Eckert, "ἐκλέγομαι," "ἐκλεκτός," in *EDNT* 1:416-17, 417-19; Gary S. Shogren, "Election: New Testament," *ABD* 2:441-44.

67. Isa 41:8; 43:10; 44:1; 45:4.

68. Deut 34:5; Josh 1:2; 9:24.

this service is to be extended throughout subsequent history by the agency of both ruler and prophet.[69] The impact of Deuteronomistic ideas on this second major section of Isaiah can be gauged statistically by noting that in chapters 40–66 the term *ʿebed* ("servant") appears 32 times with a religiously significant meaning, whereas in chapters 1–39 it occurs almost exclusively in the usual secular sense of a servant, slave, or court official.[70] Since we are concerned at present with "servants" as designating a collectivity, it is to be observed further that the plural *(ʿăbādîm)* is restricted to the last 11 chapters of the book (56–66), the so-called Trito-Isaiah. The one exception is 54:17 ("This is the lot of Yahveh's servants"), which links 40–54 with 56–66, the Servant of the Lord of chapter 53 with "the Servants" of the last 11 chapters, the last two in particular.

The last section of the book (chs. 56–66) opens with a remarkable statement in which foreigners and eunuchs — the sexually mutilated — are assured on prophetic authority of their good standing as members of the community and participants in the common cult. The assurance is given in defiance of the law in Deut 23:2-9 (Eng. 1-8), which excludes certain ethnic categories and the sexually mutilated from membership in the assembly; it is therefore an example of the abrogation of a point of law on prophetic authority. The assurance given to those of foreign descent that they may aspire to be servants of Yahveh (56:6) may refer specifically to cultic service, an idea which would clearly be unacceptable to the temple priesthood. In any case, the term "servants" is not used as a title at this point and does not imply membership in a spiritual elite within the community; so much is evident from the context. It is equally clear that the communal lament in the same section of the book (63:7–64:11 [Eng. 12]) is addressed to Yahveh in the name of the people as a whole who identify themselves as Yahveh's servants (63:17). Here too, it is the context that

69. Hence David and those in the Davidic line of succession are named servants of God in the History (2 Sam 3:18; 1 Kgs 8:24-26; 2 Kgs 19:34 = Isa 37:35), the Deuteronomistic stratum in Jeremiah (Jer 33:21-22, 26), and often in Psalms of a similar orientation (the superscriptions of Ps 18 and 36; 78:70; 89:4, 21, 40, 51 [Eng. 3, 20, 39, 50]; 132:10; 144:10). Individual prophets carry this title (1 Kgs 15:29; 2 Kgs 9:36; 10:10; 14:25), and "his servants the prophets" *(ʿăbādāyw hannĕbîʾîm)* is the standard Deuteronomistic term for the prophetic succession (2 Kgs 9:7; 17:13, 23; 21:10; 24:2; Jer 7:25; 25:4; 26:5; 29:19; 35:15; 44:4; also Amos 3:7).

70. Isa 20:3 ("my servant Isaiah") is in a brief narrative written in the style of the Deuteronomistic History; 37:35 ("my servant David") is copied from 2 Kgs 19:34; and in 22:20 ("my servant Eliakim") the reference is to a court official.

makes it clear that the term is used in a very general sense of the religious community as a whole.

The situation is quite different in the last two chapters, which open with a fierce denunciation of a "stubborn, rebellious people," of which only a remnant will escape an annihilating judgment. These survivors are designated Yahveh's servants, the progenitors of a new people who will inherit the land and settle there (65:1-12). Those whom the writer identifies as "Yahveh's servants" form a group distinct and segregated from their "brethren." The Abrahamic promise is now limited to "my servants" and "my elect":

> I shall bring forth descendants from Jacob,
> from Judah heirs to inherit my mountains.
> My chosen ones will inherit the land,
> my servants will have their abode there. (65:9)

The implied reinterpretation of the Abrahamic blessing may be compared with the words attributed to John the Baptist, that "God is able from these stones to raise up children to Abraham" (Matt 3:9).

In the following passage the contrasting destinies of these servants and their opponents, who must have included the religious authorities, are expressed in the characteristically sectarian idiom of eschatological reversal:

> My servants will eat, while you go hungry;
> my servants will drink, while you go thirsty;
> my servants will rejoice, while you are put to shame;
> my servants will exult with heartfelt joy,
> while you cry out with heartache
> and wail with anguish of spirit. (65:13-14)

This categoric statement sounds very much like a response to the taunt directed at those who tremble at Yahveh's word in the following chapter (66:5). If this is so, and assuming some consistency and coherence in this part of the book, the titles *'ăbādîm* ("servants") and *ḥărēdîm* ("those who tremble") would be alternative designations for the same pietistic and prophetic-eschatological group which, at least at the time Isa 66:5 was written, formed a distinct entity, one which existed at the margins of the Judean cult-community.

A further point is that the title *ḥărēdîm* is attested only in Isa 66:1-5 and in the account of the marriage crisis in Ezra 9–10 (9:4; 10:3), where it identifies the principal support group of Ezra. Since there is no law mandating divorce and dismissal of wife and children, support of Ezra's program by those who trembled at the word of the God of Israel implied commitment to a rigorist interpretation of the laws, in this instance prohibition of intermarriage with the local population (cf. Deut 7:3-4). We shall argue later that the Ezra "tremblers" and those referred to in Isa 66:5 describe the same group from different perspectives and at different points of its development.[71]

Another text, generally dated to the first half of the 5th century, registers a complaint of those who serve God that their religious observances and penitential way of life go unregarded by God (Mal 3:13-18). These God-servers and God-fearers then confer together, perhaps entering into a pact similar to the covenant initiated by Nehemiah (chapter 10). A document is written containing the names of those who fear God and think on his name, and they are assured they will be acknowledged as God's special possession (once again, *sĕgullâ*) on judgment day when the wicked will be destroyed and those who revere the name of YHVH will rejoice (3:19-21 [Eng. 4:1-3]). Since (as argued in an earlier chapter) these three texts (Isa 65–66; Ezra 9–10; Mal 3:13-18) are roughly contemporary and reflect, at least in generalities, the same situation during the first century of Iranian control of Judah, they can be read as testifying to an emergent sectarianism of a type which about two and a half centuries later will be more comprehensively embodied in the Damascus sect and the Qumran *yaḥad*.

The same designation, *'ebed*, *'ebed YHVH* ("servant," "servant of YHVH"), is one of the most frequent ways in which those whose voices we hear in the psalms refer to themselves.[72] Affinity between Psalms and Isaiah was pointed out earlier, and it is most clearly in evidence in those psalms which speak of the rebuilding and restoration of Zion and repossession of the land.[73] Understandably, then, the question arises whether

---

71. See p. 253.

72. Ps 19:12, 14 (Eng. 11, 13); 27:9; 31:17 (16); 35:27; 69:18 (17); 86:2, 4, 16; 109:28; 116:16; 119 *passim*; 143:2, 12. The plural *'ăbādîm* occurs somewhat less frequently: 34:23 (22); 69:37 (36); 79:2, 10; 89:51; 90:13, 16; 102:15, 29 (14, 28); 105:25; 113:1; 134:1; 135:1, 14.

73. See esp. Ps 69, 102 and the last two verses of Ps 51, on which see Henk Leene, "Personal Penitence and the Rebuilding of Zion: The Unity of Psalm 51," in *Give Ear to My Words: Psalms and Other Poetry In and Around the Hebrew Bible. Essays in Honour of Professor N. A. van Uchelen*, ed. Janet Dyk (Kampen: Kok Pharos, 1996), 61-77.

there are also points of contact between the Isaianic servants and the servants of whom the psalms speak. For Ulrich Berges, the answer is decidedly in the affirmative. He argues that a sectarian group at the time of Nehemiah, known among themselves as "Servants of Yahveh," were responsible for editing both the last chapters of Isaiah and those psalms which allude to servants, the latter, not by coincidence, occurring almost exclusively in the last two books (IV and V) of the collection. Verses were added at certain points (Ps 34:23 [Eng. 22]; 69:35-37 [34-36]; 102:13-23, 29 [12-22, 28]) with the purpose of reinterpreting the psalms in question as referring to this Servant sect. Berges maintains that the universalist perspective of the sect was eventually submerged by the integrationist ideology of the *gôlâ* group, which took over and applied to itself the designation "Servants of Yahveh," as in Nehemiah's prayer on hearing bad news from Judah (Neh 1:5-11a).[74]

Berges's argument starts out from what I take to be a correct perception of the importance of the designation "Servants" and the background shared by Isaiah 40–66 and those psalms which he takes into consideration. However, we would need much clearer indications that the term *ʿăbādîm* is used in these psalms as the appellative for a distinct group, and the few and unspecific references to "servants" in Nehemiah (1:5-11a; 2:20) fall short of proving that the Judeo-Babylonian element to which Nehemiah belonged took over the title and applied it to itself. It seems even less likely that these "servants" held and promoted a universalist ideology. Universalism, as generally understood, is not especially characteristic of sectarian thinking. Moreover, the liberal attitude to foreigners displayed in Isa 56:1-8 is not attributed to the "Servants" of the last two chapters of the book and, in any case, is directed at people within the Judean community and therefore does not illustrate attitudes to those outside the sect. In these chapters (Isa 65–66), the animus directed against other Jews leaves little room for consideration of foreigners, but what little comes through (e.g., in condemning "pagan" cults) is by no means benign.

74. Ulrich Berges, "Die Knechte im Psalter: Ein Beitrag zu einer Kompositionsgeschichte," *Bib* 81 (2000): 153-78; "Who Were the Servants? A Comparative Inquiry in the Book of Isaiah and the Psalms," in *Past, Present, Future: The Deuteronomistic History and the Prophets*, ed. Johannes C. De Moor and Harry F. Van Rooy. OtSt 44 (Leiden: Brill, 2000), 1-18. The thesis has some aspects in common with Christoph Levin, "Das Gebetbuch der Gerechten," 355-81.

While, therefore, the designation ʿăbādîm and the closely associated
ḥărēdîm are not titular in the same way as, for example, the terms Pharisee and Sadducee, since both have attached qualifications ("Servants of
the Lord," "those who tremble at his word"), in context they come close to
being used as identifying labels for minority groups, either self-
segregating or coercively segregated, among Jews of the Iranian period. It
is therefore surprising that these titles appear not to have been adopted by
the Qumran sects. The Qumran texts refer to both Moses (4Q378 22 I 2)
and David (1QM XI 2) as Servants of Yahveh and speak of prophets as
"his servants the prophets,"[75] but where the term appears in the plural in
the Qumran material the text is too fragmentary to render a meaning in
context.[76]

In keeping with traditional usage, the New Testament refers to Moses as *doulos tou theou* ("Servant of God," Rev 15:3) and to David as *pais
theou* with the same meaning (Luke 1:69; Acts 4:25). Prophets are described as God's servants only in Revelation (Rev 10:7; 11:18; 19:2), but the
same idiom may be behind the parables of the Marriage Feast and the
Unfruitful Vineyard, in which the king, or the proprietor of the vineyard,
sent out his servants who were mistreated and put to death (Matt 22:1-14;
Mark 12:1-12). The title of Jesus as *pais theou* exploits the ambivalence of
the Greek word, which can mean "child" or "servant" (Acts 3:13, 26; 4:27,
30). The allusion to the Servant of Isaiah 53 is unmistakable in the hymn
incorporated in Philippians (2:5-11), but the Isaianic connection between
this Servant and the Servants of the last chapters of the book did not
carry over into early Christianity. The closest approach is the gospel injunction about precedence among the disciples, with its clear echo of the
Servant of Isaiah 53: "Whoever among you wishes to be first must be your
servant; as the Son of Man came not to be ministered to but to minister
and to give his life as a ransom for (the) many" (Matt 20:27-28). Paul and
other church leaders often refer to themselves as Servants of God or of
Christ, but in this context the terms in question *(doulos, pais)* do not reflect systematic titular usage.[77]

75. 1QS I 3; 1QSᵇ I 27; 1QpHab II 9; VII 5.
76. 1Q25 5.4 (1QApocryphal Prophecy); 1Q36 17.3 (1QHymnic Composition); 4Q176
8-11.15 (4QTanhumim); 4Q471 2.5 reads ʿabdê ḥôšēk, "servants of darkness."
77. Paul: Rom 1:1; Phil 1:1; Gal 1:10; James: James 1:1; Peter: 2 Pet 1:1; Jude: Jude 1;
Epaphras: Col 4:12; Christians in general: Acts 4:29; 1 Pet 2:16; Rev 1:1; 2:20; 7:3; 22:3, 6.

The Saints

In the Hebrew Bible holiness is primarily a ritual rather than an ethical concept, though this dichotomy should not be overworked. Holiness characterizes those areas of social life and those individuals specially dedicated to the worship of the deity. Cult personnel are therefore holy *(qĕdôšîm)*, but any person consecrated (i.e., set aside for a special religious task) is ipso facto holy for the duration of the mission. Stringent rules were in effect to preserve the separate status of cult personnel and to prevent encroachment on holy terrain.[78] It will be obvious that these distinctions, characterizations, and restrictions could also function as a way of maintaining social control. The point is clearly made in the paradigmatic wilderness narrative of the rebellion of Levites and lay people against the exclusive authority of Moses and Aaron, a rebellion based on the claim that "all the congregation are holy, every one of them" (Num 16:3). This affirmation of democratic holiness ended predictably in defeat. The right to decide "who is holy and who will be permitted to approach God" (Num 16:5) was reasserted by Aaron. Priestly privilege remained intact.

Any place was considered holy where a numinous event had been experienced, and any place set aside as a permanent cult site was by definition a holy place. This was preeminently so with the wilderness sanctuary as prototype for the Jerusalem sanctuary or "holy place" *(qōdeš)*, together with its inner sanctum, the "holy of holies" or "most holy place" *(qōdeš qŏdāšîm,* Exod 26:33-34, etc.). The holiness of the sanctuary irradiated out along the spatial axis, affecting, in the first place, the elevated plateau on which the temple was built,[79] then the *via sacra* leading to the sanctuary (Isa 35:8), and the city which forever after would be called "the holy city" by Jews *('îr haqqōdeš)*, Moslems *(al quds)*, and Christians *(civitas sancta)*. As the property of the holy God, the land also was considered holy (e.g., Ezek 45:1-8), though the familiar expression "the holy land" *(terra sancta)* occurs only once in the Old Testament (*'admat haqqōdeš,* lit., "holy soil," Zech 2:16).

The holiness of Yahveh, God of Israel, is a characteristic Isaianic

---

78. This was common practice in ancient and some modern societies. In the Eleusinian mysteries any uninitiated person passing beyond the door into the *telestērion* was subject to the death penalty; see Walter Burkert, *Griechische Religion der archaischen und klassischen Epoche* (Stuttgart: Kohlhammer, 1977), 429.

79. Hence the typically Isaianic expression "my holy mountain" (*har qodšî,* Isa 11:9; 27:13; 56:7; 57:13; 65:11, 25; 66:20).

theme. Since the destiny of the people is in every respect dependent on its relation to Yahveh throughout the book, "the Holy One of Israel" *(qědôš yiśrā'ēl)* is the most common divine title from beginning to end of the book.[80] The acclamation of the seraphs in the great vision scene in Isa 6:1-13 — the source for the *Sanctus* in the Catholic mass, the Greek Orthodox *trisagion,* and the *kedusha* of Jewish liturgical prayer — is a classic expression of the holiness of God, well known as the motto for Rudolph Otto's at one time influential book *Das Heilige* (in English translation, *The Idea of the Holy*[81]). Isaiah's seraphic liturgy and the joyful singing of the "sons of God" (angelic beings) in Job 38:4-7 remind us that Yahveh also has a "holy habitation" in the sky (Isa 65:25) which, like its earthly counterpart, has its own officiants, "the assembly of the holy ones" *(qěhal qědōšîm,* Ps 89:6 [Eng. 5]). This idea is also represented in sectarian writings of the late Second Temple and, in fact, is still with us.

Dedicated to Yahveh, the holy God, and living in the holy land, Israelites could be referred to as a "holy people" or a "holy nation," though we have seen that in prophetic preaching the identification of the nation or the people as a whole as God's people could not simply be taken for granted. The reluctance in classical prophecy to identify any particular social or political embodiment with the ideal Israel, with the concomitant of this conviction in the concept of the holy remnant, is the essential point of departure for the long development which reached its furthest limits in the Qumran sectarian writings and the New Testament. The development can be traced through the compositional history of the book of Isaiah. One example is the prose addendum to a judgment pronouncement which foresees that the future remnant of Zion, those recorded in God's book, will be called holy:

> On that day, the shoot that Yahveh has planted will be an object of magnificence and glory, and the fruit of the land an object of pride and splendor for the survivors of Israel. Those who are left in Zion and who remain in Jerusalem will be called holy, all those who are recorded for life in Jerusalem. (Isa 4:2-3)

80. Isa 1:4; 5:19, 24; 10:20; 12:6; 17:7; 29:19; 30:11, 12, 15; 31:1; 37:23 (= 2 Kgs 19:22); 41:14, 16, 20; 43:3, 14; 45:11; 47:4; 48:17; 49:7; 54:5; 55:5; 60:9, 14. Similar titles appear fairly often in postbiblical texts inclusive of Qumran, e.g., *qěddîšā' rabbā',* "the Great Holy One," in the Genesis Apocryphon (1QGenApoc II 14; VI 15 etc.) and the Book of Giants (4Q530 II 17).

81. Rudolph Otto, *The Idea of the Holy* (1923; 2nd ed., London: Oxford University Press, 1950).

We see how redundantly the idea of the holy remnant is expressed in this text from some time in the Persian period, including "the shoot that Yahveh has planted," a figure which will be seized on by the author of the Damascus Document.[82] Another example is the scribal note at the end of Isaiah's throne room vision which identifies the stump of the felled tree, symbolizing all that remains of the people, with the "holy seed" (*zera' qōdeš*, Isa 6:13). Ezra 9:2, where the same expression is used of Ezra's Judeo-Babylonian compatriots, the *běnê haggôlâ*, segregated from the local inhabitants, provides an essential clue to the source of the gloss.

Another scribal addendum speaks of a group of penitents who will become the nucleus of a new people. It begins: "On that day the residue of Israel and the survivors of the household of Jacob . . . will rely in truth on Yahveh the Holy One of Israel" and goes on to predict that, even if Israelites were as numerous as the sand on the seashore, only a remnant of them would survive the judgment to come (Isa 10:20-23). The allusion to a people as numerous as the sand on the seashore once again reveals the subtext of the Abrahamic blessing (cf. Gen 12:1-3; 22:17; 32:13 [Eng. 12]). Who are and who are not children of Abraham will become a major focus of debate in the late Second Temple period inclusive of early Christianity (John 8:31-40; Rom 9:7; Gal 3:6-14).

Angels are also referred to as "holy ones," especially in poetic compositions. The proem to Moses' blessings on the tribes (Deut 33:2-3) presents Yahveh coming forth from Sinai accompanied by "myriads of holy ones," and the same scenario is reproduced in Zech 14:5 ("Yahveh will come, and all the holy ones with him"). The image continued to impress those with visionary propensities in the late Second Temple period.[83] These "holy ones" no doubt belong to the same category as the seraphs of Isaiah's vision[84] and the living creatures of Ezekiel's chariot throne vision. In Ps 89:6 (Eng. 5), likewise, Yahveh is praised in "the assembly of the holy ones," also referred to as "divine beings" (*běnê 'ēlîm*). The sages are familiar with

---

82. CD I 7-8; 1QH[a] XIV 15; XV 19; XVI 10.

83. E.g., the 10 myriads (millions?) of holy ones who accompany Yahveh in *1 En.* 1:9; see also *1 En* 14:22-23; 4Q204 I 15 (4QEnoch[a] Aramaic).

84. The term *śārāp* is related to a verbal stem meaning "to burn" and is also a word for a serpent, perhaps on account of the effect of the serpent's bite. The *Syriac Apocalypse of Baruch* (2 Bar 21:6) speaks of countless holy ones who are flame and fire, and 2 En 29:3 records that the hosts of heaven, the stars, the cherubim, seraphim, and ophannim (the wheels in Ezekiel's vision) were created from fire.

these heavenly "holy ones" (Job 5:1; 15:15), though Agur ben Yakeh (if that is his name) disclaims any knowledge of them (Prov 30:3).

Beginning with Ezekiel and Zechariah, prophetic visions become more interactive, with angelic figures in the vision interpreting what is going on and answering questions. In the Danielic vision of the Ram and the Goat, the seer overhears a conversation between two "holy ones" from which he ascertains how much time must elapse before the rededication of the temple (Dan 8:13). In Nebuchadnezzar's second dream, the dream of the great tree, the king sees a "holy watcher" (*'îr wĕqaddîš*, hendiadys) descending from the sky followed by judgment passed on the king by the "holy ones" (Dan 4:14 [Eng. 17]). These beings intermediate between God and humanity and are frequently active in postbiblical writings including the Qumran texts.[85] In the latter, these "holy ones" are also known as "sons of heaven," "holy ones of heaven," "luminaries" *(mē'ôrôt)*, and "divinities" *('ēlîm)*; the list is not exhaustive. In these texts there is the same intense interactivity as in the narratives and visions in Daniel. The member who has not lived up to the standards of "the men of holiness" must be shunned, since "all the Holy Ones of the Most High have cursed him" (CD XX 8). A similar situation is described in the strange hymn sung by Eliphaz and directed against Elihu in *The Testament of Job* which declares that "the Holy Ones have abandoned him" (43:10). In the Messianic Rule (1QS^a II 3-9), those with physical defects are excluded from the assembly "since the angels of holiness are among their congregation," a (to us) curious criterion for participation reminiscent of Paul's disposition about women covering their heads in the assembly "on account of the angels" (1 Cor 11:10).

The first Christians inherited the same belief in angelic beings, though there is perhaps only one instance in the New Testament where the term "holy ones" occurs as a title with reference to angels: this is where Jude 14, drawing on *1 En* 1:9, assures his readers that the Lord will come accompanied by "myriads of his holy ones" *(en hagiais muriasin autou)*. Elsewhere in the New Testament holy angels serve as escort for the second coming of Jesus (Mark 8:38 = Luke 9:26; 1 Thess 3:13). They also fulfill the

---

85. Among the numerous examples in texts other than Qumranic, see Sir 42:17; 45:2; Wis 5:5; *Pss Sol* 17:43; *T Job* 33:2; 43:10, 14-15; *2 Bar* 21:6; *Jub* 17:11; 31:14; 33:12; and the numerous references to "Holy Ones" and "Watchers" in the Enoch literature. The subject is dealt with recently by M. J. Davidson, *Angels at Qumran: A Comparative Study of 1 Enoch 1–36, 72–108 and Sectarian Writings from Qumran.* JSPSup 11 (Sheffield: Sheffield Academic, 1992).

traditional role of messengers (Acts 10:22) and interpret what is happening in visions (Rev 14:6-13).

The term *qādôš* (Aram. *qaddîš*) is therefore used as a title with reference to God and to intermediate spiritual beings in the Hebrew Bible, the Qumran texts, and the New Testament. The question must now be asked whether it also serves as a title or rubric without further qualification with reference to either Israel as a whole or a particular social entity within Israel. It seems that there is clear biblical attestation for this titular usage only in Ps 34:10 (Eng. 9)[86] and in the Danielic vision of the Ancient of Days and the Son of Man (Dan 7). The "holy ones" of Psalm 34 are urged to fear Yahveh, for nothing is lacking to those who do so. The high concentration of vocabulary characteristic of religious conventicles in this psalm, including such terms as "the humble" (*ʿănāwîm*, v. 3), "the poor" (*ʿānî*, v. 7), "the servants of Yahveh" (*ʿăbādâw*, v. 23), and, most frequently, "the righteous" (*ṣaddîqîm*, vv. 16, 18 LXX, 20, 22), raises the possibility that those addressed form a distinct cult group. In Daniel 7 the context favors the view that "the one like a human being," in contrast to the four beasts who came up out of the primeval ocean, represents "the people of the holy ones of the Most High" (v. 27). The alternative view, that "the Son of Man" is Michael the archangel, "the Holy Ones of the Most High" are angelic beings, and "the people of the Holy Ones of the Most High" are the righteous associated with the angels, does not make the best fit with the context. The Horn (Antiochus IV) may have waged war against angelic beings, but it is unlikely that he would have worn them out (Dan 7:21, 25). Moreover, judgment is given in favor of these Holy Ones, and they receive the kingdom promised to them, which would more naturally refer to human rather than angelic recipients.[87] Though no doubt allied with angelic beings, therefore, these "Holy Ones" are the members of the pietistic group to which the writer belongs and for whom the visions were written.

In the Qumran sectarian texts the "holy ones" are generally angelic beings, but it is going beyond the evidence to conclude that "there is no undisputed case in this literature. . . where the expression 'holy ones' in itself refers to human beings."[88] That God performs wonders with "the holy

---

86. Ps 16:3 *liqdôšîm ʾăšer-bāʾāreṣ* ("as for the holy ones who are in the land/on the earth") is textually uncertain.

87. Pace John J. Collins, *Daniel*, 316.

88. Collins, *Daniel*, 316. Bauckham, "The Early Jerusalem Church, Qumran, and the Essenes," 80-81, is inclined to agree, with the exception of the three occurrences of the phrase "the holy ones of his people."

ones of his people" (1QM VI 6; XVI 1) would more naturally refer to God's *human* people, and this must be so where "holy ones" are distinguished from angels:

> Who is like you, God of Israel . . . ? Who performs deeds like your great deeds and mighty feats like yours? Who is like your people Israel . . . a people of holy ones of the covenant, learned in the law, wise in knowledge, who hear the glorious voice and see the holy angels? (1QM X 8-11)

In the War Scroll, moreover, "the holy ones" occupy camps (1QM III 5), which would be unusual for angels.

In early Christian writings the holy angels fill their accustomed roles of messengers and interactive interpreters of prophetic visions (Rev 14:6-13). As a title, however, *hagioi* ("holy ones") refers to angelic beings only rarely, when they function as escort for the parousia (1 Thess 3:13; Jude 14). On the other hand, and in striking contrast to Qumran, Christians refer to themselves frequently by this title.[89] As an appellative it is especially in evidence in the salutations at the beginning of epistles and in the exchange of greetings at the end, sometimes in combination with other titles such as "the elect" or "the faithful" (e.g., Rom 1:7; Col 1:2; 3:12). It seems to have been used initially with reference to the primitive Jewish-Christian community in Jerusalem. Paul speaks of the harm he had done to the saints in Jerusalem (Acts 9:13; 26:10) and made up for it by assiduous efforts to meet their material needs (Rom 15:25-26, etc.). From Jerusalem the designation spread outward into other Christian assemblies. Needless to add that the same sobriquet continued in use throughout Christian history, for example among Cromwell's adherents and with the Puritan signatories to the Mayflower Compact.

Several explanations for the frequency of the designation "holy ones" *(hagioi)* in early Christianity are on offer. The suggestion that it reflects the Isaianic processional way to Jerusalem, the "holy way" of Isa 35:8, is suggestive in view of the overwhelming importance of Isaianic themes for early Christian self-understanding. This association could easily have come to mind, but more likely as one aspect of the holiness theme expressed so often and in many different ways in Isaiah, for example "the holy remnant" (Isa 4:3; 6:13). The "Holy Ones of the Most High" of Daniel 7 would also

---

89. In addition to numerous examples in the Epistles, Acts, and Revelation, see also Ignatius *Smyrna* 1:2; Hermas I 19, 32; *Ascen Isa* 4:13, 14, 16.

have been a factor. The appellative cannot be dissociated from the intense eschatological expectations in the early period. As *hagioi*, the first disciples anticipate the Parousia, when Jesus will return accompanied by all his holy ones (1 Thess 3:13, etc.), at which time they are destined to sit in judgment on a sinful world (1 Cor 6:2).

As to why the first Christians referred to themselves as "the holy ones" or "the saints" and the Qumran sectarians generally did not, we can only speculate. Perhaps among the latter the term had already been preempted by angelic beings with whom the members had a particularly close affinity in their assemblies. In early Christianity the title could reflect the link between the Danielic Son of Man, an expression appropriated by Jesus, and "the Holy Ones of the Most High" understood as the people to whom the kingdom is promised.

The Poor

In prophetic texts and psalms, the language of indigence, marginality, and low status tends to overlap with the language of piety and devotion, thereby taking on a religious aura. Amos, for example, speaks of the righteous and the needy as victims of oppression, as if the two terms were practically synonymous (Amos 2:6). The liturgical hymns often contrast the needy (*'ebyônîm, dallîm*) and afflicted (*'ănāwîm, 'aniyyîm*) with the reprobate (*rĕšā'îm*) and proclaim the God of Israel's predilection for the poor.[90] It is therefore not always easy to decide whether the relevant terms refer simply to economic and social status or whether they are being applied, by extension, to the devout minority and, in the latter case, whether the ones so designated form a specific subgroup or conventicle of the devout within the community as a whole. We can rarely be sure, but we can suspect that this is so where congregational language occurs. Psalm 1 speaks of the "congregation of the righteous" from which the reprobate are excluded, and in Psalm 149 the praises of God are sung in the "assembly of the devout." In Ps 14:5-6 we are told that God is with "the company of the

90. Ps 9:12-13, 18-19 (Eng. 11-12, 17-18); 10:2, 9-10; 12:6 (5); 18:28 (27); 25:9; 149:4. In translating these terms for the poor, needy, afflicted, etc., we should allow for some indeterminacy. See G. Johannes Botterweck, "*'ebyôn ['ebhyôn]*," *TDOT* 1:27-41; Heinz-Josef Fabry, "*dal*," *TDOT* 3:208-30.

righteous" and that Yahveh is a refuge for "the council of the poor" (*'ăṣat-*
'ānî). In Ps 22:26-27 (Eng. 25-26) the psalmist's commitment to praising
God and fulfilling his vows "in the great assembly" is reinforced by the assurance that "the poor (*'ănāwîm*) will eat and be satisfied, those who seek
God will praise Yahveh." The speaker who identifies himself as "poor and
needy" (*'ānî wě'ebyôn*, v. 22) in Psalm 109 complains that his opponent
pursues the poor, the needy, and the broken-spirited (v. 16). The psalmist
concludes with an assurance of divine assistance common in this type of
psalm:

> With my mouth I will give Yahveh abundant thanks,
> In the midst of the Many I will praise him,
> for he stands at the right hand of the needy. (109:30-31)

Much of what these psalms have to say about the righteous poor is
replicated in Isaiah. In Isaiah no less than in Psalms, the cause of the poor
is pleaded and it is the duty of those in power to defend the rights of those
of low social and economic status.[91] A prominent theme in both Psalms
and Isaiah is the assurance that the righteous poor will possess the land. In
one of the many pronouncements against hostile neighbors in Isaiah the
assurance is given that, once Yahveh has established Zion, "the afflicted
among his people (*'ăniyyê 'ammô*) will find refuge there" (Isa 14:32). The
theme is heard more insistently in the last section of the book (chs. 56–66),
except that now it can no longer be taken for granted that those addressed
or spoken of as the poor, the afflicted, the elect, those who take refuge in
Yahveh, are the people of Israel as a whole. The imprecatory Psalm 37, one
of several acrostic psalms, is closely parallel. In this composition the contrast between the reprobate on the one side and the poor and needy (v. 14)
on the other is thematic throughout, and it is stated with equal frequency
that it is the latter who will inherit the land. The same theme is taken up by
the author of the Qumran Psalms pesher, who assures "the congregation
of the poor," that is, the congregation to which the writer belongs, that it is
they who will possess the land.[92]

One of three brief thanksgiving psalms in Isaiah 24–27 (the so-called

---

91. For the ruler as protector of the rights of the poor, see Isa 11:4; cf. Ps 72:2-4, 12-13.

92. 4Q171 (4QpPs^a) II 9 on Ps 37:11 and II 16-20 on Ps 37:14-15. The expression "the
congregation of the poor" (*'ădat 'ebyônîm*) occurs also at 4Q171 III 10, cf. *'ăṣat 'ebyônîm* in
4Q491^c (Self-Glorification Hymn) fr. 1 3-4.

"Isaian Apocalypse") speaks of the triumph of the oppressed and the poor (*'ānî, dallîm*) and commands that the gates of the city be thrown open that a righteous people may enter (Isa 26:1-6). The wording is close to that of the processional psalms, and especially to Ps 118:19-20 discussed earlier in the chapter. It was suggested there that verse 20 ("This is the gate of Yahveh, the righteous shall enter through it") serves to explain the command to open the gates, presumably the gates leading to the temple. At any rate, the Qumran Psalms commentator reinterpreted the passage to refer to entrance into the symbolic temple, namely, the community of the righteous, the community to which the interpreter himself belonged (4QPs^b fr. 5).

In both Qumran and early Christianity the poor, in the fuller sense attested in Isaiah and Psalms, are the recipients and beneficiaries of the good news anticipated for the messianic age. According to the Messianic Apocalypse (4Q521), the spirit of God's Anointed "will hover over the poor," and the Lord "will heal the wounded, bring the dead back to life, and proclaim good news to the poor" (fr. 2 II 6, 12). This prediction corresponds to what the gospels represent as actually taking place in the ministry of Jesus: the blind see, the lame walk, lepers are cleansed, the deaf hear, the dead are raised, and the poor have the good news proclaimed to them (Matt 11:5; Luke 7:22). Both Qumran and the gospels are enacting a persistent Isaianic theme, and both are claiming to fulfill the mission of the prophetic messenger in Isa 61:1-3, who is anointed and commissioned to announce good news to the poor.

In this vision of the future the poor certainly include those of low economic and social status, but the Qumran sectarians took over the fuller and more explicitly religious connotation of the term and applied it to themselves. The author of the *Hodayot* refers to himself as God's poor one,[93] and speaks of the members of the *yaḥad* as "the poor of lovingkindness," if that is the proper translation of *'ebyônê ḥesed* (1QH^a XIII 22). Elsewhere, the sectarians are referred to as "the poor redeemed by God" (1QM XI 9, 13; XIII 13-14), and the author of the Damascus Document speaks of them as "the poor ones of the flock," a term borrowed from Zech 11:11 (CD XIX 9). The expression "the poor in spirit" (*'ăniyyê rûaḥ*, 1QH^a VI 3; 1QM XIV 7) is somewhat ambiguous, but probably refers to the humble demeanor of one oppressed by hostile forces or adverse circumstances rather than detachment from the goods of this world, what might

93. 1QH^a X 32; XI 25; XIII 16, 18.

be called spiritual poverty. The same would probably be true of the "poor in spirit" *(ptōchoi tō pneumati)* of the gospel Beatitudes (Matt 5:3; cf. Luke 6:20, which omits the qualifier).

The history of Western Christianity in the Middle Ages, and for some time afterwards, provides many examples of sectarian movements recruited from among the poor, movements such as the Franciscan Spirituals, the Beghards, and the Brethren of the Free Spirit. The fact that these groups claimed to reproduce the evangelical poverty of the first Christians did not exempt them from suspicion of heresy and active persecution. What we know or can reasonably surmise about the social situation of the Jesus movement and the first generation of Christians suggests that they were drawn more from the artisan and professional classes than from the indigent and socially marginal. At any rate, they did not refer to themselves as "the poor" *(hoi ptōchoi)*, and we have just seen that the "poverty of spirit" of the first beatitude (Matt 5:3) refers to a situation which, like mourning, hunger, thirst, and subjection to persecution, must be and will be abolished. The involuntary poverty of the Jerusalem church, the alleviation of which called for special measures (Rom 15:26; Gal 2:9-10), was something quite different.[94]

The Penitents

Christian ideas about penitence include both repudiation of past sin and a firm purpose of amendment, but the emphasis tends to be more on the past than the present and the future. The verbs used in early Christian writings, *metanoein* and *epistrephein*, do not exclude regret for the past but connote more directly a change in the direction of one's life in the present, a turning one's life around. The Hebrew verb *šûb* (usually "turn," "return") and the corresponding substantive *tĕšûbâ* (in Mishnaic and Modern but not Classical Hebrew with this meaning) convey the idea of changing direction, getting on to the right way, perhaps by retracing one's steps in order to find the right way from which one has departed.

In the most obvious and direct sense, to repent, is to turn to or re-

---

94. On the different social and economic strata in early Christian communities, see the discussion by Ekkehard W. Stegemann and Wolfgang Stegemann, *The Jesus Movement: A Social History of Its First Century* (Minneapolis: Fortress, 1999), 303-16.

turn to God, and with this meaning it occurs often in prophetic texts including Isaiah.[95] When it is used of the people as a whole, returning to God is more often than not associated with returning from exile. The "Moses" of Deuteronomy, for example, predicts that Israelites exiled as a result of sin will return to Yahveh (Deut 4:30; 30:1-3). Here as elsewhere the ambivalence of the verb *šûb* allows for a combination of the people's return to God (repentance) with the prospect of a return to the land and a restoration to be brought about by God. God will restore their fortunes and will do so by enabling their return to the land — "Your God will once again restore your fortunes" (*wĕšāb 'ĕlohêkā 'et-šĕbûtkâ*, Deut 30:3). This phrase, *šûb šĕbût*, combines the prospect of return from exile with the idea of a change in fortune in general. There is also in the background the need for "turning," repentance, as a necessary precondition for this change to take place.[96]

A further linguistic complication arises from the similar verbal stem *šbh*, "take captive," with the associated substantive *šĕbî*, "captivity." In Ezra-Nehemiah the latter can stand, either by itself or with *haggôlâ*, for the Diaspora, perhaps an abbreviation of "those who came from the captivity" (*habbā'îm mēhaššĕbî*).[97] Wherever the Qumran texts speak about the past, it is evident that the exile and return constitute the defining moment in the history of Israel. However, lack of vowel markers in these texts leaves some uncertainty as to whether at certain places we should read *šĕbî yiśrā'ēl* ("the captivity of Israel") or *šābê yiśrā'ēl* ("the penitents of Israel," "the 'returnees' of Israel").[98]

Two Isaianic texts, both from a late stage in the history of the formation of the book, were of special interest to the Qumran sectarians. The final stanza of the first poem in the book, a radical repudiation of contemporary Judean society, begins as follows:

---

95. Isa 9:12 (Eng. 13); 19:22; 31:6; 44:22; 55:7.

96. The expression is used with reference to exile and return in Amos 9:14; Zeph 3:20, and often in Jeremiah, while a psalmist prays to Yahveh to "bring about our restoration" (*šûbâ YHVH 'et-šĕbûtēnû*, Ps 126:4). The more general sense of restoration is not confined to Israel. Jer 48:47; 49:6, 39; Ezek 29:14, e.g., refer to the future restoration of neighboring countries including Egypt. However, *šĕbût* is not attested in Biblical Hebrew with the meaning "conversion," but it has this meaning in the Qumran Community Rule, which requires full and unqualified conversion (*šĕbût*) for acceptance into the group (1QS III 3).

97. Ezra 2:1; 3:8; 8:35; Neh 1:2-3; 7:6; 8:17.

98. See above p. 115n.46.

> Zion will be saved in the judgment,
> her penitents *(šābîm)* in the retribution,
> but rebels and sinners will be destroyed together,
> those forsaking Yahveh will be consumed. (1:27-28)

Most critical commentators agree that this stanza (1:27-31) comes from a time in the postdestruction period when the received Isaianic tradition was being remodeled and reshaped in accord with a pietistic and quasi-sectarian perspective. It also makes a kind of inclusion with the last chapters of the book, in which the contrast between the penitents on the one side and rebels and sinners on the other is a central theme. The other text is from this last section, where it concludes a passage describing the final intervention of Yahveh in judgment and salvation:

> He will come to Zion as Redeemer
> for those in Jacob who turn from transgression. (59:20)

"Those who turn from transgression" *(šābê pešaʿ)*, that is, the true penitents, comprise the few who will experience redemption when that day comes. Both texts express a strong polarity between these *šābîm* and the reprobate majority. We do not know whether, in referring to these true penitents, the speaker had in mind a distinct, segregated group, but it is of interest to note that 59:20 is followed immediately by an assurance addressed to an individual seer that the prophetic spirit-endowment and the gift of inspired utterance will remain with him and his disciples:

> As for me, this is my covenant with them, declares Yahveh: my spirit that rests upon you and my words that I have put in your mouth will not be absent from your mouth, or from the mouths of your descendants, or from those of the descendants of your descendants, from this time forward and for evermore. (59:21)

These texts would have resonated among the Qumran sectarians since they saw themselves as a penitential group, those who had turned from transgression,[99] in stark contrast to the unregenerate majority, and the descendants of those first survivors of the exile who returned to the land and segregated themselves from its inhabitants. An obscure allusion

---

99. CD II 5 = 4Q266 2 II 5; XX 17; 1QS I 17; X 20; 1QH^a VI 24; X 9; XIV 6.

in the Damascus Document refers to Zadokite priests who are "the penitents of Israel *(šābê yiśrā'ēl)* who left the land of Judah" (CD IV 2-3). In the midrash on the poem in Num 21:18 about digging a well in the desert, the well stands for the law and the diggers are the penitents of Israel who left the land of Judah and sojourned in the land of Damascus (CD VI 3-7). Digging a well to get access to living water is an appropriate and telling metaphor for study of the law, a representation which corresponds to the interpretation of Isa 40:3 in the Community Rule, according to which the way of Yahveh is to be prepared by study of the law (1QS VIII 13-14). Both these texts are referring obliquely to the founding of the self-segregating desert community.

Elsewhere in the Damascus Document we hear that these same "penitents of Israel" turned aside from the way of this people, following the example of Isaiah: "Yahveh warned me against walking in the way of this people" (CD VIII 16).[100] We conclude from these scattered references in the texts that the designation "penitents" *(šābîm)* was appropriated by the dissident, self-segregating group which settled eventually at Qumran, which saw itself as in direct line of descent from those few who survived the Babylonian exile with their faith intact and returned to Judah (the alternative meaning of the verb), and which formed around a core of Zadokite priests.[101] The same identification is implied in the sectarian commentary on Isa 10:20-23, which itself contains a comment on Shear-yashub, the name of Isaiah's son (7:3), and which speaks about the few who constitute the remnant or residue of Jacob who will return from exile to the God of Might.

The designation "Penitents" is not attested in early Christian texts, perhaps because of the lack of an appropriate Greek term corresponding to Hebrew *šābîm*. But the necessity of a radical change in spiritual and moral orientation *(metanoia)* is a central theme in early Christian preaching as it is in the message of Jesus. In this respect, early Christianity took over the message of the Baptist both in its substance and in its eschatologi-

---

100. A literal translation of Isa 8:11. In 4QFlorilegium (1 I 14-17) those who heed the warning are identified with the Zadokites of Ezek 44:15.

101. The alternative meaning "return" is more directly expressed in the phrase *šābê hammidbār* ("the 'returnees' of the wilderness") in the pesher on Ps 37:19 (4Q171 1 + 3-4 III 1); cf. "When they return from the wilderness of the peoples" *(běšûbām mimmidbār ha'ammîm,* 4Q161 5-6.2). The priestly character of these "penitents" and "returnees" is further evidenced in the identification of the *šābîm* with Korahite Levites in 4Q171 3-10 IV 24.

cal motivation (Matt 3:2, 8, 11). It also took over from the Baptist the practice of immersion in water as symbolic of the change of life implied by
metanoia (Matt 3:11). The function of the rite was different in early Christianity since it was exclusively a rite of initiation into a community, signifying a fundamental change of status, and we note at several points a concern to emphasize the difference.[102] While certainty is beyond our reach,
an original connection between the early Christian baptismal rite and the
Qumranic rite of immersion in "the waters of purification" and in "seas
and rivers," mediated through John the Baptist, seems plausible at least in
the sense that both were, if in different ways, "for the forgiveness of
sins."[103]

The Mourners

In ancient Israel, as in other societies, mourning the dead was governed by
convention with respect to place, time, and expression. The closer the relationship, the more intense the expression, the most intense being the
mourning for close relatives (Ps 35:14) and, among relatives, for an only
son (Amos 8:10; Zech 12:10). The survivors would congregate in the "house
of mourning" (Jer 16:5; Qoh 7:2, 4) and there would be a mortuary meal
(Jer 16:7) during which the deceased would be commemorated. The period
of mourning seems to have been variable. In contemporary Judaism shiva
lasts seven days, the same as the mourning for Jacob (Gen 50:10). Moses,
the preeminent figure in the tradition, was mourned for 30 days (Deut
34:8). During that period it was customary to exhibit visible signs of distress, including a dishevelled appearance, torn garments, and ashes sprinkled on the head, as is still customary for the *avel* in Jewish mourning ritual. Fasting invariably accompanied these mourning rites. One also

---

102. In the disavowals of the Baptist himself (Matt 3:11 and par.), the prologue to the
Fourth Gospel (John 1:6-9), and the encounter with the disciples of Apollos at Ephesus who
knew only the baptism of John (Acts 18:24–19:6).

103. See esp. 1QS III 4-5, 9; also 4Q255 2.4; 4Q512 1-6.4. 1 QS III 4-5 refers to sanctifica-
tion in seas and rivers, which suggests immersion rather than sprinkling, and 1QS III 9 refers
to *mê dôkî*, "waters of purification" or "waters of repentance," the latter according to
Florentino García Martínez and Eibert Tigchelaar, *The Dead Sea Scrolls Study Edition*, 1:75.
The Qumran immersion rite should be distinguished from the occasional purification rites
of a ritual nature in the fragmentary text 4Q512 (4QRitual of Purification B).

mourned after a natural disaster (famine, drought, locusts) or some other grave misfortune or with the purpose of obviating an anticipated disaster.

After the fall of Jerusalem and the deportations, mourning and fasting rites became one aspect of a strongly emphasized penitential piety and a regular feature on the liturgical calendar. Fasts in the fourth, fifth, seventh, and tenth months commemorated successive stages in the disaster of the Babylonian conquest from the beginning of the siege to the assassination of the local administrator Gedaliah (Zech 7:1-7; 8:18-19). In the course of time only the fast of Yom Kippur survived (Lev 16:29) together with the festival of Tishe b'Av commemorating the fall of Jerusalem to both Babylonians and Romans. But in the postdestruction period we see the beginnings of a transformation from an occasional, ad hoc practice to a more generalized type of penitential piety which found expression in psalms of communal lament and confessional prayer, generally accompanied by fasting. Isaiah 58:1-14, for example, reads like an interactive homily on genuine fasting and piety. On hearing the news about Judeo-Babylonians intermarrying with local women, Ezra kept a night-long vigil in the temple, fasting and mourning the faithlessness of his colleagues (Ezra 10:6). On hearing bad news from Judah, Nehemiah in distant Susa sat down, wept, and went into mourning for days, during which he fasted and prayed (Neh 1:4). In due course this type of piety came to be characteristic of the sects of the late Second Temple period, perhaps also in the expectation that fasting prepared one for a vision or other extraordinary religious experience. Daniel, for example, had his vision by the Tigris River after a three-week period of fasting and mourning (Dan 10:2-4).

Mourning as a *modus vivendi,* a way of being in the world, was characteristic of prophetic disciples and associations of the devout long before the time of Daniel. In the last section of the book of Isaiah (chs. 56–66) we hear the term "mourners" (*'ăbēlîm, mit'abbēlîm*) used as a descriptive designation with reference to a specific group in Judah. Here and elsewhere (e.g., Isa 57:14-19) mourning is a reaction to the anger, or the silence, or the hiddenness of God. It is the appropriate response in a time of Godforsakenness. Those who mourn are those among the people who are contrite and obedient, those who "wait for God," another Isaianic expression. They do not as yet form a self-segregating group, but we see that some of the conditions for the formation of such groups are already in place.

Mourning also describes the attitude of those who live in the expectation of the final intervention of God in human affairs, when their mourning will be changed to rejoicing. This typically sectarian theme of eschatological reversal is prominent in the final chapters of Isaiah (65:13-14; 66:5, 10-11) and in the penultimate passage in Malachi discussed earlier (Mal 3:13-18). Here the devout complain that God makes no difference between the righteous and the reprobate and ask rhetorically "what good does it do us when we observe his charge and live a penitential life?" (hālaknû qĕdōrannît).[104] They are then reassured that they will be, and will be seen to be, God's special possession on judgment day. At this point we are not far removed from the eschatological dualism of the Qumran sects.

Neither the Qumran sectarian writings nor the New Testament employ the designation "mourners" as it occurs in Isaiah 65–66, but both hold out the promise of a transition from a state of mourning to one of eschatological rejoicing. A sectarian text (4Q177 = 4QCatena A III 8) speaks of a presumably permanent state of mourning for the children of light during the dominion of Belial, while another (4Q417 = 4QInstruction^c fr. 1 I 12) urges the members to bear in mind the everlasting joy to come in place of present mourning. In interpreting Hos 2:13 (Eng. 11) ("I will bring all her rejoicing to an end"), 4QpHos^a II 17 paraphrases: "Their joy will be changed into mourning." The same assurance of a reversal will be familiar to readers of the New Testament. The Epistle of James abjures sinners to mourn and weep while assuring them that their laughter will be turned to mourning (Jas 4:8-9). In his farewell talk, Jesus reminds his disciples that "you will weep and mourn, but the world will rejoice; you will have pain, but your pain will be turned into joy" (John 16:20). This assurance is reinforced with the image of a childbearing woman (16:21), a borrowing from Isaiah 65–66, where the image of the joyful birth of children to mother Zion follows assurances addressed to Yahveh's servants and those who tremble at his word (Isa 66:7-11). The Isaianic pronouncement about the change of fortune in store for the opponents of the servants of Yahveh (65:13-14) is even more clearly reflected in the gospel Beatitudes (Matt 5:3-12), which in one of the versions (Luke 6:20-26) are followed by woes. Here too, the contrast is stated programmatically: "Blessed are those who mourn, for they will be comforted" (Matt 5:4); "Woe to you who laugh now, for you will mourn and weep" (Luke 6:25).

---

104. The adverb qĕdōrannît is hapax but related to the verb qdr, meaning "to darken"; cf. Ezek 31:15, where wā'aqdīr (Hiphil) means "I obscure," in the context "I cause (Lebanon) to mourn."

The Devout

The lament for a dead *ṣaddîq* in Isa 57:1, with whom certain *'anšê ḥesed* ("devout") were associated, was noted earlier:

> The Righteous One has perished, and no one takes it to heart;
> the devout are swept away, and no one gives it a thought. (57:1)

The designation *ḥāsîd* does not occur in Isaiah, but since *'anšê ḥesed* is synonymous with *ḥăsîdîm*, and since this designation becomes a standard way of referring to self-segregating pietistic groups in late antiquity, a brief note is in order. In normal Jewish usage the *ḥāsîd* is a person of exemplary piety *(ḥăsîdût)*, a member of a group dedicated wholeheartedly to Torah observance and with its own distinctive religious practices. The "First Hasidim" *(ḥăsîdîm ri'šōnîm)*, often mentioned in Jewish sources,[105] were those virtuosos of piety like the great Hillel, some of whom in addition worked miracles like Honi the Circle-Drawer and Hanina ben Dosa. In the Hebrew Bible the term is one of a cluster of epithets for religiously faithful Israelites as opposed to the irreligious, ungodly, and unfaithful. As such, the frequency of its occurrence in Psalms is exceeded only by the closely related terms "Servants of the Lord" *('abdê YHVH)* and "Righteous" *(ṣaddîqîm)*.

For the most part, there is no suggestion that this is more than a conventional way of referring to the true devotees of Yahveh. But here and there we find indications of a more polarized situation, one which points forward to the "Hasidic" groups which emerge into the clear light of day in the late Second Temple period. The polarization is in evidence where a sharp distinction is made between the devout and the reprobate (e.g., Ps 1, 37, 52) or where the death of the *ḥāsîd* is mentioned, as it is in Isa 57:1-2.[106] Psalm 149 is especially intriguing in this respect. The praises of God are sung "in the congregation of the devout" *(biqěhal ḥăsîdîm, v. 1)*, this devout company exults and sings for joy on their couches (v. 5), and they visit judgment on their enemies thus winning glory for themselves (v. 9). It may not be coincidental that *ḥăsîdîm* are named at the beginning, the end, and

---

105. E.g., *m. Ber.* 5:1; *b. Ned.* 10a; *b. Men.* 40b-51a.

106. Ps 79:2-3, which speaks of the desecration of Jerusalem and the violent death of God's servants and devotees *(ḥăsîdîm)*, is cited in 1 Macc 7:17 in connection with the treacherous murder of a group of Asideans *(sunagōgē asidaiōn)*. It is not out of the question that it comes from so late a time.

the exact center of this brief psalm. They identify themselves with Israel, and they combine the psalmodic praise of God with a warlike posture, having two-edged swords in their hands ready for use. About the social background of this psalm we can only speculate, but we should not discount the possibility that it derives from a "Hasidic" group of the kind which for a time fought alongside the Maccabees, including the *asidaioi* of 1 Macc 2:42, who are described as "mighty warriors of Israel." It may also at one stage have served as the excipit to the collection corresponding to Psalm 1 as its incipit.

Echoes of Psalm 149 can be heard in some of the Qumran apocryphal psalms. In 11Q5 XVIII (Syriac Psalm II), we are told that "her (Zion's) voice is heard from the gates of the righteous and her singing from the congregation of the devout." The psalm goes on to speak of these devout ones banqueting and meditating on the law of the Most High, reminiscent of the devout singing for joy on their couches in Psalm 149. Other psalms in the same collection (XIX 7-8; XXII 3-6) assign high status to the *ḥăsîdîm*.

One of several proposed etymologies for the title "Essene" derives it from *ḥasyā* (plural *ḥăsayyāʾ*), the Aramaic equivalent of Hebrew *ḥāsîd*, *ḥăsîdîm*, a proposal which is consonant with Philo and Josephus, both of whom associate the title "Essene" with *hosioi*, the LXX translation word for *ḥăsîdîm*.[107] If this is correct, it would reinforce the connection between the Essenes and the *asidaioi* of 1-2 Maccabees, perhaps in the sense that the Essenes developed out of a "Hasidic" conventicle of the kind referred to directly in 1-2 Maccabees and indirectly in other texts. One of the *Psalms of Solomon* alludes to conventicles of the devout *(sunagōgai hosiōn)* taking refuge in the wilderness to segregate themselves from evil *(Pss Sol* 17:16).

In the Qumran sectarian writings the devout, together with the righteous, the poor, the faithful — all of which terms designate members of the sect — are among those who will participate joyfully in the final coming of God in judgment and salvation. According to 4QMessianic Apocalypse (4Q521 2 II 5), at the end of days the *ḥăsîdîm* will sit on the throne of an everlasting kingdom. The implied scenario is an act of judgment, and it

---

107. For this derivation, see J. T. Milik, *Ten Years of Discovery in the Wilderness of Judaea* (London: SCM, 1959), 80-81; Frank Moore Cross, *The Ancient Library of Qumran*, 54; and for alternative proposals, see Todd S. Beall, "Essenes," in *EDSS* 1:262-69. On the ancient authors mentioned, see Philo *Good Person* 12:75; 13:91; and Josephus *War* 2:119.

brings to mind the sectarian commentary on Hab 1:13, according to which God will assign the final judgment to his chosen ones (1QpHab V 5). It also recalls the promise of Jesus to his disciples that they would sit on 12 thrones judging the 12 tribes of Israel (Matt 19:28).

Like the Qumran sectarians, the first Christians read the psalms as composed by David "through (the spirit of) prophecy given to him from the presence of the Most High" (11QPs XXVII 11). This made it possible to argue that the *ḥāsîd* of Ps 16:10 referred prophetically not to David but to Jesus himself (Acts 2:27; 13:35). Jesus is also given this title by virtue of his status as eternal high priest (Heb 7:26) and is acclaimed under the same title by martyrs and angels (Rev 15:4; 16:5). While *hosiotēs* ("devotion," "holiness of life") is often inculcated (e.g., Titus 1:8), this language is not particularly prominent in early Christian writings, and *hosioi* was not adopted as a descriptive title or label among the first Christians. Each of these titles represents a facet of the religious identity of the Qumran sects and early Christians as viewed from within. Taken together, they reproduce on a smaller scale organizational features of the parent body (congregation, assembly, community).

CHAPTER 7

Exile in the Interpretation of Isaiah

The Prophetic Idea of the "Remnant of Israel"

This strange-sounding concept is rooted in reflection on the possibility of surviving the many dangers which threaten the existence of a community, nation, or humanity as a whole, whether in the form of natural disasters, warfare, internal disintegration, or whatever. The more specific point of departure is the biblical motif of the few who survive a catastrophic disaster. The idea is expressed in prophetic texts by certain key terms,[1] but also by the use of a wide range of figurative language. The basic image is that of a small number of survivors of a catastrophe such as a foreign invasion, the capture and sack of a city, a massacre, or defeat in battle. Since disasters of this kind were no less frequent in the ancient Middle East than they are in the contemporary Middle East, it is not surprising that the language of a remnant or residue occurs often throughout the region from the time of the Sumerians in the 3rd millenium B.C.E. onwards. The prophetic books themselves refer frequently, often with a good dose of *Schadenfreude*, to the "remnant" of hostile nations including Babylon (Isa 14:22), Moab (15:9;

---

1. The relevant terminology, chiefly *šĕʾērît, šĕʾār, pĕlêtâ,* is set out and discussed in Hans Wildberger, "שאר *šʾr* to remain," *TLOT* 3:1284-92; and other works of reference. See also Gerhard F. Hasel, *The Remnant: The History and Theology of the Remnant Idea from Genesis to Isaiah,* 2nd ed. AUM 5 (Berrien Springs: Andrews University Press, 1974), with some updating in *IDBSup,* 735-36; W. E. L. Müller and H. D. Preuss, *Die Vorstellung vom Rest im Alten Testament,* 2nd ed. (Neukirchen-Vluyn: Neukirchener, 1973); Lester V. Meyer, "Remnant," *ABD* 5:669-71.

16:14), Edom (Amos 9:12), Syria (Isa 17:3), and the Philistine cities (Amos 1:8; Isa 14:30; Jer 25:20; Ezek 25:16).

Applied internally to Israel as a way of either affirming, calling into question, or negating the possibility of a future, depending on the context, the concept is first taken up in Amos as an integral aspect of his message. Amos captures the basic image in his description of a defeated army in headlong but unsuccessful flight after a battle (2:14-16):

> Flight will fail the swift,
> the strong won't preserve their strength,
> warriors won't save their lives,
> archers won't hold their ground,
> nor the swift of foot find safety.
> Horseman won't save their lives,
> the hardiest of warriors will flee
> stripped of their arms on that day.

His presentation of the concept is predominantly figurative. The standard term *šĕʾērît* ("remnant," "residue") occurs only once in the book with reference to Israel, at the conclusion of a brief passage — "Perhaps Yahveh God of hosts will be gracious to the remnant of Joseph" (5:15), which however derives in all probability from a later editor.[2] The basic idea is nevertheless expressed often in metaphoric and symbolic language. In the first of several vivid cameos, the remnant of Israel is compared with all that is left of a sheep devoured by a lion:

> As the shepherd rescues from the mouth of the lion a couple of legs or a bit of an ear, in like manner the people of Israel who live in Samaria shall be rescued. . . . (Amos 3:12)

The same point is made by depicting an almost but not quite annihilated army:

> The city that marched out a thousand strong
> will have but a hundred left;

2. Together with 5:4-5 and 5:6-7, 5:14-15 is a passage in which the prospect of survival is contemplated on condition of seeking Yahveh, a homiletic theme dear to the Deuteronomists, who had a significant role in editing the prophetic corpus. The possibility of a reprieve contradicts the uncompromising negative prospect for the future in evidence elsewhere in the book.

the city that marched out a hundred strong
will have but ten left. (5:3)

A particularly striking and somewhat cryptic cameo describes impressionistically the results of an earthquake, perhaps the one at the beginning of the book which establishes the date of Amos's activity:

> It will come about that if ten men remain in one house they will die. If a close relative, one whose duty it is to cremate the dead, carries the remains out of the house, and calls to someone in the inner parts of the house, "Is anyone still in there with you?" he will answer "No one," and he will add: "Hush! We must not invoke the name of Yahveh." (6:9-10)

To invoke the deity is to compel the deity's presence, destructive or salvific as it may be, an old belief with its own remnant in our expression "Speak of the devil and he will appear." In Amos, death and destruction are everywhere, from the death dirge over Israel intoned by the prophet (5:2) to the vision in which, by a play on words, the basket of summer fruit *(qāyiṣ)* betokens that "the end *(qēṣ)* has come upon my people Israel" (8:1-3).

This idea of the remnant is taken over by Isaiah from Amos, together with much else, and applied to the kingdom of Judah. It seems as if Isaiah set out deliberately to apply the message of Amos, addressed to the kingdom of Samaria, to Judah. Prophets do not, as a rule, acknowledge borrowings and adaptations from prophetic or nonprophetic predecessors, but even though Isaiah never mentions Amos, Isaianic sayings from the earliest period of the literary history of the book reproduce motifs and language from Amos even in detail. This is not the place for a close study of these borrowings, but examples would include Isaiah's criticism of contemporary worship (Isa 1:10-17; cf. Amos 5:21-24), his rebukes addressed to the political elite and their wives (Isa 3:16–4:1; cf. Amos 4:1-3), and earthquake as an instrument of divine punishment (Isa 9:9, 18 [Eng. 10, 19]; cf. Amos 1:1; 4:11). There may even be an oblique reference to Amos himself at Isa 9:7 (8), where Isaiah speaks of a message directed against Jacob which will fall on Israel.

Isaiah draws on Amos in two other important respects. The first is the threat of deportation and exile; in Amos the place of exile is Harmon (Amos 4:2-3)[3] or beyond Damascus (5:27), a location which will assume

---

3. A location otherwise unattested, perhaps a textual error for Hermon; see Shalom M. Paul, *A Commentary on the Book of Amos*. Herm (Minneapolis: Fortress, 1991), 135-36.

great significance for the members of the Damascus sect (CD VI 5, etc.). In Isaiah, the place of exile is of course Babylon. The second line of continuity between Amos and Isaiah starts out from the ominous threat of a coming Day of Yahveh. Whatever the origins of this prophetic topic, it expressed a positive concept which envisaged in the first instance an anticipated act of benevolence for Yahveh's people and trouble for their enemies. As it appears in Amos, however, it is one of several examples of a deliberate and systematic subversion of the expectations of his contemporaries (Amos 5:18-20):

> Woe to you who are longing for the Day of Yahveh,
> What good will the Day of Yahveh do you?
> It will be darkness, not light.
> As when one flees from a lion only to encounter a bear,
> Or comes home, leans his hand on the wall, and a snake bites him.
> Surely the Day of Yahveh will be darkness, not light,
> Gloom, with no glimmer of light in it.

Isaiah 24:17-18 presents a similar series of disasters with strong eschatological overtones, an obstacle race in which there will be no winners. This is a text which will resonate among the Qumran sectarians (e.g., CD IV 13-19):

> Terror, the trap, the deep pit
> await you who dwell on the earth!
> If you flee from the sound of the terror
> you will fall into the pit;
> and if you get out of the pit
> you will be caught in the trap.

The origin of the much-discussed topic "the Day of Yahveh" need not concern us. We can accept provisionally the *opinio communis* that it expresses the expectation of a decisive victory brought about by divine intervention, perhaps reproducing one or other of the spectacular interventions of Yahveh memorialized in Israel's traditions as, for example, "the day of Midian" (Isa 9:3 [Eng. 4]) referring to the victory recorded in Judges 6–8. Appropriated by Amos, this topos underlies the many predictions of what will happen "on that day": it will be a day of punishment (Amos 3:14), of defeat and slaughter (2:16), a bitter day of lamentation and wailing (8:3, 9-10), an evil day (6:3). This too is taken up and taken further in Isaiah, where predictions of future events, both good and ill but mostly ill, are typically introduced by the same "on that day" formula. It will be a day of punishment (Isa 10:3), a day of God's burning anger (13:13), and, ominously, a day of great slaughter when the towers come crashing down (30:25).

While the implications of the concept of the remnant can be positive — in the sense that at least some will survive the disaster — in the form in which it appears in Amos it is overwhelmingly negative; the idea of the day of Yahveh has been completely turned on its head. When taken over in the book of Isaiah, its negative connotations are still clearly in evidence.[4] In sayings generally assigned to the earliest redactional strand in chapters 1–35, principally chapters 1–12 and 28–31, the dominant message is not essentially different from that of Amos: Israel (Judah) has forfeited its status as God's chosen people and now faces rejection. The message is most clearly stated in the throne-room vision narrative with its dark saying about the hardening of hearts, the closing of eyes and ears, and the prospect of annihilating judgment (Isa 6:9-13). The same figurative language of decimation occurs here as in Amos (6:13a; cf. Amos 5:3), but the survivors have no future and their land will no longer be cultivated. What is left will be like the stump of a great oak which has been cut down.

At this point we find a clue to a development in the idea of the remnant which is characteristically Isaianic. A scribe reading the vision narrative after the fall of Jerusalem and the deportations has added a gloss identifying the remaining stump with the "holy seed" (*zera' qōdeš*, 6:13b). The only other place where this expression occurs is Ezra 9:2, where it describes the self-segregating immigrant, Judeo-Babylonian community in Judah of the Persian period. The self-identification of this group with the old prophetic concept of the remnant of Israel is important for understanding developments internal to the book of Isaiah and the reception of the book by the sects of the Greco-Roman period. Exile from which a few return as the core of a new people is the Isaianic concept which proved to be most productive and generative for the future. As encapsulated in the symbolic name of the prophet's son, *Shear-yashub* ("a remnant will return"), it presages both destruction and restoration, an end and a new beginning. It rep-

---

4. On the *Forschungsgeschichte* of the concept in the book of Isaiah up to the time of writing, see Ursula Stegemann, "Der Restgedank bei Isaias," *BZ* N.S. 13 (1969): 161-86. Note, however, that the author's principal aim is to determine the nature and scope of the concept in the authentic sayings of the 8th-century prophet.

resents a much more radical response to disaster than that of the Deuteronomists or even of the Priestly writers. It anticipates the creation of a new people to prepare for the final intervention of God in the affairs of Israel and human affairs in general, the final showdown. Because of the ambiguity of the verbal element in the name Shear-yashub, it also connotes both a physical return from the land of exile and repentance, a turning away from a sinful history. It is therefore open to becoming quite explicitly an eschatological concept. As such, it provided a powerful impulse not only to the development of a sectarian and apocalyptic way of thinking, evident already in the book of Isaiah itself, but also to the actual formation of eschatological and apocalyptic sects throughout the period of the Second Temple.[5] The remainder of this chapter will consist in an attempt to give substance to this statement about the interpretation of the book.

Our point of departure is, therefore, the name of the prophet's son. The naming of Isaiah's children may have been suggested by the symbolic names of Hosea's three children, Jezreel, Lo Ruhama, Lo Ammi, generally translated, respectively, Jezreel,[6] Not Pitied, Not My People. The sequencing of the names signifies the progressive dismantling of the covenant between Yahveh and the kingdom of Samaria, leading to the annulment of the relationship: "You are not my people (*'attem lo' 'ammî*) and I am not your I AM" (Hos 1:4-9). For those who accept that Immanuel (Isa 7:14) is also Isaiah's son, a third in addition to Shear-yashub (7:3) and Maher-Shalal-Hash-Baz (8:1), the parallel with Hosea would be closer, but this is by no means assured. We assume that the presence of Shear-yashub ("a remnant will return") with Isaiah in his fateful encounter with King Ahaz at a moment of political crisis and high drama (Isa 7:3) was intended in a positive sense. It would have made the point that, even if diminished, Judah would by one means or another survive the crisis of the threatened attack on Jerusalem by the Syrian-Samarian axis.

The earliest interpretation of this name of ominous threat for the future and promise beyond threat is found in the book of Isaiah itself (10:20-23). Here it is detached from its original historical situation, which permits

---

5. According to Otto Kaiser, *Isaiah 1–12*, 2nd ed. OTL (Philadelphia: Westminster, 1983), the name Shear-yashub "sets out the programme of the entire preaching of Isaiah."

6. Jezreel is an allusion to the town of that name in which Jehu carried out a bloody coup against the Omri dynasty and therefore connotes the condemnation of Jehu's own dynasty by the prophet.

it to take in a much wider field of vision. By exploiting the ambivalence of the Hebrew verb *šûb*, which can refer to a physical return, in this instance return from exile, and a metaphorical turning or returning to God by repentance (hence the word for "repentance," *tĕšûbâ*, derived from the verb), the name Shear-yashub comes to represent the few who survived the exile and returned to Judah. As such, they constituted the true remnant, the beginnings of a new community, and at the same time exemplified and prefigured those who would survive the annihilating judgment of the end time. The passage in question reads as follows:

> On that day the remnant of Israel and the survivors of the household of Jacob will no longer rely on the one who struck them, but they will rely in truth on Yahveh, the Holy One of Israel. A remnant will return (*šĕʾār yāšûb*), the remnant of Jacob, to the God of Might; for even if your people were as numerous as the sand of the sea, only a remnant of them will return. Destruction is decreed, with vindication abounding; for the Sovereign Lord, Yahveh of the hosts, will bring about the destruction that is decreed in the midst of the earth. (Isa 10:20-23)

We can see why this text, interpreted eschatologically in two of the Qumran pesharim, both unfortunately badly damaged,[7] would appeal to sectarians in the late Second Temple period.

The adaptation in this statement of expressions and images from other parts of the book, and its use of language reminiscent of the book of Daniel, counsel a date late in the Second Temple period. In the passage immediately preceding, Assyrian hubris is rebuked, and the rebuke ends with the image of deforestation, a not inappropriate metaphor in view of Assyrian boasts of cutting down trees wherever their campaigns took them. The author of 10:20-23 seems to have taken his cue from the final verse of the preceding passage:

> The remnant of the trees of his (Assyria's) forest will be so few
> that a child can count them and write them down. (10:19)

Turning from Assyria to Israel, the author of Isa 10:20-23 thinks of the few remaining trees as the small number destined to survive the judgment of exile. These few are redundantly described as "the remnant of Israel" (*šĕʾār*

---

7. 4QpIsaᵃ 2-6 II 1-9; 4QpIsaᶜ II 10-21.

yiśrā'ēl), "the survivors of the household of Jacob" *(pĕlêṭat bêt ya'ăqōb),* "the remnant of Jacob" *(šĕ'ār ya'ăqōb).* They are the *šābîm* (from the verb *šûb),* namely, "those who return," but they are also "penitents," the same term derived from the same verb.

The survival of the elect few also brings to mind the story of the great deluge, the archetypal disaster which only eight individuals survived as the progenitors of a new humanity (Gen 7:1-5; 8:15-19). In Isa 54:9 "Noah's floodwater" is one figurative rendering of the exilic experience, to be followed by the restoration of Jerusalem formerly abandoned by God (vv. 10-17). The story of the deluge may well have been in the mind of the author of Isa 10:20-23, but the allusion to a people as numerous as the sand of the sea leaves no doubt that the Abrahamic promise was the author's principal subtext (Gen 22:17; 32:13 [Eng. 12]). The implication appears to be that the promise has now become problematic, even subject to drastic revision. The question about the identity of the "children of Abraham" will be a central issue for the sectarians of the Greco-Roman period no less than for the first Christians. It recalls John the Baptist's statement that "God is able from these stones to raise up children to Abraham" (Matt 3:9) and Paul's argument that the Abrahamic promise is extended to all who share the faith of Abraham (Rom 4:1-25; 9:6-9).

The author of Isa 10:20-23 then moves without a pause from the judgment of exile to a final annihilating judgment "in the midst of the earth," a move which will not be lost on later readers of the book. The author of the Danielic visions was certainly familiar with this passage, as we may see by comparing the Isaianic text with the conclusion of Daniel's vision report in which he receives the true meaning of the 70 years of Jeremiah from the angel Gabriel.

> Destruction is decreed, with vindication abounding; for the Sovereign Lord, Yahveh of the hosts, will bring about the destruction that is decreed in the midst of the earth. (Isa 10:22-23)[8]

---

8. The term *ṣĕdāqâ* is usually translated "righteousness," but in later Isaianic texts it refers to judgment rather than to social justice, and specifically to eschatological judgment which involves punishment for some, vindication for others (Isa 1:27; 51:6, 8; 59:9, 16-17; 61:10-11; 63:1); *kālâ wĕneḥĕrāṣâ,* hendiadys, means "decreed destruction"; the Niphal participle of *ḥrṣ,* "decree," occurs only in Isaiah and Daniel and is expressive of a strong sense of divine foreknowledge and predestination.

Its end will come with a flood . . . desolations are decreed . . . until the destruction that is decreed is poured out on the desolator. (Dan 9:26-27)

These linguistic parallels — together with a number of others — point to the existence of an interpretative trajectory from Isaiah to Daniel and beyond, one to which we will have occasion to return. They also provide another indication of the key role of the book of Isaiah in the formation of the eschatological-apocalyptic worldview in the late Second Temple period.

We conclude, then, that the concept of the remnant of Israel was taken over from Amos into the book of Isaiah, where it came to be encapsulated in the name of the prophet's son, Shear-yashub. It is possible that the prophet Isaiah's disciples mentioned in 8:16-18 were seen, and saw themselves, as the remnant of Israel committed to preserving the teachings of the master. It is even possible, though incapable of proof, that this discipleship continued in existence long after the time of Isaiah and was linked with prophetic figures and prophetic groups attested in later strands of the book's redactional history. At all events, the disasters of the 6th century B.C.E. ending with deportation and exile led to a reinterpretation of the concept of the remnant focusing on the group of penitents who returned from the land of exile to form "the holy seed," the nucleus of a new community.

Exile and Return in Sectarian Writings from the Greco-Roman Period

It is a curious fact that, while the biblical narrative provides practically no information on the exile as a historical episode, the exile as symbolic representation, as idea, is fully developed. For the Historian, the exile represents the final punishment for infidelity manifested especially in the worship of deities other than Yahveh. If we bracket the final paragraph of the History as an epilogue added at a later time, one which narrates the accession of the Babylonian king Evil-Merodach (Amēl-Marduk), successor to Nebuchadnezzar, and the release of Jehoiachin from prison after 37 years (2 Kgs 25:27-30), we are being told that the history that began in Egypt has now come to an end in Egypt (25:26). With the prospect of the collapse of the Babylonian Empire in view, an Isaianic prophet took the more benign view of the exile as a time of indentured service, of the amortizing of debts, a dark age but one now about to come to an end (Isa 40:1-2). The detachment of the exile from its historical moorings, its presentation as concept or theological locus rather than event, is, however, most clearly in evidence in the Chronicler's interpretation of Jeremiah's 70 years of exile in terms of the Levitical Jubilee law (Lev 25:1-12). The basic idea is that the land, now emptied of its inhabitants, is to enjoy its belated sabbatical rest (2 Chr 36:20-21). In this view, the exile is not an end but an interim period allowing for recuperation and eventual restoration.

The interpretation which would have the most profound consequences for the future, however, was the identification in the book of Isaiah of the return from exile with the exodus from Egypt, and of those who returned with the prophetic remnant.[9] It is remarkable how often in Jewish sectarian texts from the Greco-Roman period the Babylonian exile is described as the defining moment in the religious history of Israel, followed by a long period of apostasy. Often, too, the sects which emerged at that time found in the earliest interpretation of the name Shear-yashub in Isa 10:20-23 essential clues to their own identity and their place in the religious history of Israel. No one who reads these texts, which reflect in one way or another the crisis of that age, can fail to notice how large the Babylonian exile looms in the attempt to understand the present in the light of the past.[10] The land of exile is regarded as the most fitting location for edifying narrative, and the time of the exile the most fitting time frame for visions and revelations. Didactic narratives such as Daniel 1–6, Tobit, and Judith are set in the eastern Diaspora, and the Qumran text *The Apocryphon of Joseph* (4Q371-373) even locates the story of the patriarch Joseph in an exilic context following on the fall of Jerusalem. Vision reports such as those of *4 Ezra* are also backdated to the exilic period. Though composed in the late 1st or early 2nd century c.e., *4 Ezra*, or the Ezra Apocalypse, presents Ezra, also known as Salathiel, living in Babylon

---

9. On the exile and return as concept, see Peter R. Ackroyd, *Exile and Restoration: A Study of Hebrew Thought of the Sixth Century B.C.* OTL (Philadelphia: Westminster, 1968), 237-56; Rainer Albertz, *Israel in Exile: The History and Literature of the Sixth Century B.C.E.* (Atlanta: SBL, 2003), 4-44. On exodus typology in Isaiah 40–55, see my *Isaiah 40–55*, 111-12.

10. In what follows I am much endebted to Michael A. Knibb, "The Exile in the Literature of the Intertestamental Period," *HeyJ* 17 (1976): 253-72; "Exile in the Damascus Document," *JSOT* 25 (1983): 99-117; "Exile," *EDSS* 1:276-77.

shortly after the fall of Jerusalem in 586 B.C.E. Backdating to the time of the Babylonian exile or its immediate aftermath is, however, by no means confined to this text, as we shall see presently. The practice may have been anticipated in Ezra's genealogy in Ezra 7:1-5, which presents him as the son of Seraiah, the last preexilic high priest executed by the Babylonians after the fall of Jerusalem (2 Kgs 25:18-21), thus eliminating the gap between the beginning of the exile and Ezra's mission almost a century and a half later. In one way or another the Babylonian exile is the great divide in the history. In its interpretative afterlife it will be the rite of passage which one must traverse in order to belong to the gathered community of the new age.

These perspectives take on a special sharpness of focus in sectarian writings. Both the edifying stories in the first half of the book of Daniel and the visions in the second half are set in the eastern Diaspora, "the land of Shinar" (Dan 1:1-2). The time is the exilic age, towards the end of Neo-Babylonian rule and the beginning of the Persian Empire. In the opening narrative (ch. 1), Daniel and the three other Judean youths at the Babylonian court serve as a small-scale model for the apocalyptic sect in which and for which the book of Daniel was composed almost four centuries after the time in which the stories are set. The choice of setting and period is deliberate. The link between the exilic situation and the critical present of the composition of the book, resulting from the persecution launched against his Jewish subjects by the Seleucid king Antiochus IV, corresponds to the conviction that those for whom the stories and vision accounts were written were the successors and continuators of the pietistic group which formed in the Babylonian exile and which would eventually return to Judah. The linkage in effect cancels out the intervening centuries, which is to say the entire Second Temple period down to the emergence of the group for which the book of Daniel was written.

These ideological contours of the book of Daniel call for further elaboration. In the Diaspora stories Daniel and his companions are supernaturally endowed with wisdom, knowledge, and understanding. They are also learned in the Babylonian intellectual tradition including Akkadian, having been put through a three-year academic curriculum. But Daniel, one of the group, is singled out as possessing special God-given competence as visionary and dream interpreter, endowments which the following narratives will exemplify (1:4, 17). His status vis-à-vis the others may therefore be taken to reflect the status in the vision reports of the leaders, the *maśkîlîm* ("wise teachers"), vis-à-vis the *rabbîm*, the "Many," a term used, though not always consistently, for the members of the group.[11]

The intellectual endowments of the youths at the Babylonian court are subordinated to strict observance of the Jewish law, with special reference to the dietary prescriptions and an uncompromising rejection of idolatry exemplified by their refusal to worship the gold statue (3:17-18). Their activities are carried out in an atmosphere of penitential prayer, including praying towards Jerusalem (6:10), asceticism, and familiarity and converse with angelic beings.[12] This is not unlike the milieu in which Daniel is represented as living and acting in the vision reports. He prays (9:3-19), mourns, fasts in sackcloth and ashes (10:2-3), and receives communications by means of angelic intermediaries from "the God who reveals mysteries" (2:28). The four youths, therefore, comprise a small-scale model of the emergent sectarianism of the middle decades of the 2nd century B.C.E.

The stories about Daniel and his companions in the first part of the book also illustrate the technique of eschatological interpretation, of the kind which will elicit from a close reading of Isaiah, for both Qumranites and early Christians, new truths of overwhelming import. The text to be interpreted could be a dream, even a dream which the dreamer has forgotten, or a few words written on the wall. It could also be a biblical text, "decoded" in an atmosphere of penitential prayer and fasting. The God who reveals mysteries uses Nebuchadnezzar, the mad tyrant, as an unconscious means for communicating eschatological truths, just as he used Jeremiah, also unconscious of the full and true import of his words, as a means to reveal through a later intermediary the time of the last events. This is not essentially different from the theory and practice of interpretation at

---

11. Dan 11:33, "The wise leaders of the people will give guidance to the many," is more likely generic usage in spite of the article, but in the reference in 12:3 to those who vindicate the many (*maṣdîqê hārabbîm* with the article), parallel with *maśkîlîm, hārabbîm* is almost certainly used in a technical sense of the (sectarian) community as a body, esp. in view of the evident dependence on Isa 53:11b. The occurrence of the term in Dan 12:10 is less clear, in spite of the fact that what is said of them is said in 11:35 of the *maśkîlîm*, since it is without the article. John J. Collins, *Daniel*, 385, 393, 400, understands the term in a generic sense as "the common people," adding that it was adopted in the Qumran Community Rule (1QS) as a technical term.

12. If this may be deduced from the mysterious presence alongside the three youths in the fiery furnace (3:24-25). The Aramaic *bar-'ĕlāhîn* is the equivalent of Heb. *ben-'ĕlōhîm*, one of several terms for an angelic being; the angelic nature of the fourth is in any case acknowledged by Nebuchadnezzar (3:28) and is explicit in LXX.

Qumran. The terminology is also similar to that of the Qumran pesher type of interpretation. Daniel's interpretations of Nebuchadnezzar's dreams are introduced in the telegrammatic manner characteristic of the pesher-type commentary: this is the dream, here is its interpretation (*pišrā'*, 2:36; 4:21 [Eng. 24]).

That the choice of an exilic setting for the stories and visions was deliberate is reinforced by the symbolic history which the visionary Daniel draws out of the 70 years of Jeremiah's prediction.[13] While seeking to understand the hidden meaning of the text, Daniel is visited by an angelic being who proposes to give him its true meaning, to "impart understanding" *(lĕhaśkîl bînâ)*, as Daniel the *maśkîl* must in his turn impart it to the other initiates in his group. But what follows is a genuinely different interpretation from that of the "original meaning" of the text, since it rejects the idea implicit in the Jeremian text that the exilic period has come to an end. The 70 weeks are therefore extended into 70 periods of seven years, therefore leaving the exilic period open-ended. Following the predestined and predetermined course of events, this extended period corresponds to the history of Israel from the permission to return in the early Persian period to the rededication of the temple.[14]

Gabriel informs Daniel that the 490 years must run their course so that transgression may be brought to an end, the measure of sin completed, iniquity expiated, everlasting righteousness introduced, the prophetic vision sealed, and, finally, that a most holy place be anointed (9:24). Most scholars have concluded that this last requirement refers to the rededication of the temple, which took place in 164 B.C.E., somewhat later than the composition of the book. The implication is that transgression and iniquity have characterized the history up to that point, a period of time corresponding to the greater part of the Second Temple period. More specifically, it is predicted that the 62 weeks from the time of Joshua (or Jeshua), first high priest after the return, to the murder of the high priest Onias III, therefore in our terms from 520 to 171 B.C.E., will be a troubled time, a time of distress and oppression.[15]

13. Dan 9:24-27; Jer 25:11-12; 29:10.

14. It is futile to attempt to bring the 70 weeks of years chronology into agreement with the known history of the Second Temple period. Counting 490 years from 538 B.C.E. results in a date far too low, and it is evident in any case that the author is not well informed on the Persian period.

15. The Hebrew term *ṣôq* is hapax, but the general sense seems tolerably clear. Collins,

This negative view of the period of the Second Temple is not confined to Daniel and not even to explicitly sectarian writings. In the historical introduction to *The Book of Jubilees,* the Babylonian exile is the time when God hid his face from Israel. It is followed by a period during which the law was neglected and worship corrupted (1:14), a period which is brought to an end only with the emergence of God's new plant of righteousness and the final ingathering of the faithful (*Jub* 1:7-18). In broad lines, this presentation of the history corresponds to that of the Damascus Document (CD I 7) and the Enochian "Apocalypse of Weeks" (*1 En* 93:9-10). Erasing from the record the entire Second Temple period down to the emergence of the sect or conventicle within which the text in question was composed left the way open for the claim to continuity with the exilic remnant, those who survived the exile and returned as the penitents of Israel.

In a passage in *1 Enoch* which has much in common with both Daniel and Qumran (*1 En* 93:1-10 + 91:12-17), the history is laid out in 10 "weeks" from the beginning of humanity in the first week to the final judgment. At that time the first heaven shall pass away and a new heaven appear, one of several eschatological scenarios taken from Isaiah (Isa 65:17; 66:22). The sixth week, corresponding to the preexilic period, is a time of blindness and folly and ends with the destruction of Jerusalem and exile in Babylon. The seventh week, meaning the postexilic period, is no better, being described as an "apostate generation" (*1 En* 93:9). At its conclusion, the elect, the righteous remnant, will be chosen and set aside. In Isaianic terms, they will be a root or plot planted by God (93:10; cf. Isa 60:21; 61:3). They, and they alone, will be the privileged recipients of the revelations communicated to Enoch at the beginning of history.[16]

We find a similar reading of Israel's past in the part of Enoch's

---

Daniel, 356, translates "in distressful times"; R. H. Charles, *A Critical and Exegetical Commentary on the Book of Daniel,* 237-52, "even in troublous times," but rejects MT in favor of LXX and Syr., "at the end of the times"; S. R. Driver, *The Book of Daniel, with Introduction and Notes* (Cambridge: Cambridge University Press, 1912) also translates "in troublous times" and appeals to the similar formation in Isa 33:6 which he translates "the stability of your times."

16. See George W. E. Nickelsburg, *1 Enoch* 1. Herm (Minneapolis: Fortress, 2001); and the new translation of the relevant passages in Nickelsburg and James C. VanderKam, *1 Enoch* (Minneapolis: Fortress, 2004), 140-43. A seven-line fragmentary Qumran text, 4Q247, mentions a fifth week and a period of 480 years, suggesting affinity with the Enochian "Apocalypse of Weeks."

Dream Visions, which relates the history of Israel from beginning to end and which includes the section known as "the Animal Apocalypse," composed later than the book of Daniel but earlier than the assumption of the high priestly office by Jonathan Maccabee in 152 B.C.E. (*1 En* 89:68–90:5). The distinguishing feature of this section of *1 Enoch* is theriomorphic symbolism: Israelites are sheep, foreign oppressors are wild animals who feed on the sheep (another Isaianic image; see Isa 56:9-12), the Hellenistic rulers are birds of prey, the Pietists are lambs, and so on. In this somewhat surreal symbolic narrative, the destruction of Jerusalem, return from exile, and rebuilding of the temple inaugurate a period marked by the corruption of temple worship, violence, and oppression by aliens (89:65–90:5). This situation continues until lambs are born, who are therefore the symbolic counterpart to the elect and righteous in the "Apocalypse of Weeks." One of these lambs is killed by ravens, an event usually decoded to refer to the murder of the high priest Onias III at the instigation of Menelaus in 170 B.C.E.[17] The story ends with the final judgment, the new Jerusalem (again dependent on Isaiah; see Isa 54:11-12; 60:1-22), the conversion of the Gentiles (cf. Isa 64:2; 66:12, 19-21), and the eschatological consummation (*1 En* 90:20-39).

The way in which the history is presented in the *Testament of Levi*, also from the 2nd century B.C.E., is similar.[18] The emphasis is on the moral turpitude of the priesthood, which resulted in the destruction of the temple and exile in Babylon (*T Levi* 14-15). The increasing corruption of the priesthood is narrated in successive jubilees or weeks of years, as in Daniel and Enoch. The last three of these correspond to the period from the return from exile to the time of the composition of the text, perhaps, like the book of Daniel, during the reign of Antiochus IV Epiphanes. All three periods are times of darkness. During the fifth week the deportees or their descendants return to the land and rebuild the sanctuary. The seventh week witnesses, once again, the total depravity of the Jerusalem priest-

---

17. For the translation, see Nickelsburg and VanderKam, *1 Enoch*, 120-36; and for critical comment Patrick A. Tiller, *A Commentary on the Animal Apocalypse of 1 Enoch*. SBLEJL 4 (Atlanta: Scholars, 1993). R. H. Charles, *The Apocrypha and Pseudepigrapha*, 2:257, identifies the lambs as "Chasids," i.e., the *asidaioi* of 1 Maccabees. This is certainly plausible, but since Onias III was not as far as we know a member of one of these groups, the term "Chasid" would have to be taken in a broader sense.

18. For the text, see Howard Clark Kee in *The Old Testament Pseudepigrapha*, ed. James H. Charlesworth, 1:788-95.

hood, no doubt with reference to the auctioning off of the high priestly office during the reign of Antiochus IV (17:10-11). The sixth week, covering the entire period from the rebuilding of the temple in the early Persian period to the time of the composition of the text in the Seleucid period, is passed over in silence. The prophecy concludes with the raising up of the eschatological priest and the final consummation.

The division of the history into jubilees also shows up in a fragmentary Qumran text which presents itself as a *Testament of Moses* (4QPseudo-Moses). It is based on a biblical model of last admonitions and predictions (the Blessings of Moses in Deuteronomy 33) and is comparable to the Testaments of the Twelve Patriarchs. Following this well-established pattern, Moses — presumably at the point of death — predicts the course of the future in the form of *vaticinia ex eventu*. Here, too, the priesthood comes in for severe criticism both before and after the exile. The account of the postexilic period reads as follows:

> They (the sons of Aaron) will do what is evil in my sight in keeping with all that Israel had done in the first days of its kingdom, with the exception of those who were the first to go up (to Judah) from the land of their captivity to build the sanctuary. . . . But in the seventh jubilee of the devastation of the land they will forget precept, festival, sabbath, and covenant. They will disobey everything and do what is evil in my sight. I will hide my face from them and deliver them into the hands of their enemies and abandon them to the sword. But I will leave over from among them survivors *(wĕhiš'artî mēhem pĕlêṭîm)*, so that they will not be annihilated by my anger and the hiding of my face. (4QpsMoses^e = 4Q390 fr. 1)

As in the *Testament of Levi,* the history between the first return from the Babylonian exile to the seventh jubilee is passed over in silence. It is implied that those who survived the wrath of God and the hiding of God's face during this seventh jubilee were in line of succession to those who returned from the Babylonian exile, the only ones exempt from condemnation.[19] Comparable in this respect is the fragmentary *4QAges of Creation*

---

19. See Devorah Dimant, "New Light from Qumran on the Jewish Pseudepigrapha — 4Q390," in *The Madrid Qumran Congress: Proceedings of the International Congress on the Dead Sea Scrolls, Madrid 18-21 March 1991*, ed. Julio Trebolle Barrera and Luis Vegas Montarer. STDJ 11 (Leiden: Brill, 1992), 2:405-48.

(4Q180, 181) according to which, in the seventh and presumably final age of creation, some are chosen by God out of the prevailing corruption to belong to a community of "divine beings" *(yaḥad 'ēlîm)* and a "holy congregation" *('ădat qôdeš)*.[20]

An equally somber view of the Second Temple period informs *The Testament of Moses*, often referred to as *The Assumption of Moses*, in its original form from the reign of Antiochus Epiphanes IV (175-164 B.C.E.), roughly contemporaneous with the book of Daniel. Here, too, the return from exile is followed by a time of general moral corruption, with special reference to the profanation of temple worship. Israel will be punished through the agency of Antiochus, and the persecution launched by this ruler will reach its climax with the martyrdom of the mysterious Taxo and his seven sons. Then the kingdom of God will appear accompanied by cosmic upheavals and Israel will be saved. While there is nothing explicitly sectarian about this text, the proposal of Taxo and his sons to retreat into a cave and die rather than transgress the commandments is reminiscent of those *asidaioi* ("Pietists") who retired to caves in the wilderness and died there rather than profane the sabbath (1 Macc 2:29-38). The martyrdom of Taxo and his sons is rewarded by their being raised to the heights and fixed firmly in the heaven of the stars *(T Moses* 10:9) — the same promise of astral immortality, therefore, as is pledged to the *maśkîlîm* in Dan 12:3.[21]

A final and particularly explicit example of the same historiographical pattern appears in the opening Admonition of the Damascus Document (CD). The title of the homily, addressed to "all who know righteousness and understand the actions of God" (CD I 1), is taken verbatim from Isa 51:7. The admonition itself follows the good biblical precedent of an indictment *(rîb)* in the form of historical recital.[22] It presents the historical experience of Israel as, for the most part, a history of religious infidelity, a theme to which the Damascus Document returns several times,

20. See Devorah Dimant, "The 'Pesher on the Periods' (4Q180 and 4Q181)," *IOS* 9 (1979): 77-102.

21. See George W. E. Nickelsburg, *Jewish Literature between the Bible and the Mishnah* (Philadelphia: Fortress, 1981), 80-83; ed., *Studies on the Testament of Moses* (Cambridge, Mass.: SBL, 1973); Emile Schürer, *The History of the Jewish People in the Age of Jesus Christ,* rev. ed., 1:278-88; for the text, see John Priest in Charlesworth, *The Old Testament Pseudepigrapha,* 1:919-34.

22. Deut 32 is often taken to be the prototypical *rîb,* though the term itself does not occur in it; other examples are Hos 12:3 (Eng. 2) and Mic 6:2, both against Judah.

and which itself is not without biblical precedent.[23] The initial recital reads as follows:

> When they (Israel) were unfaithful, in that they abandoned him (God), he hid his face from Israel and from his sanctuary and delivered them up to the sword. But when he recalled the covenant of the ancestors he allowed a remnant to survive for Israel *(hišîr šĕʾērît lĕyiśrāʾēl)* and did not deliver them up to destruction. Then, at the end of the period of God's anger,[24] 390 years from the time when he delivered them into the hand of Nebuchadnezzar king of Babylon, he visited them and caused a plant root *(šôreš maṭṭāʿat)* to sprout from Israel and Aaron, to take over his land and to flourish on the goodness of his soil. They realized their iniquity and acknowledged that they were guilty men; they were like the blind, like those who grope along the way, (and they were like this) for twenty years.
>
> But God appraised their deeds, for they were wholeheartedly seeking him, so he raised up for them a Teacher of Righteousness to lead them in the way of his heart. (CD I 3-11)

There is no question of offering a detailed commentary on these historical allusions,[25] but the basic pattern in this first survey is tolerably clear. The destruction of Jerusalem and the temple was the outcome of a sinful history. The initial survivors of the exile constituted the prophetic remnant, after which the subsequent history to the origins of the Damascus sect 390 years later is passed over in silence. The 390-year interval is thematic rather than the result of precise calculation, based as it is on Ezekiel's sign-act where he is instructed to lie on his side for 390 days to bear the punishment of Israel (Ezek 4:4-5). Some commentators on the Damascus Document de-

---

23. Good examples are Ps 78, 105, 106. In Ezek 20, the historical survey traces infidelity, exceptionally, back to the sojourn in Egypt.

24. Florentino García Martínez and Eibert Tigchelaar, *The Dead Sea Scrolls Study Edition,* 1:551, translate *bĕqēṣ ḥārôn* by "at the period of wrath," but neither in Biblical Hebrew nor, as far as I can tell, in the Qumran texts does *qēṣ* means "period of time." Cf. the expression *'maet qēṣ,* "the time of the end" (4Q372 1.15 and elsewhere). The context suggests that the period of divine anger ended with the emergence of the Damascus sect.

25. I am especially in debt to Philip R. Davies, *The Damascus Covenant;* see also "The 'Damascus' Sect and Judaism," 70-84; and his article, "Damascus Rule (CD)," in *ABD* 2:8-10 with bibliog.

mote the phrase "390 years after handing them over to Nebuchadnezzar king of Babylon" to the status of a gloss. This seems to me to be unnecessary and therefore undesirable. The passage is present in the alternative versions 4QD^a and 4QD^b, and, based on the translation offered above, the time of wrath is the entire period from the exilic remnant to the writer's own day. It is also chronologically plausible since, calculating from the destruction of Jerusalem and the temple (CD I 3), it takes us down to 196 B.C.E., by which time movements of religious renewal must have been well under way in Jewish communities under Seleucid rule.

In the second section of the Admonition (CD II 2-13) we find the same overlap between the exilic generation and the Damascus sect. The section is addressed to "all who enter the covenant," the same covenant described elsewhere as "the new covenant in the land of Damascus" (VI 19). They are identified as those who repent of sin (šābê pešaʿ, II 5) and the survivors (pĕlêṭâ) who will inherit the land (II 11). There follows another survey (II 14–IV 10) which begins with the fallen angels, here referred to as the Heavenly Watchers (cf. Gen 6:1-4), and traces Israel's religious infidelity from the sojourn in Egypt to the devastation of the land. After the exile there is more guilt and more punishment, but, again, nothing is said about the long period preceding the covenant which God made with those "left over from among them" (III 13). The nucleus of this covenanting sect is those Zadokite priests who "left the land of Judah and dwelt in the land of Damascus" (III 21–IV 4; VI 5), namely, the land of exile.

The interpretation of "the land of Damascus" has been and continues to be much discussed. In view of the differences of opinion among those who have labored long over these texts, it would be out of place for me to be apodictic, but it seems arguable that leaving the land of Judah and dwelling in the land of Damascus means going into exile and that therefore the land of Damascus is the land of exile, hence Babylon. This appears to be suggested by the context of CD VI 5, which speaks of the devastation of the land and of God remembering his covenant, language associated with the Babylonian conquest and deportations. It is supported by the midrash on Amos 5:26-27 in which Damascus — or somewhere beyond Damascus — is a place of exile (CD VII 13-19).

Another historical survey, attributed in Acts 7 to the deacon Stephen, a Greek-speaking Jewish-Christian, cites the same Amos passage as the author of the Damascus Document (Acts 7:42-43; CD VII 13-18 with reference to Amos 5:25-27), but substitutes "Babylon" for "Damascus" as the place of exile.[26] The theme of the rejection and persecution of the prophets is also common to both texts (Acts 7:51-52; CD VII 17-18), but Stephen is more radical, since for him the historical survey comes to an end with the building of Solomon's temple, the crowning act of a history of apostasy that began with the golden calf. The rejection of the temple as the indispensable center of religious life, supported by citing Isa 66:1-2, is also consistent with the polemic against the temple cult and denunciations of the temple priesthood in the sects of the late Second Temple period surveyed earlier.

Exile and Return in the Isaianic Interpretative Tradition

In Isaianic terms, therefore, those who survived the exile and returned constitute the holy remnant and embody the Abrahamic promise. Identification with these first *šābîm* ("those who returned," also "penitents") provides the basic legitimation for the Qumran sects and, indirectly, for the original followers of Jesus as a distinct entity within 1st-century C.E. Palestinian Judaism. It is this nucleus of a new community which is encapsulated in the name of Isaiah's son Shear-yashub: they are the holy remnant, they are the ones who repented, and they returned from exile. According to the seminal text Isa 10:20-23, those who return are few in number: "Even if your people Israel were as numerous as the sand of the sea only a remnant of them will return." This passage is given an explicitly eschatological interpretation in one of the Qumran pesharim on Isaiah (4QIsa[a]), most of which unfortunately is lost. The pesher on the previous passage, Isa 10:15-19 (4QpIsa[c]), is also lost with the exception of the concluding verse, which predicts that "the remnant of the trees of his forest will be so few that a child can count them and write them down." This drastic thinning out of the forest is interpreted in the one legible fragment of the pesher as indicating the eschatological "diminution of humanity" *(mĕʿût hāʾādām)*, resulting in the few who will survive the final judgment, a characteristic link-

---

26. The interpretation of Damascus as a symbolic name for Babylon, the place of origin for the Damascus sect — and therefore for the Essenes — has been argued in numerous publications by Jerome Murphy-O'Connor, most recently in *EDSS* 1:165-66. His principal arguments were evaluated by Knibb, *JSOT* 25 (1983): 99-117.

ing of the fate of Israel and other nations with that of the world, of humanity as a whole.[27]

The belief that, just as only a few survived the exile with their faith intact, so only a few will survive the final judgment is not confined to the Qumran pesharim on Isaiah. In *4 Ezra*, the visionary Ezra also known as Salathiel is told that, just as base metals are plentiful and precious metals few, so in this age the godless abound while the righteous are few. At the final judgment God will rejoice over these few elect ones who will be saved (*4 Ezra* 7:60). Elsewhere in this work we hear that this world is for the many, the world to come for the few (8:1) and that "many have been created but only a few shall be saved" (8:3). The statement in this text that only a few will be saved brings to mind the gospel saying of Jesus that "many are called but few are chosen" (Matt 22:14), and the same point is made figuratively in the gospel saying about the narrow gate (Matt 7:13-14). In one of the logia in the *Gospel of Thomas*, Jesus says that "I shall choose you, one out of one thousand and two out of ten thousand, and they shall stand as a single one." The few faithful ones who survived the exile to be the nucleus of a new community, the holy remnant of Israel, therefore typify and prefigure the few elect of the last days who will survive the annihilating judgment.

The Christian editor of *4 Ezra*, writing some time in the 3rd century, takes up the same theme in describing the world in its final state as a place of silence and solitude, with a few stragglers wandering about in a shattered landscape (*4 Ezra* 16:26-34).

The dark side of the experience of exile can be expressed metaphorically in many different ways. In biblical texts, the Babylonian exile is the time of Godforsakenness, the time when the God of Israel moved away from his people. The sense of abandonment is frequently stated as the time of God's hiding his face from Israel. The image of hiding the face, that is, turning the face away from a suppliant, derives from language and protocol associated with the palatine courts and audience chambers of the great empires. It would therefore naturally come to the mind of one whose prayer goes unanswered or who is experiencing a sense of abandonment by God.[28] Turning away the face is a natural expression of displeasure or

27. See above pp. 114-15.

28. Ps 13:2 (Eng. 1); 22:25 (24); 30:8 (7); 51:11 (9); 69:18 (17); 88:15 (14); 102:3 (2); 143:7; Job 13:24; 34:29.

anger and is done in silence. Hence the exile is also the time of the silence of God; God has moved away out of earshot of his people.

This language about seeking God's face, or God turning away his face from the suppliant, or God remaining silent has strong liturgical undertones and would therefore be particularly apt to describe the sense of deprivation after the destruction of the Jerusalem temple. Thus, the author of Psalm 27, who desires to live in the house of Yahveh all the days of his life, begs Yahveh not to hide his face from him. The Targum on Isa 54:8, which speaks of God hiding his face during the exile, interprets the expression as the absence of the Shekinah, and we have seen that the Damascus Document speaks of God hiding his face from Israel and from the sanctuary (CD I 3; cf. II 8-9). With reference to the exilic experience, its use is not confined to Isaiah,[29] but it is nonetheless identifiably an Isaianic theme:

> For a passing moment I abandoned you,
> but with great compassion I will gather you;
> With wrath overflowing for one moment
> I hid my face from you,
> but with never-failing love I have pitied you,
> says YHVH your Redeemer. (Isa 54:7-8)[30]

That this saying is referring to the Babylonian exile is clear from the immediate context and from a reading of the book as a whole. The only difference is that the 70 years of Jeremiah are, in God's time, now seen as but a passing moment *(rega' qāṭon)* rather than 490 years.

In a fragmentary Qumran text, which appears to contain revelations to Moses (4QpsMoses[b] 3 III), we pick up a much less positive view of the exile. Speaking, we assume, to Moses, God says, "I will remove the people and I will abandon the land (leaving it) in the hands of destroying angels, and I will hide my face from Israel." This corresponds to the seventh of the jubilees according to which the history of Israel is periodized, the jubilee of the devastation of the land, as stated in another fragment of the same work quoted earlier (4QpsMoses[e] fr. 1). The historical introduction to the book of *Jubilees* likewise predicts that God will hide his face from Israel and deliver them to the nations as captives (*Jub* 1:13-14; also 4Q216 II 14), and the brief survey of the history at the beginning of the Damascus

---

29. Deut 31:17-18; Jer 33:5; Ezek 39:23-24.
30. See also Isa 8:17; 57:17; 59:2; 64:6 (Eng. 7).

Document, discussed earlier, expresses itself in much the same way (CD I 3; cf. II 8-9).

The Babylonian exile therefore marked an ending, but it was also a new beginning. The second major segment of the book of Isaiah opens with the consoling proclamation that the time of indentured service is coming to an end and that a way is to be cleared in the wilderness for return to the land and a new beginning. This familiar passage reads as follows:

> A voice proclaims:
> "Clear in the wilderness a way for Yahveh;
> level in the desert a highway for our God!
> Let every ravine be filled in,
> every mountain and hill flattened out;
> the crooked made straight, the rough places leveled.
> Then the glory of Yahveh will be revealed;
> all humanity as one shall see it." (Isa 40:3-5)

The proclamation does not refer explicitly to return from exile, but the preceding announcement of the end of servitude implies that the way to be cleared is the way leading from the land of exile. That it is also said to be a preparation for the coming of God and the revelation of the divine glory made it easier for devout sectarians of the late Second Temple period to apply it to the *final* coming of God in glory and to hear the command to prepare as addressed to them.

For the Qumran sectarians, this Isaianic text served as the scriptural basis for their own legitimacy and the foundation for their own self-understanding. The author of the Community Rule *(serek hayyaḥad)* adapted the text, in its Masoretic form, to the situation of the group to whom the Rule was addressed. He did so by omitting the voice of the one proclaiming and presenting the words as a divine command to prepare the way of Yahveh in the wilderness, which was in fact where they were. This section of the Rule runs as follows:

> When they have become a community *(yaḥad)* in Israel in keeping with these procedures, they are to be segregated from the dwelling of sinful men by going into the wilderness to clear that way there, as it is written: "In the wilderness clear the way of Yahveh, level in the desert a highway for our God." This signifies the study of the law which God commanded through Moses, so as to act in keeping with everything

revealed from one age to the next, and in keeping with what the prophets have revealed through his Holy Spirit. (1QS VIII 12-16)[31]

This passage calls for a brief comment.[32] In the first place, the self-segregation in the wilderness was not understood in a purely metaphorical way but realistically as a physical relocation. Physical segregation was meant to facilitate a close and attentive study of the law — not just the "plain meaning" of the law but the hidden meanings revealed through the leaders of the sect, and in the first place the Teacher of Righteousness revered as the inheritor of a long history of inspired prophecy.[33] The goal of this activity was certainly the living of a holy life according to their lights, but also, by penetrating the hidden meanings of scriptural texts, learning what was their place in the great scheme of things, what they were to do as a community now living through the final countdown to the end.

The same Isaianic text stands at the beginning of the gospel story in all four versions.[34] In order to relate it more closely to the situation of John the Baptist, who was in the wilderness, the gospels cite it according to the LXX version, which parses it differently from the Hebrew text: "The voice of one proclaiming in the wilderness: 'Prepare the way of the Lord. . . .'" John's proclamation encapsulates the eschatological message common to Qumran and the first followers of Jesus. The call to repentance — *metanoia*, the Greek translation of *tĕšûbâ* — proclaimed by John and taken up by Jesus, also reflects the self-description of the Qumran sectarians as *šābîm*, "penitents." Most importantly, the call to prepare the way of the Lord presides over the origins of both the Qumran *yaḥad* and the Jesus movement, providing both with their *raison d'être*. The link between John the Baptist's followers and those of Jesus is in evidence throughout early Christian writings. We remarked earlier how, according to John 1:35-42, Jesus recruited his first disciples from the Baptist's following and made his first public appearance, proclaiming the same message, immediately after John was removed from the scene (Mark 1:14). If, as many scholars would argue, John was a one-time member of the Qumran sect who went his own way, taking the eschatological message of the sect into the world for anyone who would listen,

31. Also in two recensions: 4QS^d VI 6-7 (4Q258) and 4QS^e III 2-6 (4Q259). In 4Q176 (4QTanhumim) 1-2 I 4-9, Isa 40:1-5 is cited without comment.

32. George J. Brooke, "Isaiah 40:3 and the Wilderness Community."

33. See esp. 1QpHab II 7-10; VII 1-4; CD I 11-12.

34. Matt 3:3; Mark 1:2-3; Luke 3:4-5; John 1:23.

the interpretation of Isa 40:3 would constitute one of the strongest links between Qumran, the Baptist community, and the first Christians.[35]

The citation of Isa 40:3 as the keynote text for the Qumran *yahad*, the Baptist group, and the first Christians is therefore a link in an exegetical chain, the crowning moment in an interpretative continuum, the first stages of which must be recovered from the book of Isaiah itself. In the second segment of the book, "the way in the wilderness" is a major theme. To mention only two examples: Isa 35:8-10 presents a more ample and developed scenario:

> There will be a highway there;
> it will be called The Way of Holiness;
> the unclean will not pass by that way,
> it will be for the use of pilgrims,
> fools will not wander along it. . . .
> Those ransomed by Yahveh shall return;
> shouting for joy, they shall enter Zion
> crowned with joy everlasting.

In envisioning the future, Isa 62:10-11 uses the same figure of the processional way:

> Pass through, pass through the gates, clear a way for the people!
> Build up the highway, build it up, clear away the stones!
> Raise a signal over the peoples!
> See, Yahveh has proclaimed from one end of the earth to the other:
> "Tell daughter Zion, 'See, your salvation comes;
> see, his reward is with him, his recompense precedes him.'"

In these and other places in Isaiah,[36] "the way" is removed from the historical particularities of 40:3, where the reference is to the return of the deportees or their descendants from Babylon, and nudges the metaphor in the direction of the end-time perspective of judgment and salvation. This is the perspective which is taken up in Qumran and early Christianity.

35. On the Qumran-John the Baptist-Jesus connection, see above, pp. 138-47.
36. Elsewhere in Isaiah the way is the miraculous highway through the Papyrus Sea and the route through the wilderness leading to the promised land (Isa 11:16; 48:21; 51:10-11). It also has an ethical connotation in 57:14, introducing a homily on true piety: "Build up, build up the road and clear the way,/remove every obstacle from my people's path."

The question now arises as to the identity of those who embarked on the way leading out of exile. Here, too, the Qumran sectarians found an answer in their close reading of the book of Isaiah. In keeping with a feature in evidence throughout the book, the first poem, a fierce indictment of the prophet's contemporaries and especially the political and religious leadership (1:2-31), is rounded off with a typically universalizing and eschatologizing epilogue (vv. 27-31), introduced as follows:

> Zion will be saved in the judgment,
> her penitents *(šābêhā)* in the retribution,
> but rebels and sinners will be destroyed together,
> those forsaking Yahveh will be consumed.

The rebels and sinners destined for destruction are the unrepentant members of the Judean community whose fate is vividly described in the last verse of the book in terms of unextinguishable fire (66:24). Those who will survive the final judgment are the *šābîm*, those who have repented, who have made *těšûbâ*, the true "turning," and who later in the book are described as the ones who have turned away from transgression *(šābê pešaʿ, 59:20)*.

The ambiguity of the verb *šûb* has been noted more than once. It allows for the identification of these penitents with those who returned from the exile as the nucleus of a new community,[37] and was exploited by the author of the Damascus Document in arguing that the sect to which he belonged was the successor and continuator of the first of those who returned from exile. The Zadokite priests are "the penitents of Israel *(šābê yiśrāʾēl)* who went out from the land of Judah, the Levites are those who joined them, and the sons of Zadok are the elect of Israel, famous men, who are to serve (God) in the latter days" (CD IV 2-4). Described in Isaianic terms, they are "those who turn away from transgression" *(šābê pešaʿ)*[38] or simply "the penitents of Israel" *(šābê yiśrāʾēl)*, who are also those who returned from exile as the nucleus of a new commu-

---

37. For the idea of a physical return, see Isa 9:12; 21:12; 37:7, 8, and for return from exile, 35:10 and 51:11. For *šûb* = repent, with the strong sense of giving one's life a new direction, see Isa 6:10; 19:22; 31:6; 44:22; 55:7. Further possibilities were presented by similarity with the verb *šābāh*, "take captive"; in Ezra-Nehemiah the Judeo-Babylonian element in the province of Judah is often referred to as "those who came/came up from the captivity" *(miššěbî)* (Ezra 2:1; 3:8; 8:35; Neh 1:2-3; 7:6; 8:17).

38. CD II 5; XX 17, taken from Isa 59:20.

nity.[39] From the way the argument is developed in this text, it seems unnecessary to chose one or other of the options implicit in the verb: the
group which returned also repented.[40]

The Damascus Document also describes the sectarians for whom
this rule book was written, or perhaps their immediate antecedents, with
the organic metaphor of a "plant root" which God caused to sprout:[41]

> At the conclusion of the time of God's anger, 390 years from the time
> when he delivered them into the hand of Nebuchadnezzar king of
> Babylon, he visited them and caused a plant root *(šôreš maṭṭāʿat)* to
> sprout from Israel and Aaron, in order to take over his land and to
> flourish on the goodness of his soil. (CD I 5-8)

However the redactional history of the text is viewed, the author is posit-
ing a connection between the faithful remnant of the exile and the members of the Damascus sect. He seems to be saying that, just as God brought
about a new beginning with the survivors of the exile, so now, many years
later, in a situation which provoked the divine anger in equal measure,
God planted a new seed which would develop into a new people.

The plant metaphor occurs frequently in the Qumran sectarian writings. The community itself is an everlasting plant *(maṭṭāʿat ʿôlām)*.[42] It is a
garden of Eden in which God brings forth a holy shoot, the true plant
planted by God (1QH[a] XVI 9-11). Eden must also have been in the mind of
the author of the *Hodayot,* the Thanksgiving Hymns, where we are told
that the root, that is, the community, "will sprout like a wild flower forever,
causing a shoot to grow into branches of an everlasting plant" (1QH[a] XIV
14-15). This organic metaphor can also be traced back to a diligent reading
of Isaiah:

---

39. CD VI 5; VIII 16 = XIX 29.

40. The meaning of a physical return from exile was defended by Samuel Iwry, *ErIsr* 9
(1969): 80-88; and Jerome Murphy-O'Connor, "An Essene Missionary Document? CD II,
14–VI, 1," *RB* 77 (1970): 212-13. See the discussion of the issue in Knibb, *JSOT* 25 (1983): 105-9.

41. If the 390-year interval from the Babylonian conquest to the sprouting of the root
is an editorial addition, the root would refer to the first of those who returned from the exile.
But the subsequent course of this brief historical account (CD I 8-12), and the parallels
noted below, strongly suggest reference to the origins of the sect itself. Martin Hengel, *Judaism and Hellenism,* 1:175, identified "the root for planting" with the *asidaioi,* whom he took
to be the spiritual ancestors of the Essenes.

42. 1QS VIII 5; XI 8; 1QH[a] XIV 12-15; XV 18-19; 4Q418 81.13.

Your people, righteous one and all,
will possess the land forever,
the shoot that I myself planted,[43]
the work of my hands so that I might be glorified.
The least will become a thousand,
the youngest a numerous nation.
I am Yahveh!
At the appointed time swiftly will I bring it about. (Isa 60:21-22)

The prediction occurs in an apostrophe to Zion which reactivates once again the Abrahamic promise of land and progeny, the allusion to which is unmistakable in these verses. That this was noted by the author of the Damascus text, and applied to the group for which he was writing, is indicated by the statement that the new shoot was planted by God "to possess his land and to flourish on the goodness of his soil" (CD I 7-8). We find a parallel in the alphabetic Psalm 37, in which, repeatedly, the promise of land is addressed to the lowly, the humble, the righteous — all terms used of themselves by the Qumran sectarians.[44]

The popularity of this Isaianic metaphor for the sowing by God of the seeds for a new people is also attested in *Jubilees,* where the survivors of the exile are described as a "righteous plant" (*Jub* 1:12-18). In a statement running parallel with the historical introduction of the Damascus Document, the "Apocalypse of Weeks" in *1 En* 93:9-10 refers to "an eternal plant of righteousness" which will appear at the end of the seventh week, corresponding to the emergence of movements of religious renewal in the latter part of the Second Temple period. The same organic metaphor for the founding of a new community was familiar to early Christian writers. In the course of a controversy with Pharisees, the Jesus of Matthew's gospel affirms that "every plant which my heavenly Father has not planted will be rooted out" (Matt 15:13). Using the same metaphor, Paul tells the Corinthian church that they are God's cultivation, God's field. He (Paul) planted it, Apollos watered it, but it was God who gave the increase (1 Cor 3:6, 9).

The long trajectory which ends with the emergence of sects in the late Second Temple period, inclusive of the Christian movement, can therefore be traced back to the refusal of the first generation of prophets,

---

43. *nēṣer maṭṭāʿay* (emended text); cf. 61:3. The term *nēṣer,* "shoot," is a metaphor for the community in 1QH^a XIV 14-15; XV 18-19; XVI 6, 9-11.
44. The terms in question are *ʿănāwîm, ʾebyônîm, ṣaddîqîm.*

in the first place Amos and Isaiah, to confer absolute validity on contemporaneous political institutions. The refusal is expressed through the idea of the remnant (*šĕʾār, šĕʾērît,* and related expressions) and the reversal of the traditional topos of the "Day of Yahveh" as foreshadowing a final, annihilating judgment. In the book of Isaiah, the remnant, encapsulated in the name of the prophet's son Shear-yashub, is identified with the survivors of exile as the nucleus of a new community. As the book continued to be expanded in the direction of the apocalyptic worldview, the exile according to Isaiah came to be viewed as a prefiguring of the end time and its survivors as the community of the end time. In this way the interpretation of the book of Isaiah served as a powerful stimulus to the formation and consolidation of the well-known sects of the late Second Temple period.

CHAPTER 8

The Many Faces of the Servant of the Lord

The Beginnings in the Book of Isaiah

In one of the many vivid incidents described in Acts (8:26-35), an unnamed high Ethiopian official, probably a "God-fearer" returning from a
pilgrimage to Jerusalem, is shown reading Isaiah 53 en route. Somewhere
between Jerusalem and Gaza he meets Philip, a Christian missionary, and
on reaching verse 7 of the chapter, about the Servant led like a sheep to the
slaughter, he asks Philip: "About whom, may I ask, does the prophet say
this, about himself or someone else?" Philip then took this text as the starting point for instructing the official about Jesus as the fulfillment of this
biblical prophecy. The incident makes us wonder whether others had anticipated this official's inquiry — whether, in other words, there was an interpretative tradition behind Philip's appropriation of this text. This is the
question we want to address in this chapter.

The "Suffering Servant" passage (Isa 52:13–53:12) is one of four in the
second section of Isaiah (42:1-9;[1] 49:1-6; 50:4-9; 52:13–53:12) which profile
the servant of the Lord who serves as an agent of the God of Israel. While
the ancient reader obviously knew nothing about Second Isaiah, first isolated as a distinct section of the book in 1781 by Johann Christoff
Döderlein, professor at the University of Altdorf, or about the *Ebedlieder*
("Servant Songs"), first clearly identified as such by the German scholar

---

1. Bernhard Duhm limited this first *Ebedlied* to 42:1-4; 42:5-9 is distinctive in that it
has its own heading; it may have been added, but continues the theme of vv. 1-4.

Bernhard Duhm in 1892, the practice of reading the Scriptures as an inter-connected whole would have sharpened the reader's eye for such linguistic parallels and themes as are shared by these texts. Without excluding the possibility of a collective interpretation, which would not in any case nec-essarily have excluded reference to an individual prophetic figure, the highly individualized language of these four texts, over against the many allusions to Israel/Jacob as the Servant of the Lord, frequent in Isaiah 40–55, would have been noted by a reader in late antiquity without benefit of modern literary-critical techniques. One small indication that the distinc-tive character of these passages was noticed is the space separating Isa 42:1-4 from the following verse in the complete Isaiah scroll from the first Qumran cave (1QIsa^a) and in one of the fragmentary copies of the book from the fourth cave (4QIsa^h).

What, in other words, would have been recognized by our *dôrēš hammiqrâ* ("searcher of the Scriptures") in late antiquity as a possible reading would have been the profile of a prophetic individual acting as God's agent on behalf of the people of Israel, an individual inspired and spirit-possessed (Isa 42:1; 50:4), the object of a special divine election (41:8-9, etc.) from the first moment of life (44:2; 49:1, 5), a teacher who therefore fulfills his mission by speaking (49:2; 50:4) and one whose mission led to opposition, abuse, violent death, and ultimate vindication (49:4-5; 50:5-9; 52:13–53:12) by the God whom he served. The profile would not necessarily have been limited to passages which identify the subject explicitly as the Servant of the Lord, since there are other texts in the book of Isaiah in which a prophetic voice is heard[2] or which could have been understood to refer to the same individual (e.g., 57:1-2). In the present chapter we shall see how this composite image served as a model or template for prophetic agency in some of the great crises in late Second Temple Judaism.

It will be well to repeat a point made at the beginning of our inquiry, namely, that *the first stage in the interpretation of a prophetic book is to be found in the book itself.* Most commentators today would no longer be pre-pared to accept Duhm's view that the four Servant passages were inserted into the book of Isaiah haphazardly, wherever there was space on the papy-rus copy.[3] But even if Duhm was right, it does not follow that these pas-sages were exempt from the kind of expansive comment and reinterpreta-

2. Isa 40:6; 48:16b; 59:21; 61:1-4.
3. Bernhard Duhm, *Das Buch Jesaja*, 311.

tion in evidence elsewhere in the book. Two examples may be given. The self-presentation of a prophet in Isa 61:1-3 draws on the first of the Servant passages in 42:1-9: both are endowed with the spirit of God and both bring good news to the poor, the broken in spirit, metaphorically described as the bruised reed and the dimly burning wick. Isaiah 51:4-6, on the other hand, can be read as a fairly drastic reinterpretation of the first of the four Servant "songs." In 42:1-9, the imposition of law and justice is the task of the one addressed, certainly a political figure, almost certainly Cyrus described as "a light to the nations" *('ôr goyîm)* and later as Yahveh's anointed (45:1).[4] In 51:4b, on the other hand, law and justice themselves are to serve as "a light to the peoples" *('ôr 'ammîm)*, and they now proceed directly from God. In 42:4b the coastlands wait for law administered by God's representative in the political sphere, whereas in the reinterpretation they wait for God directly, without a human intermediary (51:5b). It seems that 51:4-6 comes from a stage of development, much in evidence in Isaiah 56–66, when it had become clear that Cyrus was not about to fulfill the expectations placed on him by his Jewish subjects and that therefore only the direct intervention of God could secure a better future.

The three Servant poems in Isaiah 49–55, in the first two of which the Servant speaks in his own name, reveal the profile of a prophetic teacher and preacher with a mission to restore Israel and announce salvation to the Gentile world, a mission which has provoked opposition and abuse and will eventually lead to a violent death. None of the three passages mentions disciples, but it would be natural — assuming some degree of coherence and consistency in the book — to conclude that "the Servants" of Isaiah 65–66, also opposed and marginalized, were the disciples of the Servant of the three texts in question. This association of "Servants" with the Servant was argued earlier in our inquiry. The comment following the Servant's account of his mission and the physical abuse he had suffered because of it (50:4-9) evidently comes from one who feels authorized to speak on behalf of the Servant and to pass judgment on his opponents (50:10-11). The most natural conclusion is that the speaker is a disciple who has internalized the message of the prophetic master. The panegyric pronounced on the dead Servant in 53:1-11 also makes best sense if delivered by a disciple, perhaps one recently converted to discipleship. The "offspring" (*zera'*, lit., "seed") mentioned towards the end of the

4. On Isa 42:1-4 as *originally* referring to Cyrus, see my *Isaiah 40–55*, 209-12.

panegyric (53:10) would then, in the context, refer to disciples of the martyred prophet.

The same prophetic leader associated with disciples could be alluded to in other passages in the book not identified by Duhm as *Ebedlieder*, especially passages in which a prophetic figure speaks self-referentially in the first person. Thus, several scholars in the modern period have added Isa 61:1-4, the text of Jesus' sermon in the Nazareth synagogue (Luke 4:18-19), to the Servant passages. Isaiah 59:21 is an oracular divine utterance addressed to an anonymous prophet promising that the prophetic gift will remain with him and his "seed" for the indefinite future and that in this way God's covenant with the people will be fulfilled.[5] One or two cryptic passages, relevant to our theme, seem to have been written for the small circle of those who could be expected to get the point. The first of these, Isa 30:19-21, reads as follows:

> You people in Zion who dwell in Jerusalem, you shall weep no more. He will surely show you favor when you cry for help, and he will answer when he hears you. The Sovereign Lord may give you the bread of adversity and the water of affliction, but your teacher will no longer remain hidden. Your eyes will see your teacher, and whenever you turn aside to the right or to the left your ears will hear a word spoken behind you: "This is the way, keep to it."

Practically all critical commentators assign this text to the Second Temple period, and later in the period rather than earlier.[6] The previous passage makes it clear that those addressed are not Jerusalemites in general but "those who wait for God," in other words, the remnant of Israel who form the core of the new community which comes increasingly into focus throughout the long editorial history of the book.[7] They will have more to

5. Cf. Isa 42:6 and 49:8, where the Servant is referred to as "a covenant of the people" (*běrît ʿam*).

6. Duhm, *Das Buch Jesaja*, 221-25; Georg Fohrer, *Das Buch Jesaja*, vol. 2: *Kap. 24-39*. ZBK (Stuttgart: Zwingli, 1967), 102-3; R. E. Clements, *Isaiah 1–39*. NCBC (Grand Rapids: Wm. B. Eerdmans, 1980), 250 (Persian period); Jacques Vermeylen, *Du Prophète Isaïe à l'apocalyptique*, 1:419. Otto Kaiser, *Isaiah 13–39*. OTL (Philadelphia: Westminster, 1974), 301-2, attributes the text to an eschatological teacher comparable to and contemporary with the *maśkîlîm* of Daniel who was forced into hiding during the persecution of Antiochus IV.

7. The same "people who dwell in Zion" are addressed in Isa 10:24 in a passage (10:20-27) which speaks about the remnant of Israel more clearly and insistently than in any other

suffer, and there will be more uncertainty and disorientation (turning to the right or the left), but they will have a teacher to guide them and move them in the right direction. The situation is strikingly reminiscent of the 20 years disorientation (groping like the blind) of the Damascus sectarians which came to an end with the advent of their Teacher (CD I 8-11).

Commentary has naturally focused on the identity of this teacher. The Hebrew substantive with suffix *(môrêkâ)* can be singular or plural; both 1QIsa[a] and LXX have the plural, but the decisive consideration is that the verb is in the singular. We are being told that this teacher has a special association with those addressed, that he is at present inaccessible to them, but that he will once again come into view, at which time he will instruct and guide them. The strangest bit of information, however, is that he will speak and be heard *behind them (mēʾaḥārêkâ)*. Following the lead of the Targum and Rashi, many commentators have identified the teacher as God, in keeping with indications elsewhere in the Hebrew Bible of a God who instructs and guides (e.g., Job 36:22, "Who is a teacher like him?).[8] But the fact that the Sovereign Lord is named in the same sentence suggests that access to the guidance of a *human* teacher is precisely how God will answer their prayers and show them favor. And what would it mean for God to speak and his voice to be heard behind them? Bernhard Duhm and John Skinner, two of the great names in Isaianic interpretation, imagined God as father directing his children as they walk ahead of him, while Georg Fohrer opted for God in the guise of a maternal guide ushering her children along.[9] Edward Kissane, the most distinguished Irish commentator on Isaiah in the modern period, originally pictured God as shepherd, but when he realized that shepherds, biblical shepherds at any rate, lead their sheep from the front, he emended *môrêkâ* ("your teacher") to *maʾărahkâ* ("your pathfinder"), a form which, however, is not attested in

---

part of the book and concludes with language reminiscent of the book of Daniel (10:23; cf. Dan 11:36). It is not surprising that the implications of this passage were seized on by the authors of the Qumran *pĕšārîm* (4QpIsa[a] 2-6 II 1-9; 4QpIsa[c] II 10-21).

8. Karl Marti, *Das Buch Jesaja erklärt.* KHC 10 (Tübingen: J. C. B. Mohr, 1900), 225; Duhm, *Das Buch Jesaja,* 223; J. Fischer, *Das Buch Isaias.* HSAT 7/1A (Bonn: Peter Hanstein, 1939), 203-4; Clements, *Isaiah 1–39,* 250; Brevard S. Childs, *Isaiah.* OTL (Louisville: Westminster/John Knox, 2001), 227.

9. Duhm, *Das Buch Jesaja,* 223; John Skinner, *The Book of the Prophet Isaiah: Chapters I-XXXIX,* 2nd ed. CBC (Cambridge: Cambridge University Press, 1915), 246; Fohrer, *Das Buch Jesaja,* 2:103.

Biblical Hebrew.[10] More recently, Wim Beuken took the first *môrêkâ* as referring to human teachers and the second to God, resulting in the rather odd translation, "Your teachers shall not be pushed aside any more, but your eyes shall be looking upon your Teacher." I am not sure how Beuken arrived at this translation, but in any case the problem of the voice heard from behind remains unsolved.[11]

A more promising point of departure is the account of Ezekiel's commissioning, in which he sees the great and sublime vision of the *merkaba*, the chariot throne, but hears the sound of the winged living creatures and the wheels *behind him* (*wā'ešma' 'aḥăray qôl ra'aš gādôl*, "I heard behind me a great roaring sound," Ezek 3:12). Much later, exiled in Patmos, John the Divine witnesses phantasmagoric scenarios; like Ezekiel he sees the living creatures around the throne (Rev 5:6), but at the outset of the vision hears a voice like a trumpet behind him (*opisō mou*, 1:10). While no more than chance clues, these may indicate the existence of a trope according to which auditory revelations were thought to come from behind the recipient. There is the further and more significant point that the relevant preposition *'aḥar ('aḥărê, mē'aḥărê)* can have a temporal as well as a spatial connotation, or a temporal sense can be expressed in spatial terms, as when we say "I now have that experience behind me." The sense may then be that those addressed are being assured that the guidance they will receive from their teacher will come to them from the past.

Briefly: the proposal to which these considerations are leading, and the solution which seems least open to objection, is that those addressed in Isa 30:19-21, a minority group which thought of itself as the prophetic remnant of Israel, are being promised an expression of divine favor in the form of the teaching and example of a prophetic leader now inaccessible in person, perhaps in hiding, perhaps in prison,[12] more likely dead. After a time of deprivation and sorrow they will see him, not in person, as no doubt

10. Edward J. Kissane, *The Book of Isaiah*, rev. ed. (Dublin: Browne and Nolan, 1960), 1:338, 346.

11. Willem A. M. Beuken, "What Does the Vision Hold: Teachers or One Teacher? Punning Repetition in Isaiah 30:20," *HeyJ* 36 (1995): 451-66; "Isaiah 30: A Prophetic Oracle Transmitted in Two Successive Paradigms," in Craig C. Broyles and Craig A. Evans, *Writing and Reading the Scroll of Isaiah*, 2:371.

12. Cf. Isa 51:14: "The one who now cowers will soon be released/he will not go down to death, to the pit/he will not lack for food." The verse is, however, textually and linguistically obscure; the context permits but does not demand a connection with 30:19-21.

they had done in the past, but as an inspiring presence in their lives, and they will find strength and guidance in his remembered example and teachings. If this is so, this teacher would prefigure other teachers with other disciples and would fit a pattern of prophetic leadership and discipleship familiar from many times and places, including the Qumran sectarian texts and the New Testament.

The teacher-disciple bond is occasionally explicit but generally tacit in the Servant poems. The Servant's mouth is a whetted sword (Isa 49:2). He has been given the tongue of the instructed so that he may sustain the dispirited by word of mouth (50:4-9). He is therefore a teacher and leader, and he discharges his mission in the face of opposition which has reached the point of physical abuse. As I noted earlier, the comment attached to this third Servant passage (50:10-11) has every appearance of coming from a disciple of the abused Servant:

> Whoever among you reveres Yahveh, let him heed the voice
>   of his Servant;
> whoever is walking in the dark and has no glimmer of light,
> let him trust in the name of Yahveh, and rely on his God.
> But all you who light your own fire, and set your own
>   firebrands alight,
> walk by the light of your fire and by the firebrands you
>   have kindled!
> This is my message for you: You shall lie down in torment!

The syntax of 50:10 is unclear. In the translation offered above I have taken "walking in darkness" to refer to those addressed who are urged to abide by the Servant's teaching. If, however, the phrase is taken to refer to the Servant rather than to those who heed the Servant's voice there could be an allusion to the hiddenness of the teacher in 30:19-21.

The teacher-disciple relationship is also implicit in the fourth Servant poem (Isa 53), in that the panegyric is recited by one who, after sharing the common interpretation of the Servant's misfortunes as divine punishment, came to grasp their true significance, in all probability only after the Servant's death. The intensity of the language and its arcane, recondite character mark it as the language of discipleship no less clearly than in the previous poem (50:10-11). These two texts, therefore, refer to one and the same prophet and teacher. From casual abuse in the first we move to injury and death in the second. As the Servant of the earlier text anticipates that God will be his vindicator (*maṣdîq*, 50:8a), so the Servant of the later one will vindicate "the many," but will do so posthumously (*yaṣdîq ṣaddîq 'abdî lārabbîm*, "my righteous servant will vindicate/render righteous the many," 53:11), a statement which will assume great importance in early Christianity, as we shall see. It seems that the expression "the many" (*hārabbîm*) anticipates technical usage in Qumran and early Christianity, where it designated a circle of disciples. It was also understood in this way in Dan 12:3, where the *maśkîlîm*, the leaders of the sect, are the ones who vindicate/render righteous the many (*maṣdîqê hārabbîm*), the circle of disciples.[13]

Prophetic texts are notoriously reluctant to provide information of a chronological, historical, or social nature, but if we may assume a degree of internal coherence in Isaiah 40–66, the teacher now hidden but to be revealed to his followers through his example and teaching could well be either the abused and martyred Servant himself or one of the servant-disciples who filled the same leadership role after his death. However that may be, Isa 30:19-21 provides a glimpse of a pattern of prophetic teacher-disciple relationship which will be reproduced in the relation between the *maśkîlîm* and the *rabbîm* in Daniel, the Teacher of Righteousness and the sectarians of Qumran, and both John the Baptist and Jesus and their respective followers.

The description of the Servant as *ṣaddîq* ("righteous") in Isa 53:11b creates an intertextual link with another cryptic passage of relevance to our theme. Isaiah 57:1-2 reads as follows:

> 1 The Righteous One has perished, and no one takes it to heart;
> the devout are swept away, and no one gives it a thought.
> It was on account of evil that the Righteous One was swept away.
> 2 He enters into peace.
> They repose in their last resting places.
> He is upright in his conduct.

While *ṣaddîq* can have a collective meaning with reference to righteous or innocent people, especially in Psalms, the fact that it occurs here with the article and at the beginning and end of verse 1 favors a reference to an indi-

---

13. On *hārabbîm* as a technical term for members of a community or sect, see pp. 66-70.

vidual righteous one associated with a group of the devout (*'anšê-ḥesed*, the equivalent of *ḥăsîdîm*). Commentators have struggled to make some sense of verse 2, sometimes by recourse to more or less drastic textual surgery. My proposal is to accept the text of verse 2 as it stands, but to read it as a collection of three glosses on the preceding verse arranged in the same order, the first and third referring to the individual *ṣaddîq* and the second to the *'anšê-ḥesed*. Both verses would therefore be set out in an a-b-a pattern. If we read it with the Isaianic Servant in mind, the affinities are difficult to ignore, apart from the possibility that the epithet *ṣaddîq* may have been added to 53:11b precisely to create an intertextual link with 57:1-2.[14] The Righteous One and the Servant are, respectively, "gathered" and "taken away," euphemisms for death, and their passing goes unregarded ("Who gives a thought to his fate?" 53:8a). For both, death is in some way the result of evildoing, though neither has done anything evil (53:8b, 9). Both passages refer to burial (53:9a),[15] and while the Righteous One enters into peace, the Servant will see light and be satisfied (53:11a). Finally, and most importantly, the Righteous One associated with a group of the devout (lit., "men of devotion") matches the Servant, who is promised his own "offspring," namely, disciples.

The conclusion to which these exegetical considerations are leading is that an integrative approach to Isaiah 40–66, and for that matter to the book as a whole, permits us to see prophetic agency in general, and the profile and mission of the Servant of the Lord continued by his disciples in particular, as a central theme in the book, and one by no means confined to the four *Ebedlieder* passages identified by Bernhard Duhm.

The Servant as Protomartyr and Eschatological Figure

It has occasioned some surprise that the Servant texts, especially the Suffering Servant text, seem to have had relatively little impact in the pre-Christian period. In this as in other respects we must be content to work with what we have, the relatively few writings which have survived from

---

14. In Isa 53:11b, *yaṣdîq ṣaddîq 'abdî lārabbîm*, *ṣaddîq* overburdens the verse and is placed anomalously before the substantive.

15. In the second of the three glosses, *yānûḥû 'al-miškĕbôtām*, "They repose in their last resting places," I assign the meaning "bier," "grave" to *miškāb*; cf. Isa 14:11; Ezek 32:25; 2 Chr 16:14 and LXX *hē taphē autou*.

the latter part of the Second Temple period, in the uneasy awareness that conclusions drawn from such severely limited source material remain subject to revision. Some commentators have found an allusion to the Isaianic Servant in that most obscure and baffling passage in Deutero-Zechariah which speaks of mourning for one who has been pierced:

> On that day I purpose to destroy all the nations that attack Jerusalem. I will pour upon the house of David and upon the inhabitants of Jerusalem a spirit of compassion and supplication, and they shall look on him[16] whom they have pierced, and they shall mourn for him as one mourns an only son, and weep bitterly over him as one that weeps bitterly over a firstborn child. (Zech 12:9-10)

It will not be necessary to discuss the many historical figures with whom the Pierced One of this text has been identified, extending over half a millennium from Josiah in the 7th century to Onias III in the 2nd century B.C.E. Early Christians referred it to Jesus (John 19:37; Rev 1:7), and a rabbinic tradition (*b. Sukkah* 52a) identified the Pierced One with Messiah ben Joseph, the forerunner of the Davidic Messiah, destined to die in battle fighting the enemies of Israel. Others have had the Suffering Servant of Isaiah 53 in mind. But the only feature which the Pierced One has in common with the Isaianic Servant is that both died a violent death, a fate which befell all those whose names have been proposed. It is, moreover, difficult to imagine why the house of David would mourn the Servant's death, even if there was a house of David at the time the death took place. If we read on to the next paragraph, it is even more difficult to envisage mourning for the dead Servant like the mourning for the god Hadad-rimmon in the plain of Megiddo.[17] Dependence on Isaiah 53 is equally improbable with respect to the shepherd struck down by command of Yahveh in Zech 13:7, since "shepherd" is a traditional metaphor for a ruler, not for a prophetic figure.

---

16. Reading *'ēlāw* ("on him") for MT *'maelay* ("on me").

17. The connection with Isa 53 was made by Douglas Rawlinson Jones, *Haggai, Zechariah, Malachi*. TBC (London: SCM, 1962), 163; and, in dependence on earlier commentators including Karl Elliger and Ernst Sellin, more recently by Martin Hengel, "The Effective History of Isaiah 53 in the Pre-Christian Period" in *The Suffering Servant: Isaiah 53 in Jewish and Christian Sources*, ed. Berndt Janowski and Peter Stuhlmacher (Grand Rapids: Wm. B. Eerdmans, 2004), 85-90.

With the elimination of Zech 12:9-10 and 13:7, the earliest allusion to the Isaianic Servant texts is to be found in Jesus ben Sirach's Hymn of Praise to the Ancestors (Sir 44–50). Elijah is one of the great figures of the past mentioned in this encomium, and the task assigned to him on his return in the messianic era is to restore the tribes of Jacob (*katastēsai phulas Iakōb*, Sir 48:10). Since the identical commission is laid on the Servant in the second of the four texts (*tou stēsai tas phulas Iakōb*, Isa 49:6), we can take this statement of Sirach, writing in the early 2nd century B.C.E., as the earliest example of the eschatologizing of the Isaianic Servant and his mission.[18] A few scholars have claimed to find evidence for an eschatological-messianic interpretation of the Servant in the complete Qumran Isaiah Scroll (1QIsaᵃ) and the LXX of Isaiah, both commonly dated to the mid-2nd century B.C.E. But we shall see in the next section of this chapter that the few variants in the Isaiah Scroll in comparison with the received text can be more easily explained otherwise than in a messianic sense, and there is nothing in the LXX of Isa 52:13–53:12 to suggest a messianic or eschatological *Tendenz*. In general, the LXX of Isaiah is more concerned to contemporize the text than to move it in the direction of an eschatological or messianic rereading.[19]

The situation is different with the book of Daniel and the conventicle within which and for which it was written, in or about 165 B.C.E., during the persecution launched by the Seleucid ruler Antiochius IV against his Jewish subjects. Several indications of an Isaiah-Daniel link were noted earlier in our study, for the most part pointing to the final scenario of salvation and judgment.[20] Daniel's fourth and last vision concludes with a

---

18. See Joachim Jeremias, "παῖς θεοῦ," *TDNT* 5:686-87.

19. See Isac Leo Seeligmann, *The Septuagint Version of Isaiah: A Discussion of Its Problems* (Leiden: Brill, 1948), 4; Arie van der Kooij, "Isaiah in the Septuagint," in Broyles and Evans, *Writing and Reading the Scroll of Isaiah*, 2:513-29; "Zur Theologie des Jesajabuches in der Septuaginta," in *Theologische Probleme der Septuaginta und der hellenistischen Hermeneutik*, ed. H. Graf Reventlow (Gütersloh: Chr. Kaiser, 1997), 9-25. Following Walther Zimmerli ("παῖς θεοῦ," *TDNT* 5:676-77), Hengel ("The Effective History of Isaiah 53," 134-36) builds up a case based on the emendation in Ziegler's Göttingen LXX Isa 53:2 of *anēggeilamen* ("we announced") to *aneteile men* ("for he rose up"), giving the reading *aneteile men enantion autou hōs paidion* ("he rose up in his presence as a child"). *aneteile* can then be related to the messianic code name *anatolē* (the east, the ascendancy of a star), and *paidion* calls to mind the messianic child of Isa 9:5 (Eng. 6); 7:14-16. But apart from the risk of basing a theory on an emendation, the context does not favor a messianic sense.

20. The principal Isaianic texts are 10:20-23, 25; 24:16; 26:19; 66:24.

prediction, at once terrifying and consoling, of the final outcome of the persecution described in terms borrowed from the prophetic books, in the first place Isaiah (Dan 12:1-5). After a period of tribulation unparalleled in history Daniel's people will be delivered, meaning not the people of Israel as a whole but only those whose names are written in the book, the same book as the one in Mal 3:16-18, in which the names of those who revered God are written. Many of the dead will arise, some to everlasting life, others to shame and everlasting contempt, a prospect which combines the awakening of those who lie in the dust (Isa 26:19) with the lurid scene described in the last verse of the book (66:24).[21] We are then told that

> The wise leaders *(maśkîlîm)* will shine like the brightness of the firmament, those who vindicate the Many *(maṣdîqê hārabbîm)* like the stars forever and ever. (Dan 12:3)

Here the debt to Isa 52:13–53:12 is clear. After passing through suffering and death the Servant will see posterity, prolong his days, and be the means of fulfilling God's plan. He will see light and be satisfied, and his life and death will have a positive and salvific effect on others:

> By his knowledge my [righteous] servant will vindicate the Many, it is he who bears the burden of their iniquities. (53:11)

The author of Daniel has given the Servant of Isaiah 53 a collective interpretation in order to serve as a model for the *maśkîlîm,* the leaders and teachers in the Danielic sect. The verb here translated "vindicate" *(hiṣdîq)* is ambivalent since it can also mean to declare someone innocent or render someone righteous, however that might be understood. In Isa 53:11 the Servant's knowledge plays a part, and this too is echoed in Dan 11:33, where we hear that the *maśkîlîm* confer understanding on many (or "the Many").

In short, the Isaianic text was intended to provide these leaders with essential clues to understanding their mission and destiny, their relation to the Israelite people as a whole and the members of their group known as "the Many" *(hārabbîm),* and, in general, their place in the great scheme of things. In his painful life and death the Servant took on himself the burden of the sufferings and the sins of others (53:4-6, 8, 11-12). The same is not

---

21. The verb *hāqîṣ* ("awake") appears in Isa 26:19 and Dan 12:2, and *dērā'ôn* ("an object of contempt or horror") occurs only in Isa 66:24 and Dan 12:2.

said in so many terms of the sufferings of the Danielic *maśkîlîm* during the persecution of Antiochus IV, but something of this may be implied in the use of the verb we have been discussing, and perhaps also in the reference to the refining, purifying, and cleansing brought about by the death of those *maśkîlîm* who had already paid the ultimate price during the persecution (Dan 11:33; 12:3). In Daniel, therefore, the Servant is presented as model for prophetic leadership, as protomartyr, and as the foreshadowing or typecasting for an eschatological savior figure.[22]

Most scholars now agree that, in spite of its absence from the Qumran archive, the Similitudes of Enoch (*1 En* 37–71) is a work of Jewish origin composed some time before the fall of Jerusalem in 70 c.e.[23] This part of the Enoch cycle has attracted great interest on account of its description of a superhuman "Son of Man," a savior-figure concealed with God, exalted on a heavenly throne, who will enact eschatological judgment on the kings and great ones of the earth. Dependence on the vision of the Ancient of Days and the Son of Man in Daniel 7 is clear (*1 En* 46:1; cf. Dan 7:13), though whereas the Danielic Son of Man (*kĕbar 'ĕnāš*, "one like a human being") represents a collectivity, namely, the "saints of the Most High," the Enochian Son of Man is an individual figure, finally identified with Enoch himself (*1 En* 71:14).[24] Several scholars have also proposed that the Isaianic Servant texts in Isa 42:6; 49:4; and 52:13–53:12 have contributed to the profile of the Enochian Son of Man.[25] If this could be shown to be

---

22. On the Isaianic background of Dan 11–12, see James A. Montgomery, *A Critical and Exegetical Commentary on the Book of Daniel*, 47-48; H. L. Ginsberg, "The Oldest Interpretation of the Suffering Servant," *VT* 3 (1953): 400-404; John J. Collins, *Daniel*, 390-94; Hengel, "The Effective History of Isaiah 53," 90-98.

23. John J. Collins, *The Scepter and the Star*, 177; *The Apocalyptic Imagination*, 2nd ed. BRS (Grand Rapids: Wm. B. Eerdmans, 1998), 177-78, argues against the thesis of Christian origin; cf. J. T. Milik, *The Books of Enoch: Aramaic Fragments of Qumrân Cave 4* (Oxford: Clarendon, 1976), 89-98. Michael A. Knibb, "The Date of the Parables of Enoch: A Critical Review," *NTS* 25 (1978/79): 345-59; and "'Isaianic Traditions in the Book of Enoch," in *After the Exile: Essays in Honour of Rex Mason*, ed. John Barton and David J. Reimer (Macon: Mercer University Press, 1996), 217-29, seems to favor a post-70 c.e. date: "The Parables form the latest section within the present Ethiopic book; they date in my view from towards the end of the 1st century c.e., after the fall of Jerusalem in 70, but they could be from earlier in the century" ("Isaianic Traditions," 219).

24. On the problems connected with this identification in *1 En* 70:1 and 71:4, see Collins, *The Apocalyptic Imagination*, 187-91.

25. J. Jeremias, *TDNT* 5:687-88; Johannes Theisohn, *Der auserwählte Richter.* SUNT 12

the case, it would be relevant and important for the study of the gospels, in which the Servant and the Son of Man are combined in the person of Jesus. Dependence on these Isaianic texts is, however, far from glaringly obvious. The attribution to the Son of Man of the titles "the Righteous One" and "the Chosen One" is worth considering, since the former is attached to the Suffering Servant (1 En 38:2-3, etc.; Isa 53:11) and the latter occurs regularly in Isaiah 40–55 in parallelism with Servant ('abdî, bĕḥîrî, "my servant," "my chosen one"). On the other hand, these titles are fairly common and contextually too isolated to establish a firm connection. The same can be said for the hiddenness of the Son of Man (1 En 48:6), presumed to derive from the statement in the second Servant passage, that "He (God) hid me in the shadow of his hand" (Isa 49:2).[26] The list of parallels between the Suffering Servant text and 1 Enoch 62–63 drawn up by George Nickelsburg, designed to establish dependence of the latter, is equally unspecific, and there is no case of linguistic overlap. For example, the exaltation of the Servant in Isa 52:13 (the Servant will be "highly honored, raised up, and greatly exalted") could be shown to be the source of 1 En 62:2a ("The Lord of Spirits sat on the throne of his glory") only if the Servant were presented as enthroned in heaven, as is the Son of Man in Matt 19:28 ("When the Son of Man is seated on the throne of his glory . . ."). The Matthean text is therefore a genuine parallel and the Isaianic text is not.[27] The only really clear case of dependence is the description of the Enochian Son of Man as a "light to the nations," also said of the Servant in the first two Servant texts (1 En 48:4; cf. Isa 42:6; 49:6).

A clearer example of a reworking of the Suffering Servant text can be found in the Wisdom of Solomon, probably from the late 1st century B.C.E. The first part of this work (Wis 1–6) presents the persecution and death of a righteous person (dikaios) at the hands of ungodly reprobates (2:12-24), his postmortem vindication by God (3:1-9; 4:7-15), and the stunned and

---

(Göttingen: Vandenhoeck & Ruprecht, 1975), 114-24; Matthew Black, "The Messianism of the Parables of Enoch," in The Messiah. Developments in Earliest Judaism and Christianity, ed. James H. Charlesworth (Minneapolis: Fortress, 1992), 156-61; Hengel, "The Effective History of Isaiah 53," 99-101.

26. Theisohn, Der auserwählte Richter, 123-24.

27. George W. E. Nickelsburg, Resurrection, Immortality and Eternal Life in Intertestamental Judaism. HTS 26 (Cambridge, Mass: Harvard University Press, 1972), 70-74. In this connection we might mention the anonymous exalted one of 4Q491c, to be considered shortly, who claims to have "taken his seat on a throne in the heavens."

fearful reaction of the perpetrators (5:1-8). The pattern is therefore close to if not identical with that of the Isaianic Servant in Isa 52:13–53:12. The persecuted *dikaios* (cf. *ṣaddîq*, Isa 53:11) calls himself *pais theou*, a servant (or child) of God (Wis 2:13), his death is a sacrificial offering (Wis 3:6; cf. *'āšām*, "guilt/reparation offering" in Isa 53:10), and in the time of their visitation the righteous will shine forth (3:7), as the Servant is assured that he will see light and be satisfied (53:11; cf. Dan 12:3). The same passage provides further, if indirect, confirmation of the connection with the death of the Righteous One and his devout disciples in Isa 57:1-2 argued earlier. Like the *ṣaddîq* in Isa 57:1-2, the despised and persecuted righteous one in Wisdom of Solomon has been removed by death on account of evil (Wis 4:11, 14). He has entered into peace and is at rest (Wis 3:3; 4:7), but those who observed this did not take it to heart (4:15; Isa 57:1; cf. 53:8). Allusion in the same passage to eunuchs who are promised a place in the temple of the Lord (Wis 3:14) and to children of adultery (v. 16), reminiscent of passages immediately preceding and following Isa 57:1-2,[28] reinforces both the reference to the fate of the *ṣaddîq* in 57:1-2 and the identification of the *ṣaddîq* with the Servant of the Lord of Isa 52:13–53:12.

We hear only uncertain allusions to the Isaianic Servant texts in the *Psalms of Solomon*. The author invokes the salvation of the Lord on his servant Israel (*Pss Sol* 12:6), and in pouring out his soul almost to death he may have had Isa 53:12 in mind (16:2). These uncertain echoes apart, nothing more is heard of the Isaianic Servant until after the rise of the Christian movement.[29] Justin's *Dialogue with Trypho* illustrates how the use of Isaiah 53 as a messianic proof text from the Christian side of the debate raised the question of a suffering and dying Messiah. Trypho, the Jewish interlocutor, was prepared to accept a Messiah who suffers and dies, and to do so on the basis of Isaiah 53, but objected to the manner of Jesus' death since, according to Deut 21:23 LXX, "the one hanged on a tree is under God's curse" (*Dial.* 90:1). The idea of a dying Messiah, though far from prominent, seems not to have been unknown in Judaism of the 1st century of the era. In the Ezra Apocalypse, from the end of that century, the seer is told that "my son the Messiah" will be revealed in the last age and will die after a

28. "The eunuchs who observe my sabbaths . . . to them I shall give in my house and within my walls a memorial and a name better than sons and daughters" (56:4-5); "As for you, draw near, children of the sorceress, offspring of an adulterer and a whore" (57:3).

29. Reference to the Servant in the Qumran texts is left over to the next section of the chapter.

reign of 400 years. In the roughly contemporary *Syriac Apocalypse of Baruch,* the Messiah, elsewhere referred to as "my servant the Messiah" (70:9-10), will return in glory to heaven, whether after death or not we are not told, at which time the dead will be resurrected (*2 Bar* 30:1). Isaiah 53 is not cited in either work, and there is no reference in either to suffering, but the titles "son" and "servant" *(pais, 'ebed)* permit the assumption that the authors may have had Isaiah 53 in mind. Whether the idea of the death of Messiah was already in circulation before the rise of Christianity is impossible to say with certainty. If the Armenian version of the *Testament of Benjamin* represents the original text, we would have a pre-Christian prediction that a descendant of Joseph, one without blemish or sin, would die for impious men (*T Ben* 3:8). But the language in which the prediction is made sounds very Christian, and both the idea and the language are without parallel in any Jewish text from the late Second Temple period.[30]

The messianic interpretation of the Servant, muted in the Ezra Apocalypse and the *Syriac Apocalypse of Baruch,* is explicit and sustained in the Targum and Jerome's *editio vulgata.* It seems that Targum Jonathan on Isaiah is the product of at least two generations of meturgeman activity before and after the Bar Kokhba war (132-135 C.E.), though the more explicitly messianic statements are more likely to have been written before than after that traumatic episode.[31] The Messiah is explicitly identified as the Servant of the Lord in *Tg. Isa.* 43:10 ("You are witnesses before me, says the Lord, and my Servant the Messiah with whom I am pleased"), and in the first of the Servant passages the identification is clearly assumed ("Behold my Servant, I will bring him near," 42:1).[32] Perhaps fired by the expectations raised by the second revolt against Rome, the Targum version of the fourth of the passages (Isa 52:13–53:12) presents the fundamentally different profile of a triumphant Servant-Messiah who will scatter the nations hostile to Israel (Rome in the first place), reduce their rulers to silence, and establish the messianic kingdom. His intercession will bring

30. Hengel, "The Effective History of Isaiah," 137-40, argues for a pre-Christian origin and believes that such ideas could have existed at the margins of Jewish society.

31. Bruce D. Chilton, *The Isaiah Targum: Introduction, Translation, Apparatus, and Notes* (Collegeville: Liturgical, 1990) with generous bibliog.; Jostein Ådna, "The Servant of Isaiah 53 as Triumphant and Interceding Messiah: The Reception of Isaiah 52:13–53:12 in the Targum of Isaiah with Special Attention to the Concept of the Messiah," in Janowski and Stuhlmacher, *The Suffering Servant,* 189-224.

32. Several MSS add *mĕšîḥā'*, "the Messiah"; Chilton, *The Isaiah Targum,* 80.

about the forgiveness of sins; he will free the land of Israel from foreign rule and rebuild the temple destroyed on account of sin, activities which indicate a date after 70 C.E. The unprepossessing appearance of the Servant is transferred to Israel long deprived of its Messiah (*Tg. Isa.* 52:14), the sufferings of the Servant are reassigned to hostile Gentile nations (53:3, 7), and the Servant-Messiah only risks his life but does not lose it (53:12).[33]

Jerome was certainly convinced that the Servant passages spoke about Jesus and indeed that the entire book contained, as he put it in the Prologue to his commentary, "the totality of the mysteries of the Lord" *(universa Domini sacramenta)*.[34] Unlike the Targumist, however, he was engaged in translating the Hebrew original (the *Hebraica veritas*) as accurately as possible and therefore could not permit himself the freedom to indulge in the kind of paraphrase which is routine in *Targum Jonathan*. This he left to his commentary on the book. Hence, messianic allusions could be insinuated only where some uncertainty or ambiguity in the original left room for them. The best known of these instances is probably his use of the term *virgo* (rather than an alternative term such as *puella, iuvencula*) for Hebrew *ʿalmâ* at Isa 7:14, but there are others. At several points he allows himself the exegetical license to substitute concrete for abstract wording in order to bring out a messianic sense — *iustus* ("the Righteous One") for *ṣedeq* ("righteousness"), *salvator* ("Savior") for *yešaʿ, yĕšûʿâ* ("salvation"), for example.[35] As far as I can determine, the Servant passages offered Jerome only one opportunity of this kind. The Hebrew of Isa 53:7a is fairly straightforward, as may be seen from a selection of modern English translations:

> NRSV: He was oppressed, and he was afflicted
> JPS and NEB: He was maltreated, yet he was submissive
> AB: He was abused, yet he was submissive.

This is in marked contrast to the Vulgate's

> He was offered up because he willed it.
> *(oblatus est quia ipse voluit)*

---

33. In *Tg. Isa.* 53:12, "He handed over his soul to death," the Aramaic expression *mĕsar napšāʾ*, "he handed over the soul (life)," is idiomatic for "he risked his life." See Ådna, "The Servant of Isaiah 53," 219-20.

34. *PL*, XXIV 18.

35. Isa 45:8; 51:5; 62:1-2, 11.

Jerome's version would have conveyed to his readers a quite clear and deliberate christological meaning, but one not as arbitrary as it might appear since it can be explained as an attempt, however forced it may seem, to translate the Hebrew *niggaś wĕhû' na'ăneh*.[36] The approach, therefore, is less direct, no doubt because explicating the christological significance of the texts was considered to be the task of the commentator rather than the translator.

The Servant of the Lord at Qumran

All four Servant texts are reproduced in the complete Isaiah Scroll from the first cave (1QIsaᵃ), dated to the middle to late 2nd century B.C.E. This version of the texts contains numerous minor variations from MT, most of them orthographic (e.g., frequent use of the conjunction to avoid asyndeton) but few of major interpretative significance. The addition of the word *'ôr* ("light") at Isa 53:11a gives the reading "after his painful life he will see light and be satisfied," but this reading is also attested in 1QIsaᵇ and 4QIsaᵈ in addition to LXX and the Syriac and Vulgate versions. In Isa 52:14b, "so marred was his appearance beyond human semblance," the equivalent in 1QIsaᵃ of the hapax legomenon *mšḥt* (*mišḥat*, presumably from *šḥt*, "destroy," "ruin") is *mšḥty*. Both E. Y. Kutscher and Dominique Barthélemy parsed this as *māšaḥtî*, "I have anointed," with the idea that it could be understood of priestly anointing or even in a messianic sense.[37] But one does not anoint someone's appearance, and the additional letter could be either *hireq compaginis* (GKC §90 *l*) or a simple slip.[38] 1QIsaᵃ also has frequent changes from singular to plural and vice versa and from third to second person and vice versa. In one instance (51:5), where MT reads "my arms will govern the peoples, the coastlands (or islands) wait for me, in my arm they hope," 1QIsaᵃ reads "*his* arm will govern the peoples, the coastlands

36. Jerome may have read some form of the verbal stem *ngš* rather than *ngś*, though the meaning "make an offering," lit., "bring near," requires the Hiphil theme; *na'ăneh* (Niphal *'nh*) with the meaning "accept with submission" is close to *voluit*.

37. E. Y. Kutscher, *The Language and Linguistic Background of the Isaiah Scroll (1QIsaᵃ)*. STDJ 6 (Leiden: Brill, 1974), 262; Dominique Barthélemy, *Critique Textuelle de l'Ancien Testament, 2: Isaïe, Jérémie, Lamentations*. OBO 20 (Göttingen: Vandenhoeck & Ruprecht, 1986), 387-90.

38. See the textual note in my *Isaiah 40–55*, 347.

wait for *him,* in *his* arm they hope." This reading could suggest a messianic interpretation together with an allusion to the Servant who speaks and is spoken of in 50:4-11,[39] but here too other possibilities exist. There is certainly no consistent messianic interpretation traceable throughout this version comparable to *Targum Jonathan* or Jerome's *editio vulgata.*

The other Isaiah text from the first cave, the incomplete 1QIsa[b] from which 42:1-4 is absent, is even closer to MT. In addition, some scraps of text from the four Servant passages have survived among the 4Q fragments but, again, with no significant variants affecting the meaning apart from the omission of *yiśrā'ēl* ("Israel") from Isa 49:3 in 4QIsa[d].[40] Unfortunately, no pesher on any of the four passages has survived. The Damascus Document (CD V 13) cites from the comment following the third Servant passage, which refers to those who "light their own fires and kindle their own firebrands" (Isa 50:10-11). In the Isaianic context, those who do so are the opponents of the prophetic Servant whose voice is heard in the previous six verses, but in the Damascus Document they are identified with the opponents of the sect. Also worthy of note is the pesher-like interpretation of Isa 52:7 in *11QMelchizedek* (11Q13), which identifies the herald who brings good tidings with the one anointed with the spirit in Isa 61:1. The prophetic-authorial voice heard in Isa 61:1-4 has enough in common with the Servant passages, especially 42:1-4, to justify putting it in the same category, as indeed several commentators in the modern period have done. Isaiah 61:1-4 proved to be a popular text at Qumran, as also in early Christianity (e.g., Luke 4:18-19).

We turn now to the compilation of thanksgiving hymns known as *Hodayot* ("Thanksgiving Hymns," 1QH[a]). Practically all scholars who have studied these hymns have accepted a distinction between Community Hymns and Teacher Hymns, one aspect of a fairly complicated redactional history.[41] The distinction is occasioned principally by complaints by the

---

39. Hengel, "The Effective History of Isaiah 53," 101-2.

40. "Israel" in Isa 49:3 MT, 1QIsa[a], LXX, and the Targum is widely taken to be a gloss since it is inconsistent with a mission *to* Israel consigned to an individual in vv. 5-6.

41. Gert Jeremias, *Der Lehrer der Gerechtigkeit.* SUNT 2 (Göttingen: Vandenhoeck & Ruprecht, 1963), 171-73. Jeremias identifies the following as Hymns of the Teacher: 1QH[a] II 1-19; II 31-39; III 1-18; IV 5–V 4; 29; V 5-19; V 20–VII 5; VII 6-25; VIII 4-40 (note that columns II–VIII in the original edition correspond to X–XVI in Florentino García Martínez and Eibert Tigchelaar, *The Dead Sea Scrolls Study Edition*); H.-W. Kuhn, *Enderwartung und gegenwärtiges Heil.* SUNT 4 (Göttingen: Vandenhoeck & Ruprecht, 1966), 23, adds II 1-19 but

speaker in the central part of the text (cols. X to XVI or XVII) about sickness, persecution, being driven into exile, and having to live in a foreign country (e.g., XII 8-12; XIII 5), none of which can easily be referred to a plurality. Since so much emphasis is placed on trials and tribulations in this central section, we might take the statement in 1QH^a IX 33, partially restored, as the introduction to the author's *historia calamitatum:* "[Let me announce in the assembly of the s]imple ones the (divine) judgments of my afflictions." The existence of Teacher Hymns may be accepted, but the distinction between teacher and community in the hymns as generally accepted is not written in stone. Unsolved problems about first person discourse in the canonical psalms, especially psalms of lamentation, whether they be individual or communal, will make it easier for us to accept that there is still much in the central section that could be referred to the group, and there are statements in the rest of the collection which could readily apply to an individual (e.g., "I defiled myself with impurity," III 19). The prudent course therefore will be to read all of the hymns, attending where necessary to the different recensions, bearing in mind that the authorial first person may imply an individual reference, or the voice may be that of a representative of the group. By the same token, allusions in the hymns to the Isaianic Servant may, depending on the context, be understood in an individual or collective sense.

Somewhat unevenly throughout the hymns the speaker refers to himself as God's servant, *'ebed.* [42] In biblical usage *'ebed* is a synonym for *nābî',* "prophet," and there is no doubt about the speaker's prophetic self-consciousness: he has been sprinkled with or drenched in the Holy Spirit (IV 26),[43] he knows divine mysteries on account of the spirit which God has placed in him (V 24-25; also XX 11-12), and he has been purified by the Spirit (VIII 20). This kind of language is consistent with the manner in which the Isaianic Servant describes himself and his mission, but there are more specific parallels. The speaker in the hymns is acknowledged by God

---

omits II 31-39 and III 1-18 and the hymns in IV–V are less extensive. For an updated list, see Eileen Schuller, "Hodayot," in *Qumran Cave 4.XX: Poetical and Liturgical Texts, Part 2,* ed. Esther Chazon et al. DJD 29 (Oxford: Clarendon, 1999), 74-75.

42. IV 11, 23, 25, 26; V 24; VI 8, 11, 25; VIII 19, 21, 23, 27; XIII 15, 28; XV 16; XVII 11; XVIII 29; XIX 27, 30, 33; XXII 16; XXIII 6, 10.

43. The verb (*nôp* Hiphil) occurs only in Ps 68:10 (Eng. 9), where it refers to heavy rainfall, and in Prov 7:17, where the reference is to a woman sprinkling her bed with fragrant herbs and spices.

from the womb (XVII 29-30), just as the Isaianic Servant was called when still in the womb (Isa 49:1). His ear is uncovered to hear divine revelations (IX 21), just as the Servant's ear is "awakened" (Isa 50:4). His tongue is like those taught by God (VI 11; XV 10; XVI 36), just as the Servant was given "the tongue of those who are instructed" (Isa 50:4). By this means — by speaking and by teaching — the author can "support the weary with a word" (XV 36) in imitation of the Isaianic Servant (Isa 50:4b). Like the Servant, he suffers both from sickness[44] and the contempt and violence of his enemies.[45] There is, finally, the expectation of future exaltation (XI 20-22) and of light which will enable the speaker to enlighten the Many (XI 3; XII 27-28), which also reflects quite closely the language in which the final destiny of the Servant is expressed:

> See, my servant will achieve success,
> he will be highly honored, raised up, and greatly exalted. . . .
> After his painful life he will see light and be satisfied.
>
> (Isa 52:13; 53:11a)

While there is no suggestion that contempt and lack of esteem, and the catalogue of miseries in XVI 27-36, were thought to have redemptive value for others, there are solid grounds for the conclusion that the profile of the Isaianic Servant formed a significant aspect of the self-image of the author of the hymns.[46]

That the Teacher of Righteousness was author of at least some of

---

44. The language of affliction (*nega'*, XII 36; XIII 28, etc.) and pain (*mak'ôb* XVII 6, cf. XIII 28; XVI 28) is reminiscent of Isaiah 53: *nāgûa'*, v. 4b; *'iš mak'ōbôt*, v. 3a.

45. He speaks of those who despise him (*bôzay*, XII 22); the Servant likewise was despised (*nibzeh*, Isa 53:3ab); both were held of no account (*lo' yaḥšĕbûnî*, XII 8; *lo' ḥăšabnuhû*, Isa 53:3b).

46. The evidence is assessed cautiously by John J. Collins, "Teacher and Servant," *RHPR* 80 (2000): 37-50. The contrary view, that the Servant passages had only slight influence on the author of the *Hodayot*, was defended in the early days of Qumran studies by J. Carmignac, "Les Citations de l'Ancien Testament, et spécialement des Poèmes du Serviteur, dans les Hymnes de Qumran," *RevQ* 2 (1960): 357-94, esp. 383-94; and Jeremias, *Der Lehrer der Gerechtigkeit*, 299-307. Using a rather mechanical and quantitative method, Carmignac concluded that only three Servant texts can be identified in the hymns (Isa 49:4; 50:4; 53:3), while Jeremias reduced these to one, i.e., 50:4 (pp. 306-7). Hengel, "The Effective History of Isaiah 53," 118, relying on Carmignac and Jeremias, dismisses the possibility of any influence of the Suffering Servant on the Teacher of Righteousness. My assessment of this issue in *Isaiah 40–55*, 86-87, I would now consider too cautious.

these hymns is no less controvertible, though widely accepted. It is consistent with the frequent mention of possession by the Holy Spirit, the spirit of prophecy, together with the equally frequent allusions to persecution and suffering consistent with what we hear about the Teacher in other Qumranic texts, especially the Habakkuk commentary. The speaker has a leadership role, and it is in his role as leader that he encounters opposition: "You (God) have set me up as a reproach and an object of mockery for the traitors . . . on account of the iniquity of the reprobates I have become the target of slander on the lips of the violent, while the scoffers grind their teeth. I have become a laughing-stock for transgressors, and against me the assembly of the reprobates is aroused" (X 9-12).[47] The voice we are hearing is certainly the voice of a teacher. Like the Isaianic Servant, his tongue is like that of those who learn from God, God's disciples, and by his speech he supports the weary and dispirited (XV 10; XVI 36; cf. Isa 50:4a). It is no doubt by means of his teaching that he enlightens the face of the Many, that is, the members of the group to which he belongs (XII 27; cf. Isa 53:11b).

At this point, the so-called Self-Glorification Hymn (4Q491c) calls for comment.[48] This text, reconstructed out of several fragments, is a first person address of a teacher who, though at one time despised and shunned, now claims to enjoy divine or quasi-divine status in the company of the angelic hosts. The text was first published by Maurice Baillet in 1982 as 4Q491 fr. 11 I, later designated 4Q491c. Baillet assigned it on paleographical grounds to the War Scroll from Cave 1 (1QM) and entitled it *Le Cantique de Michel* ("the Canticle of Michael") on account of the role of the angel Michael in the eschatological war of the Sons of Light against the Sons of Darkness.[49] Since then, the publication by Eileen Schuller of fragments from a recension of the *Hodayot* from Cave 4, one of which has clear parallels with our text, has made it apparent that it has more in common with the *Hodayot* than the War Scroll (1QM).[50] Meanwhile, four small fragments,

47. Cf. 1QpHab I 12–II 10; V 10-12; XI 5-8.
48. I say "so-called" because, as I will try to show, the central first person affirmation in this text is not really a hymn at all. In any case, I prefer the title "Hymn of Exaltation" suggested by Martin G. Abegg, Jr., "4Q471: A Case of Mistaken Identity?" in John C. Reeves and John Kampen, *Pursuing the Text*, 137.
49. Maurice Baillet, *Qumrân Grotte 4, III (4Q482–4Q520)*, 26-29. See also García Martínez and Tigchelaar, *The Dead Sea Scrolls Study Edition*, 2:978-81, for one or two alternative readings.
50. Eileen Schuller, "A Hymn from Cave Four *Hodayot* Manuscript 4Q427 7 i and ii,"

two of which contain only one word each, also originally thought to be part of the War Scroll, turned out to have language in common with 4Q491c. Designated 4Q471b, this fragmentary and much-reconstructed text provided a fourth witness to the "hymn" together with 1QH[a] XXVI, 4Q427 7 I, and 4Q491c.[51] All four are dated on palaeographical grounds to the late Hasmonean–early Herodian period, but the criteria are not precise enough to allow us to put them in chronological order.

The existence of even fragmentary variants provides some help in reconstructing 4Q491c, but by no means all the gaps can be filled in. It has much in common with both 4Q427 and 4Q471b and appears to overlap with 1QH[a] XXVI, though unfortunately the first five lines and much of the rest of this column are missing. Our text would fit before the first lines of 1QH[a] XXVI, which could be plausibly reconstructed if the limited space permitted it, but this appears not to be the case. It begins and ends by addressing the congregation as the Righteous, the Saints, and the Poor and does so in a way stylistically similar to the canonical community hymns. First person speech in the middle of the passage (lines 5-11/12)[52] introduces a quite different style, certainly not hymnic, but rather declarative in the manner of first person prophetic discourse well represented in Isaiah 40–55. This central part contrasts sharply with the balanced and parallel lines of verse detectable before and after it (lines 2, 3, and 13).[53] It is also noteworthy that the seven rhetorical questions beginning in line 8 are reminiscent of the self-designation and self-vindication of the Servant in Isa 50:6-9: "Who dares to bring an accusation against me? . . . Who will pass judgment on me? . . . Who is the one who will condemn me?" Even if it were

---

JBL 112 (1993): 605-28; also "Hodayot," 69-123, esp. 96-108. The fragment would fit, if anywhere in the *Hodayot*, at the top of col. XXVI of 1QH[a]. Abegg, "4Q471: A Case of Mistaken Identity," 136-47, argued on palaeographical grounds against 4Q471 belonging to the War Scroll (1QM).

51. Esther Eshel, "4Q471[b]: A Self-Glorification Hymn," *RevQ* 17 (1996): 175-203; "Self-Glorification Hymn," in Chazon et al., *Qumran Cave 4.XX*, 421-32. For a synopsis of the three versions, see Devorah Dimant, "A Synoptic Comparison of Parallel Sections in 4Q427 7, 4Q491 11 and 4Q471B," *JQR* 85 (1994): 157-61.

52. The large ל (*lamed*) at the left extremity of line 12 probably marked a major break corresponding to the conclusion of Baillet's *Cantique de Michel*.

53. The original and intriguing reading of 4Q491 fr. 11 by Morton Smith, "Ascent to the Heavens and Deification in 4QM[a]," in *Archaeology and History in the Dead Sea Scrolls*, ed. Lawrence H. Schiffman. JSPSup 8 (Sheffield: Sheffield Academic, 1990), 181-88, is based on a metrical structure which relies too heavily on reconstruction to be entirely persuasive.

possible to detect a metrical pattern by dint of picking one's way through the textual debris and inserting a few words here and there, it would not alter the fact that the first person declarative section in the core of the text is *generically* different from the psalmlike introduction and conclusion. The closest parallels that come to mind are first person self-descriptions and self-praise of personified Wisdom (e.g., Prov 8:22-31) and aretalogies minus the miracles, for example, the self-praises of the exalted goddess Isis. Clearly, more work needs to be done on this issue of genre.

The following tentative translation is my own but, needless to say, it owes a significant debt to previous attempts.[54] It will be obvious that it is not an attempt to produce a technically correct version, much less to improve on Baillet's *editio princeps* (see n. 49), and it will be equally obvious that some of the readings are speculative. For the most part, I have translated only what can be read consecutively with the help of the parallel versions, and I have had recourse to reconstruction as seldom as possible; where I have done so, the proposed reconstruction is set out in square brackets. The reader may check the translation against the *editio princeps* and the translations referred to above.

2a	Let the righteous exult in his mighty power!
2b	Let the holy ones rejoice with righteousness [in his salvation]
3a	. . . Israel he established it from of old,
3b	His truth and the mysteries of his wisdom in all generations
4a	VACAT
4b	and the Council of the Poor as an everlasting congregation . . .

4b . . . Among the everlasting blameless ones [he gave me] 5 a mighty throne in the congregation of the angels on which none of the kings of old has sat, and their nobles shall not . . . 6 . . . My glory is without compare, and no one but me is exalted, nor can any oppose me; as for me, I have taken my seat on [a throne] in the heavens, and there is none . . . 7 . . . I am reckoned among the angels, and my abode is in the

54. Baillet, *Qumrân Grotte 4, III*, 28-29 (with a system of numbering lines now abandoned); García Martínez and Tigchelaar, *The Dead Sea Scrolls Study Edition*, 2:981; Michael O. Wise, "מי כמוני באלים: A Study of 4Q491c, 4Q471b, 4Q427 7 and 1QH^A 25:35-26:10*," *DSD* 7 (2000): 178-83; Smith, "Ascent to the Heavens," 184-85; Israel Knohl, *The Messiah before Jesus* (Berkeley: University of California Press, 2000), 77; Hengel, "The Effective History of Isaiah 53," 142-43.

holy congregation. My desire is not after the flesh, rather, all that is precious to me (consists in) the glory 8 [of the] holy dwelling. Who has been accounted an object of contempt like me, yet who can compare with me in glory? Who is the one who, like those who cross the sea, will come back and tell? . . . 9 . . . [like] me. Who bears [all] afflictions like me, and who b[ears the burden] of evil to compare with me? There is none. I have been instructed, and no teaching compares with 10 [my teaching]. Who will attack me when I open [my mouth]? Who can contain the flow of my speech? Who can contend with me and equal me in my judgment? 11 [There is none to compare with me] for I am reckoned with the angels. My glory is (to be) with the sons of the king. To me belongs refined gold and to me belongs gold of Ophir . . . 12 VACAT

13a   . . . [Exult] O righteous ones in the God of [glory]
13b   In the holy abode sing psalms to him! . . .
14a   . . . Let exultation resound in the [house of] meditation (?)
14b   . . . in everlasting joy; and there is none like . . .
15   . . . to set up the horn of . . . . . .
16   . . . strongly to make known his power . . .
17   VACAT

Notes

1 Only two words with several uncertain letters are preserved from 1, perhaps *hiplā' nôrā'ôt*, "He (God) has done wonderful and awesome deeds."

2 Neither here nor in line 3 is the translation meant to reproduce a regular metrical bicolon since several words are missing at the beginning and the end of the line; the parallelism is nevertheless easily detected. The call to exult and rejoice is addressed to the members of the community in liturgical session, often referred to in the sectarian texts, as in the canonical Psalms, as *ṣaddîqîm* ("righteous") and *qĕdôšîm* ("saints," "holy ones").[55]

2b Rejoicing (verbal stem *gîl*) in the salvation offered by God is a frequent theme in Psalms (Ps 9:15 [Eng. 14]; 13:6 [5]; 21:2 [1]), but the restoration is uncertain.

---

55. See above pp. 187-91, 207-8. Wise (*DSD* 7 [2000]: 184) takes the call as addressed to the angels and therefore prefers *'ĕlohîm* ("gods") to Baillet's (26) *ṣaddîqîm* ("righteous").

3a The antecedent of "it" (the suffix of *hēkînô*) is lost; probably a phrase containing the word *ḥokmâ* ("wisdom") par. with *'ormâ* ("prudence"); cf. Prov 8:12.

4b Most of the second half of the line is missing. Wise (*DSD* 7 [2000]: 183) supplies "and [they are to say, 'Blessed be God who has seated me among] the [et]ernally blameless . . . ,'" implying that the hymn continues on without a break. Smith ("Ascent to the Heavens," 184-85) suggests "Amen, Amen" with a blank space indicating that what follows is a distinct section of the text. But since the missing verb governing *kissē' 'ōz*, "a mighty throne" (perhaps *nātan lî*, "he gave me"), must have been in the second half of v. 4, the self-glorifying must begin in that verse.

5 "angels" = *'ēlîm*, lit., "gods," also in lines 7 and 11; "kings of old" = *malkê qedem*, better than "kings of the east." In nonbiblical Qumran texts *qedem* occurs with the meaning "east" only in the description of the temple in the Temple Scroll (11Q19 XXXVIII–XXXIX). In Biblical Hebrew "the east" is usually *qādîm; qedem* occurs only in the locative form *qēdmāh*. Smith ("Ascent to the Heavens," 183-84) extracts from this verse the meaning "No Edomite shall be like me in glory" with reference to the Idumean Herod, but the space between *dwmy* and the *aleph* would seem to exclude this reading.

6 "nor can any oppose me": *wĕlo' yābô' bî'*, lit., "will not come against me"; the claim is comparable with claims made by the Teacher in 1QH^a XXVI 6-7; 4Q427 7 11; 4Q471b 7-8.

7 "The holy congregation" (*'ădat qōdeš*), a title which can refer either to the earthly (1QS V 20; 1QSa I 9, 12-13; 4Q181 I 4) or the heavenly congregation (1QM XII 7; 1QH^a V 14); here the latter.

8 *bî'* in the phrase *mî' lĕbûz neḥšab bî'*, here translated "Who has been accounted an object of contempt like me?" would more normally mean "on account of me," "à cause de moi" (Baillet), but this does not make good sense in the context; I therefore agree with Esther Eshel's translation of the same phrase in the reconstructed 4Q471b line 2, "Who has been accounted despicable like me?" ("Self-Glorification Hymn," 431). The last part of the verse is very uncertain, as the editor admitted ("la lecture est désespérée"; Baillet, *Qumrân Grotte 4, III*, 28), but if "like those who cross the sea" (*kĕbā'ê yām*) is correct, it could be an allusion to Deut 30:13, "It is not across the sea that you should say, 'Who will cross over the sea for us and get it for us,'" understood as the quest for esoteric wisdom, with the last phrase in the line, "Who will come back and tell?" based on a very confusing scribal correction; compare the question of Agur ben Yakeh in Prov 30:4, "Who has ascended to heaven and come down?"

9 I follow Eshel's proposal in 4Q471b 2, but with *sbl* rather than *ysbl*, namely, *mî' sābal ra'*, "Who has borne the burden of evil as I have?" rather than Wise: "Who compares to me for lack of evil?"; cf. 4Q471b line 12. Wise argues at length for reading "and never have I been instructed" (verb *šnh* Niphal) in spite of the grammatical anomaly of *'ên* followed by a finite verb. The instances cited by Wise from Biblical Hebrew are not persuasive: Exod 3:2 can be read as a (rare) Pual participle without the *mem* (GKC §52 s); Jer 38:5 and Prov 5:17 are not followed by finite verbs; Eccl 8:11 can be repointed as a Niphal participle, leaving Job 35:15, *'ên pāqad 'appô* as the one anomalous case, perhaps incorrect (GKC §52 k), but even if in order not a sound basis for Wise's reading.

11 In the final clause of this verse I read *lî'* ("to me") with García Martínez and Tigchelaar, *The Dead Sea Scrolls Study Edition*, 2:980, rather than the negative particle *lô'* (Baillet, *Qumrân Grotte 4, III*, 27); cf. 4Q427 7 I 12, *lo' bĕpaz 'aktîr lî*, "I do not crown myself with (a crown of) refined gold"; for gold of Ophir, *ketem 'ôpîr* (here the plural *'ôpîrîm*) par. with *paz* ("refined gold"); see Isa 13:12.

14 *hašmî'û bĕhegî' rinnâ*, lit., "Let your jubilation be heard in meditation"; here "the place of meditation" in parallelism with "the holy abode"; the place in question was no doubt where "the Book of Hegi" (both vocalization and the identity of this book are uncertain) was "murmured," i.e., read aloud and studied (cf. Josh 1:8; Ps 1:2).

Read as an alternative version of 4Q427 and 4Q471, which appear to fit with the extremely lacunous column XXVI of the *Hodayot*,[56] the so-called Self-Glorification Hymn has a literary affinity of some kind with 1QH[a]. The intense interest in the alternative universe of angelic beings is appar-

---

56. John J. Collins and Devorah Dimant, "A Thrice-Told Hymn: A Response to Eileen Schuller," *JQR* 85 (1994): 151-55, argue on the basis of style and content that 4Q427 could not have belonged to the *Hodayot*. The problem is the extremely fragmentary state of col. XXVI 6-16, from which less than a score of words or, more often than not, parts of words has survived. In spite of the danger of creating a lion out of a claw, it seems to me that the positioning of these fragments justifies the reconstruction of a text parallel to and practically identical with 4Q427 fr. 7 I 10-20.

ent throughout both the exaltation text and the *Hodayot*. In the latter, the speaker's ears have been opened to wonderful mysteries (IX 21, etc.), his face has been lit up, a condition which is perhaps meant to recall the transfiguration of Moses in Exod 34:29-35 (XI 3), he is radiant with a sevenfold light (XV 24; cf. Isa 30:26), he has been raised to an everlasting height and walks on a boundless plain (XI 20-22). In some respects, notwithstanding, the exaltation text goes beyond anything claimed by the speaker throughout the *Hodayot*, whether in his own person or as representing the aspirations of the members of the group. This is especially the case with the claim to occupy a throne in heaven, which puts him on a par with the Son of Man of the book of Daniel (Dan 7:9) and the gospels (Matt 19:28; 25:31), as well as Metatron of the Hebrew *Book of Enoch* and certain Tannaitic traditions.[57] The exaltation text may therefore have been composed on the model of the last column of the Hymns (XXVI) and appended to the collection. There is no way to be sure.

We are now in a position to inquire whether the Isaianic Servant texts, especially the last of the four dealing with the humiliation, suffering, death, and ultimate vindication of the Servant, have contributed to the exaltation text.[58] The glorification claimed by the writer (*kābôd*, "glory," occurs four times in our text) recalls the assurance that the Servant will be "highly honored, raised up, and greatly exalted" (Isa 52:13).[59] Likewise, the theme of the subordination of kings and rulers is common to both the last of the Servant passages (52:15) and the exaltation text (lines 5-6). The Isaianic Servant is taught by God and fulfils his mission by teaching (Isa 53:11a; cf. 49:2; 50:4), and the exalted one of the Qumran text boasts of his incomparable gift as a teacher (lines 9-10). In appealing to Servant passages other than Isa 52:13–53:12, I am aware that whoever wrote the exaltation text was not familiar with historical-critical work on the book of Isaiah and had not read Bernhard Duhm's commentary. But the practice of reading a text like Isaiah

57. Collins, *The Scepter and the Star*, 141-46; Gershom Scholem, "Metatron," *EncJud* 11:1443-46.

58. Hengel, "The Effective History of Isaiah 53," 143-44, refers briefly to the common themes of exaltation, opposition to kings and princes, and sufferings. Knohl, *The Messiah before Jesus*, 44-45, has also noted the similarity at the linguistic level. Collins, *RHPR* 80 (2000): 46, finds only echoes of Isaiah 53 in the text.

59. With Isa 52:13 *yārûm* ("he will be exalted"), cf. *wělô' yěrômēm zûlātî*, "no one but me has been exalted," line 6. For the third verb in this verse (Isa 52:13) LXX substitutes *doxasthēsetai*, "he will be glorified."

as an integrated whole with interconnected parts, and the demonstrated exegetical skill in picking out and exploiting linguistic similarities demonstrated by Qumran authors, would have sharpened his eye to note the close connections between Servant passages with distinctive individual traits.

The most significant parallel is the language in which the experience of humiliation and suffering is described. The two compositions share the same verbs: both subjects are despised (verbal stem *bzh*), and in describing their positive acceptance of suffering the paired verbs *(nś', sbl)* occur in both texts.[60] What is lacking as an *explicit* element in the Qumran text is the self-sacrificial and atoning quality of the contempt and suffering borne by the Isaianic Servant, but even here we cannot speak with too much assurance. The text is lacunous, and in any case line 9 (also lacunous) can be reconstructed to render a sense close to the language in which the atoning function of the Isaianic Servant is expressed:

> Who bears all afflictions like me?
> And who bears the burden of evil to compare with me?

Cf. Isa 53:3-5, 11-12:

> He was despised, and we held him of no account.
> Yet it was he who bore our affliction,
> he who bore the burden of our sufferings. . . .
> He was wounded because of our transgressions,
> crushed on account of our iniquities.
> On him was made the chastisement that made us whole,
> we found healing because of his wounds. . . .
> By his knowledge my servant will vindicate many,
> it is he who bears the burden of their iniquities. . . .
> He bore the sin of many,
> he interceded for their transgressions.

While the differences are obvious, the language of the Qumran text suggests the possibility that something more is intended than a retrospective

---

60. For *bzh:* Isa 53:3 twice; line 8 of our text; cf. 4Q471b line 2 (reconstruction following Eshel, "Self-Glorification Hymn," 428); elsewhere in the *Hodayot* the speaker is treated as an object of contempt (לבוז, 1QHᵃ X 33-34; cf. XII 22). For *nś'/sbl*, see Isa 53:4a, 11b, 12c; line 9 of our text, and 4Q471b line 2. In both versions the verbs occur in a reconstructed text, but the reconstruction is plausible and has been generally accepted.

on a personal history of sickness, misfortune, and oppression; and this would be more clearly the case if the speaker can be identified with the Teacher whose voice is heard throughout the *Hodayot*.

This brings us to the issue which has understandably loomed large for readers of this text: Who is the incomparable teacher who makes these remarkable claims? Since a connection with the War Scroll is no longer accepted, Baillet's identification with Michael the archangel[61] has been dropped by practically all commentators in favor of a human figure. Morton Smith, one of the first to offer an interpretation of the text, read it as an ecstatic experience of ascent and deification associated with practices or techniques designed to induce a state of transformed consciousness — the earliest example of a kind of ecstatic mysticism with which, so Smith claimed, Jesus was also familiar.[62] Perhaps influenced by local (Brazilian) liturgical practice, Paolo Augusto de Souza Nogueira understands it as the speaker's summons to the congregation to participate ecstatically in the heavenly worship.[63] Others have adopted, generally with some hesitation, a collective interpretation, one in which the speaker represents the group.[64] John J. Collins, who has returned to this text several times over the last few years, suggests that the speaker is an eschatological figure, a high priest who will atone for sin at the end of the age. One problem with this hypothesis is the need to rely on the fragmentary 4Q541 (4QApocryphon of Levi[b]) for support, a somewhat risky case of *obscurum per obscurius*.[65] Collins was

---

61. *Qumrân Grotte 4, III*, 26-29.

62. Smith, "Ascent to the Heavens," 181-88; also "Two Ascended to Heaven — Jesus and the Author of 4Q491," in *Jesus and the Dead Sea Scrolls*, ed. James H. Charlesworth (New York: Doubleday, 1992), 290-301.

63. Paolo Augusto de Souza Nogueira, "Ecstatic Worship in the Self-Glorification Hymn (4Q471B, 4Q427, 4Q491C)," in *Wisdom and Apocalypticism in the Dead Sea Scrolls and the Biblical Tradition*, ed. Florentino García Martínez. BETL 168 (Leuven: Leuven University Press, 2003), 385-94.

64. Emile Puech, *La Croyance des Esséniens en la Vie Future: Immortalité, Résurrection, Vie Éternelle?* EBib N.S. 21-22 (Paris: Gabalda, 1993), 492-95; Hartmut Stegemann, "Some Remarks to 1QSa, to 1QSb, and to Qumran Messianism," *RevQ* 17 (1996): 479-505; Hengel, "The Effective History of Isaiah 53," 145.

65. Collins and Dimant, *JQR* 85 (1994): 151-55; Collins, *The Scepter and the Star*, 136-53; *Apocalypticism in the Dead Sea Scrolls* (London: Routledge, 1997), 147; *RHPR* 80 (2000): 45-47. Esther Eshel takes the same line in *RevQ* 17 (1996): 175-203; "The Identification of the 'Speaker' of the Self-Glorification Hymn," in *The Provo International Conference on the Dead Sea Scrolls: Technological Innovations, New Texts, and Reformulated Issues*, ed. Donald W. Parry and Eugene C. Ulrich. STDJ 30 (Leiden: Brill, 1999), 619-35; "Self-Glorification Hymn," 427-28.

no doubt aware of this and stated his conclusions with due caution, admitting that the identity of the speaker remains mysterious.[66]

No such caution inhibited Israel Knohl, who identified the speaker with Menahem the Essene, an older contemporary of Herod the Great mentioned in passing by Josephus (*Ant.* 15:373-79), whom he conflates with the Menahem who "went forth" (whatever that means) in *m. Ḥag.* 2:2 and other rabbinic texts.[67] While skepticism is also in order with respect to the name Michael Wise has assigned to the Teacher of Righteousness, namely, Judah, I find appealing the idea that 4Q491c derives from and was recited by a disciple of the Teacher as a celebration of his life, death, and postmortem exaltation.[68] If, as I have argued, the profile of the Teacher is modeled on that of the equally anonymous Isaianic Servant of the Lord,[69] we would have a striking parallel with the panegyric pronounced by a disciple after the Servant's violent death (Isa 53:1-11). The most obvious difference is that the self-exaltation text is in the first rather than the third person. This might imply that, while reflecting an intensely personal experience, it could be appropriated as a model to which the Teacher's disciples could also aspire.

In these questions of literary dependence and the social realities behind the texts, all we can aspire to do is present a plausible hypothesis. I have argued that the self-presentation of the speaker in both the *Hodayot* and the exaltation text draws on the profile of the Isaianic Servant. I have accepted as a working hypothesis that the voice we are hearing in at least some of the hymns and the exaltation text is that of the leader of the sect in

66. *Apocalypticism in the Dead Sea Scrolls*, 147-48. Fragment 4 of 4Q541 has some terms indicating suffering vaguely reminiscent of Isa 53; fr. 9 speaks of someone who has a mission which involves teaching and atoning for others, but we are not told how the atonement is carried out; fr. 24, the most obscure in a very obscure text, has a few words which *could* indicate crucifixion, but in any case without reference to the Isaianic Servant. See Collins, *The Scepter and the Star*, 88-89, 124-26; Hengel, "The Effective History of Isaiah 53," 106-18; George J. Brooke, *The Dead Sea Scrolls and the New Testament* (Minneapolis: Fortress, 2005), 140-51.

67. Knohl, *The Messiah before Jesus, passim.* See reviews by John J. Collins in *JQR* 91 (2000): 185-90; and Eileen Schuller in *Shofar* 21 (2002): 153-56.

68. Michael O. Wise, *The First Messiah* (San Francisco: HarperSan Francisco, 1999); also *DSD* 7 (2000): 216-19.

69. Proposals to find his name in Isa 42:19 (Meshullam) or 49:3 (Israel) are as hypothetical as the names Menahem and Judah assigned by Knohl and Wise, respectively, to the Qumranic Teacher.

and for which both the *Hodayot* and the exaltation text were written, namely, the anonymous Teacher of Righteousness. This further thesis is less susceptible to demonstration, and in any case depends on an assessment of what we learn about the Teacher from those texts in which he is explicitly mentioned. This will occupy us in the following and final section of the chapter.

The Anonymous Teacher and Jesus of Nazareth as Servant Figures

The title *môreh haṣṣedeq* ("Teacher of Righteousness")[70] was probably suggested by a typical Qumranic exegesis of Joel 2:23, "for he (God) will give you the early rains *(hammôreh)* for your vindication *(ṣĕdāqâ)*." The genitival phrase could be translated "legitimate teacher" or "righteous teacher," but the allusion in CD VI 10-11 to "one who teaches righteousness in the end days" *(yôreh haṣṣedeq bĕ'aḥărît hayyāmîm)* suggests reading the title as an objective genitive, meaning "a teacher who teaches righteousness." The information on the Teacher provided by the surviving texts is not abundant. In the historical introduction to the Damascus Admonition (CD I 5-12), the appearance of the Teacher brought to an end a period of 20 years disorientation in the parent body of the Qumran sect, described as "the root of God's plant" (cf. Isa 60:21). Since the sectarians believed themselves to be living through "the last generations" *(dôrôt 'aḥărônîm*, CD I 12), the Teacher must have been regarded as an eschatological figure. According to a sectarian interpretation of Ps 37:10, all the wicked will disappear from the earth at the end of time after a period of 40 years (4QpPs^a II 7-8 = 4Q171). The 20 years of CD I 10 may therefore have been understood to be the halfway mark to the final intervention of God. But it appears that the death of the Teacher led his followers to reset the eschatological clock, since we hear in the text of the Damascus Document from the Cairo geniza that 40 years will elapse between the "gathering" of the Teacher (cf. Isa 57:1-2) and the destruction of those who have defected from the sect (CD XX 13-15).

In keeping with traditional role performance, the Teacher is also a priest. The Psalms pesher interprets Ps 37:23-24 (Eng. 22-23) ("though he

---

70. Also *môreh ṣedeq* without the article, *môreh haṣṣĕdāqâ* with the same meaning, *môreh hayyaḥîd* ("unique teacher").

stumble, he shall not fall, for Yahveh holds him by the hand") as a reference to "the Priest, the Teacher of Righteousness whom God chose . . . he established him to found for himself the congregation of his elect" (4Q171 III 14-16). Stumbling often goes with groping, so this statement is consonant with the appearance of the Teacher according to CD I 10-12, though at this point the Damascus Document suggests that the Teacher was the leader of a splinter group rather than a founder in the stricter sense of the term. The subsequent account makes it clear, moreover, that his appearance was the occasion for controversy and schism within the group (CD I 13–II 1).[71]

The Teacher is therefore both priest and prophet. We have just seen that he is described as a priest in the pesher on Psalm 37, and another fragment of a Psalms pesher speaks of the teachings of the *môreh haṣṣedeq* in connection with the priest of the last age (4Q173 fr. 1). The Habakkuk pesher refers to the priest placed by God in the congregation to interpret all the words of his servants the prophets (1QpHab II 7-8), and this priest is certainly to be identified with the Teacher. The Teacher is also a source of halakhic rulings which we know from other Qumran texts to have been the occasion for bitter controversy. He is not to be identified with the Priest Messiah, however, since the B section of the Damascus text speaks of an interval, no doubt the same 40 years, between the death of the "Unique Teacher" *(môreh hayyaḥîd)*[72] and the advent of the Messiah from Aaron and Israel (CD XIX 35–XX 1). Needless to say, we must allow for ideas about messianic figures and end-time schedules and scenarios changing considerably even over a quite brief period of time.

The Teacher is preeminently a prophetic figure, and his prophetic gift consists in the first place in providing the eschatological and therefore definitive interpretation of the prophecies. This aspect of the Teacher's role is most clearly stated and exemplified in the pesharim. The one in Hab 2:2 who is to read the vision while running is therefore identified with the Teacher "to whom God has made known all the mysteries of the words of

---

71. Opposition, both internal and external (the "Wicked Priest"), is thematic in the pesharim, especially the Habakkuk pesher, but the identification of the Teacher's opponents and the glimpses into his *historia calamitatum* which the pesharim provide are not part of our present agenda. See the extensive treatment of these opponents, internal and external, by Gert Jeremias, *Der Lehrer der Gerechtigkeit*, 10-139.

72. The temptation to emend this to *môreh hayyaḥad*, "the community teacher," should probably be resisted.

his servants the prophets" (1QpHab VII 1-5). For the members of the Qumran sect, faith in the eschatological doctrine of the Teacher, based on his interpretation of the prophecies, was an essential condition for membership in the group and, by implication, for a blessed outcome in the judgment soon to come.

The "gathering" of the Teacher is alluded to in the Damascus Document (CD XIX 35–XX 1, 13-14), reminiscent of the "gathering" of the Righteous One in Isa 57:1-2 referred to earlier, but we are given no indication that he died as the result of violence.[73] The midrash on the well in CD VI 1-11 ends with a reference to the emergence of "one who teaches righteousness at the end of the days," and this has been understood to reflect the expectation in the Qumran community of the return of the Teacher in the end time, comparable to the expectation of the Second Coming in early Christianity.[74] On the basis of this text alone it is impossible to decide whether this is the case, or whether this *yôreh haṣṣedeq* ("the one who teaches [or 'will teach'] righteousness") referred to here is merely a counterpart to the Teacher.[75] We can at least say that there is interest in the generation subsequent to the Teacher's death, since we hear that this period of about 40 years must pass before the internal opponents of the Teacher's disciples are destroyed (CD XX 13-15). Forty is a number consecrated by the tradition; we might think of the 40 days following the death of Jesus in Acts 1:3.

This, then, is what can be said about the anonymous Teacher with a reasonable degree of assurance and on the basis of which we can inquire to what extent the profile owes a debt to the Isaianic Servant. Like the Servant, he is both teacher and prophet, his mission encounters opposition and persecution, and he inspires disciples to follow him. The rest is much less assured, but if we are hearing the Teacher's voice in the hymns, at least in those designated Teacher Hymns,[76] and in the exaltation poem, the par-

73. This was the opinion of André Dupont-Sommer in the early days of Qumran studies, based on his reading of the pesher on Hab 2:7-8 helped out with some rather dubious reconstruction. See his *The Dead Sea Scrolls* (Oxford: Blackwell, 1952), 33-37; and "Le Maître de justice fut-il mis à mort?" *VT* 1 (1951): 200-215.

74. Philip R. Davies, "The Teacher of Righteousness and the 'End Days,'" *RevQ* 13 (1988): 313-17.

75. As Michael A. Knibb, "Teacher of Righteousness," *EDSS* 2:921.

76. On the subject of the Teacher as author of these hymns, Gert Jeremias makes a shrewd point: "It is completely unthinkable that in the shortest space of time there were two

allelism will be strengthened. The speaker refers frequently to himself as God's servant, he exhibits an intense prophetic self-consciousness, he has been favored by God from the womb, and his ear has been opened to divine revelations. He is taught by God and can therefore support others by his teaching. All of this replicates what is said of the Servant of the Lord in the Isaianic *Ebedlieder*. Not least important, the pattern of abasement followed by exaltation, which is thematic in the panegyric on the Servant in Isaiah 53 and is only hinted at in scattered passages in the hymns, comes to more explicit expression in the exaltation poem.

In making the same inquiry about Jesus we have more data but also more problems. André Dupont-Sommer, author of one of the most popular books on the Dead Sea Scrolls in the early days, ended his study by comparing the Essenism of Qumran with early Christianity and the Qumran Teacher with Jesus.[77] While taking pains to point out the basic phenomenological differences between these two prophetic figures separated by almost two centuries — Jesus was a layman not a priest, his ministry was peripatetic and took place principally in Galilee not Judea, he did not practice a Qumranlike asceticism, and rather than segregating himself and his followers he took his message of salvation through the forgiveness of sins out into the world — Dupont-Sommer maintained that what most justifies comparison is precisely the fact that both are presented in terms which draw on the Isaianic Servant of the Lord. On this point he takes a maximalist position:

> If the Teacher of Righteousness as Doctor and Prophet cannot fail to be compared to the Servant of the Lord, how much more must this be so in his capacity as the suffering just man, disgraced, persecuted and beaten? He is indeed the replica of that Man of Sorrows whose tragic destiny, and whose valour in the face of blows and final exaltation are described in the fourth 'Servant Song.'[78]

The principal reason for taking seriously the Isaianic Servant model with respect to Jesus was noted in an earlier chapter: it was the death by cruci-

---

men in the Qumran community who came before the community with the revolutionary claim of bringing about salvation through their teaching, and that both were accepted by the community"; *Der Lehrer der Gerechtigkeit*, 176.

77. André Dupont-Sommer, *The Essene Writings from Qumran* (Oxford: Blackwell, 1961), 358-78.

78. *The Essene Writings from Qumran*, 364, 372.

fixion which ensured that the suffering and dying Servant of Isaiah 53
would be a constitutive and irreplaceable element in the structure of early
Christian faith, since only by reference to this text could the death of Jesus
be made theologically intelligible.[79] Appeal to Isaiah 53 would therefore
feature prominently in Christian-Jewish polemic — in chapters 89–96 of
Justin's *Dialogue with Trypho*, for example — but it would also be central
in writings circulating within Christian communities.

We can make the point by a brief reference to Paul's Epistle to the
Romans, written in the mid-50s of the 1st century, about two decades before the earliest of the gospels. It is agreed that this is Paul's most seminal,
comprehensive, and carefully thought-out statement about the identity,
mission, and meaning of Jesus. He begins and ends the epistle by insisting
that the message contained in his gospel corresponds to a revelation disclosed ages ago in prophecy, a mystery long hidden but now revealed (Rom
1:1-2; 16:26). This *inclusio* provides an important clue to what the epistle is
about, and the point is not essentially different from that of the pesharim
and other Qumranic texts. The argument begins by affirming the univer-
sality of sin among Jews and Gentiles alike. This raises in an acute form the
possibility of achieving righteousness. The answer, Paul claims, is contained in his gospel, in which the *dikaiosunē* of God is made manifest. The
usual translation of this word, "justification," is inadequate and even mis-
leading; we are usually not at our best when engaged in justifying ourselves. Without undertaking a full-scale linguistic investigation,[80] we can
say that, as it occurs in Romans, the term indicates either the quality of
righteousness possessed in a unique way by God or the act by which God
brings it about that one becomes righteous or acceptable to God. There is
no one term corresponding to this second meaning in Biblical Hebrew

79. In her contribution to a conference on Isaiah 53 and Christian Origins held at
Baylor University in February 1996, Professor Morna D. Hooker reiterated her thesis argued
years before in *Jesus and the Servant* (London: SPCK, 1959) which questioned the unique
contribution of Isa 53, insisting that the Old Testament is full of the sufferings of the righteous. The statement is true but beside the point since it ignores the unique understanding
of the impact on others of the sufferings and death of the Servant of the Lord in Isa 52:13–
53:12. Professor Hooker also underestimates the significance of the Isaianic text by limiting
herself to the eight explicit citations which she finds in the New Testament. See her essay
"Did the Use of Isaiah 53 to Interpret His Mission Begin with Jesus?" in *Jesus and the Suffering Servant: Isaiah 53 and Christian Origins*, ed. William H. Bellinger, Jr. and William R.
Farmer (Harrisburg: Trinity Press International, 1998), 88-103.
80. Zimmerli and J. Jeremias, *TDNT* 5:654-717.

(the nearest modern Hebrew equivalent would be *haṣdāqâ*), but the corresponding verb *haṣdîq* (the Hiphil or causative conjugation of *ṣdq*) is used in a judicial framework meaning to acquit, vindicate, declare some one to be in the right.[81]

The only biblical instances which go beyond this forensic context are Isa 53:11, the Servant who makes the many righteous, and Dan 12:3, where the Servant is given a collective interpretation with reference to the *maśkîlîm*, the leaders of the Danielic sect, who vindicate, or make righteous, the many. Paul sums it up in a passage for the understanding of which recourse to Isaiah 53 is essential:

> But now, apart from the Law, God's power to bring about righteousness *(dikaiosunē)* has been made manifest, attested by the Law and the Prophets; that is, God's power to bring about righteousness *(dikaiosunē)* through faith in Jesus Christ in all who believe, for there is no distinction; all have sinned and have fallen short of the glory of God. Now, however, they are rendered righteous *(dikaioumenoi)* freely, by the grace of God, in the redemptive act effected through Christ Jesus. God put him forward as an atoning sacrifice *(hilastērion)* in his blood, effective through faith, in order to demonstrate his own righteousness *(dikaiosunē)*, since in his divine forbearance he had passed over sins previously committed; to show forth at the present time both his own righteousness *(dikaiosunē)*, in that he is himself righteous *(dikaion)* and renders righteous *(dikaiounta)* the one who has faith in Jesus. (Rom 3:21-26; the translation is my own)

We see that the term *dikaiosunē* is used here both for the righteousness of God and for the act by which God brings it about that the sinner becomes righteous. The argument is based transparently on Isaiah 53 and especially on one verse, 53:11b, the Hebrew text of which reads as follows:

> *yaṣdîq ṣaddîq 'abdî lārabbîm wĕ'āwōnōtām hû' yisbōl*
> My righteous servant will render righteous the many; it is he who bears the burden of their iniquities.

Paul's decision to follow the Hebrew text was no doubt deliberate since the Greek is quite different. Both for the author of Isaiah 53 and for Paul it is all

---

81. Exod 23:7; Deut 25:1; 2 Sam 15:4; 1 Kgs 8:32 = 2 Chr 6:23; Isa 5:23; Prov 17:15.

God's doing; all that Paul adds to Isaiah 53 is that what God offers is available to those who have faith in Jesus Christ.[82]

Since from a very early stage the interpretation of the doctrine of justification has been expressed in forensic terms,[83] it is important to note that for Paul the rendering righteous is brought about, not by God as judge acquitting the sinner, but by the death of Jesus as an atoning sacrifice through his blood *(hilastērion . . . en tō autou haimati)*. The term *hilastērion*, which in the New Testament occurs only here and in Heb 9:5, belongs to the vocabulary of sacrifice. Generally, if problematically translated "mercy seat" (Heb. *kappōret*), this object was located above the ark of the covenant, often represented as the lid of the ark, and was sprinkled with sacrificial blood on the Day of Atonement (Lev 16:14-16).

We might note a similar extended use of the term *hilastērion* which appears in the account of the martyrdom of the mother and her seven sons in 4 Macc 17:22: "Through the blood of these devout ones and their death as an atoning sacrifice *(hilastērion)* divine providence preserved Israel." While there is no evidence that Paul drew on this text, it corresponds closely to his understanding of the death of Jesus. At the same time, he remains faithful to the intention and wording of Isaiah 53, which uses metaphoric language drawn from the sacrificial cult rather than from the forensic sphere to express what, up to that time, had never been expressed. The sacrificial element is poignantly insinuated in the comparison of the Servant with a sheep or a lamb led to the slaughter (53:7), but the key term is *'āšām* (53:10a). The verse in which this term occurs is textually obscure; one way of translating it would be "If his life is laid down as a guilt offering, he will see posterity, he will prolong his days." The term *'āšām* is used in the Hebrew Bible in the forensic sphere with reference to guilt or the consequences of a verdict of guilty (e.g., Gen 26:10; Num 5:7-8), but also in the cultic sphere with the meaning "guilt offering" or "reparation offering" (Lev 5–7; 1 Sam 6:3-4, 8, 17).[84] The re-

---

82. Cf. 1QpHab VII 17–VIII 3, in which Hab 2:4b ("The righteous will live by faith") is interpreted as applying to those who have faith in, or remain loyal to, the Teacher of Righteousness; cf. Rom 1:17.

83. See the classic study of Alister E. McGrath, *Iustitia Dei: A History of the Christian Doctrine of Justification* (Cambridge: Cambridge University Press, 1986).

84. The forensic connotation is defended by Otfried Hofius, "The Fourth Servant Song in the New Testament Letters," in Janowski and Stuhlmacher, *The Suffering Servant*, 163-88, following Rolf Knierim, "אָשָׁם *'āšām* guilt," *TLOT* 1:191-95; cf. the same title but different emphasis in Diether Kellermann, "'ašām," *TDOT* 1:429-37.

markable and original achievement of the unknown author of Isaiah 53 was to take over a metaphor from the sacrificial cult to express the meaning of a life and a death which, for him, had transcendent significance, and it is this insight which is at the heart of Paul's understanding of the death of Jesus.

Scholars of early Christianity also entertain the possibility that this insight, drawing on Isaiah 53, was already part of early Christian catechesis before Paul wrote the Epistle to the Romans. It has been pointed out that Rom 4:25 has the sound of a traditional formula:

Delivered over to death *(paredothē)* on account of our trespasses,
Raised on account of our righteousness *(dia tēn dikaiōsin hēmōn)*.

This looks like a summary of Isaiah 53.[85] That the Servant was delivered over to death — use of the passive avoids the mention of God as agent — is stated twice, and with the same language (LXX *paredothē*), towards the end of the poem (Isa 53:12), and the resurrection of Jesus would have been seen as foretold in the exaltation of the Servant and the assurance that he will see light (Isa 52:13; 53:11). In one of the first sermons recorded in Acts, Peter speaks of the resurrection as God glorifying his servant (child) Jesus (*ho theos . . . edoxasen ton paida autou Iēsoun*, Acts 3:13), another echo of the fourth Servant text: "Behold my servant shall understand; he shall be exalted and glorified exceedingly" (Isa 52:13-14 LXX). The association is also expressed in Jesus delivering himself to death, or being delivered to death by God (using the same verb *paradidōmi* as in Isa 53), an expression which is thematic in the Epistles (Rom 8:32; Gal 2:20; Eph 5:2). As it appears in the traditional eucharistic formula (*en tē nukti hē paredideto*, 1 Cor 11:23), it brings to mind, as we noted earlier, both the delivery of Jesus to his enemies by Judas and the self-delivery of Jesus in accepting his death, for both of which the same verb is used.[86]

Turning now to the gospels, we should say first that the presentation of Jesus as Servant of the Lord, and as a messianic figure destined to suffer and die like the Servant of Isaiah 53, can be considered independently of the much-debated question whether this interpretation goes back to Jesus himself. Having said that, I would add that I can come up with no compelling reason to deny that the tradition about Jesus as Ser-

---

85. As observed by Hofius, "The Fourth Servant Song in the New Testament Letters," 180-82.
86. See pp. 167-68.

vant, which we have just seen was more probably taken over by Paul than created by him, is rooted in Jesus' own understanding of his mission. This opinion is reinforced by the narrative logic of the gospel story, in which, as we noted earlier, the close relation between Jesus and John the Baptist is an important element the historicity of which few would deny. Following on the execution of the Baptist, Jesus seems to have concluded that his own death was foreordained, and therefore foretold prophetically, and from that point on the suffering and death of the Servant casts a dark shadow forward over the narrative.[87] We have also observed that several of the narrative details in the account of the death serve to draw the attention of the reader to the same source — the silence of Jesus during his trial (Matt 26:63; Isa 53:7), the rich man from Arimathea (Matt 27:57; cf. Isa 53:9), and death in the company of transgressors (Luke 22:37, which cites Isa 53:12).

Death, and the manner of the death, are also anticipated in a saying of Jesus uttered in the apparently inconsequential context of a dispute about rank and priority among his disciples (Matt 20:28 = Mark 10:45). The solution is simple: if you want to be first in rank you have to be the servant — or slave (*doulos,* not *pais*) — of all. The reason: "The Son of Man did not come to be served but to serve, and to give his life as a ransom for (the) many *(lutron anti pollōn)."* The term *lutron* corresponds to Hebrew *koper,* which signifies either the price to be paid to release someone from indentured service, or compensation for services rendered, or even hush money. It therefore does not have the same meaning as *'āšām* ("guilt offering" or "reparation offering") in Isa 53:10, but the Suffering Servant context is apparent notwithstanding. "To give his life" *(dounai tēn psuchēn autou)* is equivalent to "he poured out his life blood to death" (Isa 53:12), and in both Matt 20:28 and Isaiah 53 the death is on behalf of "the many."[88] That this expression — *anti pollōn,* alternatively *huper pollōn* and *peri pollōn* — entered very early into the vocabulary in which the death of Jesus

---

87. The note of predestination and necessity is expressed in the three predictions of suffering and death in Mark 8:31 (Matt 16:21; Luke 9:22); 9:30-31 (Matt 17:22-23; Luke 9:43-44); 10:32-34 (Matt 20:17-19; Luke 18:31-34). The note is intensified as we approach the betrayal and death (Matt 26:24, 54, 56).

88. It does not seem likely that this logion is meant to recall Isa 43:3, "I have set aside Egypt as your ransom, Ethiopia and Seba in your stead," esp. in view of the Suffering Servant context; pace Peter Stuhlmacher, "Isaiah 53 in the Gospels and Acts" in Janowski and Stuhlmacher, *The Suffering Servant,* 150-51.

was spoken of in early Christian circles is evident from the eucharistic words of institution as recorded in Matthew (26:28, *peri pollōn*) and Mark (14:24, *huper pollōn*).[89]

The creative impact of Isaiah 53 is not confined to the circumstances and meaning of the death of Jesus; it bears on his entire life and especially on his healing activity. That the healing and exorcizing activity of Jesus is so prominent in the gospels is not accidental. It must be seen against the background of the deeply ingrained belief that sickness and demonic possession are symptomatic of a sinful condition and that therefore healing is the outward sign of the forgiveness of sin. The healings and exorcisms are also diagnostic, indicating for those who can read the signs, and read them in the light of certain texts from Isaiah (esp. 35:5-6 and 61:1), that the end of the age is approaching: Jesus is the One to Come in that age since he has brought it about that "the blind see, the lame walk, lepers are cleansed, the deaf hear, the dead are raised, and good news is proclaimed to the poor" (Matt 11:5).

Matthew 8:16-17, one of several summary statements about the healing ministry of Jesus in this gospel, also one of the formulaic fulfillment sayings, provided an occasion for quoting Isa 53:4a:

It was he who bore our afflictions,
he who bore the burden of our sufferings.[90]

In this instance the citation follows the Hebrew rather than the Greek, since the latter speaks of the Servant bearing the burden of our sins rather than physical afflictions, therefore not directly relevant at this point.[91]

The longest citation concerning the Servant in Matthew's gospel occurs, significantly, at the center of the fivefold arrangement discussed in an earlier chapter.[92] It will remind us of a point made earlier, that the motivated ancient reader would have noticed, without benefit of the historical-

---

89. See the discussion of Mark 10:45 against the background of the Suffering Servant by Rikki E. Watts, "Jesus' Death, Isaiah 53, and Mark 10:45: A Crux Revisited," in Bellinger and Farmer, *Jesus and the Suffering Servant*, 125-51.

90. The citation is missing from the parallels in Mark 1:32-34; Luke 4:40-41.

91. In view of the texts we have discussed, I find Marinus de Jonge's affirmation, that evidence for the use of Isa 52:13–53:12 in early Christianity is slight, simply incredible; *Jesus the Servant Messiah* (New Haven: Yale University Press, 1991), 49.

92. See above pp. 161-62.

critical approach and Duhm's commentary, that several passages in Isaiah speak of a Servant of the Lord in terms which are at once applicable to an individual. The passage cited at Matt 12:18-21, like the voice from heaven at the baptism and transfiguration (3:17; 17:5), is from the first of the four *Ebedlieder*, Isa 42:1-4, here presented as fulfilled in the healing activity of Jesus and his hiddenness — the latter with reference to the injunction that those healed should not publicize the healer (Matt 12:15-16):

> Here is my servant whom I sustain,
> My chosen one in whom I take delight;
> I have put my spirit upon him.
> He will establish a just order for the nations;
> he will not shout, he will not raise his voice,
> or let it be heard in public places.
> A broken reed he will not crush,
> a dimly smoldering wick he will not extinguish . . .
> until he has set up a just order on the earth;
> in his name the Gentiles will hope.

To summarize: what we have been trying to do in this chapter is to view the Teacher of Righteousness and Jesus along the same plane of observation, namely, the powerful interpretative trajectory generated by the Servant passages in Isaiah, especially the panegyric on the dead Servant in Isaiah 53. The results will be skewed for several reasons, and not just authorial bias. One obvious factor is the incomplete nature of the source material at our disposal, especially the data available for the Teacher. Another is the very different character of the source material. Early-generation Christians pioneered the gospel genre, for example, but wrote no biblical commentaries. On the subject of healing, one Qumran text duplicates Matt 11:5 in foreseeing the removal of physical disabilities and the proclamation of good news to the poor in the messianic age (4QMessianic Apocalypse = 4Q521 II fr. 2, II), but none of the sectarian texts provides evidence for healing activity on the part of the Teacher or indeed of anyone else.[93] Like-

---

93. Michael O. Wise, "Healing," *EDSS* 1:336-38, mentions the healing of the pharaoh by Abraham in the Genesis Apocryphon (1QapGen XX 21-29), the Jewish exorcist who cured Nabonidus of a painful disease which required that he be quarantined (4QPrayer of Nabonidus = 4Q242), and what appears to be a claim by a *maskil* to exorcize demons (4Q510 fr. 1).

wise, information provided by Josephus on the Essenes in general and individual Essenes emphasizes the prophetic gift rather than the gift of healing.[94] On the other hand, information on the attributes and activities of the Teacher is much more limited than material available for the mission of Jesus. If we had more information, and if the texts that we do have were more forthcoming, the situation might look different.

The character and situation of the groups within which the texts were produced were also different in some fundamental respects. The Qumran authors were more learned, scribal, and sedentary, several of them evidently originating among the upper echelons of society, including the priestly aristocracy. The first generation of Christians, on the other hand, seems to have been drawn for the most part from the artisan class, to which Jesus himself belonged. At any rate, they were of lower social status and not for the most part learned scribes, legal experts, and expositors of Scripture, as were the contemporary Qumranites (witness the fact that we have to wait more than two centuries for the first Christian commentary on a biblical book). But both groups, in their different ways, found in the Isaianic Servant of the Lord a way of grasping and articulating the identity and destiny of their respective founders and, by implication, their own identity and destiny.

94. He tells us that they are accurate predictors of the future (*War* 2:159) and records prophecies uttered by Judas (*Ant.* 13:311) and Menahem (*Ant.* 15:374-79), both Essenes. The Essenes treat diseases and are interested in folk medecine (*War* 2:136), but Josephus attaches no particular significance to these features.

Bibliography

Bailett, Maurice. *Qumrân Grotte 4, III (4Q482-520)*. DJD 7. Oxford: Clarendon, 1982.

Bauckham, Richard. "The Early Jerusalem Church, Qumran, and the Essenes." In *The Dead Sea Scrolls as Background to Postbiblical Judaism and Early Christianity*, ed. James R. Davila, 85-89.

Ben Zvi, Ehud, and Michael H. Floyd. *Writings and Speech in Israelite and Ancient Near Eastern Prophecy*. SBLSymS 10. Atlanta: SBL, 2000.

Black, Matthew. *The Scrolls and Christian Origins*. New York: Scribner's, 1961.

Blenkinsopp, Joseph. "The Formation of the Hebrew Bible: Isaiah as a Test Case." In *The Canon Debate*, ed. Lee Martin McDonald and James A. Sanders, 53-67. Peabody: Hendrickson, 2002.

————. *History of Prophecy in Israel*. Rev. ed. Louisville: Westminster, 1996.

————. *Isaiah 1–39*. AB 19. New York: Doubleday, 2000.

————. *Isaiah 40–55*. AB 19A. New York: Doubleday, 2000.

————. *Isaiah 56–66*. AB 19B. New York: Doubleday, 2003.

————. "A Jewish Sect of the Persian Period." *CBQ* 52 (1990): 5-20.

————. "Judah's Covenant with Death (Isaiah XXVIII 14-22)." *VT* 50 (2000): 472-83.

————. *Prophecy and Canon*. Notre Dame: University of Notre Dame Press, 1977.

————. "Second Isaiah — Prophet of Universalism?" *JSOT* 41 (1988): 83-103. Repr. in *The Prophets*, ed. Philip R. Davies, 186-206. Biblical Seminar 42. Sheffield: Sheffield Academic, 1996.

————. "The Servant and the Servants in Isaiah and the Formation of the Book." In *Writing and Reading the Scroll of Isaiah*, ed. Craig C. Broyles and Craig A. Evans, 1:155-75.

————. "The 'Servants of the Lord' in Third Isaiah." *PIBA* 7 (1983): 1-23. Repr. in

Bibliography

"The Place Is Too Small For Us": The Israelite Prophets in Recent Scholarship, ed. Robert P. Gordon, 392-412. Winona Lake: Eisenbrauns, 1995.

————. "Who is the Ṣaddiq of Isaiah 57:1-2?" In *Studies in the Hebrew Bible, Qumran, and the Septuagint Presented to Eugene Ulrich,* ed. Peter W. Flint, Emanuel Tov, and James C. VanderKam, 109-20. Leiden: Brill, 2006.

Brooke, George J. *Exegesis at Qumran: 4QFlorilegium in its Jewish Context.* Sheffield: JSOT, 1985. Repr. Atlanta: SBL, 2006.

————. "Isaiah 40:3 and the Wilderness Community." In *New Qumran Texts and Studies,* ed. Brooke and Florentino García Martínez, 117-32. STDJ 15. Leiden: Brill, 1994.

Brownlee, William H. *The Meaning of the Qumrân Scrolls for the Bible, with Special Attention to the Book of Isaiah.* New York: Oxford University Press, 1964.

Broyles, Craig C., and Craig A. Evans, ed. *Writing and Reading the Scroll of Isaiah.* 2 vols. VTSup 70. Leiden: Brill, 1997.

Charles, R. H. *The Apocrypha and Pseudepigrapha of the Old Testament in English.* Vol. 2: *Pseudepigrapha.* Oxford: Clarendon, 1913.

Charlesworth, James H., ed. *The Old Testament Pseudepigrapha.* 2 vols. Garden City: Doubleday, 1983-85.

Collins, John J. *Daniel.* Herm. Minneapolis: Fortress, 1993.

————. "From Prophecy to Apocalypticism: The Expectation of the End." In *The Encyclopedia of Apocalypticism,* 1:130-34.

————. *The Scepter and the Star: The Messiahs of the Dead Sea Scrolls and Other Ancient Literature.* New York: Doubleday, 1995.

————. "Teacher and Servant." *RHPR* 80 (2000): 37-50.

————, ed. *The Encyclopedia of Apocalypticism.* 3 vols. New York: Continuum, 1998.

Cowley, A. E. *Aramaic Papyri of the Fifth Century B.C.* 1923. Repr. Osnabrück: Otto Zeller, 1967.

Cross, Frank Moore. *The Ancient Library of Qumran.* 3rd ed. Sheffield: Sheffield Academic, 1995.

Davies, Philip R. *The Damascus Covenant: An Interpretation of the "Damascus Document."* JSOTSup 25. Sheffield: JSOT, 1983.

————. "The 'Damascus' Sect and Judaism." In *Pursuing the Text: Studies in Honor of Ben Zion Wacholder on the Occasion of His Seventieth Birthday,* ed. John C. Reeves and John Kampen, 70-84. JSOTSup 184. Sheffield: Sheffield Academic, 1994.

Davila, James R., ed. *The Dead Sea Scrolls as Background to Postbiblical Judaism and Early Christianity.* STDJ 46. Leiden: Brill, 2003.

Duhm, Bernhard. *Das Buch Jesaja.* 2nd ed. HKAT. Göttingen: Vandenhoeck & Ruprecht, 1922.

Eshel, Esther. "Self-Glorification Hymn." In *Qumran Cave 4.XX: Poetical and Li-*

turgical Texts, Part 2, ed. Esther Chazon et al., 421-32. DJD 29. Oxford: Clarendon, 1999.

Fitzmyer, Joseph A. "The Use of Explicit Old Testament Quotations in Qumran Literature and in the New Testament." *NTS* 7 (1961/62): 297-333.

García Martínez, Florentino, and Eibert J. C. Tigchelaar, ed. *The Dead Sea Scrolls Study Edition*. 2 vols. Grand Rapids: Wm. B. Eerdmans, 1997-98.

Hengel, Martin. "The Effective History of Isaiah 53 in the Pre-Christian Period." In *The Suffering Servant*, ed. Berndt Janowski and Peter Stuhlmacher, 85-90.

————. *Judaism and Hellenism*. 2 vols. Philadelphia: Fortress, 1974.

Hooker, Morna D. "Did the Use of Isaiah 53 to Interpret His Mission Begin with Jesus?" In *Jesus and the Suffering Servant. Isaiah 53 and Christian Origins*, ed. William H. Bellinger, Jr. and William R. Farmer, 88-103. Harrisburg: Trinity Press International, 1998.

Horgan, Maurya P. *Pesharim: Qumran Interpretations of Biblical Books*. CBQMS 8. Washington: Catholic Biblical Association, 1979.

Iwry, Samuel. "Was There a Migration to Damascus? The Problem of שבי ישראל." *ErIsr* 9 (1969): 80-88.

Janowski, Berndt, and Peter Stuhlmacher, ed. *The Suffering Servant: Isaiah 53 in Jewish and Christian Sources*. Grand Rapids: Wm. B. Eerdmans, 2004.

Jenni, Ernst, and Claus Westermann, ed. *Theological Lexicon of the Old Testament*. 3 vols. Peabody: Hendrickson, 1997.

Jeremias, Gert. *Der Lehrer der Gerechtigkeit*. SUNT 2. Göttingen: Vandenhoeck & Ruprecht, 1963.

Klijn, A. F. J., and G. T. Reinink. *Patristic Evidence for Jewish-Christian Sects*. NovTSup 36. Leiden: Brill, 1973.

Knibb, Michael A. "Exile in the Damascus Document." *JSOT* 25 (1983): 99-117.

————. "The Exile in the Literature of the Intertestamental Period." *HeyJ* 17 (1976): 253-72.

————. "'Isaianic Traditions in the Book of Enoch." In *After the Exile: Essays in Honour of Rex Mason*, ed. John Barton and David J. Reimer, 217-29. Macon: Mercer University Press, 1996.

Knohl, Israel. *The Messiah before Jesus*. Berkeley: University of California Press, 2000.

Levin, Christoph. "Das Gebetbuch der Gerechten: Literargeschichtliche Beobachtungen am Psalter." *ZTK* 90 (1993): 355-81 = *Fortschreibungen: Gesammelte Studien zum Alten Testament*. BZAW 316. Berlin: de Gruyter, 2003, 291-313.

Murphy-O'Connor, Jerome. "Damascus." *EDSS* 1:165-66.

Nickelsburg, George W. E. *Jewish Literature between the Bible and the Mishnah*. Philadelphia: Fortress, 1981.

Rofé, Alexander. "Isaiah 66:1-4: Judean Sects in the Persian Period as Viewed by

Trito-Isaiah." In *Biblical and Related Studies Presented to Samuel Iwry,* ed. Ann Kort and Scott Morschauser, 205-17. Winona Lake: Eisenbrauns, 1985.

Sanders, Jack T. "The Prophetic Use of the Scriptures in Luke-Acts." In *Early Jewish and Christian Exegesis: Studies in Memory of William Hugh Brownlee,* ed. Craig A. Evans and W. F. Stinespring, 191-98. Atlanta: Scholars, 1987.

Sanders, James A. "Isaiah in Luke." *Int* 36 (1982): 144-55.

Sawyer, John F. A. *The Fifth Gospel: Isaiah in the History of Christianity.* Cambridge: Cambridge University Press, 1996.

Schiffmann, Lawrence H., and James C. VanderKam, ed. *Encyclopedia of the Dead Sea Scrolls.* 2 vols. New York: Oxford University Press, 2000.

Schürer, Emil. *The History of the Jewish People in the Age of Jesus Christ.* 3 vols. Rev. and ed. by Geza Vermes, Fergus Millar, and Matthew Goodman. Edinburgh: T. & T. Clark, 1983-87.

Seeligmann, Isac Leo. *The Septuagint Version of Isaiah: A Discussion of Its Problems.* Leiden: Brill, 1948.

Seitz, Christopher R. *Zion's Final Destiny: The Development of the Book of Isaiah.* Minneapolis: Fortress, 1991.

Stegemann, Ekkehard W., and Wolfgang Stegemann. *The Jesus Movement: A Social History of Its First Century.* Minneapolis: Fortress, 1999.

Talmon, Shemaryahu. "The Sectarian יחד — a Biblical Noun." *VT* 3 (1953): 133-40.

Westermann, Claus. *Isaiah 40–66.* OTL. Philadelphia: Westminster, 1967.

Wise, Michael O. *The First Messiah.* San Francisco: HarperSanFrancisco, 1999.

Zimmerli, Walther, and Joachim Jeremias. "παῖς θεοῦ." *TDNT* 5:654-717.

Index of Subjects

Abrahamic promise, 115, 199, 229, 241
Ages of Creation, 237-38
Amos, absent from Deuteronomistic History, 39-40; Day of Yahveh in, 225-26; deportation and exile in, 224-25; relation to Isaiah, 31; "remnant" in, 223-24
Anabaptists, 171
Angels, 205-9
"Animal Apocalypse," 236
Antiochus Epiphanes IV, 85, 232, 236-37
"Apocalypse of Weeks," 86
Apocalyptic, "Animal Apocalypse" in *1 Enoch*, 25; in Isaiah and Daniel, 14-16; "Isaian Apocalypse," 16-17, 76, 189, 210-11; New Testament Apocalypse (Revelation), 25-26
Apocryphon of Joseph, 231
Apollos, 184
Ascension of Isaiah, 49-51
asidaioi, 77, 83, 84-85, 171, 219-20, 238
associations in late antiquity, 171

Barnabas, Epistle of, 180
Baruch, Syriac Apocalypse, 266
"Blessings of Moses," 173
books in antiquity, 1-4; Isaiah as a book, 9-14; sealed books, 13-14; "Book of Truth," 21

canon, biblical, 4-6; Isaiah as canonical, 27
Cathars, as a sect, 171, 185
Chronicles, books of, on Ahaz and Hezekiah, 44-45; on Isaiah, 43-44
Citation formulas in Matthew's gospel, 147-68
Clement of Alexandria, 2
Community Rule (Qumran), 174-75

Damascus Document (CD), 70-71, 76, 78, 82, 86; and the Damascus covenant sect, 87-88; history in, 238-40; ideological boundaries, 62; "the Many" in, 174; Prince of the Congregation in, 117; Teacher of Righteousness in, 125, 191, 211; on the two branches of the sect, 189
Daniel, book of, prophetic historiography, 86; Isaianic interpretation in, 14-18; mystery *(rāz)* in, 17; sealed books in, 18-19
David, as Servant of the Lord, 198
Day of Yahweh, 79, 225-26, 250
Deuteronomistic History, 38-43, 197-98

Index of Biblical and Other Ancient Texts